Rand McNally Book of
THE GARDEN

Published by Rand McNally & Company
Designed and produced for Rand McNally by
Intercontinental Book Productions

ISBN: 0-528-81094-4
Library of Congress catalog card no. 79-83543

Printed in Italy

Rand McNally Book of THE GARDEN

Written by Peter Seabrook
Illustrated by Brian Edwards
Michael Strand and Sara Silcock
Edited by Peter McHoy

Peter Seabrook

Contents

Garden Planning	6
Lawns	22
Hedges	34
Trees	40
Shrubs	50
Climbing Shrubs	64
Conifers	68
Garden Flowers	82
Houseplants	102
Roses	114
Fruit	122
Vegetables	140
Herbs	162
Greenhouses	166
Calendar of Work	180
Pests and Diseases	186
Garden Chemicals	188
Index	189

Foreword

I am particularly pleased to be asked to write a Foreword for Peter Seabrook's new book, the Rand McNally *Book of the Garden.* Peter and I have worked together for a number of years, and I know of his ability to convey the fundamentals of gardening to people the world over. His popular television programs for the BBC have effectively aided millions of people who want help in growing their gardens.

Peter has widely diversified interests in horticulture and enormous grasp of the whole subject. He is as interested in growing a beautiful lawn as he is in producing fine vegetables, or cut flowers, or perennials, or plants for indoor gardens.

While doing a series of television programs together in England and in the United States, we have developed a great feeling of friendship for one another. Peter is a warm and genuine person with a real desire to help people experience the pleasures of producing a flourishing garden. So many are afraid to begin; they need to be reminded that the trees and grasses of our woodlands grow without man's help. Plants will grow in almost any garden; and with a little bit of coaxing, they will do wonders for us.

I may not have told Peter this, but part of my own early training was under a British gardener. In the field of horticulture the term "British gardener" evokes utmost respect because of the rigorous training. The men and women who pass the national horticulture examinations in Britain are very, very skilled in their work.

Peter Seabrook belongs to this fine tradition of British gardeners — and in Peter's case, he has a happy ability to share his broad knowledge in a particularly open and friendly manner. He is especially proficient at teaching the basics of gardening, and the principles he stresses apply to gardens everywhere.

Every time Peter appears as a guest on my own television program, Crockett's Victory Garden, I get a flash flood of letters saying, "I didn't get the name of the person you had on the show but he was great and he really knows his stuff." That's just what I want to say to the readers of this book. Peter Seabrook does "know his stuff" and is able to convey his knowledge and love of gardening to others. It is for that reason — as well as many others — that I commend this book to you. I know that it is sure to become one of the most usefu' reference books in your gardening library

Jim Crockett

James Underwood Crockett

Garden Planning

It is always a problem to know where to start when you take over a garden. Often it is easier starting absolutely from scratch, even if more work is involved improving the soil. Established gardens really need watching for a full growing season to see just what treasures the garden contains. Start chopping into the soil with a spade and all too soon hidden bulbs come up clearly dissected. Old, and on first sight apparently neglected, trees and bushes can produce the finest flowers and fruits, proving them well worth attention and rejuvenation.

In a perfect world previous owners would no doubt leave behind a detailed plan with every planting named and labelled. Sadly few of us have the time for such perfection, but it is worth sketching out ideas and attempting to include the many requirements needed from the average home plot.

Most of us are in a tearing rush to get things growing in much the same way we need curtains up and rooms redecorated indoors. But gardening isn't easy to rush and the first burst of enthusiasm is best directed at preparing the soil for hedges, trees and lawns.

Hedges need to go in first to give the whole garden shelter as quickly as possible and perhaps some privacy. Trees take time to give shade and fill the site allocated to them and the sooner they are in the better. Don't skimp on the soil preparation, however, because once in there is no second chance to improve soil around deeply penetrating roots.

Levelling the garden and establishing the lawns comes next. It is quite easy to dig beds and borders out from the grassed area but not very easy to get good edges to lawns where the flower and vegetable beds were planted first.

Trees will give height and depth to the smallest garden and it is well worth checking through neighborhood gardens to see which kinds are growing well. This is a good idea for other plants too in due course.

A colorful low hedge, attractive wall plants, specimen tree, conifers, lawn and summer bedding plants are used in this attractive small garden.

Container-grown specimens are recommended not only for the option to plant all the year round even in full leaf, but more for the ability to site for a few days where you propose to plant. Then you can really look at the positioning and move a plant a foot or two to get a nice positioning when viewed from house and garden.

Such permanent features as paved terraces, walls and fences can follow but keep an overall plan in mind with path access to sheds and service areas.

UNDERSTANDING SOIL

There is a tremendous variation in soil types; invariably gardeners wish they had a different kind to suit a particular kind of plant. Even within one garden the soil types can vary from quite light sandy soil to heavy clay as a result of work during house construction.

Excepting those gardens where topsoil was cleared before the house was built and new topsoil brought in after building, there is little chance of changing the basic soil types. There are three main classifications: light sandy and stony soils, which are free-draining and very hungry; heavy clay soils, which are difficult to work but once mastered can be heavy yielding; and loams which contain varying amounts of sand and clay and with the addition of humus become the best gardening soils. Some soils are strongly alkaline and must be amended for ericaceous plants (azaleas etc.).

Most soil types are improved by the addition of bulky organic matter, an exception being a naturally peaty soil.

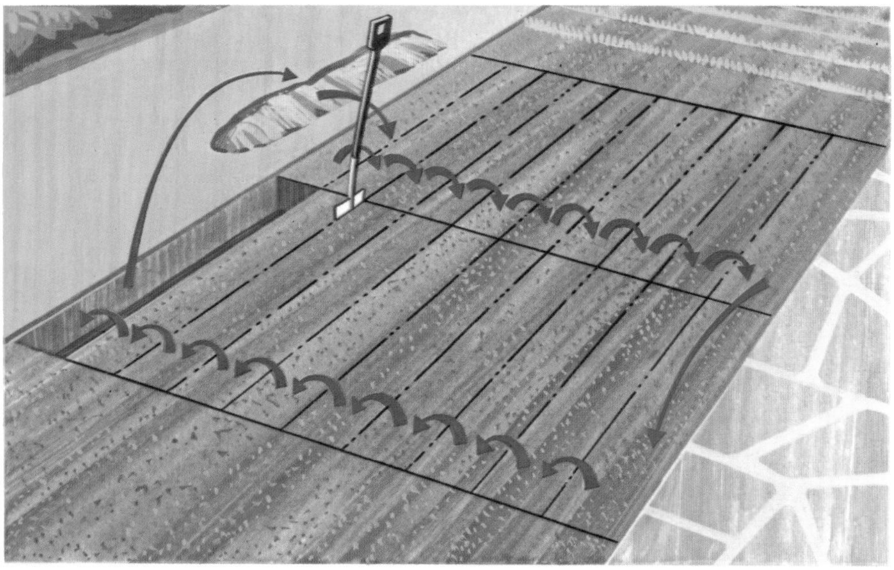

When single digging a large plot, the first trench of topsoil should be stacked as shown here; on a small plot, simply stack at the opposite end.

It is important to distinguish between rotted-down organic matter (garden compost, manure, leaf mold, sawdust and peat moss) which improve soil texture, and concentrated plant foods contained in fertilizers.

Generally the problem is getting sufficient organic matter. Even the heaviest clay soils and thinnest sandy soils will be easily worked and produce excellent plant growth if a 4—6 in. (10—15 cm) layer of organic matter is thoroughly incorporated.

Don't spread organic matter thinly over a large area. You never see the benefit this way. Really concentrate the application and spread thickly over a relatively small area before digging. Then when more rotted compost is available and more peat moss can be bought treat another patch and gradually improve the garden overall.

When buying peat moss and other organic matter to improve soil always buy by volume, never by weight, which is so much influenced by the moisture content.

Bark, usually in the form of chips, is another organic material offered for soil improvement. I prefer to use this as a long-term mulch. The woody fiber resists weathering and lasts a long time. Dug into the ground it can draw too much nitrogen from the soil.

Although peat moss is sold by all garden centers and nurseries, it is expensive, so the thrifty gardener should search for local sources of organic materials that are free. These can include pine needles, sawdust, wood chips, seaweed and fallen leaves.

Organic matter in the soil helps light soil retain moisture, it improves the drainage in heavy soils, reduces the alkalinity of some soils and encourages the desired fibrous root growth.

By far the best method of incorporation is to mix well into the soil during autumn and winter digging. Spreading a good layer of compost over wet soil helps to keep the feet clean and makes the digging job much easier.

Mixing sand, ashes and other coarse material into heavy clay soils will improve drainage and make cultivation easier but don't over-do it. Equally, heavy clay soil brought in to mix with light sandy soils will improve the structure.

Whatever the soil type some form of annual cultivation is necessary in ornamental, fruit and vegetable gardens. Digging one spade's depth in autumn or winter is a good start.

Cultivation

There is no substitute for hand digging, and done in moderation, a small area at a time, it really is a most satisfying task. Use a spade which is comfortable for you, the handle smooth, the blade clean and shiny. Shiny blades are especially important when digging heavy, wet soil which sticks to everything.

Stony soils may on occasions be more easily dug with a fork but it is more difficult to get a level finish. Quite apart from the tool, I like to keep my footwear clean when digging. A scattering of peat moss or compost over wet surfaces helps here.

Single digging requires a good trench, the depth and width of a spade taken out first. On large plots divide in half and heap the soil from the trench across one half against the top of the other half. Just stack it at the other end of small plots.

Taking a 3—4 in. (7.5—10 cm) wide strip of soil at a time, cut out a clean

Do not remove large slices of soil when digging — 3-4 in. (7-10 cm) is right.

Try to ensure that the soil is inverted, so that weeds are buried completely.

Heavy soils are best left in lumps, but in spring may be broken down.

slice of soil and invert it. When winter digging leave the large clods for the weather to break down. If you have to dig in spring then chop the surface down fine as you work back.

Watch what you are doing as the soil is inverted. Throw it over neatly so that surface weeds are thoroughly buried, rotted compost or peat moss mixed in and the final surface left level across the plot. At the end of the plot fill in the trench with the soil heaped from the first trench.

Double digging involves cultivating to two spades' depth and is usually only needed where trees are being planted, hedges set out in poor soil or very thorough preparation is being made for growing flowers and vegetables for exhibition.

Where you want to give a bit of extra-special treatment dig over the bottom of the trench when single digging. Cultivating the lower soil in this way is nearly as good as double digging.

Always pick out the roots of perennial weeds as you dig across. On heavy soils try to dig in drying weather conditions. Heavy rain can cake the surface on freshly turned wet soil and destroy the crumbly texture we are trying to produce. This is especially so with spring digging.

Where mechanical cultivators are used, rainfall immediately after chopping the soil fine and before the surface dries a little can be disastrous.

Alkalinity

The only sure way of finding the acidity or alkalinity of your soil is by chemical tests. There are cheap soil test kits available and if your soil registers below 7.0 pH (the term used to indicate an approximately neutral soil), then it is acid to some degree. Most plants do well between pH 5.8 to 6.8.

If the soil is above 7.0 pH it is alkaline, and can be brought back to neutral and acid by adding peat moss, which is naturally acid, by using acidic fertilizers such as sulfate of ammonia, or by adding powdered sulfur.

Soil Conditioners and Plant Foods

Decaying organic matter, whether composted garden waste, rotted down leaves or peat moss, improves the soil for plants and encourages better root development, but it contains little plant food.

Chemical fertilizers are one source of concentrated plant foods and well-rotted animal manures provide a combination of organic matter and plant food.

Regular digging, incorporating plenty of organic matter, will build up a good workable soil. Take out a good trench at the start.

Quite large quantities of organic matter are needed year after year to improve and retain a good tilth with crumbly and easily worked soil.

It is not possible for most gardeners to get plenty of bulky animal manure. Peat moss and garden compost are the solution, backed up with concentrated chemical plant foods.

You will find it difficult to add too much organic matter to the garden but chemical fertilizers can be overdone, in extreme cases reducing plant growth.

One source of organic matter is 'green manure'. Here crops like buckwheat, vetches, Italian and winter rye are sown, then when well established dug into the soil. Vetch and other legumes have the advantage of adding nitrogen to the soil, and grass roots are very fibrous which improves soil structure.

Part of the green manure principle is included in garden cropping. Legume crops like sweet peas and beans enrich the soil by leaving behind extra nitrogenous plant food. The fibrous nature of leek roots will do much to break up heavy soil.

All of these are secondary, however, to the great quantity of soil-improving organic matter from composted garden waste.

Warmth, moisture and air are needed to rot down organic matter and if any one of these is absent the speed of breakdown is dramatically reduced. Shake up a great mixture of garden debris in mid-summer, damp it over and add a compost activator chemical to get a dramatic rise in temperature in days. This will quickly produce well-rotted material.

At other times of the year it will take longer and the easiest way is to have two heaps. Stake out a rectangle at least 5 ft × 3 ft (1.5 m × 1 m) using any convenient material for the sides. All non-weedy plant remains can be stacked in the bin. Once full to over-flowing I like to empty this out, ideally restacking the second bin.

Mix soft green lawn mowings with tougher bean and flower stems as you refill. See that all the material is damp and dust over with a chemical compost maker to speed the rotting down. Cleanings from the cat litter box and other animal cleanings are a good alternative for activation. This heap can then be left and the second one filled. Once the first is well rotted and dark brown it can be used either to dig in or mulch beds.

Some of the material on the top of the first heap may remain undecayed and this can be left behind to mix in with the material in the second bin. Using the warmth of summer to get

Lime is best applied in late autumn or during the winter, but as not all soils need lime it is best to test the soil first, using a special kit. Plant needs for lime also differ.

compost well rotted quickly provides material for autumn digging. Bins are then quickly refilled with fallen leaves and other crop remains.

Fertilizers

N.P.K. are the initials of nitrogen, phosphorus and potash respectively, and these are the main soil-borne plant foods. They can be applied in natural organic form—usually more expensive—and as inorganic chemical fertilizers.

Nitrogen, the main food in organic fish manure and inorganic sulfate of ammonia, improves leafy growth. Use this to green-up lawns, to give a new vigorous boost to green leafy vegetables, and to encourage strong growth on bearing fruit trees.

Where plants have suffered from lack of water, hot sun and checks from cold, they can often be reinvigorated with nitrogenous fertilizers. They must not be used excessively in damp shaded conditions as they encourage leafy growth and susceptibility to disease.

Phosphorus is the principal plant food in organic bonemeal and inorganic superphosphate. It encourages root development and helps seeds and fruit to mature. It is not generally used alone, although a dusting can be applied before raking down a seed bed.

Potash is very much the counterbalance to nitrogen. Where lack of sun gives excessive leaf growth and poor flowers, increasing the potash improves the growth.

Wood and bonfire ash is a good source of organic potash while sulfate of potash is the main inorganic source.

Complete fertilizers contain these three elements as well as amounts of the minor trace elements. A general purpose formula is 5-10-5 (5% N, 10% P and 5% K). Most lawn fertilizers are high in nitrogen, while tomato and rose fertilizers are high in potash.

Apply general fertilizers at 2 oz per sq yd (60 g per sq m) early in spring, working them well into the soil. Never apply directly on or near the seed drill.

When transplanting woody subjects add the peat moss and organic matter immediately, mixing them well into the soil, then topdress with fertilizers subsequently. This fertilizer is then slowly washed with rain to the developing roots.

It is a good idea to split the application to fruit and other trees, half in late summer to be taken up by the tree and held ready for the spring burst of growth. The second application in spring will improve summer growth. Well-fed plants are more resistant to frost damage.

Do not apply any general fertilizer in late autumn or winter as much will be washed out with winter rain.

While the general fertilizer applied in the initial soil preparation will do much of what is required, a little top-up material is helpful. Liquid fertilizer can be applied to pole beans, tomatoes, sweet peas and evergreen hedges, for example. A higher potash topdressing to currants, gooseberries and tomatoes will improve flavor. Quick-acting nitrogenous fertilizers like liquid fish can be used to speed lettuce and spinach into spring growth.

Quickest acting of all are foliar fertilizers — the plant food here being taken up by the leaves and any run-off subsequently reaching the roots. They can be applied through the rose of a watering can and through sprayers.

The response will be seen in a few days if the weather is warm enough for rapid growth. All leafy subjects including lettuce, beets, spinach, carrots, hostas, peas and strawberries respond well to foliar feeds.

Remember, if you keep cropping the soil and taking goodness out then organic matter and plant foods must be replaced. The immediately available plant foods are, of course, soluble and easily taken up by the plant roots. In light sandy soils, which drain freely, these plant foods are quickly leached.

A compost heap is an important part of any garden; it is useful to have two heaps, so that the compost can be turned and a new heap started.

Paved edge at flower border makes for easier maintenance.

Apply fertilizers little and often on these soils.

PLANNING AND DESIGN

Once you have listed everything to be contained in your garden, the jigsaw puzzle, fitting them all in, can start. It is a good idea to list the requirements in priority because something may have to be left out.

Many gardens today are so small that landscape design and garden planning in the old sense have to give way to garages, fuel storage, off-street parking space, children's sand boxes and play areas, to name a few.

Even so a little careful planning and some good design ideas can make a small plot look larger than it is. Unsightly buildings and living areas can be screened or hidden behind decorative borders.

I quite like the serried ranks of neat vegetables growing vigorously in a small plot quite close to the house. Others may prefer such areas to be screened and well away from the back door. Greenhouses need regular attention and must be near the house, convenient to heat and water connection.

Bringing buildings like sheds and garages very close to the house often makes them easier to hide, rather than taking them down the garden where the vista from indoors widens. A small area for the compost heap and storage of peat moss bales is best reserved well away from the house.

Scale plans are fine for gardeners practiced in working from a measured drawing. The less experienced may find it easier to mark the various areas out with pegs and strings. Plotting them then on squared paper helps keep the record.

When making or reconstructing a garden, first level the site and mark out the proposed features and areas for buildings.

Here ×*Cupressocyparis leylandii* is being planted to screen the background.

Gardens constantly change as plants grow. Compare this picture of a bed in the author's garden, with the one below, taken six years later.

The small silver *Chamaecyparis pisifera* 'Boulevard' in the picture above is now 5 ft (1.5 m) high, and the pyracantha has screened the wall.

Don't forget the speed of growth of trees and shrubs. Marking the site and likely size in ten years can be quite a revelation. A storage shed or greenhouse may not look anywhere near so big once the space it will occupy has been marked out.

Paved areas, to serve as terraces or patios, are often constructed by the builder of the house. If not, this outdoor living area is one of the first elements of the landscape that you should consider.

Terraces and patios are usually adjacent to the house where they serve many purposes from providing a sitting-out area for relaxation and for enjoying the view of the garden beyond to giving a dry area to clean shoes before entering the house. Terraces can become gardens themselves — raised flower beds can be made from boards, railroad ties or bricks, tubs and pots can be set out and even small water gardens constructed.

Having the water garden above soil level reduces the chances of someone — especially children — falling into the pool by mistake. Raised gardens of any kind, at 20 in. (50 cm) high, with a broad surrounding ledge, are convenient places to sit.

The surface materials or pavement for a terrace or patio can be of gravel (wooden blocks or flagstone rounds or slabs can be set in the gravel), flagstone, patio blocks, brick or poured concrete. Flagstone, blocks and brick can be set in mortar for a more permanent surface or in sand. If they are set in sand this will permit later expansion or re-arrangement of the terrace and will leave space for low plants, such as creeping thyme, that can endure some traffic.

In addition to access from the house to the terrace, there must also be ready access from the terrace to the garden. Steps may be necesary and paths laid out that lead to other parts of the garden.

On small properties especially, avoid planting too many evergreen shrubs along the house foundation. A few low-growing shrubs as accents at entrances with ground-cover plants are more satisfactory.

Along the boundaries of properties, tall-growing evergreens or hedge shrubs can be usefully placed to provide privacy and screen out undesirable views.

Try to keep the lawn area in one large piece rather than cluttering it with random, unrelated plantings. Of course it is often not necessary to have a lawn at all. Some properties are wooden in structure, thus providing a place for a natural garden of wildflowers and shade-tolerant shrubs.

Variations on a plan

The rectangular garden shape is the most common. Some of the permutations in design can easily be illustrated by taking the plan shown opposite.

Working from the house we start with the paved area. The example has a 9 ft × 12 ft (3m × 4m) vegetable plot set in the paved area. But this could equally well be an attractive greenhouse structure, a sand box or a raised water garden.

A small deciduous tree at the end of the terrace provides a little shade, is attractive in itself and from it bird

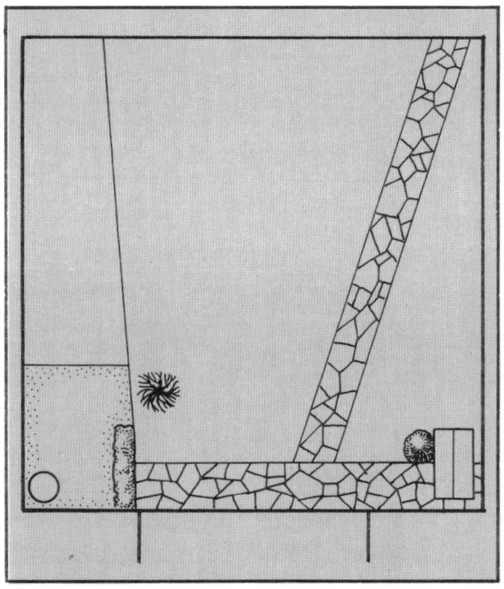

Paths and borders help to make a square garden look more spacious.

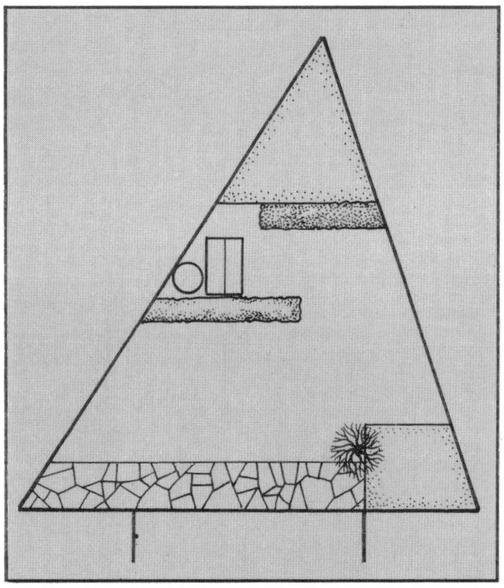

Cleverly placed hedges help to hide the converging lines of a triangle.

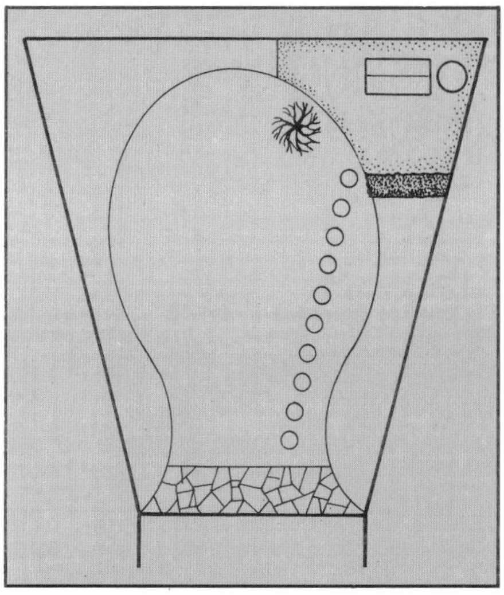

Planting shrubs close to the house helps to hide closely fenced boundaries.

feeders can hang in the winter.

Two borders run out on either side, one on the left filled with dwarf conifers, heathers, azaleas and rhododendrons underplanted with bulbs and given height by a silver birch. The other border has a manhole screened by camellias and is filled closer to the house with hardy perennials and flowering annuals.

Two upright trees (1) and (2) mark the tips of the two borders and give a walk through to a possible vegetable plot (A), and fruit plot (B). These plots could of course be reversed if any taller fruit trees needed to be sited to the north of the plot to avoid casting shadows.

This design has been used to good effect in a plot bordered on east, north and west by very high walls. It could equally well be used in an open site with hedges planted around the boundary for shelter.

Just as long as each section gets a little direct sunshine each day most plants can be grown. Where the area is totally shaded, however, only plants which thrive in shaded conditions should be chosen.

While books and catalogs indicate the conditions best for each plant, remember quite adequate growth is usually obtained with siting compromise. For example planting camellias away from east-facing walls is often recommended because rapid thawing in morning sun can turn the petals of open flowers brown. In practice the number of times this happens in a year is hardly significant and it is much better to plant east-facing if that is the only site available rather than have to manage without this plant.

Move the various features in the plan to achieve the best overall layout. Trees 1 and 2 mark the path through to vegetable and fruit plots A and B.

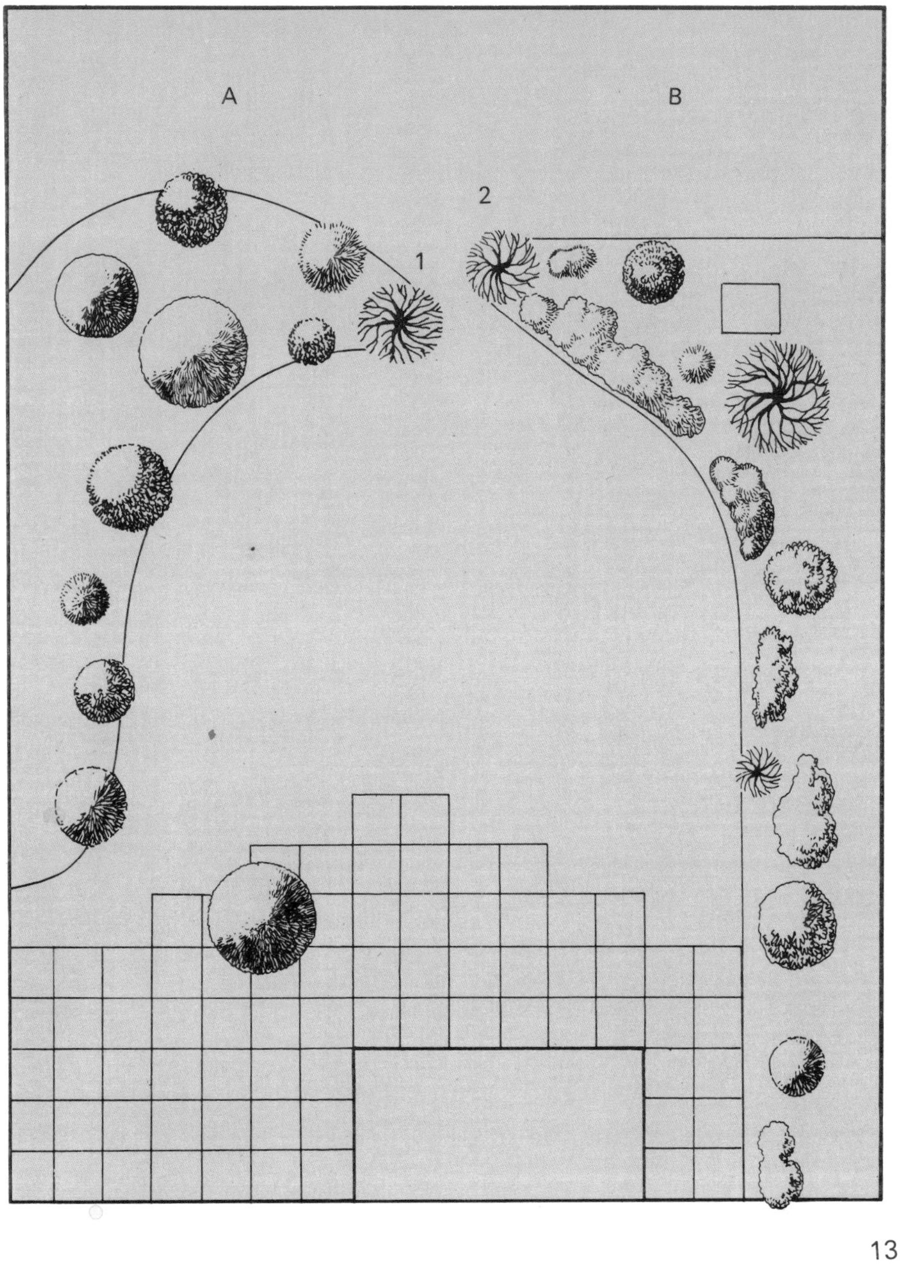

An evergreen close to the house screens the fence and a triangular rose border gives a greater feeling of space in a short narrow garden.

Camellias prefer a sheltered site but after they had been planted in the high wall-surrounded garden (illustrated on page 13), fierce wind turbulance between the walls stripped leaves off the camellias and yet they still thrive and flower.

Efforts are being made to plant more bushy shrubs to reduce the wind damage and get better growth, proving that for from ideal sites can be mastered, with worthwile results.

PROPAGATION

Plants from Seeds

Gardeners repeatedly refer to good tilth, crumbly fine soil and the need for sterile seed and potting composts because this is what you require for high germination of seed.

All seeds need the right amount of moisture, ample oxygen and the right temperture to break dormancy and germinate.

There are some alpine, shrub and tree seeds which need a period of cold, even frosty conditions before they will germinate. This cool treatment is called stratification and often involves storage outside all winter in a layer of sand. Even after stratification these seeds still need warmth, air and moisture to grow.

Overwatered soil "caps" and excludes air, waterlogged compost has insufficient air, dry soil prevents seeds absorbing moisture, swelling and cracking into growth. This may sound a formidable list but in practice it means sow in nicely moistened sterile compost indoors and in damp crumbly soil outdoors when the temperature is warm enough for growth.

If you sow too early, when the temperature is low, moistened seeds are very susceptible to fungus diseases.

Sowing outdoors

Winter frosts, the warming and cooling, wetting and drying all break down winter-dug soils to give good surface conditions for spring seed sowing. Where spring and summer cultivations have given hard lumpy soils try mixing a good layer of well moistened peat moss into the top 1—2 in. (3—5 cm).

When preparing all dug soils for seed sowing knock the lumps down with a fork or cultivator. Then tread over the surface to consolidate the soil somewhat before raking through to get a fine tilth.

Seeds can be sown broadcast and just raked into the surface — as you would for lawns or hardy annual flowers. More often we draw out a shallow drill with draw hoe, trowel tip or piece of wood. The larger the seeds the deeper the drill can be. In practical

Break cloddy soil with a fork. If soil is sticky, wait, or work in damp peat moss.

Large seeds, such as broad bean, can be sown with a trowel.

A piece of wood can be used to draw out the seed drills.

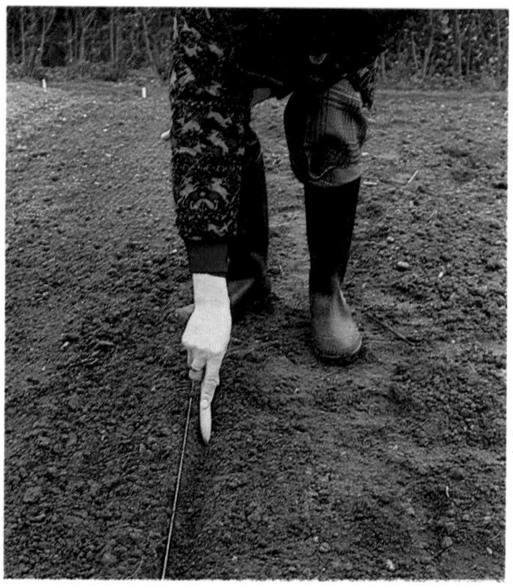

terms this means sufficient soil just to cover the seed and 1 in. (2.5 cm) is sufficient for most.

Where the soil is rather wet and you cannot reach to draw the drill and sow from the path, tread on a wide board to prevent soil compaction. Large seeds such as broad beans and sunflowers can be sown individually with a trowel.

Most of us are tempted to sow seeds too thickly and while it is perhaps an insurance to sow plenty, the more seeds that germinate the more time we need to spend thinning out the seedlings to the required spacing.

Soil can either be shuffled back over the seeds, using the toes of both shoes, or pulled over with a rake. If using a rake be careful not to rake the seeds out when pulling the soil over.

If you don't know what the emerging seedlings will look like mix a little fast-germinating lettuce or radish with them. Once they germinate you will see where to hoe and exactly where the desired seedlings will follow. The indicator seeds are pulled out with the thinnings.

Thinning is best done in two stages, the first to half the final spacing; this reduces the possible losses from slugs, birds or other pests.

There are one or two other guidelines with seeds. Peas and beans are best sown in soil on the dry side — don't soak them in water before sowing as this depresses germination and subsequent root growth.

Accumulation of fertilizer in the surface reduces germination, especially where the whole season's fertilizer application is applied before sowing. Sowing seeds with low germination percentage, for example old seed, will often give less vigorous growth. More vigorous seeds give more vigorous plants, under these conditions.

When storing seeds, every time the temperature is dropped 5°C the life-span is likely to be doubled, between 50°C and 0°C. Keep foil-packed seeds cool to maintain high germination. Seeds in paper packets need dry storage because again each time moisture content is lowered by 1 per cent (within the range from 14 per cent to 4 per cent) the germination life is doubled.

A cool, airtight tin is by far the best storage place for most seeds.

If seedlings become tall and drawn see they are planted well down in the compost when pricked out singly. Use fluorescent lights to obtain stocky seedlings indoors.

Space seeds carefully down the row to reduce the need to thin out later.

Keep the soil between the seedlings hoed to control weeds.

Sowing indoors

Seed and potting composts must in no way be confused with well-rotted garden compost used to improve soil outside. Seed compost is designed to germinate seeds and can be used to root some cuttings. Potting composts are used to grow seedlings on into larger and mature plants.

The name compost probably comes from the original constituents for mixes when good turf was cut and stacked to rot down — that is, be composted — to provide loam, and leaves from beech and oak were given the same treatment to provide leaf mold. These two materials formed the basis of many recipes used by skilled gardeners.

Today we increasingly come across the term "growing medium" and this more aptly describes the very carefully formulated mixes for seed raising and container plant cultivation.

The British John Innes Institute did

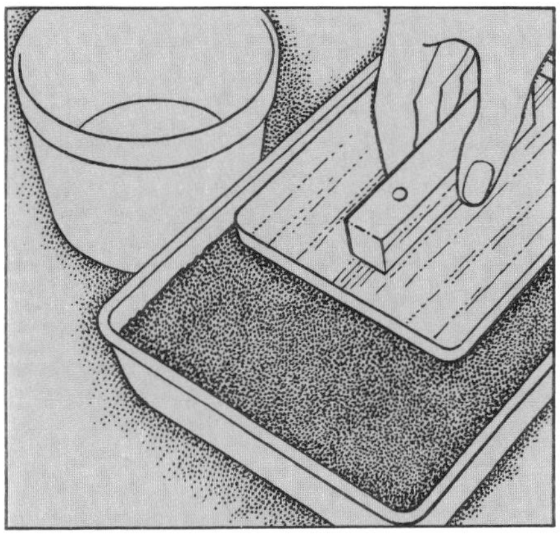

Loosely fill the container before firming the compost evenly.

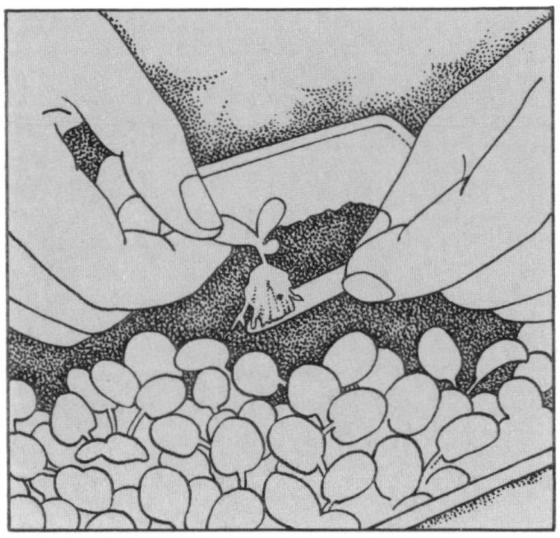

Always handle seedlings by their leaves, lifting with a stick.

much basic research and brought about a reduction in the number of recipes. They introduced a seed compost and a potting compost with a range of fertilizer strengths, but the basic ingredients are the same.

These were later followed by the University of California (U.C.) soilless mixes based on peat moss and sand, and the Cornell mix which uses vermiculite instead of sand. Now we have many commercial brands of soilless mixes, including Jiffy Mix, Redi-Earth and Pro-Mix, to name a few.

These soilless mixes can be used as growing media for seeds and seedlings, cuttings and mature plants; there is no need to have different mixes or composts for each growing procedure. They are convenient and free from diseases and weed seeds. However, since the commercial mixes vary somewhat, it is recommended that you always read the bag label and follow instructions suggested by the packager.

If you prefer to use garden soil (mixed with sand and peat moss) for indoor seed sowing, pasteurize it in the oven at 140°C (60°C) for 30 minutes. Allow about a half hour for the soil mixture to heat up and the same time for it to cool before use.

Cover all but the smallest seeds with a light sprinkling of compost.

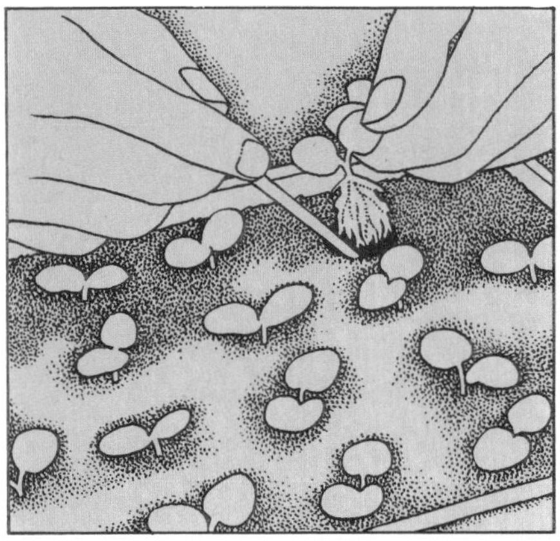

Seedlings should be pricked off into boxes or pots, and spaced evenly.

For those who want to make their own soilless mix, here is a formula from the U.S. Dept. of Agriculture:

- 1 bushel (36 liters) peat moss
- 1 bushel (36 liters) vermiculite
- 11/4 cups (300 milliliters) ground dolomitic limestone
- 1/2 cup (100 milliliters) superphosphate (20 per cent)
- 1 cup (250 milliliters) 5-10-5 fertilizer.

Use a shovel to mix the ingredients, over and over again for a thorough distribution of each element. A little water can be added to reduce the dust during mixing if the pile is very dry.

Mixing base fertilizers evenly right through the peat of soilless mixes, especially the small quantities of trace elements, is difficult. It is better to buy branded formulations and follow the maker's recommendation on subsequent liquid feeding.

You may find it easier to prick off seedlings from peat-and-sand composts because the sand produces a finer root more easily separated from the compost and its neighbors. You can even add a little lime-free sand to all peat compost when seed raising, to make transplanting easier.

Moisture content of all composts is important, especially at seed sowing and seedling transplanting — the pricking-off and potting-on stages. The moisture content is right for all soil-based mixes when a squeezed handful cracks open in one largish crack when you release the grip. Where the compost just crumbles when pressure is released it is too dry and if the lump retains the fingers and hand shape, without cracking, it is too wet.

Soilless composts are sufficiently damp if moisture just oozes from between the fingers when a handful is tightly squeezed. Shallow containers just 1 in. (2.5 cm) deep can be used for fine seeds and these will use less compost, but remember that these shallow containers dry out quickly if not thoroughly watered.

Sow small quantities of seed in flower pots and seed pans — like flower pots but half the depth — larger quantities in seedboxes. Loosely fill the container to the brim with moist compost. Firm a little into corners and around the edge with fingers and then use a flat object; this will leave the firmed compost level $^1/_2$ in. (1—2 cm) or so from the top.

Space seeds over the surface; you can mix very small seeds with some fine dry sand to make the spread more even. Then sprinkle a little more compost over the seeds. Very fine seeds can be covered with fine sand.

Cover the sown seeds with glass to retain moisture and paper to reduce light. Alternatively place in plastic bags to achieve the same ends. A temperature of 55—80°F (13—27°C) is needed for quick germination of most

Seedlings damp off (see box on right) if sown too thickly in dirty boxes.

seeds. Some such as pepper, tomato, eggplant and petunia require warmer temperatures 80—90°F (27—32°C).

Watch the sown pots daily and as soon as you see the first signs of emerging shoots remove the covers, and water overhead with a fine mist to keep the compost damp. Move the pots to a sunny window or place under fluorescent lights, 4 in. (10 cm) from the tubes, for 12—14 hours per day.

Once the first two leaves have unfolded and as soon as they are large enough to handle, prick them off singly into potting compost. Always handle seedlings by the leaves and never bruise the tender stem. Where the seedlings have become a little drawn it may help to lower the stem well into the hole when transplanting.

To take a softwood cutting, select a shoot with six fully developed leaves.

Trim off cleanly just below the bottom two leaves, then cut off the two leaves.

Use a hormone rooting powder, and put cuttings round outside of pot.

Cover with a plastic bag and place in a light, warm position.

PLANTS FROM CUTTINGS

Softwood Cuttings

Very many plants can be increased by taking 2—3 in. (5—7.5 cm) long cuttings from soft young growing tips. More than half of the popular foliage house plants are propagated in this way. A lot of hardy shrubs and many flowering plants, from geraniums and fuchsias to heliotropes and double lobelia.

The method for all of them is the same. Trim the cutting just below a pair of leaves and remove the two bottom leaves. Use rooting hormone if you want to increase the number of roots and to get roots more quickly. Place the cutting in a damp, open compost. Moist sand or vermiculite will do, although the most common rooting compost is an equal mixture of peat moss and clean sharp sand.

Cuttings need light so the leaves can continue to manufacture plant food, but not so much sun that they wilt badly. Covering with a polyethylene bag and placing in a sunny position is fine, except in spring and summer when the cuttings are better out of direct sunlight.

Remove the bag for a little while — half an hour or so — occasionally, to dry the leaves and reduce the chance of wet rot affecting the leaves. Once the cuttings remain turgid with the bag off dispense with the bag. Misting over at midday from then on will help the cuttings to grow away.

Rooted cuttings are then removed and potted up singly.

Hardwood Cuttings

Once again cuttings are prepared from the current year's growth. Here we need the well ripened brown-barked wood, hence the term hardwood. These cuttings are taken in the autumn, winter and spring, during dormancy.

Plants propagated in this way include hedge plants such as privet, flowering shrubs such as deutzia, forsythia, weigela, and fruit bushes (currants and gooseberries for instance), as well as trees like poplar and willow.

Vigorous straight growth 6—8 in. (15—20 cm) long, excluding the soft tip of growth in most cases, is pushed into soft sandy soil 6 in. (15 cm) deep in a greenhouse or cold frame. Or in the garden, make a slit with a spade, line the base with sand, put the cuttings in the slit and tread the soil back firmly.

Twelve months later the young plants prepared in this way should have rooted well and will then be ready for transplanting.

Because hardwood cuttings do not lose moisture as rapidly as softwood cuttings, there is little benefit in providing them with a close humid atmosphere.

Semi-hardwood Cuttings

Young growth with the stem just starting to harden and through a variety of stages to almost hard wood provides cutting material for many plants. Generally the more difficult subjects come under this heading. Plants propagated from half-ripe wood include cotoneaster, jasminium, pyracantha and evergreen barberries, rhododendrons and azaleas as well as many conifers.

It is best to tear off 4 in. (10 cm) long cuttings of conifers with a piece of the older wood at the base for good rooting.

Mist bench propagators and warm humid conditions are needed for the best results. Some of the hardier shrubs can be rooted in peat moss and sand under plastic within a cold-frame.

July to September is the usual time to take this type of cutting but the stage of wood maturity is important and varies with the different plants. Cuttings are likely to take from just over a month to eight months to root depending on the type of plant and rooting conditions.

Root Cuttings

Short lengths of root are the other means of producing new plants from cuttings. Horseradish, oriental poppy, anchusa and phlox, raspberry and shrubby trees such as *Rhus typhina,* can all be propagated in this way.

Relatively thick pieces of root are selected to provide food reserves. Most cuttings are 3—4 in. (7.5—10 cm) long, taken in the dormant season and spaced in sandy soil outside to root.

TOOLS

Good gardens and satisfaction from gardening do not come from a great shed full of tools and equipment. Lay hands on a good spade and very many of the garden tasks can be completed adequately.

There are literally thousands of clever gadgets and redesigned pieces of equipment, but few beat the well tried basic tools that have been developed over years of use.

One piece of advice I strongly recommend is to buy the best to suit your needs. A really good spade will last the ordinary gardener a liftime. By good I mean a really comfortable handle and well-made cutting blade. If you are not too strong choose a smaller, lighter spade but one that is still of good quality.

Second choice must be a good pair of pruners and once again the better quality will give the longest life and best value for money. Third in line for the average garden with a mixture of plants are a lawnmower and shears. Remember with shears that stainless steel does not keep a good sharp cutting edge. You will get better value and a sharper cut for a longer period if you choose a steel with what is best described as a "non-stick" finish. Metal which has been treated in the same way as non-stick cooking pans stays sharp and, like stainless steel, does not rust when accidentally left wet and dirty.

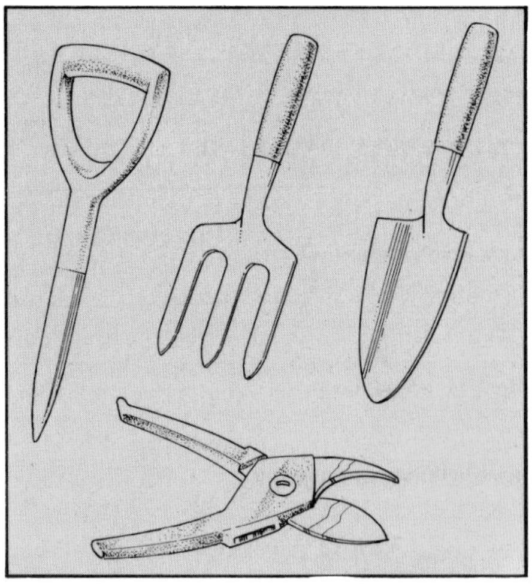

A good set of small hand tools and stainless steel pruners are invaluable.

A good selection of hand tools which will allow most gardening jobs to be executed easily and quickly. Buy the better quality for a lifetime's use.

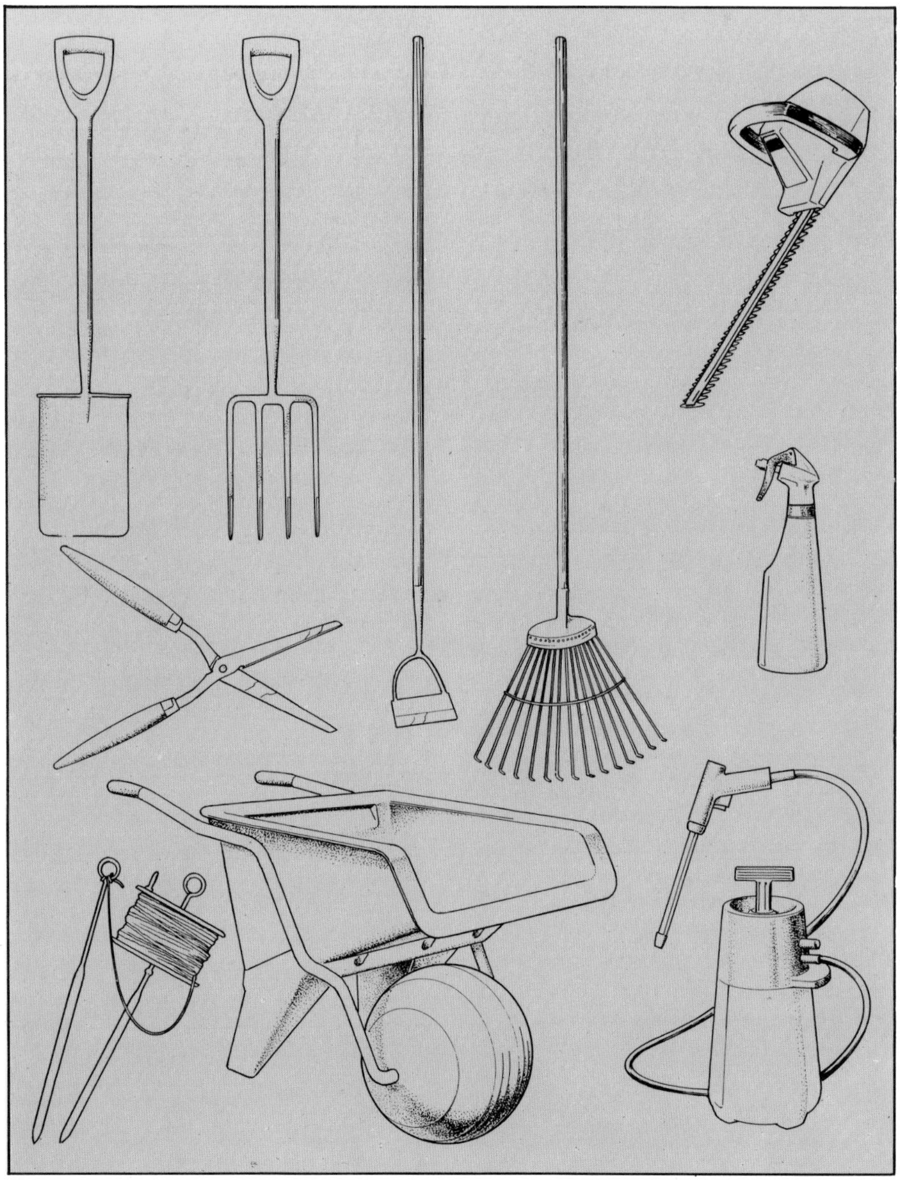

All gardens with fertile soil will have their share of weeds and a regular surface hoe will kill off everything if used often enough and long enough. The Dutch or push hoes are best in my view. You work backwards with these and leave nice crumbly soil free of footprints. Where the draw hoe is used and one works forward, inevitably some of the weeds are firmed back into the soil.

New gardens and established ones being redesigned often need soil moved to change levels. Cement and sand have to be moved for paths and walls. All too often gardeners go out in a hurry and by the cheapest wheelbarrow to move these materials. The carrying box is made of thin galvanized metal which rots in no time as rain collects in the bottom.

A barrow with a pliable plastic box will give much longer service. Unfortunately, this sort of wheelbarrow is not yet available in the U.S.A.

When it comes to sprayers for pesticide application there are small cheap plastic hand models which do an adequate job. We often need just a little insecticide or fungicide in smaller gardens and the small models hold just the amount for this.

Where you have a fruit tree or from 12—18 roses which need spraying regularly, the half gallon (2.27 liter) pump-up plastic models will give good service for many years. Be sure to use up all the diluted chemicals and wash out and drain the sprayer after use. Just a little water left in the nozzle or pump mechanism can split the plastic if it freezes.

Spring-tine lawn rakes serve several puposes and can be used for lawn renovation, leaf gathering and the production of a fine tilth for seed sowing. Where the amount of money to be spent is limited choose the wire spring-tine rake rather than one with rigid tines.

Power tools can be used to speed and ease the workload, especially in larger gardens. Battery operated tools are safest and quiet to use.

Where house electricity is used for hedge trimming and mowing, work systematically across the area to avoid cutting cables.

Layflat plastic tubing can be very useful for watering, and is one of the simplest and most efficient forms of irrigation.

WATERING

Plants have tremendous powers to suck up water from the ground; just think of the distance from root to branch tip of large trees. Water evaporating from the leaves starts the power force which draws up moisture.

Where a plant cannot absorb water quickly enough the foliage wilts to conserve moisture. Occasional wilting will do little harm, although every check of this kind inevitably reduces growth.

Shallow cultivation breaks the soil crust and eliminates weeds, but both purposes are more easily served by mulches.

Waterlogged soil conditions suffocate plant roots and with a checked and less efficient root system plants are more susceptible to drought when weather conditions change. Soils which remain flooded need the drainage improved. Pipe drains are the ideal way of achieving this, draining out from the pipes into boundary ditches. This is not practical however for many suburban areas where gardens are small and packed closely together.

The only answer here is to raise up the soil level of those areas where fruit bushes, vegetables and flowers are to be grown. Select plants which are able to withstand the wet in the remaining garden areas.

Something like 1 in. (2.5 cm) of rain evaporates from the soil via the plant leaves in 8—10 days of sunny warm weather. The more plants there are and the more leaves, the faster moisture will be lost.

Replacing the water loss is best done in good heavy doses applied occasionally. Just wetting the surface does more harm than good.

A watering can is the number one piece of equipment and long-spout designs are easiest to use. The longer the spout the lower the angle it is to the ground. Thus when tipped the water doesn't shoot out quite so forcefully and can be more gently applied to soil around plants.

Where deep water penetration is required a slowly dripping nozzle is most effective. Sprinklers which spray water right up into the air in a great arch suffer a loss from evaporation before the water hits the soil.

Simple and cheap black "lay-flat" plastic tube with holes punctured every 6—12 in. (15—30 cm) along its length will drip or produce light water jets close to the soil. The wider the hole spacing the longer the run of tubing you can use on the ordinary household hose.

The same principle can be used to help recently transplanted trees suffering in hot weather. Tie a large, thick walled plastic bag to the tree stake. Fill the bag with water and prick a small hole in the base so that the water drips out against the trunk and runs down the root deep into the soil. This is a good system for watering small fruit trees in the garden.

Oscillating sprinklers, self-rotating sprinkler heads and a wide variety of nozzles can be used to irrigate lawns and areas of ornamental and food gardens where there is an abundant water supply.

Repeated watering in this way can damage the soil structure. A mulch will protect the soil surface and reduce the need for frequent watering. Mulching materials include garden compost, leaves and leaf mold, pine needles, hay, bark and wood-chips. Apply 2—3 in. (5—7.5 cm) deep.

Where it is not practical to lay proper land drains, wet soils can be worked quite satisfactorily by raising the level of the beds.

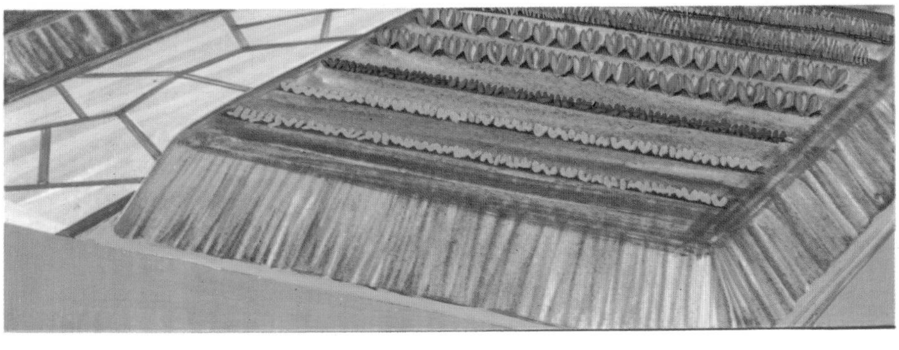

Trees and shrubs can be bought with bare roots, like those the author is holding, and conifers are often balled, but most are sold in containers.

CONTAINER PLANTS

Over the past ten years there has been a complete change in the way nurserymen grow very many plants. Up to the mid 1960's, nearly all but a few species of shrubs, conifers, herbaceous plants, trees, fruit bushes, roses and climbers were grown in open fields. Transplanting was then restricted to the dormant late autumn to early spring period for deciduous plants, and spring and autumn for evergreens.

Now most plants are available grown in pots or are, to use the accepted term, "container grown". Quite apart from the commercial implications of this change, it allows the gardener to plant perennial subjects the year round, as long as the soil is unfrozen and not too wet. Container-grown plants are also transplanted with virtually no root damage and the chance of losses after planting are very much reduced, if not entirely eliminated.

Plants grown in the open field and lifted to dispatch to gardeners, either bare-root in the case of trees and shrubs or with a burlap-retained soilball in the case of conifers and evergreens, are still available and sometimes cost less when delivered by public transport. Such plants still serve the gardener well if planted carefully, but the trend is very much to container growing.

It is important to check that container plants are well established and fully rooted into the pot. Growers often lift plants from the field and containerize them. If purchased before they are fully rooted into the pot they have as much root disturbance as the plants sold straight from the field and the container-grown advantages are lost.

There are several ways of checking container-grown plants. First, if you lift the plant carefully by the stem the compost and container will come too with no harm done. Freshly potted plants will come out of the compost. If when you start to lift you see the compost cracking on the surface and feel the plant starting to come from the pot, replace quickly and leave until it is fully rooted.

Container-grown plants will often have roots coming out of the base of the pot, showing the roots are right through the compost. Avoid plants which have great quantities of root through the base. This usually means they have outgrown their pot and may well be root-bound (masses of root in the pot) and the growth starved and checked as a result.

Young plants growing strongly without experiencing a check to growth will always be the best buy. Larger and older plants appear to be better value for money, but if they have been short of food and water such that growth is checked, the younger stock will grow away more quickly and be the better buy.

One other sure sign of plants fully rooted in the container is mossy and small weed growth on the surface. Newly potted plants have fresh clean compost on the surface; as they stand in the open and the compost settles some form of green inevitably develops.

Very many different materials are used to make the container, such as soft and rigid plastic, some from biodegradable material, and metal. Where plants are in metal containers be very careful with the cut edges when transplanting because they are very sharp and hazardous to handle. I prefer to remove *all* containers when planting. Even the biodegradable ones will sap up nitrogen at the plant's expense if left in place. Even worse, in dry soil conditions and dry weather the container can dry right out and isolate the root-ball within the container.

Follow all the good soil preparation rules, whatever kind of propagation and growing method has been used. Once the soil has been dug over one or two spade's depth and plenty of peat and/or well-rotted compost mixed into it, take out a good-sized hole.

Remove the container before planting, which is easy with the plastic type.

Always water the container well before planting. It is a wise precaution to water and leave for several hours and water again to ensure the container is wet right through. A little liquid fertilizer in the last watering will give the plant a good start in life, especially where the container is full of roots.

Place the container-grown plant in the hole and check that the depth is right. This will leave the compost in the container 1 in. (2.5 cm) or so lower than the soil surface. It is ideal if the compost is just covered after the soil has settled.

Once the hole is right remove the container. I also like to unravel some roots very carefully if they have fully circled the base of the container. Spread these roots out around the bottom of the hole and fill in with good soil, firming the area with your feet as you work.

A final watering to settle the soil around the plant roots will be needed in dry soil and dry weather. Mulch with peat or compost to cover the surface soil and reduce the rate of drying. Where the soil is wet and sticky at planting time, mixing in peat will make the texture crumbly and easier to handle. It is wise not to firm wet soil too much or it will cake hard once it dries. Another firming may well be needed if planted in wet soil, once it has dried a little.

Tall-growing shrubs, conifers and trees will need some form of support until the root system is fully established in the soil. Larger specimens in big containers will have a heavy root ball to help anchor the plant against wind but the larger the stem and branches above ground, the greater the wind resistance.

Pushing a stout cane right through the compost and into the soil below gives good anchorage for many plants, including young trees. Where stout stakes are needed it is often best to insert them into the ground at a 45—60^0 angle to the stem and away from the root-ball to avoid excessive root damage.

Secure the uppermost part of tree stems to the stake for maximum support. Check the ties every 2—3 months during the growing season. Fast-growing conifers can have the soft bark girdled in weeks if tight plastic or wire ties are not loosened regularly.

If for any reason it is necessary to lift and transplant a container-grown plant after a season or two, you will find the root-ball in the container remains firm and makes transplanting easier.

If roots have encircled the base of the container, carefully tease some of them free without damaging the main ball of roots, which must remain intact.

To give the plant a good start, it is wise to work a liberal quantity of peat into the surface. Alternatively compost can be used.

Lawns

An area of neatly trimmed grass can make a garden complete, and it is difficult to imagine the average home garden without its patch of lawn.

Grass is so versatile that we can use it for many purposes, from purely utilitarian grass paths and play areas, to beautifully kept lawns, which can be a perfect foil to formal ornamental gardens.

It is too easy to take the lawn or grassed area for granted and forget that plants are involved — plants which are subjected to constant cutting and wear. Give grass the same care bestowed on vegetables and flowers, and the effort will be repaid many times.

PREPARING THE SITE

Grass grows well in nearly all situations, although densely shaded areas and very steep banks are best avoided. In fact, where the slope is great it is more sensible to cover it with shrubs. The soil must be graded sufficiently to give a surface level enough to mow, although a slight slope overall is no bad thing.

Heavy clay soils and those which can lie wet should ideally be drained, although the small garden owner often has nowhere to drain the excess water. Should you have a ditch or water course at the lowest point of your garden, then a 3 in. (7.5 cm) diameter line of pipes set 18 in. (46 cm) deep across the area to be grassed would be an advantage. Cover the pipes with 12 in. (30 cm) of either clinker or gravel before filling with the last 6 in. (15 cm) of topsoil.

If the laying of drainage pipes is not possible, the next best thing is to add peat moss and coarse sand to improve drainage. Raising the surface slightly overall will also help. At least 14 lb (6.3 kg) of sand to each square yard or meter and a 1 in. (2.5 cm) depth of peat will be needed for good results.

Light sandy soils present no drainage problems but they dry out very quickly in hot weather. it is equally important, therefore, to add plenty of organic material to these soils.

Debris left by builders is best removed from the site. It is sometimes possible to bury sub-soil at the same time as bringing buried topsoil up to the surface. Should the site only have very inferior topsoil, then either a 6 in. (15 cm) depth of topsoil will need to be brought in or a very heavy dressing of organic material worked into the soil. Since both these improvements may be too costly, especially when large lawn areas are planned, for many the solution may be heavy fertilizing and watering. And as the lawn ages, grass clippings and root decay can improve the soil to some degree.

The majority of lawn grasses thrive in moderately acid to slightly alkaline soils (5.5—7.5 pH), so unless a soil test indicates a very acid soil, liming may not be necessary.

It is much easier to cultivate, level and grass down the whole area, cutting out beds and borders later. In any case digging the young turf into such areas considerably improves the soil for other plants.

MAKING A LAWN

Where an area of cultivated garden is just left and the resulting weed growth regularly mown, an area of indigenous grasses will quickly become established. These can form an acceptable play area and a quite reasonable sward and are useful for reducing cultivated areas in large gardens. Commercial fruit growers call this "tumble down" grassing.

Whether the lawn is made by seeding, laying sod (turf), or by planting sprigs (divisions), the initial preparation is the same. Ideally, you should prepare the soil in early autumn for spring lawns, or in spring for autumn lawns to give the soil a chance to settle. Also, ideally late summer and early fall are the best times to sow grass seed throughout most of the USA. In the South, spring and early summer are preferred. However, home gardeners are often impulsive and choose the times convenient for them.

After rough clearing to remove tree stumps and roots, stones and other debris, the soil is ready for cultivation — *if* it is not excessively wet. This is a good time to add lime (if needed),

To level a site, prepare pegs with the top 2 in. (5 cm) marked off. Use a straight edge and spirit-level to align them, then level soil against the marks.

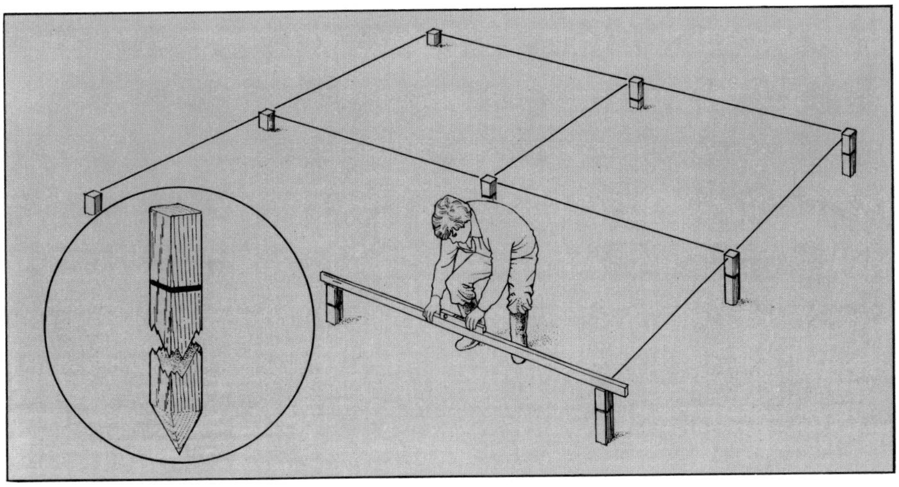

organic material (if the soil is very sandy or more sub-soil than top-soil) and fertilizer.

A soil test by a professional (contact your regional extension agent, listed in the telephone book under county government, for information) to determine if lime (or its opposite, sulfur, for some regions of very alkaline soil) is needed. However, very acid soils will invariably be improved by a general recommendation: add 75 lb (22.68 kg) of ground limestone to 1000 sq ft (90 sq m).

The organic matter, spread about 3 in. (7.62 cm) deep, can be peat moss, well-rotted manure or garden compost and anything else you have access to, including spent mushroom soil.

A new lawn's fertilizer should be high in phosphorus to encourage root development of the grasses. Mixing it in the soil at the time of cultivation will put the phosphorus where the roots can reach it. (Higher nitrogenous fertilizers will be spread over the new grass later.) A safe recommendation for an initial fertilizer application is 5-10-5, distributed uniformly by a spreader at the rate of 40 lb (18.15 kg) for 1000 sq ft (90 sq m).

The depth of cultivation should be from 6—8 in. (15—20 cm). Limited areas can be forked over by hand but a rotary tiller is preferable for larger properties and can be rented if you don't own one. The soil and added materials should be mixed well but avoid over-cultivation that will reduce the soil structure to dust.

Levelling

A smooth lawn, free of bumps and hollows, begins with careful preparation. Gentle slopes across the area and undulation can improve the appearance of some garden designs, but a flowing surface is needed to prevent mowers cutting into the soil. Flowing but even and perfectly flat surfaces are achieved by careful raking, and this is the final stage of levelling.

Before final raking, though, a primitive but time-honored practice for levelling the surface after cultivation is to drag, by rope, a ladder (placed flat on ground) sideways across the surface. This operation will break down bumps and fill up hollows and help firm the soil faster than raking which will be the final step.

SEED OR TURF

Whether you create a lawn from seed or turf depends on what you want from your lawn, and the advantages and disadvantages of each method are set out in the table opposite.

Without question I prefer to use seed, though new methods of growing turf using loamless composts and good seed mixtures are promising. Such turf is likely to be more expensive than seed but it will be quicker to establish as a lawn.

Kinds of Grasses

There are many different kinds of grasses and mixtures of two or more kinds are usually planted together. Both seed mixtures and turf sod available from local outlets are blends formulated for the soils and climates of the region. There are also special blends for shady and play areas. However, many grasses are sold separately, especially by mail-order seed companies, so the enterprising gardener can make his own blends or follow recommendations of the local extension agent or state agricultural experiment stations.

Some of the well-known grasses are listed below.

Grasses for the North

Bent grasses (*Agrostis* spp.) are fine-leaved and make attractive lawns. They do best in cool, humid regions, such as in the Pacific North-west. Elsewhere they are mostly used on golf courses where they can receive the special attention they need.

Kentucky blue grass *(Poa pratensis)* and its many improved varieties such as 'Merion', 'Adelphi', 'Delta', 'Fylking', 'Pennstar' and 'Windsor' are the most important northern grasses. Kentucky blue grass is often blended with fescues to form a dense lush turf.

The fine-leaved fescues such as Chewings *(Festuca rubra commutata)* perform best in cool, humid regions but some of its variants, such as 'Jamestown' and 'Highlight', are vigorous enough to thrive with blue grass selections in most areas.

Perennial ryegrass *(Lolium perenne)*, although coarse-leaved and considered short-lived, grows fast. It is now available in many improved varieties with finer-textured leaves. A few are 'Pennfine', 'Manhattan' and 'Game'.

Zoysia grasses are useful in the North in those gardens or regions where their brown foliage in winter and early spring is not a drawback.

Since many winter lawns in the North are a mess anyway (or are under snow), this concern for the appearance of Zoysia for a few months seems trivial. Some zoysias are coarse-textured but even these are satisfactory for summer homes.

Plant Zoysia from seeds or sprigs (divisions).

Grasses for the South

Bahia grass *(Paspalum notatum)* is coarse and tough but useful in Florida and like regions where other grasses fail. It is fast-growing and requires frequent mowing to remove its tall seed heads.

Bermuda grass *(Cynodon dactylon)* withstands drought and traffic and is often blended with perennial rye-grass. There are superior hybrids which must be planted from sprigs rather than seeds.

Since Bermuda grasses turn brown in cool weather, they are often overseeded with annual and perennial ryegrass, blue grass and some bents for winter greenery.

Carpet grass *(Axonopus affinis)* is fast-growing, requires little fertilizing and grows well on very acid, damp soils. It needs frequent mowing to remove its seed heads.

Centipede grass *(Eremochloa ophiuroides)*, popular in the Deep South, is low-growing and easy to mow. It needs acid soil and only moderate feeding but unfortunately is susceptible to varying kinds of pests and diseases.

St. Augustine grass *(Stenotaphrum secundatum)* does well in neutral to slightly alkaline soils and is shade tolerant. It is susceptible to chinch bug attacks.

Zoysia and its named improvements such as 'Meyer' and 'Emerald' are disease resistant and make dark green, dense turf.

They can be overseeded for winter color but their dense growth makes this difficult.

Sowing

You need to sow when the soil is damp and day temperatures are warm enough for speedy germination and nights are cool for root establishment. This ideally means spring or early autumn, periods when rainfall is likely over most of the country.

The standard seed rate is 3 lbs (1.36 kg) per 1000 square feet (9.0 sq m), although with the cheaper, coarser mixtures and with ideal growing conditions sowing rates can be a little less than this.

After raking the surface, divide the seed to be broadcast into two equal

SEED OR TURF?

SEED

The case for	The case against
Cheaper to buy. Easier to put down, less weight to handle. Easy to purchase and hold until weather conditions are right. Choice of grass mixtures to suit site and purpose.	Takes longer to get established. Can suffer more from weed competition. Birds can damage emerging grass seedlings. Seedling grass can be infected by disease in cold, wet conditions.

TURF

The case for	The case against
Quick to establish and ready to use earlier. Less soil preparation needed as long as site is level. Longer period of time when turf can be laid successfully.	Difficult to obtain in good quality. Heavy to handle and takes more time to lay. Must be put down within a day or so of delivery More expensive. Turves shrink and gaps open in dry weather.

halves and apply one half, walking over the area in one direction. Then sow the remainder walking at right angles, to get an even spread. (Except for the smallest plots, a spreader, 24 in (61 cm) wide, is recommended for uniform distribution of the seed. Set the spreader for the openings given on the seed bag).

When the soil is moist and the surface dry, choose a calm time and keep the hand well above the soil to spread seed. Cast the seed gently upwards and it will float down to give an even spread. If you have not sown grass seed before, practice first with an equal volume of dry peat moss to get the knack.

Right: To achieve even coverage scatter seeds gently upwards into the air. *Below:* Broadcasting too close to the soil will result in uneven coverage.

Once sown, just very lightly rake into the surface; running the back of the rake over the soil is often all that is required.

Do not roll and water only gently in order to avoid caking the surface and damaging the good crumbly conditions.

Do not worry either about some seed remaining on the surface, or about birds taking seed. The sowing rates are ample to allow for some of these minor losses.

When very dry weather follows sowing, it may be necessary to water the seeded area often, even daily. Frequent light waterings—an exception to the usual gardening instructions — are better than prolonged soakings that may eventually cause the seeds to be washed away.

A light mulch of moist peat moss or clean straw scattered over the grass seed can protect the soil from drying and washing and discourage birds from taking dust baths. The grass will grow through the mulch which adds humus as it decays.

A Lawn from Turf

Many sod farms specializing in fine turf are in existence. Sometimes you can buy directly from the farm but more often the sod is sold through garden centers. Look for healthy, weed-free turf that has not dried out. There are also specialists who sell plugs or sprigs

Stack turf carefully until you are able to lay it, which should be as soon as possible. Start at one corner of the plot and stagger the joins. Work from a plank to avoid damaging the newly laid turf.

of zoysia and other mild-climate grasses.

Laying Turf

Once delivered the turf should be laid within a day or two. Should wet weather prevent laying then unroll and unfold each piece in a shady place and keep well watered until it can be put down properly.

Spring and Fall in the North, whenever the soil is frost-free and not too wet, is the best time to lay. If this job is carried out in late spring and summer, hot dry weather will cause shrinkage and cracks between the

This unusual lawn of sedum shows what imagination can do for a garden.

turves, unless regular heavy watering can be given.

Start putting the turf down from one corner or one side of the plot. Once the first row or two is down, place a board on the laid turf and work outwards over the unturfed area. At the edges overlap the turf to leave sufficient for edging back in a few months' time to give the final straight edges.

Stagger each row of turf to give a brick-laying pattern and lightly roll the whole area twice in opposite directions to finish off. Tight contact between turves and soil ensures rapid root establishment into the new soil and the complete knitting of roots between the edges of each turf. Water thoroughly, and frequently thereafter if rainfall is inadequate.

Turf laid in autumn or early winter is unlikely to need cutting before the spring. Don't be afraid to mow grass as soon as it is $1^1/_2$—2 in. (4—5 cm) long, but keep the mower blade high, just trimming off the tips or not removing more than a third of the blades.

Sprigs or plugs of zoysia are usually planted about 6 in. (15.24 cm) apart in rows 6 in. (15.24 cm) apart to achieve complete coverage in about 18—24 months.

GRASSLESS LAWNS

Plants other than grass can be used to cover the ground and a few, like chamomile *(Anthemis nobilis)* much seen in Europe and Britain, even give the close-knit look of grass. Small divisions of this are set 4—6 in. (10—15 cm) apart and are best grown in sun and rather sandy soil.

Mother-of-thyme *(Thymus serpyllum)* is another low, creeping plant for sun and sandy soils. *Sedum acre,* the well-known rock garden plant, with its ground-hugging habit and bright yellow flowers is another possibility for sun but it will not withstand traffic.

In the Southwest and southern California, dichondra *(Dichondra micrantha)* with its close-growing rounded leaves gives the effect of a lush green lawn all year round. It can also be mowed.

Periwinkle or creeping myrtle *(Vinca minor)* has ever-green foliage and pretty lavender-blue flowers in spring. Its 6 in. (15 cm) viney growth does not resemble grass in the least but as a carpeting plant under trees or on shaded slopes, it is unexcelled.

Other hardy ground covers for shade include pachysandra *(Pachysandra terminalis),* sweet woodruff *(Asperula odorata)* and the common English Ivy *(Hedera helix).*

CUTTING GRASS

The average lawn will be cut many

In Britain, a good lawn is one with neat alternating stripes. These are achieved by mowing in the method described below, but a reel type of mower is required for this effect.

times a year and it is this treatment which will have more effect on the sward than any other. Very fine grasses will stand quite close mowing, say $^1/_2$in. (13 mm), and regular close mowing is one way of reducing rough, coarse grasses.

Most lawns with a wider mixture of grasses are best maintained at a height of $1^1/_2$—2 in. (4—5 cm) and cut at least once, and in spring twice, a week to give the best turf.

Experts differ on the necessity of collecting the grass clippings. Collecting is much tidier, supposedly reduces the build-up of dead organic matter on the surface and reduces the spread of weed seeds. But succulent clippings decay quickly, returning some nutrients and humus to the soil.

Start mowing in spring with the blade set high, at $1^1/_2$ in. (4 cm), reducing the height as speed of growth increases. It is advisable to raise the mower blade slightly in very hot weather.

A longer grass leaf is better able to sustain good green color in hot, dry conditions in high summer.

Drawing either a large brush or heavy sack over the lawn before mowing knocks off dew and speeds drying. It also helps to scatter worm casts and lifts and exposes straggly stems to the mower.

It is best to cut grass when the surface is dry, and brushing early in the day will certainly help to achieve this in spring and in fall.

Cut two widths of the mower at the top and bottom of the lawn before cutting the remainder in parallel lines. While it is easier and quicker to cut in the direction of the length of the lawn, occasionally cut in the right-angle direction to remove the more stubborn straggly stems.

To create a striped effect, first cut across both ends of the lawn, then mow in alternate directions in even widths.

Choice of Mower

The reel mower is essential for the best finish on lawns and golf greens. It can be manually pushed, or powered by gas engines.

The parallel stripes typical of an English lawn are only achieved with a reel mower. The more blades to the cylinder and the more cuts per yard, the finer will be the finish.

See that the cylinder and base blade are finely set to cut the grass clean and avoid leaving bruised and browning ends. The test for correct setting is the ability to cut thin paper the length of the base blade by rotating the cylinder by hand.

Where the cylinder is set just touching the base blade and yet is still easy to rotate, the cylinder is virtually self-sharpening. After 15 years of regular use my mower has required no sharpening or repair. The only requirements are a stone-free surface, the occasional drop of oil and the blades and rollers kept clean, especially after cutting damp, clinging grass.

Rotary blade mowers are best for longer grass and for wet and rougher conditions, especially on banks and under trees. There is a choice between rotary mowers powered by gas (the most common), electricity and battery. Modern designs powered by electricity are very easy to use and keep quite large areas of grass under control. Battery mowers are comparatively quiet, easy to use and avoid the risk of cutting a live power cable, but you must remember they are heavier than other machines and it is necessary to keep the battery charged.

Once the garden exceeds $^1/_4$—$^1/_2$ acre (1,000—2,000 sq m), then a ride-on mower becomes a great work and time saver.

Size of machine required is related to the area to be cut. Hand pushed mowers of 12—14 in. (30—15 cm) are adequate for the average small garden. Increase the mower cut from 12 to 18 in. (30 to 45 cm) and you increase the area cut in a given time by two and a half times.

A motor mower with a 30 in. (75 cm) wide cut will cover an acre (4047 sq m) in approximately an hour.

LOOKING AFTER THE LAWN

Repeated mowing and the regular treading as people use a lawn inevitably compacts the surface on all but the most sandy, free-draining soils. Decaying old leaves and roots also accumulate to cause an unsightly matted surface.

Regular maintenance is needed to counteract this wear and tear, and September or October is the best time for this. First, thoroughly rake the surface using a spring wire-tined rake or a thatch rake. A thatch rake works for small areas where the layer of decayed organic matter known as "thatch" is not extensive. For large lawns it is better to rent dethatching equipment powered by a gas engine or hire a professional crew with both

Some of the many types of mowers. Top row, from left to right: ride-on rotary mower, gas rotary, electric rotary; bottom row, from left to right: rotary grass collection hopper, reel hand mower, wheeled hand mower.

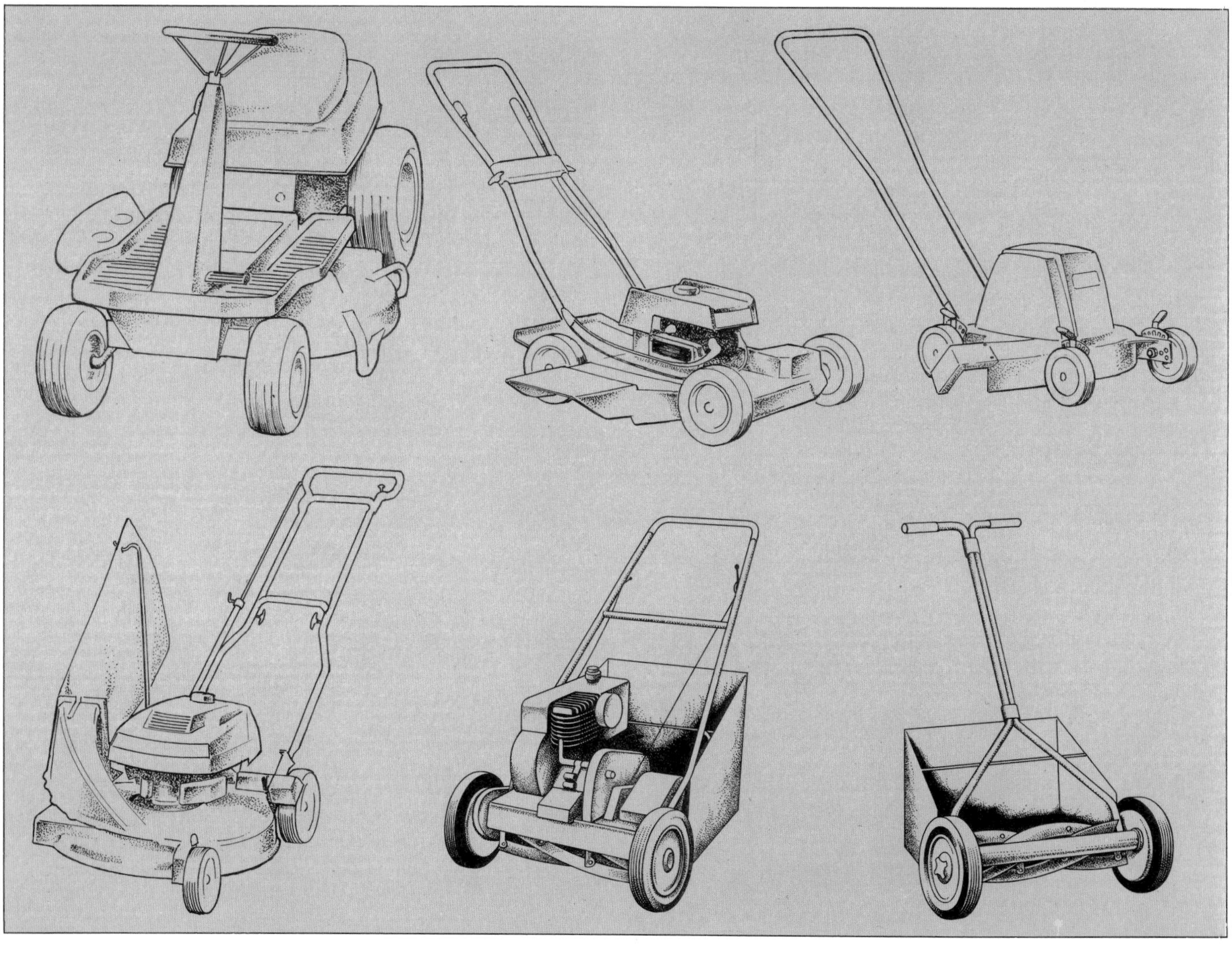

Sweeping the lawn early in the morning with a wide broom knocks off the dew, and the grass dries more quickly for mowing. Worm casts are also spread.

dethatching and aerating equipment.

After you rake, aerate with a special tool, such as a hollow-tined fork, or by piercing some 4—6 in. (10—15 cm) deep with an ordinary garden fork. The garden fork, a hollow-tined fork and really strong machine-powered aerators are best.

Aeration holes should then be filled by brushing or raking in a turf dressing at 2—7 lb per sq yd (1—3 kg per sq m). The dressing can be peat moss and sand, screened soil and sand, or similar combinations of material which will encourage new root growth and improve drainage from the surface.

It is important not to apply so deep that the grass is suffocated. Rubbing the mixture into the surface with the back of a rake works it into holes and hollows as well as uncovering the grass. Or drag a steel door mat over area. If wet weather prevents autumn treatment, aeration can be undertaken in early spring.

Slight hollows in the lawn can be filled at the time of top dressing, although it may take several years to build up to the required level.

Dips and hollows are more quickly straightened by cutting the turf over the area in question, lifting it back and either removing soil or infilling before rolling back the turf. Where gaps are left between returned turves they should be filled with a soil mixture similar to that for aeration treatment and seeded.

Keeping a Trim Edge

Neatly trimmed edges to the lawn are almost as important as a well cut surface — the both give a finishing touch to a good garden. Once or twice a year it is necessary to cut the grass and soil back to a line. A guide is needed for the half-moon edging tool and this can be either a string line between two posts or the straight edge of a piece of timber. Curved edges can be marked out with a supple hose (stiff hoses are more likely to fall to the desired shape if warm). Really sharp, even curves can be cut using a string as radius attached to the edging iron.

Make sure the cut edge slopes outwards at the base, as this strengthens the edge and reduces the chance of it breaking away. Once soil has been cut subsequent trimming is best done with long-handled shears. Here the secret is to hold the left hand still and work the right-hand handle to achieve the cut. The left hand moves the shear along after each cut as the right hand opens up the shear to take the fresh cut of overhanging grass.

Where a small area of edge breaks back it can be repaired by cutting out a rectangle of turf, reversing the turf so that the hole is inside and filling this with compost ready for seeding. Paths which have become too narrow by repeated edging can also be widened by cutting turf along each edge, moving the turf outwards, then infilling the center and seeding. This retains a good outside edge of well-established turf.

It is unwise to have a grass path much narrower than say $2\frac{1}{2}$—3 ft (75—90 cm), for convenience of cutting.

A half-moon edging tool is used with a batten to cut a straight edge.

A length of hose can be used to create an evenly curved edge.

Watering

Generally speaking the average garden lawn is best left unwatered. Where a rich green lawn is required right through the summer then irrigation should start before the soil gets really dry and be continued right through any

YEAR-ROUND LAWN CARE						
Operation	**Mar-Apr**	**May-June**	**July-Aug**	**Sept-Oct**	**Nov-Dec**	**Jan-Feb**
Sow lawn seed or plant sprigs (new lawns or worn patches)	●	○	●	●		
Overseed dormant lawns for winter color (South only)				○	○	
Lay turf (new lawns or worn patches)	●	○		●	●	
Apply selective weedkillers	●○	●○	●○	○		○
Check for pests and diseases		○	●○	○		
Apply high nitrogen fertilizers	●	○	○		○	○
Apply low nitrogen fertilizers	○		●	●	○	○
Test soil and add lime if needed	●○			●○	●	●
Aerate and dethatch		○	○	●		
Rake up leaves	●			●	●	
Mow*	●	●○	●○	●○	○	○
Water, as necessary	○	●○	●○	●○	○	○
Service mower				○	●○	●

Key ● NORTH ○ SOUTH
Note Operations overlap from month to month according to climate and region.

* set blades higher in summer and do not remove more than one third of grass growth at one time

dry period. Occasional watering will just encourage surface roots which soon shrivel back with the first really hot, dry day.

Some 5 gallons (22 liters) of water will evaporate from a square yard in a week of hot weather, so even small lawns will need considerable quantities of water to retain all the moisture needed. Aeration in the autumn to encourage deeper rooting is far better than occasional watering.

Either oscillating lawn sprinklers or trickle hoses are needed to apply all the water needed slowly and gain good penetration. The higher the spray of water the greater will be the loss in evaporation before the much needed water actually reaches the grass.

There are many sprinklers for lawns. Choose a size to suit the area.

Feeding

While raking in a lawn top dressing after aeration feeds the lawn, additional fertilizers will be needed to retain a rich green color. The same general principles apply for grass as for other crops when selecting fertilizer. Nitrogen is needed for strong green leafy growth in spring and summer. Superphosphates encourage root growth and are best applied in autumn and early spring. Potash is not required in great quantity but a little at some stage in the year encourages good strong growth, and gives resistance to dry conditions, wear and disease.

Lime may or not be required, and alkaline conditions encourage unwanted clover. Occasionally, however, old lawns on thin acid soils will become excessively acid, particularly when organic matter has built up on the surface. A sure sign of this is greener grass along the lime-washed lines for sports areas. Where this does occur, then lime should be applied according to test results.

The average lawn only needs one dressing of autumn lawn fertilizer and one general lawn fertilizer in the spring. However, frequency of feeding depends on soil fertility and local climates as well as type of fertilizer used.

Above: Spike the turf with fork tines in the autumn.

Right: After tining, work in a lawn dressing with the back of a rake.

Most of us are well served by the proprietary brands of fertilizer and can rely on the directions for rate applications and frequencies included on the bag. Most modern lawn fertilizers contain nitrogen in two forms of availability: immediate and slow release (urea form). However, the following recipes are for those who wish to mix their own.

Autumn dressing: 7 parts (by weight) bone-meal to 3 parts sulfate of potash, applied at 2 oz per sq yd (60 g per sq m).

Spring dressing: 2 parts (by weight) sulfate of ammonia, 1 part cottonseed meal (or similar slow release nitrogenous fertilizer), 2 parts superphosphate, 1 part steamed bone-meal and 1 part sulfate of potash. Apply at the same rate as the autumn dressing.

Select a time when the soil is damp to apply general fertilizers, and should the weather remain very dry for a day or two after applying, it is wise to water it in well.

Care must be taken when applying lawn fertilizers because uneven distribution will cause uneven coloring, and perhaps scorch where an excess is put down. Hand application is still the most widely used method and if the fertilizer is bulked up and well mixed with *dry* sand, soil or peat, even distribution is easier to achieve.

Like grass seed application, it is best to split the quantity to be applied in half and apply one half walking in one direction and the remainder walking at right angles.

Special mechanical fertilizer spreaders can be purchased and sometimes rented from garden centers and these make spreading easier. Do a test run over newspaper and weigh the delivery to a given area to check the correct rate is being applied. Be sure the spreader covers the whole area with no gaps or overlaps to avoid discoloration in lines across the lawn.

Diluters to attach to the hose are also available for the easy application of liquid lawn fertilizers.

When deciding to feed the lawn, remember that much grass is being removed with repeated cutting, yet excessive nitrogen fertilizer will give tremendous soft leafy growth, which will increase the need to mow. Keep things in balance to provide a good color without the need to mow excessively. Rich and heavy soils will need less fertilizer than poor, sandy soils to maintain balanced growth.

Weeds

The importance of starting as free of weeds as possible has already been stressed, but some will still appear. Many germinating with newly sown grass seeds will be destroyed with repeated mowing. Strong growing, healthy grass will also smother out weeds, while raking and brushing before mowing exposes the trailing stems of weeds like clover to the mower. Removal of large single weeds by hand can prevent weed spread on small lawns.

Apart from these mechanical methods of weed control there are the chemicals. The oldest, used in England, is *lawn sand* whereby the caustic action of the mixture scorches broad leaved weeds and mosses but falls from the upright grass. Lawn sand is made from 3 parts (by weight) of sulfate of ammonia, 1 part sulfate of iron, and 20 parts dry sand. It is applied at 4—6 oz per sq yd (120—180 g per sq m) in spring, ideally when there is a touch of dew for the sand to stick to. Dead growth can be raked out after about three weeks, according to temperature (the warmer the weather the faster the effect of the lawn sand). Where there is the risk of hot, dry weather following application, make two dressings, reducing the rate by half to avoid scorching the grass.

To ensure even application of weedkillers or fertilizers, mark the area off into yard or meter squares. Bamboo canes are satisfactory for this.

It is also possible to buy wax sticks impregnated with hormones and aerosols for spot weed treatment. However, hand removal of single weeds and the very occasional use of selective weedkillers are all that are needed to keep a lawn free of weeds.

Applied correctly these materials will give adequate control of nearly all weeds but good cultural treatment is also needed to avoid regrowth and reinfestation by weeds. These hormone weedkillers are most effective when plants are growing strongly as they are then translocated rapidly.

Hormone weedkillers are also freely available, although perhaps not as freely as formerly because of environmental concerns and possible health hazards.

Chemical weedkillers are poisons and must be used accordingly. Read the label on the container and follow directions exactly.

Since regulations on use and availability of many chemicals differ from state to state, seek advice from your county extension agent if you have serious weed problems.

Weedkillers are available as sprays or in granular form. The sprays work faster but must be used on a still day. Remember that this spray will kill other garden plants if allowed to drift on them. Keep a separate sprayer for pesticides. It is possible to buy proprietary brands that include chemical weedkillers and fertilizer, permitting a one-step "weed and feed" operation in the spring.

The most common weedkiller for broadleaved weeds is 2,4D and it is used alone or in combination with other chemicals. Crabgrass is an annoying annual weed best controlled by siduron applied before its seeds have germinated in spring. It will kill other annual grass weeds as they emerge, but will not hinder the germination of "good" perennial grasses. Use DSMA, MAMA or MSMA on crabgrass plants in summer. Dicamba, often combined with 2,4D, controls wild onion, yarrow, veronica and clover in established lawns.

LAWN PROBLEMS

Bare patches are not only the result of pests and diseases. Humans and animals can also create problems. Areas which take a great deal of wear, for instance, can go bare, and the introduction of paving slabs to take this wear is one answer. There are also open, honeycomb-like bricks which can be set into the soil and seeded over. The bricks take the heavy wear and help to protect the grass, and they are ideal where cars occasionally go over the grassed area.

The main animal pests are moles and dogs! Moles seeking worms and insects burrow through newly seeded lawns and fertile soils, causing much damage. Deterrent smokes and traps can be used, and prickly leaves like holly in the tunnels will also act as a useful deterrent.

Dogs' urine, especially bitch urine, causes small brown patches. Dousing the area with water, ideally just behind

The major lawn pests are some sort of grub: Top, billbug and wireworm; bottom, sod webworm and white grub.

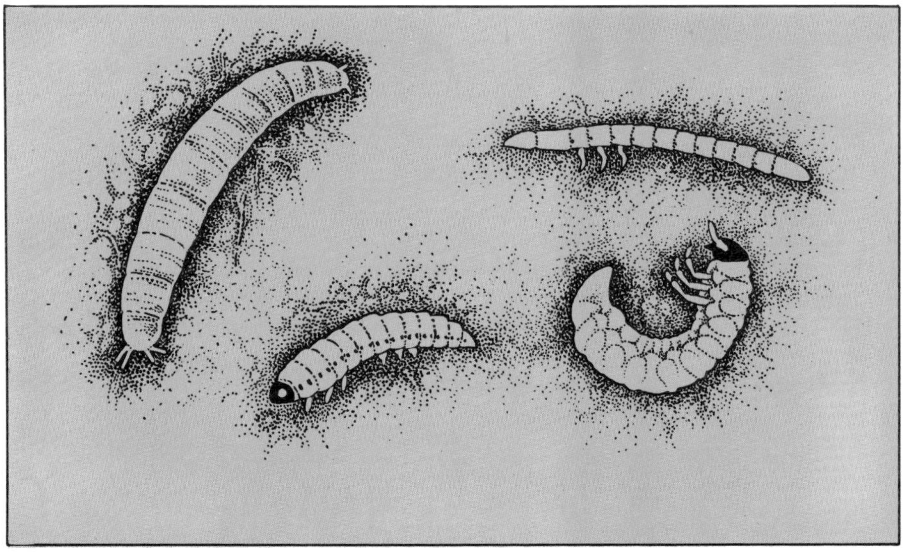

Weeds such as daisies are quickly and easily removed by hand.

Bare patches left where weeds have been removed can be reseeded.

the dog, is the only treatment.

Although birds in numbers pecking into the soil in spring after rain look horrifying, they are usually to be welcomed. They, like the moles, are after worms, and the pecking does little damage and can even help to aerate the surface.

Killing the worms and grubs with chlordane (where permitted) or diazinon should discourage the birds — and moles as well — but for many, this may be too drastic.

Moss can be another nuisance. Poor drainage and lack of soil nutrients encourage the growth of moss, and aerating the soil and raking out the dead thatch improves conditions and reduces its effect. A spring application of fertilizer should kill moss.

Diseases

White mold in the grass is caused by fusarium patch; red threads in the grass are caused by the corticium fungus. Both can be controlled by watering with a mercury-based lawn treatment (such as calomel) or benomyl in late summer and early autumn. Benomyl is best for home garden use.

Small brown patches which spread are likely to be caused by dollar spot (sclerotinia), and once again benomyl will give control.

Toadstools and fairy rings can disfigure a lawn, and need to be controlled. Start by spiking the turf and watering well to penetrate the mycelium growth of these fungi, then apply a proprietary copper or mercurial chemical.

Where fairy rings are a persistent problem the only sure cure is the removal and destruction of infected turf, digging the soil 9 in. (23 cm) deep and fumigating with a solution of formaldehyde.

Pests

Ants can be a problem, especially in light sandy soils where small ant-hills are thrown up. Several powders are available for killing ants.

The grubs of various beetles (Japanese, June, Asiatic, etc.) can seriously damage grass roots when they are present in sufficient numbers, about 8—10 grubs per sq. ft (929 sq. cm). They are white, about 1—1½ in. 3—4 cm) long and lie in a crescent position. Chlordane gives long-lasting control but its use is banned or regulated in some states. Diazinon, less persisent in soil is an alternative. There is also the milky spore disease, a biological control that is slow acting but environmentally more desirable.

Causing damage at ground level by chewing on grass blades are larvae of sod webworms, cutworms and armyworms. Drenches of carbaryl or diazinon are the usual controls, applied according to directions on the container.

Chinch bugs have replaced the Japanese beetle grubs as the most serious lawn problem in many regions. The bugs are about 1/6 of an inch long. The controls are either carbaryl or diazinon.

Six widespread and troublesome lawn weeds: top row, left to right: plantain, clover, yarrow; bottom row, left to right: buttercup, dandelion, daisy.

Hedges

First priority in any garden must be the introduction of hedges and screens. Not only is it important to mark out the boundary of your property, but you will also need the shelter and protection they will provide.

A well-chosen hedge plant, carefully planted and tended, will give years of good service. It will be much cheaper and usually longer lasting than wooden fencing.

Many hedging plants are attractive in themselves and make a very good backcloth to other planting schemes.

List the qualities you want before making the choice of plant. Protection from two- and four-footed invaders will be provided by thorns, especially the deciduous hawthorn, which remains an excellent choice for large gardens, and the evergreen holly.

All plants will provide some protection from wind. Plants are better than solid fences for this, as it is preferable that the wind filters through rather than hits an impenetrable barrier and bounces over with even greater force. The higher the hedge the greater the extension of shelter; as a general guide one unit high gives seven unit lengths of wind shelter beyond.

Even in front-yard gardens informal groups of low-growing shrubs will give valuable shelter from wind.

Privacy can also be brought to the garden with hedge plants. Fast and tall growing kinds will soon prevent private gardens being overlooked. Unsightly objects can be screened completely. The summer foliage of deciduous plants and the year-round foliage of evergreens reduce noise and help to minimize the aggravation of traffic and other unwanted sounds.

Gardeners in the past used low hedges to surround vegetable plots, and the advantages of earlier and heavier crops obtained from such shelter should not be forgotten.

On very exposed sites it is a good plan to erect either metal or concrete posts and plastic or wire netting around the boundary. The hedge plants are then planted just inside this fence. They get shelter from the netting, are supported by it in the early stages of growth, and quickly grow to cover it.

A few plants like the small-leaved evergreen *Lonicera nitida* require the support of posts and wire to prevent them blowing over when more than 18 in. (45 cm) high. They are grown in the South.

The hornbeam, *Carpinus betulus,* makes a tall hedge and is a good alternative to beech, being equally happy on alkaline or clay soils.

CHOOSING THE RIGHT PLANTS

The first step is to decide whether you want an evergreen or deciduous hedge. Remember, too, that there are a few deciduous plants like beech and hornbeam that retain russet-brown leaves through the winter if clipped regularly. Others drop their leaves to unmask richly colored bark like the purple-leaved plums, or highly colored berries in the case of plants like *Berberis wilsoniae.*

Some evergreens, like pyracantha and cotoneaster, produce masses of bright berries to contrast with the evergreen and semi-evergreen foliage.

Select those with dark foliage to throw up lighter colored plants in front of them. For example, the yellow winter-flowering *Hamamelis mollis* and pale pink *Viburnum* ×*bodnantense* are more eye-catching against a background of evergreens. Light green and golden plants contrast well with copper beech and *Prunus* ×*cistena.*

Generally speaking the evergreens make better hedges. They give year-round seclusion and offer more

Hedges do not have to be high and impenetrable to serve a useful purpose. Lavender makes a low boundary hedge that's both colorful and fragrant.

protection. Deciduous flowering plants like forsythia and flowering currant make excellent screens even if they can be seen through in winter.

Plants for Low Hedges

The plants in this group can normally be contained to form a low hedge no more than 3 ft (90 cm) high.

Common box, *Buxus sempervirens* 'Suffruticosa', will make a very low evergreen hedge and there are a number of forms with golden and creamy white leaves which grow taller. *Berberis thunbergii* 'Atropurpurea Nana' has purple foliage and the leaves turn yellow before leaf-fall in autumn. Kept trimmed this makes a neat and self-protecting low hedge, as it has sharp thorns.

The evergreen *Euonymus fortunei* 'Silver Queen', Sarcopie and others make neat hedges if kept trimmed. Some of the evergreen veronicas or hebe, are also attractive low hedge plants, best lightly trimmed once a year after flowering and allowed a less formal shape.

Lavender makes one of the most popular low hedges. *Lavandula spica* 'Hidcote' has compact growth and makes the neatest low hedge to 30 in. (75 cm), while the ordinary *L. spica* will form a much larger and somewhat rougher hedge. Trim lavender back after flowering and choose a sunny, well drained site.

Lonicera nitida, with its tiny evergreen leaves, will quickly form a neat low hedge. But it needs regular trimming to keep its shape — almost monthly through the summer. Golden privet, *Ligustrum ovalifolium* 'Aureum', does not grow as tall or as quickly as the green kind. It makes a neat low hedge and needs less frequent trimming. Both lonicera and ligustrum root easily from 8—12 in. (20—30 cm) hardwood cuttings in late autumn.

A favorite low-growing plant of mine is *Mahonia aquifolium,* best cut back after flowering in April or May and allowed to produce a natural semi-formal shape. It grows well in most soils once established, in sun or shade.

Two silver foliage plants, *Santolina chamaecyparissus* (the best for a neatly trimmed low hedge) and *Senecio laxifolius,* not hardy, can be recommended. Trim them back in spring.

The best deciduous plant for low hedging is *Prunus ×cistena,* commonly called purple leaf sand cherry. Star-like flowers in April and May are followed by rich copper foliage. Trim this plant back quite hard after flowering to retain shape and size; this will also help to produce plenty of richly colored young foliage.

Plants for Medium Hedges

The plants in this section will form a hedge up to 10 ft (3 m) high. However, there can be no hard and fast rule on speed of growth and ultimate height because both soil and the quality of the young plant will influence growth rate. This grouping is only a guide, and plants need to be clipped and pruned back to retain their size.

The evergreen *Berberis ×stenophylla* has showering branches of bright yellow flowers in April or May and makes a completely impenetrable hedge. As it is not easy to root cuttings (which should be taken in summer and kept in a cold frame), it is best to buy container-grown specimens for successful transplanting.

Much easier to propagate is *Cotoneaster simonsii,* with seed-raised plants much cheaper to buy. Upright in habit, this species is semi-evergreen with large scarlet berries close to the stem, which are more clearly seen as the leaves fall.

Less formal hedges are produced with escallonia, which is good for seaside areas on the West Coast where exposure to very cold winter winds is unlikely. Prune back after pink or red flowers have finished in late summer

Hedges do more than mark boundaries and afford privacy – they provide vital wind protection. Every meter height of hedge offers protection for seven meters.

and try to avoid cutting back too hard.

Another good seaside plant for informal screens is the Russian olive, *Elaeagnus angustifolius,* also a good choice for windy, poor soil regions of the Midwest.

The strong-growing green privet serves us very well in this size grouping. While the twice-yearly trimming may be considered by some to be unnecessary work, this plant does grow quickly in rough conditions. It is cheap to buy and easy to root from hardwood cuttings, taken in early autumn.

Plant a double row of privet if you want a dense impenetrable hedge quickly. But despite its strong growth, privet can easily be kept in bounds with an electric hedge trimmer.

Completely deciduous but with fragrant flowers is the philadelphus, commonly known as mock orange. Other informal hedges can be created with the yellow forsythia or the white-flowered *Spiraea ×arguta.* Also justifiably popular is the red flowering currant; just prune out some branches with pruners after flowering.

The purple-leaved plum, *Prunus cerasifera* 'Atropurpurea', is an attractive alternative to the usually more expensive copper-leaved beech. It does not, however, hold its leaves in winter and is not as popular as *Prunus laurocerasus,* the evergreen cherry laurel. Both, left unpruned, will reach 16 ft (5 m). On alkaline soils try to plant the darker and smaller evergreen Portugal laurel, *Prunus lusitanica.*

Another recommended evergreen, available in several forms, is the recently introduced *Thuja occidentalis,* a very neat-growing conical conifer which forms a good compact hedge. English yew, *Taxus baccata,* will grow much taller than 10 ft (3 m) but can be kept to any size by trimming in August. Other yews to consider are the Japanese yew, *T. caspidata* and its many forms and *T. ×media* and its useful cultivar 'Hicksii' which grows as a dense column.

Plants for Tall Hedges

The plants in this section will exceed 10 ft (3 m) quite rapidly. The common hornbeam, *Carpinus betulus,* is a good example of a plant that will soon reach 10 ft (3 m), then if left alone will grow into a small tree. Clipped once or twice a year it is a good alternative to beech and will thrive on alkaline or heavy clay soil.

Evergreen conifers of the Lawson type also form upright trees, but careful clipping of the young growth in August will contain their size. Seedlings of *Chamaecyparis lawsoniana* are cheapest and can give a variety of colorful foliage.

Hedges need never be dull – even in leaf. This picture illustrates how purple leaved *Prunus cerasifera* 'Atropurpurea' and *P. cerasifera* (cherry plum) provide contrast.

Hawthorns, including *Crataegus oxyacantha,* and beech, *Fagus sylvatica,* are widely used for hedges. Thorn remains the best boundary hedge, keeping out cattle and trespassers of all kinds at a low cost. Planting a double row of seedlings up to 18 in. (45 cm) tall and cutting them back by half a few weeks after planting gives the best hedge.

Seedling beech is very attractive in late April and May when different leaf color unfurls. The rich green summer foliage is then followed by brilliant autumn shades to make this a most attractive hedge and screen. Be sure to clip in August if you want beech to retain its leaves over winter. Clipping the tips off prevents the production of a hormone which causes the leaves to fall in autumn. They then drop when new growth starts in spring.

Finally, two more evergreens. *Thuja plicata* 'Atrovirens' makes a splendid hedge, being especially useful because it responds well to quite hard cutting back when space is outgrown. The other one, *×Cupressocyparis leylandii,* has become very popular in Europe and England. It will grow 3—5 ft (1—1.5 m) a year and can be clipped in August to retain size and improve its bushiness. An excellent

Beech hedging cut back hard soon shoots out growth to cover the cuts.

Upright cultivars of *Chamaecyparis* make a good screen.

Green privet makes one of the best hedges. Trim to leave it wider at the base. Try not to leave it too long between cuts, and collect the trimmings on a sheet (see below).

alternative to the dark green Leyland is ×*C. l.* 'Leighton Green', this cultivar being bushier than the green type and gray-green in May and June when new growth forms.

Always plant either pot or container-grown Leylands; and you will find that smaller specimens 20 in. (50 cm) tall get away quickly.

Planting a Hedge

Careful preparation will give a good long life and the speedy establishment usually needed. On good to average soil, digging over the site one spade deep, and adding plenty of peat moss and similar organic matter, is usually sufficient. For the very best results, however, it is worth digging out a trench one spade deep and forking organic material into the base before returning the improved topsoil. If there is grassy turf on the site, dig this into the sub-soil.

The time to transplant bare root plants is October and November or February and March. Plants in this category usually include buckthorn, privet, beech, multiflora rose and Siberian elm.

While all plants lifted from the open ground need their roots kept damp it is especially important with beech. Let their roots get dry and transplanting losses can be very high.

The closer you plant the quicker a dense hedge forms but the more it costs, as a general rule. Good specimens of the larger growing container-grown evergreens can be planted 3 ft (90 cm) or more apart. Most plants set at this spacing will give a good screen in three years.

Evergreens can be transplanted in September and October or March and April if not too old and established. It is best to spray the foliage with an antidessicant before lifting, and to take up a good ball of soil with each plant to keep root disturbance to a minimum (see the advice on transplanting conifers on page 71).

All newly-planted stock will need watering in dry weather until well established. Evergreens benefit from syringing with water in drying winds and hot weather.

KEEPING A GOOD SHAPE

Once planted and established, growth will be improved with feeding. A well-balanced general fertilizer applied in spring and autumn, hoed in lightly around the plants, will considerably speed growth.

Trimming is the only other regular cultural treatment required. The general rule here is to cut young deciduous plants back regularly to encourage branching from the base. Most coniferous evergreens are best cut back by 6—12 in. (15—30 cm) before the ultimate required height is reached. The tip growth then develops to cover

It is a good idea to stretch out a plastic or cloth sheet at the base of the hedge to catch clippings. Simply lift up four corners to carry trimmings away.

Hedging plants with large leaves can look unsightly if trimmed with shears.

the cuts and takes the hedge or screen up to the final height.

Where long, straight edges have to be cut, erect posts and string to guide the shears.

Large-leaved evergreens are best cut with pruners, pruning out branch tips. Lopers and hedge trimmers are more suited to the smaller-leaved plants and conifers where shaping the outer edges is all that is normally required.

Some plants will respond to very hard cutting back, and renovation of old overgrown hedges is easy with these. Beech, privet, thuja and yew are good examples. Hedges 3 ft (1 m) or more thick, cut back one side at a time, can be reduced by half and soon produce new growth. Evergreens like *Chamaecyparis* and *Tsuga* (hemlock) will not respond to this hard cutting.

Growth is naturally stronger at the top so clip to give a wider base and narrower top. This will not only produce more dense growth but reduce the chance of snow damage.

Where topiary work is planned it is a good idea to make a wooden jig which can easily be placed in position, and cut to this.

YOUR GUIDE TO HEDGES AND LIVING SCREENS

Plant	Common name	Spacing	Height in 4-5 years	Ultimate height	When to trim
Abelia grandiflora (E, F)	Glossy Abelia	1½-3 ft*	3 ft	6 ft	Early spring
Berberis ×mentorensis (E, B)	Mentor Barberry	1½ ft	5-6 ft	4-6½ ft	After flowering
Berberis thunbergii 'Atropurpurea Nana' (F)	—	12-20 in.	1 ft	1½ ft	After flowering
Buxus sempervirens (E)	Common Box	1½-3 ft	3 ft	4 ft	July/August
B. microphylla koreana (E)	Korean Box	1½ ft	6 ft	12 ft	July/August
Carpinus betulus	Hornbeam	1½-3 ft	5-6½ ft	20 ft+	July/August
Chamaecyparis lawsoniana (E)	Lawson's Cypress	3 ft	5 ft	20 ft+	July/August
Cotoneaster lucidus (B)	—	1½-3 ft	5 ft	10 ft	Early spring
Cotoneaster simonsii (B)	—	1½ ft	5 ft	6½ ft	July
Crataegus monogyna	Hawthorn	1 ft	5 ft	23 ft	Twice in summer
Crataegus oxycantha 'Paul's Scarlet' (F)	—	1½ ft	5 ft	23 ft	July/August
×Cupressocyparis leylandii	—	1½-2 ft	8 ft	30 ft	April and August
Elaeagnus angustifolia (B)	Russian Olive	3 ft	6 ft	15 ft	Early spring
Euonymus fortunei 'Sarcopie' cultivars (E)	—	1 ft	1 ft	4 ft	May
Euonymus japonica cultivars (E)	—	2 ft	2 ft	10 ft	June
Fagus sylvatica	Beech	1-1½ ft	5-6½ ft	20 ft	August
Hippophae rhamnoides (B)	Sea Buckthorn	2 ft	5 ft	10 ft	July/August
Ilex aquifolium cultivars (E, B)	Holly	2-3 ft	3 ft	13 ft	August
I. crenata cultivars (E, B)	Japanese Holly	1½-3 ft	3 ft+	5 ft	Spring
Juniperas virginiana and cultivars (E, B)	Red Cedar	3 ft	4 ft+	20 ft+	Spring
Lavandula spica 'Hidcote' (E, F)	Lavender	1 ft	1½ ft	2 ft	After flowering
Ligustrum ovalifolium (E)	Privet	1½ ft	5 ft	10 ft+	May to August
L. maackii (B)	Amur Honeysuckle	3 ft	6 ft	15 ft	Spring
L. valgare 'Pyramidale'	Privet	1½ ft	2½ ft	8 ft	May to August
Lonicera nitida (E)	—	1½ ft	4 ft	6 ft	May to August
Mahonia aquifolium (E, B)	—	1½-3 ft	2½ ft	3 ft	Informal — May
Prunus cerasifer 'Atropurpurea'	Pissardi Plum	1½ ft	5 ft	10 ft	July
Prunus 'Cistena' (F)	Crimson Dwarf	1½ ft	2½ ft	4 ft	May
Prunus laurocerasus (E)	Cherry Laurel	2½ ft	6½ ft	10 ft	July/August
Pyracantha (E, B)	Firethorn	3 ft	6½ ft	13 ft	June and August
Ribes (F)	Flowering Currant	1½ ft	5 ft	6½ ft	May
Santolina chamaecyparissus (E)	—	1½ ft	3 ft	3 ft	March
Taxus baccata (E)	Yew	2½ ft	3 ft	10 ft	August
Thuja occidentalis 'Smaragd' (E)	—	3 ft	3 ft	13 ft	August
Tsuga canadensis (E)	Hemlock	3 ft	4 ft	15 ft+	Late spring

Key E = Evergreen F = Flowering B = Berries

**1 ft = 0.3 m*

Trees

The steady and continuing growth of trees is quietly reassuring in this energy-demanding era. If all mineral fuels are lost, we still have trees slowly building up wood year after year, regardless of our folly.

Trees do much more for us, quite apart from the many products made from wood pulp. They, more than any plant, purify the air, taking in carbon dioxide and breathing out oxygen.

Great canopies of leaf give shade in summer, and masses of twiggy branches soften wind and help to reduce noise. And when the leaves fall they enrich the soil.

At last their many qualities are being appreciated. Each one of us has a responsibility to see that more trees are planted, but with decreasing garden size we need to be careful in selection.

I see no harm in using trees rather like indoor decoration material, replaced by other more appropriate kinds as their growth and the family's requirements change; rapid growing and relatively short-lived poplar and willow, for example, can be used to give near-instant effect in a small new garden and then be cut down as soon as they grow beyond the space available.

Slower-growing trees planted at the same time can then be left to develop once the quick-growing space fillers are removed.

While you may be unable to grow what I call forest and field trees in the garden, try at least to instigate the occasional planting in your locality, be it in town and city parks, churchyard or roadside. Real giants like the white candle-flowering horse chestnut *(Aesculus)* and the beautiful deeply grooved bark of sweet chestnut *(Castanea)*, green and copper beeches *(Fagus)*, the tough, hardy black-budded ash *(Fraxinus)*, town-pollution-withstanding London plane *(Platanus)*, huge oaks *(Quercus)*, and elms *(Ulmus)* are such a welcome feature of our land.

Robinia pseudoacacia 'Frisia' will make a colorful addition to any garden; container-grown plants transplant best.

Many people are unnecessarily worried about trees close to buildings. Very many country and town houses have stood for centuries unmoved with large trees within touching distance. A major worry is that in regions where ice storms and severe hurricanes can be expected, trees or their limbs will fall on the house.

Rapid-growing trees like willow will draw many gallons of water each day from clay soils. This causes shrinkage and soil cracks which can affect the house. Roots of these trees also seek moisture from every source when the soil is dry. Where drainage pipes have the slightest crack roots will penetrate and in extreme cases block the pipe with root.

Plant trees from one to one-and-a-half times their ultimate height away from houses to be absolutely safe. Small trees will, of course, have a much lower water requirement and closer planting is acceptable.

There is always a rush to get trees planted in a new garden to give added height and some privacy. While I am all in favor of getting trees in and away, take a little time over the choice. Never rush the selection, for the choice of species and variety can be vitally important in a small garden.

Less care is needed over the quick-growing kinds treated as expendable, but once in, the remainder are likely to be there a long time. My advice is always cultivate the soil and grass first, then hedges, screens and specimen trees can be planted.

Where trees are to be planted on the boundary and in cultivated soil, as opposed to lawn, then once the choice is made there is no need for more delay.

CHOOSING A TREE

We have tree shapes, sizes, rates of growth and leaf colors for nearly every situation with the maples, or *Acer*, as they are known botanically. Most are easy to grow in all soils and situations.

Where space is available for a specimen that will form a large shrub or small tree, choose a Japanese maple or a snakebark maple. The Japanese *Acer japonicum* and *A. palmatum* types are more often grown as shrubs, often with several stems. All have beautiful autumn leaf color and several have rich red summer leaves.

The rich yellow leaves of *A. j.* 'Aureum' will scorch in strong sunlight and the young growth burn in spring frost, so find a partially shaded site for this plant. All the Japanese maples are better given protection from wind and will thrive in partial shade. Add plenty of peat to the soil to get strong growth and the richness of young foliage. They associate well with azaleas, lilies and the natural stone of rock banks and gardens.

Autumn leaf color is an attraction on the cut-leaved Japanese maple.

Colored bark is the feature of the small tree *Acer davidii*, with green and white snake-skin-like coloring. For birch-like, papery, peeling brown bark seek out *Acer griseum.*

Very common and widely planted in gardens are *Acer negundo* 'Elegans', which has leaves margined yellow, and *A. n.* 'Variegatum', with white-edged leaves; this is commonly called box elder. They can also be grown in tubs and as tall shrubs but need any shoots of all-green foliage cut out promptly. The illustrations below show how these plants can be treated as either shrub or tree, depending on the situation.

Large trees are well covered by the Norway maples, *Acer platanoides* — the ordinary species grows quickly and has good autumn leaf color. There are rich summer colored kinds including *A. p.* 'Crimson King', with copper-purple leaves, and *A. p.* 'Drummondii', with green leaves edged cream.

Often confused with the Norway is maple sycamore, *Acer pseudoplatanus*, a very easily grown large tree which seeds freely; in fact seedlings can be a problem in the garden. There are a number of very attractive garden forms

Acer negundo can be treated as a shrub. Prune back in spring to retain size and give strong new growth.

Another example of *Acer negundo*, this time grown as a tree. There are forms with cream and white variegation.

without the seeding problem. My favorite is *A. p.* 'Brilliantissimum', with rich pink new spring growth and creamy-orange young leaves on a small mop-head tree.

Larger growing are the green, yellow and pink splashed *A. p.* 'Leopoldii' and yellow-leaved *A. p.* 'Worleei'.

The chestnuts demand space, especially the large ordinary horse chestnut, *Aesculus hippocastanum* with its sticky buds which can be cut in early spring to open in water, eye-catching white flower spikes, and prickly seed cases. Red-flowered *A.×carnea* 'Briotii' is of medium size and does not produce prickly nuts. Large-growing sweet chestnut is a different plant, *Castanea sativa,* and hot summers are needed for the best edible chestnut crops. The Chinese chestnut, *C. mollissima*, is fast growing and produces edible nuts in cold climates. It needs an acid soil.

Tree of heaven, *Ailanthus altissima*, also responds to hard pruning as a young plant. The strong new shoots carry huge attractive leaves. Left unpruned it becomes a large specimen withstanding city dirt and pollution.

Wet soils suit the alders. *Alnus cordata* is larger than the medium-height *A. glutinosa;* both are useful for shelter belt planting. Better suited to gardens is *Amelanchier*. This small tree or large shrub has white flowers and rich copper young leaves in April, beautiful is association with spring-flowering bulbs. Rich autumn leaf color and purple fruits, attractive to birds, follow the spring spectacle.

One of the few evergreen trees other than conifers is *Arbutus unedo*, the strawberry tree; it is slow to establish and eventually makes a small tree. White flowers are produced in autumn at the same time as seeds from the previous year's flowers ripen on small strawberry-like fruits. Always plant pot-grown specimens as root disturbance causes a severe check.

Most graceful of all, the birches with silver bark and rich yellow autumn leaves are superb for the garden.

Smallest is *Betula pendula* 'Youngii', a lovely weeping tree, seldom reaching more than 10 ft (3 m) unless the growing tip is kept tied upright until the wood hardens. The spreading, weeping habit produces a flat-topped tree.

All young birches have brown bark and only as they age over four to six years does the silver-white color develop. *Betula papyrifera* has really

The young yellow leaves of *Gleditsia tricanthos* 'Sunburst' are one of the attractive features of this tree. It makes a small to medium tree.

striking white bark and grows a little larger than the common birch, *Betula pendula.* Container-grown trees are easier to transplant successfully than bare-root plants.

Much more spreading but of similar medium size, *Catalpa bignonioides,* the Indian bean tree is more suited to large gardens, parks and street planting. Large trusses of white flowers with yellow and purple throats are followed by long bean-like seed pods in hot summers.

Neat, rounded, light-green leaves are the attraction of *Cercis siliquastrum,* commonly called the Judas tree because legend indicates this was the tree on which Judas Iscariot hanged himself. Masses of purple-pink flowers are produced in May on tall shrub or small tree shapes. A good hardy subject, but best transplanted from containers as it does resent root disturbance.

An almost perfect tree for the small property is the flowering dogwood, *Cornus florida*, native over a wide area of the eastern half of the country. Its inconspicuous flowers are surrounded by four large white bracts in spring. Equally striking in autumn are red berries and red and orange leaf colors. Its counterpart in the Pacific Northwest is *Cornus nuttallii* which grows taller — up to 70 feet eventually.

Very tough and easy to grow in all soils and conditions are flowering hawthorns; carmine-pink flowered *Crataegus oxyacantha* 'Paul's Scarlet' most popular of all. When planting bare-root trees be sure to keep the roots damp at all times and be patient. It may take several months into the spring before new growth develops on newly transplanted trees.

While children should be encouraged to grow oaks and horse chestnuts from seed and watch them develop over the years, impatient adults will get quicker returns from *Eucalyptus gunnii* grown from seed.

This tree, where hardy, grows fast. The young growth produces rounded silver-gray leaves and then older branches produce sickle-shaped gray-green leaves. If cut back when one to two years old, the single-stemmed seedlings will be forced to shoot up several branches. All are useful for flower arranging and the cut branches can be stood in glycerine (one part) and water (two parts) to produce excellent preserved material for indoor arrangement.

Only one beech, *Fagus sylvatica* 'Purpurea Pendula', is small enough for most gardens today. This cultivar is ideal with its very weeping branches, reaching down to the soil, covered with rich purple leaves.

The common beech and its weeping variety *Fagus sylvatica* 'Pendula' are truly graceful giants with beautiful early leaf color, rich summer green and rich autumn gold that falls to unmask the light gray bark. Even greater impact on the skyline is made by the purple-leaved *F. s.* 'Atropunicea'. Give these plants space to develop and their full beauty, as branches sweep to the ground, will be seen in future years; a perfect choice for the surrounds of sports and playing fields, and other large open areas.

Mention must be made of the ash, *Fraxinus excelsior*, to encourage planting where disease has killed stately elms. Fast growing, tough and easy to grow, the ash has black buds in winter and attractive rich green leaves in summer. In more formal planting use the yellow-barked *F. e.* 'Aurea' with its rich yellow autumn foliage, and *F. oxycarpa* 'Raywood' with more sharply defined leaves, and rich purple autumn color on more compact trees.

Autumn color on small maples seen through the spread of *Platanus orientalis.*

A good example of how plants can be combined to enhance each other. *Clematis montana* types will happily scramble through a tree such as laburnum.

Slow growing, heat and drought resistant, *Gleditsia triacanthos* 'Sunburst' makes an attractive small to medium sized garden tree. The fern-like leaves are light yellow when young and they turn light green with age. Avoid the strong-growing honey locust, *Gleditsia triacanthos*, in gardens because it grows quite rapidly to a large tree and is armed with long vicious thorns. It is, however, a good choice for public ground where young boys sometimes need to be deterred from climbing!

Another tree for our heirs is *Juglans regia*, the common walnut, which will provide edible nuts in warm summers. The wood can fetch a high price.

The common name of golden rain tree is easier to cope with than *Koelreuteria paniculata*. It gets its common name from the large clusters of dainty yellow flowers produced in August in hot sunny weather. The attractive deeply divided leaves turn rich yellow before falling in the autumn. Small to medium sized, it is suited to the larger garden.

Don't confuse golden rain with the common name golden chain tree which some people use to describe laburnum, one of the most popular flowering trees. Best for garden use is *Laburnum* 'Vossii' because it has great long trusses of scented yellow flowers and sets few seeds. It is important to remember that laburnum seeds are poisonous and best not introduced where undisciplined children play.

Giant *Populus nigra* 'Italica' need plenty of space. They make very good windbreaks but cut the tops out while you can still reach them.

Damp, but not waterlogged, and acid soils are required for *Liquidambar styraciflua*, the sweet gum. It is beautiful in autumn when the five-lobed palm-shaped leaves turn yellow, orange, red and almost purple. Given the right soil conditions it will grow to a large tree.

Newcomers to gardening sometimes confuse *Liriodendron tulipifera*, the tulip tree, with the magnolia, which follows it in so many catalogs. Liriodendron makes a large specimen with unusual shaped leaves. The greenish-yellow flowers which are cup-shaped, like a tulip, are produced at the tips of branches on well-established trees.

There is nothing to compare with the visual impact of a multi-branched, small tree-sized Specimen of *Magnolia ×soulangiana* in full flower in April ahead of the leaves. Once established—ideally transplanting container-grown specimens to avoid damaging their succulent roots—they are hardy and withstand a variety of soils, even quite heavy clay. See that plenty of peat and organic matter is mixed into the planting site for the best growth. Cold winds and spring frost can damage the April flowers so choose a protected site if possible. The flowers apart, this tree is quite hardy.

It will be advisable to provide the shelter of a wall in cold areas for *Magnolia grandiflora*, a really magnificent evergreen. The large shiny, light green leaves have a brown furry underside, and huge cup-shaped, richly lemon-scented cream flowers appear late summer or early autumn on the tips of the branches. This tree can also be planted free-standing in mild parts of the country. Older specimens are particularly interesting, with a gnarled appearance.

Jostling with *Prunus* for pride of place in providing garden trees are the *Malus*, or ornamental crabs. Small to medium-sized trees provide flowers, attractive fruits and, in the case of upright-growing *Malus tschonoski*, the bonfire tree, brilliant autumn foliage.

All the fruits are edible but pretty tart and it is as well to use only the largest fruiting kinds for jelly and wine. Best for flowering in my opinion is the neat small tree *Malus floribunda*; crimson buds open to pale pink and cover the rounded head with flowers.

Good for flowers are 'Katherine', outstanding because of its abundance of white flowers and 'Dorothea', with semi-double dark pink flowers and yellow fruits. *M ×arnoldiana* has pale pink flowers and masses of rounded rich yellow fruits which hang on well into the winter. These three crabapples are of medium size and *M. ×arnoldiana* is especially wide spreading.

There are two kinds of Siberian crab, *Malus ×robusta* — red fruited and yellow fruited; both are attractive in flower and fruit. One of the best for flower is the compact and upright-growing small tree *M.* 'Van Eseltine', while *M.* 'Profusion' and *M.* 'Royalty' have rich copper leaves, flowers and tiny fruits. The foliage of 'Royalty' is especially spectacular.

There is a delightful weeping form, *M.* 'Red Jade', with pale pink flowers, bright green leaves and small red fruits.

Taking us back to the giants is the London plane, *Platanus ×hispanica*. It is easy to grow, responsive to very hard pruning to retain size, and very

The most suitable poplar for garden use, *P. balsamifera* 'Aurora'.

The flagpole cherry, *Prunus* 'Amanogawa', makes a neat column of flowers in restricted gardens.

resistant to adverse city conditions.

Many poplars are equally large and are some of the fastest growing trees we have. They grow easily and quickly even from cut lengths of branch put in the soil in winter. Poplars are good plants for wet soils but best kept away from houses, drains and buildings.

The white underside leaf of *Populus alba* is very attractive and the yellow autumn leaf color is bright. A recent form, *P. a.* 'Racket' has upright growth as well as leaves glossy green above and gray beneath.

The only candidate for garden use is *P. balsamifera* 'Aurora', growing to medium size. Under poor soil conditions the young leaves are cream, green and pink. It is best cut back hard every year or every second year to produce plenty of young growth and colored foliage. If over-fed the leaves will stay green.

A good example of carefully sited flowering *Prunus* planted among prostrate and upright growing conifers and deciduous and flowering shrubs.

Pyrus salicifolia 'Pendula' with lead branch weeping over.

Ornamental almonds, cherries, peaches and plums all have a place in gardens. Earliest to flower are the almonds, *Prunus dulcis* (syn P. amygdalus) which will produce edible nuts and the peach, the best of which is the rich double pink *P. persica* 'Klara Meyer'. Sadly both are susceptible to the disease peach leaf curl.

More shrub than tree and easy to grow, the purple-leaved plum, *P. cerasifera* 'Atropurpurea' has masses of tiny white flowers in March or April followed by dark purple leaves.

This leaves the cherries, the most free-flowering of all trees. Nothing can compare with the flowering abundance of double pink *Prunus* 'Kwanzan', its branches stretching upwards like an umbrella blown inside out, on a medium-sized tree.

Weeping cherry *P.* 'Kiku-shidare Sakura' has flowers of similar color but this small tree with branches to the ground is ideal for small gardens. In marked contrast is the flagpole cherry, *P.* 'Amanogawa'; growing very upright and with pale pink flowers, it is also suited to small gardens.

There are many cultivars of medium-sized flowering cherry trees, but for shape of head, and large white flowers contrasting with young copper leaves, I like *P.* 'Tai-Haku'. For rich shiny mahogany bark choose *P. serrula*, the birch bank cherry, and for winter flowers select small to medium-sized *P. subhirtella* 'Autumnalis'.

Gray-leaved weeping pear, *Pyrus salicifolia* 'Pendula', is another perfect small garden tree. Left with the lead shoot untrained upwards it makes little more than a shrub. Masses of white flowers in April are followed by rich

Prunus 'Shirofugen' is one of several flowering cherries suitable for a small garden where one tree is desired.

Willows (*Salix*) are very striking and beautiful trees, but many species do need space, so careful selection is necessary. This is S. *alba*.

silver willow-like leaves. This tree seems to take everything, including soils, coastal conditions and town pollution, in its stride.

I can but plead for *Quercus,* the mighty oak; if you can find the place and the space this tree is a must. Where space is restricted the upright *Q. robur* 'Fastigiata' is the choice.

The *Robinia* is closely related to *Gleditsia* and it is easy to confuse the two. Best for the garden, a quite outstanding small tree is *Robinia pseudoacacia* 'Frisia'. Bright yellow leaves like maidenhair fern grace the branches right through from spring to autumn.

All the *Robinia* are hardy, quite quick growing and once established are easy in most soils, though preferring lighter, sandy soils and sunny conditions. Container-grown trees are easiest to transplant successfully. The branches tend to be brittle so avoid very windy situations. *R. pseudoacacia,* the common acacia, grows very rapidly and tends to sucker; also its branches are quite fiercely thorned.

Many gardeners are attracted by the yellow bark and shoots of the weeping willow, *Salix alba.* It grows much too large for most gardens, however, unless used as a temporary filler, cutting it down after a few years. The best choice of weeping willow for small gardens is *S. purpurea* 'Pendula'; very small, it is slow growing and not easy to cultivate.

Flower arrangers will like the twisted branches of *S. matsudana* 'Tortuosa', seen at its best in winter against a blue sky.

While not quite so large as the weeping willow it will still require space unless cut back regularly.

Two popular groups of garden trees are listed under *Sorbus,* the mountain ash: *Sorbus aucuparia,* and the white-beam, *Sorbus aria.* There are quite a number of different cultivars to choose from. All are easy to grow, even in dry soil. They are not terribly long lived in comparison, say, with beech, and are of small to medium size.

Although there are a variety of berry colors the red *Sorbus aucuparia* remains very popular with both gardeners and birds. I would like to see *Sorbus aria* 'Lutescens' planted more widely; its creamy white leaves are especially attractive in spring before turning to the more typical gray-green color of *S. aria* in summer and yellow in autumn.

Most of the *Sorbus* are neat and upright in habit, especially in their early years. Branches may bend over and spread out a little when carrying heavy bunches of fruit but the compact shape suits smaller gardens.

Finally the lindens, Tilia, and the elms, *Ulmus,* again need space—but we owe it to our heirs to plant more of these important landscape trees.

PLANTING

Once you have selected the kind of tree you want, be sure to purchase the right shape. Many ornamental trees are grown in just the same way that nurserymen grow bush, half-standard and standard fruit trees (see fruit training section, page 123). Where trees are in grass and need to be mown underneath, and where you plan to sit under the tree, then full standards with a trunk of 6 ft (2 m) should be purchased.

Full standards will need a good

When planting a tree or shrub, make sure there is room to spread the roots.

Use the existing soil mark on the stem as a guide to planting depth.

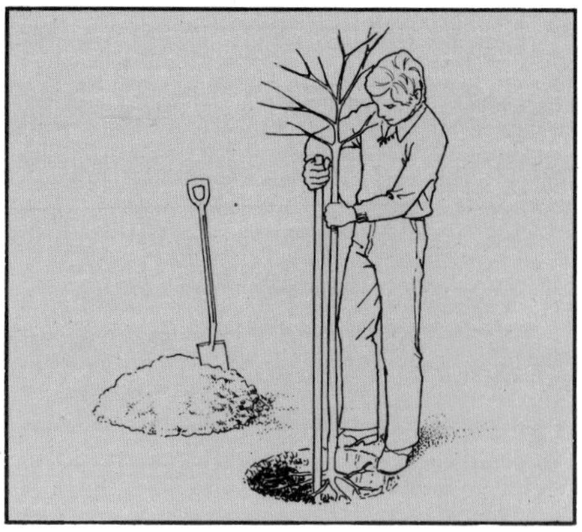

Always position the stake on the windward side before filling the hole.

Carefully return the soil to the hole, shaking it between the roots.

It is essential that the earth is firmed well, using the feet to tread the soil.

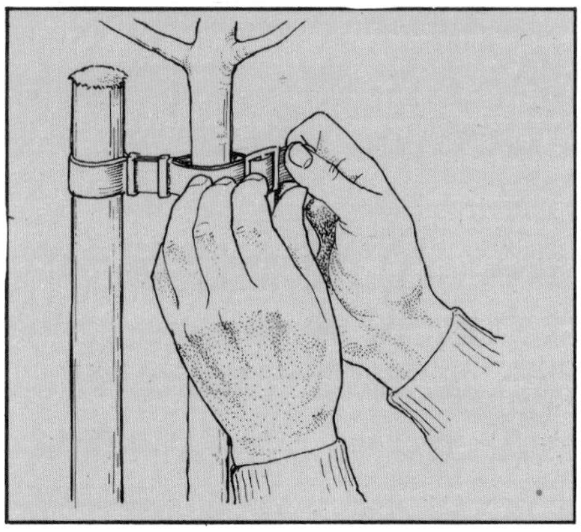

To complete the job, trees should be tied, using a specially designed tie.

strong stake at least 7 ft (2.5 m) for support until well established. One- and two-year-old trees are often sold, and the term used here is 'feathered'. This refers to the small side branches coming out from the main stem, the trunk of the tree.

Once well established the feathers can be pruned off to give the clear trunk of a full or half standard 3—5 ft (1—1.5 m). Side branches are left the first year or two to help speed the thickening of the main stem.

Soil preparation really cannot be done too thoroughly; once planted the tree may well be there for a hundred years and there will be no second chance to add well-rotted compost, peat moss or like material in order to improve water retention and drainage, to enrich the soil and speed root growth.

When planting bare-root trees in autumn to early spring, do not let the roots become dry, and prune off any roots which may have become twisted or broken.

While bare-root deciduous trees can be planted at any time the soil is not frozen during their dormant season, the earlier they are planted the more time there is for root development before the demands of new spring growth.

Container-grown trees can be planted the year round without check. Where trees are well established in the pot and roots are completely circling the base of the container, it is well worth gently unwinding them and spreading them out to improve anchorage, and get them off to a good start.

Make a cut on the underside of large branches before sawing from the top.

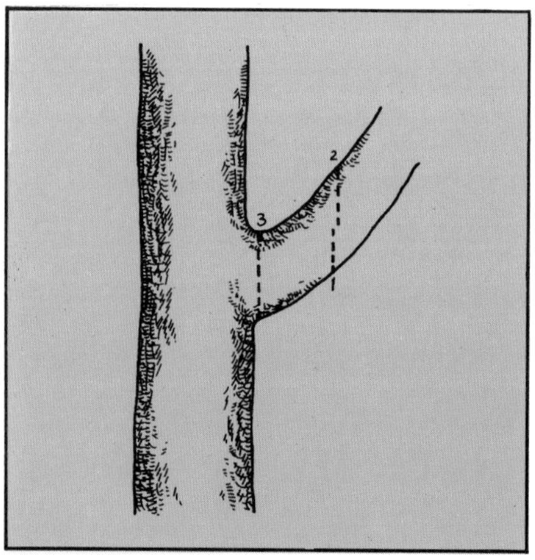

Carefully pare around the edge of the cut to leave a clean wound.

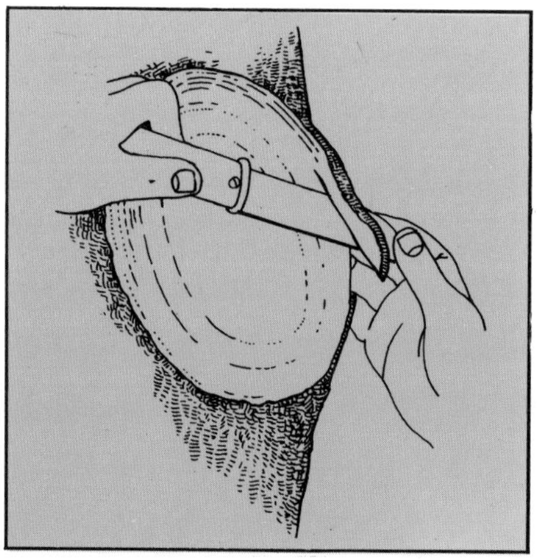

PRUNING

When cutting large limbs from trees always cut into the underside of the branch first, then finish cutting from the top. This prevents the weight of the branch breaking the last piece of wood and tearing it back.

Once the branch has been removed, carefully pare around the edge of the cut bark to leave a clean finish which quickly heals over.

GARDEN TREE SELECTOR CHART

Name	Common name	Soils	Likely ultimate height	Shape	Garden value
Acer davidii	Snake-bark Maple	A	40 ft*	1	Colored bark
Acer palmatum	Japanese Maple	N	20 ft	1	Red foliage
Acer platanoides	Norway Maple	N	80 ft	1	Easy to grow, autumn leaf color
A.p. 'Crimson King'		N	65 ft	1	Crimson-purple leaves
A.p. 'Drummondii'		N	60 ft	1	Creamy-white edged leaves
Amelanchier grandiflora	Shadbush	N/M/C	30 ft	2	White spring flower, autumn leaf color
Betula pendula	Silver Birch	N	60 ft	1	White bark, autumn leaf color
B.p. 'Youngii'	Young's Weeping Birch	N	20 ft	3	Small weeping tree
Carpinus betulus 'Fastigiata'	Fastigiata Hornbeam	N/C	50 ft	4	Spine-like shape
Cercis siliquastrum	Judas Tree	N/C/D	25 ft	2	Pink spring flowers
Cornus florida	Flowering Dogwood	N/A	20 ft	1	White flowers in spring, autumn leaf color and red berries
Crataegus laevigata 'Paulii'	Paul's Scarlet Hawthorne	N	25 ft	1	Double red spring flowers
Eucalyptus gunnii	Gum Tree	N	65 ft	1	Silver-blue leaves
Gleditsia triacanthos 'Sunburst'	Golden Honey Locust	D	33 ft	1	Thornless cultivar with rich yellow leaves
Laburnum 'Vossii'	Golden Chain	D/C	25 ft	1	Yellow spring flowers
Liquidambar styraciflua	Sweet Gum	M	65 ft	1	Autumn leaf color
Magnolia X *soulangiana*		N/M	25 ft	2	Large spring flowers
M. grandiflora	Evergreen Magnolia	N	33 ft	2	Large glossy leaves, huge scented flowers
Malus arnoldiana	Flowering Crab	N	25 ft	1	Flowers and fruits
M. 'Red Jade'	Weeping Crab	N	25 ft	3	White flowers and red fruits
M. tschonoskii	Bonfire Tree	N	35 ft	1	Upright growth and autumn leaf color
Populus balsamifera 'Aurora'	Variegated Poplar	N/M	45 ft	1	Color of young leaves
Prunus 'Amanogawa'	Flagpole Cherry	N	25 ft	4	Pale pink spring flowers
P. cerasifera 'Atropurpurea'	Purple-leaved Plum	N	25 ft	1	Dark copper leaves
P. 'Kwanzan'		N	40 ft	1	Double, pink spring flowers
P. '*Kiku-shidare Sakura*'	Weeping Cherry	N	13 ft	3	Double, pink spring flowers
P. serrula	Paperbark Cherry	N	33 ft	1	Shining coppery bark
Pyrus salicifolia 'Pendula'	Weeping Willow-leaved Pear	N	15 ft	3	Silver leaves
Robinia pseudoacacia 'Frisia'		N/D	25 ft	1	Golden-yellow foliage
Salix caprea 'Pendula'	Kilmarnock Willow	N/M	13 ft	3	Umbrella-shaped weeping tree
S. alba	Weeping Willow	N/M	65 ft	3	Golden-yellow shoots and weeping habit
Sorbus aria 'Lutescens'	Whitebeam	N/C	60 ft	1	Silver-white young leaves
S. aucuparia	Mountain Ash	N	40 ft	1	White flowers and red berries

Key N = suitable for neutral and most garden soils A = suitable for slightly acid soils C = suitable for slightly alkaline soils M = suitable for moist soils D = suitable for dryish soils

**25 ft = 7.6 m*

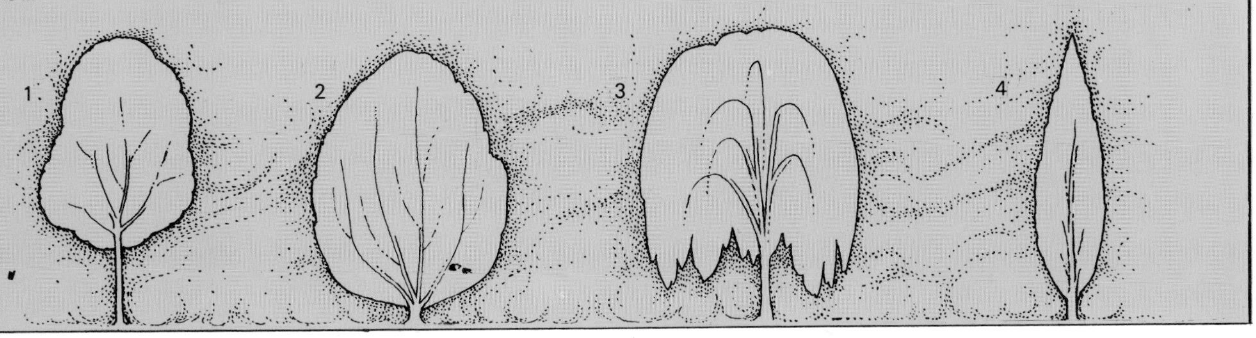

Shrubs

Shrubs are all too often neglected in smaller gardens because for many people a shrubbery conjures up a gloomy and dusty border densely planted and perhaps 7—10 ft (2—3 m) high. Shrubberies like that only exist because planting has been done carelessly, without due attention to selecting the right kinds of shrub for the right place and space. Frequently such errors in planning are made much worse by neglect of even the small amount of pruning and feeding that shrubs require.

Consider the true qualities and value of shrubs in the garden and their adaptable nature, then the invaluable contribution they make to a balanced garden soon becomes apparent.

Shrub borders in large gardens give color and interest the whole year, with the minimum of effort. Even a small shrub border can include a wide range of species that reflect the diversity of shrubs. There are shrubs in flower every month of the year. Taking the winter months, and depending on the climate, the fragrant chimonanthus and hamamelis can be in flower at the back of the border, with the sweet-smelling evergreen mahonia mid-border and heaths covering the foreground. Add to all that the winter berries and the colored barks of shrubs such as the dogwoods, and it will become apparent that there is nothing dull about shrubs even in winter. If this can be achieved in the bleak months, how much more there is to look forward to for the rest of the year, when the weather is kinder.

Shrubs play a vitally important part in any garden design. This is part of a shrub border in the author's garden.

Planning a Shrub Border

Plan a border like an artist using color, selecting each plant to build the complete but ever-changing picture. Do not overlook the importance of height — trees on a clear stem can provide this, while taller and upright-growing shrubs can be used in the center and back of the border. Prostrate, ground-hugging types should be used to cover the ground underneath larger specimens. Such ground-cover plants are attractive in their own right, but also make gardening easy by smothering weeds and reducing maintenance.

Do not overlook the usefulness of evergreens. Besides green foliage being attractive in its own right it is also a useful winter foil for winter-flowering shrubs such as hamamelis. The chapter on conifers offers many possibilities in this direction but there are broad-leaf rhododendrons, aucuba and pieris, and evergreens such as the hebes, some with attractive variegation. Evergreens are useful for furnishing the garden in winter, for filtering winds and deflecting noise.

Quantity and brightness are obvious qualities required from ornamental fruits and berries, but also important is the length of time they remain on the plant — and how attractive they are to birds. The female plants of the broad-leaf evergreen *Skimmia japonica* can be depended upon to hold their scarlet berry clusters all winter. The yellow and orange-berried pyracanthas seem to be less attractive to birds than the red kinds, and where birds are a problem this is worth considering when making a selection. One shrub that usually retains its large fruits right through the winter is *Chaenomeles,* the Japanese quince.

When young shrubs are seen in a nursery or garden center it is sometimes difficult to visualize their final size and form, yet this is vital if a balanced border is to be created.

Speed of growth and ultimate height will of course depend on district, soil and situation, and heights quoted are the averages likely to be reached under normal conditions. Impoverished soil

A few well-chosen shrubs can transform a garden. Here forsythia contrast well against silver birch and bring a spring garden to life.

and also cold, dry positions will restrict growth, while warm, rich soils and high rainfall can increase the ultimate size. Plants grown in shade may become drawn.

The other problem encountered in establishing a new border is the *rate* of growth, for some will grow rapidly, while others take many years to reach a mature height.

The appearance of a new shrub border can be improved by planting groups of perhaps three or five plants of a single kind, thinning over the years until just one good specimen remains. The extra plants will give an appearance of maturity more quickly, and three plants, to be thinned to one finally, could cover the ground in a season and save a couple of seasons of hoeing the ground every fortnight to control weeds.

Foundation Planting

It has long been the practice in the U.S.A. to use shrubs to disguise foundations of the house, and the higher and uglier the foundation, the more shrubs were planted. The result has been that the foundation is hidden, but eventually so are the windows and finally much of the house.

The trend now is toward restraint. If the foundation is nearly level with the ground, a few shrubs can be used at the entrances and perhaps at the corners of the house with ground covers or even grass in between. High foundations can still be a problem but plant shrubs that remain low, in groups of three or more of a kind.

Besides their use in borders and foundations, shrubs are an attractive feature in their own right, just like specimen trees. They also provide protection, privacy, and a pleasant vista. The range of shrubs available is wide, but the key to success is to select carefully in the first place, matching the plant to soil and situation.

Most shrubs are tolerant of quite widely differing soils, and it is usually only where extremely alkaline (limy) or acid (peat and thin sands) soils occur that special care must be taken when selecting species. The chart on page 62 indicates which shrubs will grow well on difficult soils, and if this is read in conjunction with the notes on specific plants it should be possible to select the best for your situation.

BUYING SHRUBS

How well your plants grow away after planting will depend to a large extent on the state of the root system. The roots may be bare when you buy the plant, wrapped in a soil-ball, or be growing in a container.

Bare-root plants have been lifted from the field and transported without soil, although the exposed roots should have been wrapped to keep them moist. Such plants are usually received from mail-order nurseries in spring and should be planted as soon as possible. Follow directions sent by the nurseries.

Balled plants, which have been lifted with a soil-ball and held firmly in place with sacking-like material, allow transplanting with very little root disturbance.

Container-grown plants are subject to the least disturbance of all, and unlike the others can be planted at any time of the year. Such plants grow away with no check because roots are undisturbed when transplanting.

When purchasing a container-grown plant try lifting it by the stem — an established plant will hold the full weight of the pot and compost; a recently potted specimen will not and should be avoided.

Where possible it is best to visit a garden center or nursery to choose well-shaped, vigorously growing specimens. But this is not always possible, and some shrubs may have to be ordered from a reputable nursery. Cheap offers and low-priced plants are usually inferior and are likely to prove a false economy.

Vigorous young plants will tend to

Alkaline soil turns the leaves of many shrubs yellow, even this pyracantha.

grow away quickly and become established more readily than larger specimens that suffer a more severe check when moved, especially where bare-root plants are concerned. Because the younger plants tend to grow away more strongly, they often overtake larger plants of the same kind. As younger plants are usually cheaper to buy, do not be influenced by size alone.

PREPARATION AND PLANTING

Although plants will cling tenaciously to life despite unsatisfactory conditions, they will establish themselves far more readily if they are given the benefit of well prepared soil — which is not much to ask considering the many years most shrubs decorate a garden.

The minimum depth to which the site should be dug is 1 ft (30 cm) but forking over the lower soil is advisable. Both heavy and light soils will benefit from the incorporation of peat moss and compost. Remember that although it is simple to add fertilizers later, it is not so easy to improve soil structure once the shrubs are planted.

While annual weeds are easily dealt with later, deep-rooted perennials are more difficult, so every effort should be made to clear these from the ground during soil preparation.

The newly prepared ground should be left to settle before planting.

Broom can be pruned after flowering by cutting back the previous summer's growth by about two-thirds.

Planting

Always dig a hole large enough to accommodate the roots without cramping. If there is nowhere convenient to place the earth during planting apart from the lawn, use a sheet of plastic to protect the grass and provide a clean finish to the job.

Be sure to protect bare roots from cold drying winds while preparing the holes, covering them with a damp sack or cloth if necessary. Bare roots should be spread out well in the bottom of the hole, but try not to disturb the soil-ball if there is one. When the shrub is in position, fill round the roots with peat moss and good friable soil. Bare-rooted shrubs need to be eased up and down a little during this process to make sure there are no large air pockets left in the soil.

The sacking-like burlap round balled plants can be left in place as it quickly decays in the soil. Any plastic root wrap which will not rot must be removed — and most won't!

Firm the soil as infilling progresses by treading firmly. The surface footprints should be forked out once complete however, as if left, the structure of the soil will be affected and become wet and muddy, then dry into a hard cake. For the same reason, try to avoid planting in wet conditions.

Planting should also be delayed if the ground is frozen. In wet or icy conditions it is best to wait until the weather improves. Container-grown plants will not come to any harm provided they are not allowed to dry out. Bare-rooted plants should be left in the wrapping in a frost-free place and kept damp. If plants arrive before the ground has been prepared, they can be 'laid in' temporarily by placing the roots in a spare piece of ground and covering with moist soil, gently firmed.

Container-grown plants are the easiest to handle as the hole only needs to be fractionally larger than the container, and the plant placed in the hole before removing the container. The gap can then be filled in with fine soil and firmed.

Deciduous shrubs can be planted from mid-October till the end of March. Evergreens are best planted in September and October or March and April. Container-grown plants can, of course, be planted at almost any time provided the ground is not frozen.

PRUNING

The majority of shrubs need very little regular pruning, and in many cases it is quite sufficient to remove dead flower heads and trim to retain good shape.

Although there are very many different kinds of shrubs, pruning can be simplified into four groups — spring, summer and winter-flowering deciduous, and evergreens.

Those which flower in spring and early summer such as flowering currants, forsythia and lilac, should be pruned immediately after flowering, cutting back old shoots that have flowered to fresh young growths on the main branches. Weak growths and crowded shoots should be thinned out at the same time.

Shrubs which flower in late summer or early autumn on the current year's growth, such as *Buddleia davidii* cultivars, the fuchsias, potentillas and caryopteris are best pruned hard in early spring.

Winter-flowering shrubs should have diseased and weak branches cut out in spring, otherwise just prune to keep the plants within a restricted space.

Evergreens are best pruned in spring, when they will quickly produce new growth to hide any unsightly cuts. Normally only weak, straggly or diseased shoots need to be cut out. A few plants however, such as box, lavender, rhododendrons and santolina, respond to hard pruning; if they are bare at the base and have grown too large they can be successfully cut back in spring.

Before attempting any pruning, be sure to have a good sharp pair of pruners — for the sake of the plant and your own comfort. It will be easier to remove a large branch if downward pressure is applied on the branch, and away from the blade.

The barberries are justifiably popular shrubs, with a variety of forms and leaf color. This is a deciduous species, *Berberis thunbergii* 'Rose Glow'.

SOME GOOD GARDEN SHRUBS

Acer (Maple) Some maples, though technically trees, are often grown as shrubs. The Japanese types will tolerate some lime, but they grow best in slightly acid, peaty soil. As those with finely-cut, colored leaves are easily damaged by late spring frost and strong winds, plant them in a sheltered position and out of direct early morning sunshine.

The cut-leaved forms are well suited to growing on banks, as specimen subjects in lawns, or in association with stone. Japanese maples and lilies make a good planting combination.

Acer negundo 'Variegatum', which has broad white margins to the leaves, makes a nice pot-grown tree, and is effective planted with purple-leaved prunus. Among the Japanese maples, *A. palmatum* 'Atropurpureum' is a popular purple-leaved shrub, but for a dwarfer, slower-growing plant try *A. p.* 'Dissectum.'

Amelanchier (Service Berry) This large shrub or small tree should be more widely planted. The young pink to copper foliage contrasts with clusters of massed white flowers in spring. It also associates well with spring bulbs. The leaves have rich autumn color before falling.

Prune back hard after flowering to retain a compact size.

Aucuba japonica A good town plant as the evergreen foliage will withstand shade and grime. Best planted in a position with some shelter from very cold wind. The variegated forms retain their color longest if grown in full sun. If male and female specimens are planted, red berries are produced.

Prune in May or June to restrict size and retain shape.

This versatile plant can also be grown in tubs or urns, and even makes an attractive houseplant in cool rooms.

Aucuba japonica is a good, attractive shrub for town gardens.

Azaleas There are two main groups — evergreen and deciduous. The evergreen and semi-evergreen azaleas, of which there are numerous named cultivars, vary in their hardiness and will not survive in the extreme North nor in alkaline soils. Because some flowers fade badly in strong sunlight, plant in a position sheltered from early morning sun. A partially shaded site under trees is good.

Slow-growing plants, they may take ten years to reach 3 ft (1 m). Deciduous azaleas tend to grow taller, and the flowers are larger.

All types can be grown in tubs, but keep them well watered with lime-free water.

If azalea gall shows itself as white and pale green swellings, remove the galls and spray with benomyl.

Berberis (Barberry) This is another genus with evergreen and deciduous forms — all with sharp spines which can make them useful as a deterrent hedge.

The evergreens are grown mainly for attractive deep green foliage, but some are grown for their flowers. *B. darwinii* and *B. ×stenophylla* are planted in mild climates, the latter for hedges.

Deciduous types are grown for their attractive autumn foliage and bright berries. This group is dominated by *B. thunbergii,* well known in the North.

To avoid planting losses, purchase container-grown plants. Prune only to remove weak old growth and to retain shape — the deciduous kinds in spring, the evergreens after flowering.

Buddleia (Butterfly Bush) A wonderful plant if you want to encourage butterflies to visit your garden. The most widely planted types are the July- to September-flowering *B. davidii* cultivars, but *B. globosa,* the orange ball tree, is a complete contrast with its orange balls of flowers in June.

Prune *B. davidii* hard in March, but *B. globosa,* not hardy in the North, only needs to be trimmed after flowering.

Calluna (Heather) Although some ericas (heaths) will tolerate limy soils, the callunas will not. Apart from this, the major difference between callunas and ericas is in the leaves — those of callunas being softer and thicker.

The cultivars grown for their silver, golden or red leaves generally have insignificant flowers, but others have good flowers in summer.

Full sun is needed for plenty of flower and a good color to the foliage. Trim the flower heads back lightly in March every year.

Camellia The exotic, waxy flowers of the camellia make it the shrub equivalent of the orchid. The glossy, evergreen foliage is a bonus.

The plants are not reliably hardy much beyond Washington, D.C. and in like climates but some varieties have done well as far north as Long Island and Cape Cod. In fringe-hardiness areas, the plants should be placed in the protection of house walls and out of searing winter winds and sun.

Plant in an acid, humus-rich soil. These shrubs can be put in tubs for winter in cool well-lighted rooms.

Camellias are spectactular spring-flowering shrubs that are very rewarding to grow. The variety illustrated is *C. japonica* 'Elegans'.

Chaenomeles is a hardy spring-flowering shrub, also known as flowering quince.

Ceanothus This shrub in its blue-flowered species and hybrids can be very beautiful but the plants are not hardy beyond their Pacific habitat, where they are known as California-lilac. The New Jersey tea *(Ceanothus americanus),* native from Maine to South Carolina and west to Texas, is hardy in the North and sometimes grown but its white flowers lack the spectacular beauty of the West Coast natives.

The West Coast evergreen plants need little pruning beyond shaping after flowering. Cut deciduous types back in March.

Chaenomeles (Japanese Quince) This outstanding garden plant used to be known as cydonia. It is completely hardy and thrives in all soils. The attractive spring flowers are followed by golden-yellow fruit in the autumn. The red cultivars are the most spectacular, especially against a wall.

Chimonanthus (Winter Sweet) A delightful, fragrant shrub that flowers from December to February in mild climates. A well-drained sheltered site is ideal. It responds well to the protection of a south or west facing wall. The plants take several years before they start flowering so do not be impatient; the result is worth the wait.

Choisya (Mexican Orange Blossom) The heavily fragrant flowers in May make this an ideal patio plant or for planting beneath a window. It prefers full sun, and some shelter. A well-drained soil is best. Pruning only consists of removing frost-damaged shoots in March. For mild climates.

Cornus (Dogwood) Colored foliage and bark are the reasons for growing shrubby dogwoods. Those grown for

Cotinus in the foreground of a mixed border. This used to be known as *Rhus cotinus,* and its fluffy flower heads give rise to the common name smoke tree.

the winter bark are happy in most soils. Some dogwoods have nicely variegated foliage like *Cornus alba* 'Elegantissima' one of the most popular of all shrubs. A few, such as *Cornus mas* and *C. officinalis,* are grown for their yellow flowers in spring.

Those kinds with colored bark should be cut back very hard every other spring to encourage new growth.

Corylus (Hazel) *Corylus avellana* 'Contorta', the corkscrew hazel, can be quite a conversation piece, with its twisted and contorted branches.

Totally different but still attractive is the purple-leaf filbert, *C. maxima* 'Purpurea'.

Prune in March after the catkins fade, cutting back even into three- and four-year-old wood.

Cotinus (Smoke Tree) This used to be called *Rhus cotinus.* It is grown for its fluffy flower heads that give rise to its common name. There is a purple-leaved form, 'Purpureus'. Cotinus is an excellent plant for a mixed border, contrasting with golden foliage.

Pruning is normally unnecessary, though any unwanted growth can be cut out in March.

Cotoneaster These are among our most important hardy shrubs. There are both evergreen and deciduous kinds, and a wide range of form and habit. Colorful autumn foliage and brilliant berries are their main attraction, but their ease of culture also explains why they are so widely planted.

Among the evergreen cotoneasters there are many that are good for carpeting a bank, such as *C. conspicuus* 'Decorus' and *C. dammeri,* the latter growing only a few centimeters high but each plant spreading over a 4 sq m area.

Among the deciduous contoneasters, *C. horizontalis* is one of the best, and is invaluable for north and east walls. It is also excellent on banks. The common name fish bone cotoneaster describes it well. This species has a good autumn color. Not all cotoneasters are showy in flower but an exception is *C. multiflorus* which has white flowers followed by red berries on arching branches, 6—12 ft (1—3 m) long.

There are some species best described as semi-evergreen, and this group contains the popular hedging plant *C. simonsii.*

If any trimming is necessary, do it in spring.

Cytisus (Broom) The brooms, with their tumbling sprays of spring flowers cascading like a waterfall, are excellent garden plants. They will be happy in most garden soils, provided the extremes of acid and alkaline soils are avoided. Full sun and good drainage are important.

Brooms do not take kindly to transplanting, so buy container-grown plants. Prune after flowering by cutting back the previous summer's growth by up to two-thirds. Hardened wood does not respond to pruning, so leggy specimens are best replaced with new plants.

Daphne *Daphne mezereum* is one of the most popular February-flowering plants. It has a delicious fragrance.

A well-drained soil is required, and lime is tolerated. Full sun or partial shade are both acceptable, but the soil must not be allowed to dry out. If planting near a wall, be sure to add plenty of organic matter to retain moisture.

The scarlet berries which follow the flowers are poisonous.

Deutzia These summer-flowering shrubs are often planted too closely in a mixed border, where their beauty is not seen at its best. When planting be sure

Cytisus ×*praecox* is one of the most graceful brooms, ideal for small gardens.

A ground covering of *Erica carnea* 'Vivellii' and *E. c.* 'Springwood Pink'.

A pleasing group of *Erica cinerea* 'White Dale', *E. c.* 'Pink Ice' and *E. carnea* 'Foxhollow'.

to allow sufficient space for development. An open sunny site will give the most balanced growth, but pink-flowered forms will hold their color better in the light shade of overhanging trees.

Occasional removal of old wood from the base will keep the plants vigorous and attractive.

Elaeagnus Useful evergreen or deciduous plants. *E. pungens* 'Maculata' is variegated with yellow, and is popular with flower arrangers. *E.* ×*ebbingei* has fragrant white flowers in the autumn and can be grown in coastal areas.

Ground-covering *Euonymus fortunei* 'Emerald 'n' Green'.

Any all-green shoots that appear on variegated forms should be cut out as soon as they are noticed.

Erica These useful ground-cover plants have become justifiably popular. Young plants spaced 15 in. (38 cm) apart will cover the ground in two seasons.

An acid soil is preferred, and if the soil is alkaline, choice should rest with *E. carnea, E. mediterranea* or *E.* ×*darleyensis.*

Mulch annually with moistened peat or composted bark to speed growth. Dead flower heads can be removed with shears in spring, but do not cut the plants back too hard.

Escallonia Any well-drained soil is suitable for these shrubs, and they will survive even in those that are very light and dry.

They will endure some frost but are mostly shrubs for the Sun Belt and California.

If used as a screen or hedge they should be spaced so that hard pruning is unnecessary. Trimming back should be done after flowering.

Euonymus (Spindle) The evergreen forms of euonymus are becoming popular because of their attractive foliage and compact growth.

Euonymous japonica 'Aurea' has bright yellow variegation. Several forms of *E. fortunei radicans* are excellent ground cover plants. The variegated kinds need full sun to produce the best coloring.

Forsythia One of the most brilliant of spring-flowering shrubs, it is also one of the easiest to grow. Any reasonable soil will give good results.

Besides the popular *F.* ×*intermedia* cultivars, 'Lynwood' and 'Spectabilis', there is a species with a rambling, weeping habit — *F. suspensa.* This is effective trained against a wall, on steep banks, or sprawling over fences or walls.

Do not prune too hard — only remove old flowering shoots immediately after flowering.

Branches cut after Christmas and placed in water indoors can be forced into flower.

Fuchsia Although even hardy species tend to be cut back by frost, they produce new shoots from the base in spring. Protection from severe frost can be given by covering the base of the plant with 8—12 in. (20—30 cm) of dry peat in the autumn. Open sunny sites or shade are both satisfactory.

On established plants, shoots can be pruned to ground level in spring in areas where frost causes die-back. Otherwise all that is necessary is the removal of dead wood.

Garrya elliptica The glossy evergreen foliage of this shrub will withstand the onslaught of city smoke and dirt. The real prize comes with the long tassels of catkins in January and February, which make it attractive as a free-standing bush or against a wall.

Ideally a south-facing wall is the best place for planting as cold winds burn back the leaves. It will survive on a north wall in mild, sheltered districts. In fact, it is native to the Pacific Coast and is not hardy in most of the North.

Genista Closely related to Broom, the genistas *G. hispanica* and *G. lydia* are excellent plants for covering dry banks. A hot, sunny site suits them best, and poor soil produces the most flowers.

Hamamelis (Witch Hazel) One of the most popular garden shrubs, bringing as much interest and color to the garden in mid-winter as the forsythia does in spring. Small branches can be cut to bring their fragrance into the house.

A soil heavily enriched with peat moss or leafmold is required.

The Witch hazel, *Hamamelis mollis,* is a fragrant winter-flowering shrub that enjoys a moist, acid soil.

Hebe These plants, which are mostly grown in California, have shiny evergreen leaves, some of them being variegated. The flowers, which may persist for many months, are also attractive in their own right.

Hebes are excellent coastal plants, and also stand up to the dust and grime of city life. Long, severe spells of cold can damage some cultivars.

Hibiscus These spectacular shrubs, with their large almost hollyhock-like flowers, make good solitary plants as well as mixed border subjects.

There are both very hardy species, such as rose of Sharon *(H. syriacus),* and the tropical rose of China *(H. rosa-sinensis),* often grown in tubs indoors.

Hydrangea Many hydrangeas find their way into gardens after serving their time as a pot plant indoors. These are the *Hydrangea macrophylla* cultivars, but there are other interesting species such as *H. paniculata* 'Grandiflora', which produces cone-shaped white flower heads. This is also hardier. As the *H. macrophylla* cultivars are not completely hardy they may need some protection in winter from severe frost in the form of straw or sacking. As the dead flower heads offer some protection, do not remove them until March.

Hydrangeas are useful for planting in planters or tubs, but watering must never be neglected. Some pink varieties turn blue in acid soil, but if it is not very acid 3 oz (88 ml) of aluminum sulfate dissolved in 1 gallon (1 liter) of water can be applied to ensure a good flower color. White varieties will not change color.

Large, single, yellow flowers typical of deciduous and evergreen hypericum.

Hypericum (St. John's-wort) A wonderful ground-cover plant, *Hypericum calycinum* is evergreen and has large, yellow buttercup-like flowers in profusion. It will give a good show in full sun or semi-shade, and grow freely in all but waterlogged soil. Semi-evergreen *H.* 'Hidcote' is a free-flowering taller shrub.

Ilex (Holly) In addition to the important tree hollies, such as the English and American kinds, there are a number of shrubby hollies. One of the best is the Japanese holly, *I. crenata,* a hardy species with many cultivars, more often planted than the species. They are useful in foundation plantings because they can be sheared or cut back to the base if they outgrow their space. The Japanese hollies bear black berries favored by birds in winter.

Inkberry *(I. glabra),* stoloniferous and also evergreen, is very hardy and although it is often found wild in bogs, adapts well to average conditions,

One of the most popular magnolias is *M.* X *soulangiana*, which has large tulip-like flowers in April.

including those of city gardens.

Jasminum nudiflorum (Winter Jasmine) The yellow-flowered *J. nudiflorum* makes a good wall shrub for winter flowers, but avoid an east-facing site.

Prune side shoots after flowering.

The white-flowered *J. officinalis* is summer-flowering (see climbers).

Kalmia Mountain-laurel is native to woods of Eastern North America. It needs a moist, acidic soil free from lime. A peaty soil in semi-shade is ideal.

Once established it will require no further attention except removing dead flower heads.

Kerria japonica An undemanding free-flowering plant that suckers from the base to form a many-stemmed shrub. There is a variegated form which needs the protection of a wall in cold districts.

Prune back flowered shoots in early June.

Magnolia Most gardeners are familiar with the splendid April-flowering species. The most widely planted species is *M. ×soulangiana,* which has large tulip-like flowers, but another gem is *M. stellata,* which grows only slowly to reach 9 ft (3 m), and is laden with white star-like blooms in March and April. Other species flower later in the year.

Magnolias are best in a reasonably rich, deep and lime-free soil, but they will grow in clay and stand the atmosphere of towns quite well.

Mahonia These excellent evergreen plants have sprays of yellow flowers in early spring followed by dark blue grape-like berry clusters. They are called Oregon-grape.

Although not fussy about soil, these shrubs take a season or two to settle down, but require little attention once established. *M.aquifolium* can be encouraged to maintain low and lush green growth by cutting back hard in April after flowering. Plant in partial shade to prevent winter burn of foliage.

Osmanthus This shrub will grow on most soils, in sun or partial shade.

Paeonia (Peony) The tree peonies are quite as showy as roses, but unfortunately they are not as hardy. The tender young shoots produced in the spring are sometimes damaged by late frosts, and it is worth covering them with sacking on cold nights and leaving until the frost has thawed in the morning.

Tree peonies are best planted in groups to the front of mixed borders, or as specimens in sheltered gardens if they can be given a position protected from early morning sun.

Philadelphus (Mock Orange) This plant derives its common name from the fragrance of the flowers, which is like orange blossom. It is an almost perfect garden plant, with a good habit and undemanding nature. It will thrive in the poorest conditions, including alkaline. Little pruning is required apart from thinning out old wood after flowering.

Pieris *Pieris japonica*, Japanese andromeda, is grown for its white flower panicles in early spring. Other kinds, including *P. formosa forestii* and *P.* 'Forest Flame', have new spring growth leaf that is bright scarlet; plant them in a sheltered, partly shady site.

A lime-free soil is required, and they will appreciate a bed of acid peat. Pieris are useful for planting with heathers and rhododendrons, which have similar requirements.

Potentilla For sheer flower power it is difficult to better the shrubby

Potentilla fruticosa 'Red Ace' is brightest red in cool weather.

Pyracantha 'Orange Glow' is one of the best firethorns, with its long-lasting orange-red berries carried on strong upright plants.

Rhododendrons come in great variety; choose dwarf kinds for small gardens.

potentillas, which produce their single rose-like flowers from June to the first frost. All are easy to grow, but they do best on a light well-drained soil, and although shade is tolerated they will be more prolific in full sun.

Besides being useful in mixed shrubberies and low hedges, they make a good ground cover, and some cultivars are suitable for sunny banks and the back of rockeries.

Pyracantha (Firethorn) The pyracanthas have so many uses that no garden would be complete without at least one of them. Sheets of white flowers in spring are followed by bright red or orange berries carried well into the winter. One of the best to grow is *P.* 'Mohave', a strong upright plant smothered with orange-red fruit for many months.

All garden soils, including alkaline, are suitable. They thrive in both sun and partial shade. Their thorns make the plants useful for creating an impenetrable hedge, but they look most attractive against a wall. Any pruning should be done in May or June.

Buy pot or container-grown plants to avoid transplanting losses.

Rhododendron Although rhododendrons are often seen to best effect in large stately gardens, there are species and hybrids well suited to gardens of more average size. Some remain and are suitable for quite compact planting close to the house.

All willows *Salix*, thrive in damp soil, even the low-growing shrubs.

All rhododendrons require an acid soil — lime turns the leaves yellow. An application of flowers of sulphur 4—6 oz per sq yd (100—150 g per sq m) will reduce alkalinity.

Where conditions are not right naturally, it is worth creating a peat moss bed, and watering with Sequestrene to overcome the yellowing of the leaves.

Never allow rhododendrons to become dry at the roots; leaf edges rolling under and tips browning indicate a dry soil.

Remove dead flower heads as this encourages the formation of next year's flower buds.

Rhus (Sumach) These easily grown plants have splendid autumn color, and are useful in city areas where they withstand the atmospheric pollution better than many plants. If cut back in February, vigorous new shoots will be produced. This plant tends to produce suckers round the base, and these can be a nuisance in a small garden.

Ribes (Flowering Currant) One of the earlier flowering shrubs, the flowering currant will grow well in ordinary garden soil in full sun or partial shade, though the flowers will be more colorful and profuse in a sunny situation.

Prune out old wood after flowering to keep the plants growing vigorously and to provide plenty of one-year-old wood to produce the flowers.

Salix (Willow) Although many people think of the willow as a large tree, there are shrubby species. Some, such as the prostrate woolly willow, *Salix lanata*, barely reach 3 ft (1 m) in height.

Any ordinary garden soil is suitable,

Spiraea bumalda 'Gold Flame' carries richly colored shoots in spring.

White felt-like leaves throughout the year and yellow flowers in summer are produced by *Senecio laxifolius* and the very similar *S. greyi*. Both are for mild climates.

including those that are occasionally waterlogged. Light, dry soils will need large quantities of peat moss or leafmold added when the site is being prepared.

Little, if any, pruning is required for the dwarf types, although stronger-growing kinds, selected for their colored bark, will need cutting back hard in spring.

Skimmia Skimmia is a neat evergreen shrub that grows little more than 3 ft (1 m) high. It has clusters of tiny scented white flowers in March and April. Male plants have more flowers, but the female plants have abundant brilliant red berries the size of large peas, which remain on the bush right through winter.

To be sure of having plenty of berries, plant one bush of each sex together, or one male to three females. *Skimmia reevesiana* carries male and female on the same plant.

Avoid alkaline soils. Pruning is rarely necessary.

Spartium (Spanish Broom) This plant looks like the common yellow Broom, but is more vigorous and the branches are circular in cross-section. It will tolerate a wide variety of soils, but does less well on chalk. Good drainage and full sun help it to reach its full potential.

This is a subject that resents transplanting, so buy pot or container-grown plants.

Plants which have become leggy or too tall can be cut back in spring provided that only young wood is pruned.

Spiraea The spring-flowering spiraeas have white flowers, but the summer-flowering kinds usually have pink or red flowers. The various types can add color and interest over a long period. All are easy to grow and are not fussy about soil.

Spring-flowering types need a light pruning after flowering to restrict size, but the summer-flowering kinds need harder pruning in spring to produce large flower spikes.

Stephanandra Sometimes called lace shrub because of its filmy, fernlike foliage, which is its outstanding feature. There are inconspicuous white flower clusters in spring.

The habit of growth is graceful and almost fountainlike, making this a shrub suitable for banks or as a low hedge. Prune as necessary.

It has a suckering habit which can get out of control.

Symphoricarpos (Snowberry) This is a suckering shrub which has tiny bluish-white flowers during the summer followed by shiny white berries that remain on the plant for many months. There are also some cultivars with colored berries.

Snowberries are quick to become established and will furnish the wilder parts of the garden and fill waterside banks very rapidly.

Syringa (Lilac) Few shrubs are better than lilac for fragrance, for garden decoration or for cutting. There are many very good named forms, though the flowering season tends to be rather short.

Lilacs thrive on all soils, including alkaline. However, they will languish in poor soils. Full sun is required for a good show of flowers.

One of the best methods of pruning is to cut the branches in flower for indoor decoration. Even so it will occasionally be essential to prune hard, cutting out thin unproductive wood, and this is best done immediately after flowering.

Any suckers coming from the base of the plant should be cut out.

Viburnum opulus, the guelder rose, has bright red berries in autumn.

Tamarix This shrub has a graceful habit of growth that makes it a good choice for mixed borders or as a lawn specimen.

Though delicate in appearance, it is quite tough, and will do well on most soils, though a well-drained and sunny position is preferred.

Up to two-thirds of the current season's growth should be cut out — after flowering for the early-flowering species, in winter or early spring for *T. ramosissima* (syn. *T. pentandra).*

Viburnum There are many different kinds of viburnum, with a range of qualities. It would almost be possible to furnish a garden with viburnum alone, and it is worth considering a special border of just viburnums — once established there would be interest all the year, and it would require the minimum of attention.

There are evergreen and deciduous kinds, some deliciously fragrant, others with bright autumn foliage, and yet others with richly colored fruits. Most have white or whitish flowers. Main flowering seasons are winter, spring and early summer.

All types flourish in a wide variety of soils, though those that are moisture-retentive suit them best. Some species, such as *V. rhytidophyllum,* really thrive in limestone soils.

Weigela The easy and free-flowering nature of this shrub makes it very popular. It can be used in borders, on banks, or grown against a fence.

These plants prefer a well-cultivated soil, but will grow in either full sun or partial shade.

Quite hard pruning immediately after flowering will encourage production of plenty of flowers.

SHRUBS FOR SPECIAL SITES

North Walls	Shaded Sites	Ground Cover
Camellia*	Aucuba*	Cotoneaster
Chaenomeles	Buxus	Cytisus
Garrya*	Camellia*	Erica
Kerria	Euonymus	Euonymus
Mahonia	Hedera	Genista
Pyracantha	Hypericum	Hedera
	Ilex	Hypericum
	Leucothoe	Lonicera
Climbers	Lonicera	Potentilla
Hedera	Ligustrum	Stephanandra
Hydrangea	Mahonia	
Jasminum*	Pieris	
Parthenocissus	Rhododendron	
	Skimmia	

NOTE * Of borderline hardiness and/or for mild climates

SHRUBS WITH ATTRACTIVE BERRIES OR FRUITS

Name	Deciduous	Both	Evergreen	Acid soil	Alkaline soil	Clay soil	Sandy soil
Callicarpa	×						
Clerodendrum*	×						
Colutea*	×				●	●	●
Cotoneaster		×		●	●	●	●
Hippophae	×						
Ilex			×				
Mahonia			×				
Pernettya*			×	●			
Pyracantha			×			●	
Skimmia*			×	●			
Symphoricarpos	×				●	●	
Viburnum		×			●		

NOTE * Of borderline hardiness and/or for mild climates

SHRUBS WITH ATTRACTIVE FOLIAGE OR STEMS

Name	Deciduous	Both	Evergreen	Acid soil	Alkaline soil	Clay soil	Sandy soil
Acer	×			●			
Aralia	×					●	
Aucuba*			×		●	●	
Buxus			×		●		
Cornus	×					●	
Corylus	×					●	
Cotinus	×					●	
Elaeagnus			×				●
Euonymus		×			●		
Fatsia*			×				
Garrya*			×				
Hebe*			×		●		
Laurus*			×		●		
Ligustrum			×		●		●
Lonicera		×					
Osmanthus*			×			●	
Pieris			×	●			
Rhododendron			×	●	●		
Salix	×						
Senecio*			×		●	●	

NOTE * Of borderline hardiness and/or for mild climates

SHRUBS GROWN FOR THEIR FLOWERS

Name	Deciduous	Deciduous/Evergreen	Evergreen	Color	Fragrance	Acid soil	Alkaline soil	Clay soil	Sandy soil	Jan	Feb	March	April	May	June	July	Aug	Sept	Oct	Nov	Dec
Amelanchier	×			W								●	●●	●							
Azalea		×		W, Y, O, R, P, M	×	●							●	●●	●						
Berberis		×		Y, O								●	●●	●							
Buddleia	×			M, R, B, W, O	×		●									●	●●	●			
Camelia*			×	W, R, P		●					●	●●	●●	●							
Carpenteria*			×	W											●	●					
Caryopteris	×			B													●	●●	●		
Ceanothus*			×	B	×		●							●	●						
Ceanothus*	×			P, B	×		●									●	●●	●●	●		
Chaenomeles	×			W, O, R, P				●				●●	●●	●							
Chimonanthus*	×			Y	×					●●	●										
Choisya*			×	W	×									●●	●						
Clethra	×			W	×	●				●							●●				
Cytisus	×			W, Y, R, M					●				●	●●	●						
Daphne	×			M	×						●	●●									
Deutzia	×			W, P			●	●							●●	●					
Erica/Calluna			×	W, R, P, M		●				●●	●●	●●	●●	●		●●	●●	●●	●●	●●	●●
Escallonia*			×	R, P				●							●	●●	●●	●			
Forsythia	×			Y			●	●				●●	●●								
Fuchsia*	×			W, R, M											●	●●	●●	●●	●		
Genista	×			Y										●	●						
Hamamelis	×			Y	×					●●	●●	●									●
Hibiscus	×			W, P, M, B													●	●●	●		
Hydrangea	×			W, R, P, B		●										●	●●	●			
Hypericum		×		Y			●	●							●	●●	●●	●●	●		
Indigofera	×			P		●			●							●	●●	●●	●		
Jasminum nud.	×			Y						●●	●●	●								●●	●●
Jasminum off.*	×			W												●●	●●	●			
Kalmia			×	P		●									●●						
Kerria	×			Y		●			●				●●	●●							
Kolkwitzia	×			P										●●	●●						
Leucothoe			×	W	×	●			●				●●	●							
Magnolia	×			W, P	×	●		●				●	●●	●●	●●						
Magnolia			×	W	×											●	●●				
Mahonia jap.			×	Y	×					●●	●										●
Olearia*			×	W			●								●●	●	●●				
Philadelphus	×			W	×	●	●								●●	●●					
Potentilla	×			W, Y, O											●●	●●	●●	●●	●		
Prunus	×			W, P								●	●●	●●	●						
Rhododendron			×	W, Y, R, P, M		●						●	●●	●●	●●						
Ribes	×			Y, R, P				●				●	●								
Rosa	×			W, Y, R, P	×									●	●●	●					
Skimmia*	×		×	W	×	●						●	●								
Spartium*	×			Y											●●	●					
Spiraea	×			W, P				●				●	●●	●●	●●	●●	●●	●			
Syringa	×			W, Y, R, P, M, B	×		●						●	●●	●						
Tamarix	×			P		●			●					●●		●●	●●				
Viburnum		×		W	×		●			●●	●●	●	●	●●	●●					●	●●
Weigela	×			R, P, M			●	●						●●	●						

Key

W	White	P	Pink	O	Orange
Y	Yellow	M	Mauve	*	Of borderline hardiness and/or for mild climates.
R	Red	B	Blue		

A solid dot under a soil type indicates the plant will grow well under these special conditions.

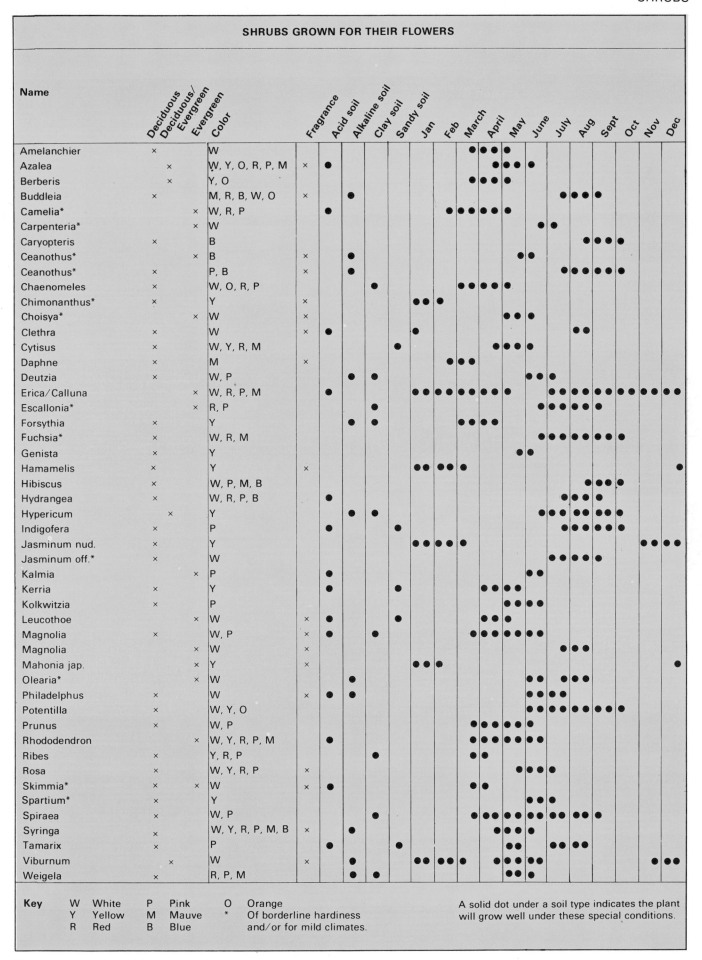

Climbing Shrubs

No list of shrubs would be complete without climbers, and there is room in practically every garden for at least a few of these useful plants.

Wherever there is a wall or fence, there's a possible site, and the great merit of climbers is that they usually clothe and enhance what would otherwise be bare areas, and for very little in the way of root space.

Many otherwise boring wooden fences can also be transformed into a living vista by careful selection of suitable climbers. Even old tree stumps that are too difficult to remove can be put to good use.

Some climbers need a little help with support until they get a grip themselves, but others such as the Virginia creeper are totally self-clinging.

Clematis

Clematis are justifiably among the most popular climbing plants, and they deserve to be in every garden. They take up little soil space yet they can transform an otherwise dull wall or fence into a blaze of color.

There are many superb large-flowered cultivars in shades of blue, white, pink and red, in single and double forms.

A collection of half a dozen will bring admiration from May till September, and from the numerous varieties available my personal selection would be:

'Duchess of Edinburgh', a large fragrant double white. Flowers in May and June.

'Ernest Markham', a glowing carmine-red that flowers from July to October.

'Jackmanii Superba', violet-purple and flowering from July to September.

'The President', a large deep violet blue. In flower from June to October.

'Nelly Moser', a pale mauve-pink with carmine bar. Flowers May to September.

'Vyvyan Pennell' is one of the best, with deep blue fully double flowers from May to July.

Pruning can sometimes be a little complicated with large-flowered clematis. Those which flower mid to late summer should be pruned hard in early spring, the others only need a light pruning immediately after flowering. If they become too straggly these too may need pruning back hard after flowering to rejuvenate them.

Of the six cultivars listed above 'Ernest Markham' and 'Jackmanii Superba' need hard pruning in early spring, the rest should be lightly pruned after flowering.

Climbers take up little root space, yet can produce a wealth of interest and color. This is a charming combination of clematis and ivy.

Equally spectacular in a different way are some of the small-flowered clematis species. These are usually much easier to establish, grow more rapidly and are easier to manage.

Many of the cultivars of *C. montana* are magnificent plants, with their abundant fragrant flowers in May, followed by decorative seed heads.

The true species *C. montana,* which has masses of white flowers, is a very rampant grower.

Two rose-pink varieties are *C. m. rubens,* which has purple-bronze young shoots, and the larger-flowered *C. m.* 'Tetrarose'.

True species with attractive silvery seed heads are the yellow-flowered *C. tangutica,* which starts blooming in July, and *C. orientalis* which flowers from August onwards. *C. orientalis* is commonly known as the orange peel clematis because the thick orange sepals curl back to resemble the freshly cut peel of an orange.

The last two species should be pruned hard in early spring, but *C. montana* is best trimmed to size after flowering.

Clematis need a rich moist soil slightly alkaline. Although they like to have their heads in the sun, the roots appreciate a deep cool run, and it is useful to provide shade in the form of other shrubs or herbaceous plants.

All clematis will benefit from a mulch of manure each spring, and this will encourage vigorous growth.

Hedera (Ivy)
One of the most attractive ways to cover a wall, fence or pillar is to plant the creamy-white variegated Canary Island ivy, *Hedera canariensis* 'Variegata', or the hardier *H. colchica* 'Dentata Variegata'. These can be grown outdoors in mild climates or indoors in the North.

In the North, English ivy *(H. helix)* and its varieties are grown as ground covers in shade and as vines. There are also variegated forms of *H. helix,* including 'Glacier', which has silvery-gray, white-edged leaves, and 'Gold Heart', which is quite showy with its bold yellow center to the leaves.

Although ivies will grow in the most impoverished soil and thrive in almost impossible situations, including dense shade, the variegated forms will have stronger colors if positioned in a sunny situation.

Ivies may need some support until the aerial roots have a chance to gain a hold. Wall plants can be pruned back in early spring.

Hydrangea
Hydrangeas do not always come immediately to mind when thinking of climbing plants, but one of the hydrangeas, *H. petiolaris* is a hardy self-supporting climber. Its large white flowers are similar to the lacecap forms of hydrangea, and these cover the plant in June and July.

The glossy green leaves are also attractive when seen against walls or old tree trunks. It is a good plant for sunless north walls, though it may need some support until the aerial roots manage to take a grip.

The same plant can be grown as a free-standing shrub, but against a wall and given ample moisture it will grow very tall.

Jasminum (Jasmine)
The common white jasmine, *jasminum officinale* is a strong grower, and given the support of a trellis or old trunk, it will grow to 30 ft (9 m) high. The clusters of fragrant white flowers are carried from mid-summer to September, though vigorous leaf growth sometimes tends to hide them. For this reason avoid hard pruning.

This jasmine is only hardy in the Deep South and mild regions of the Pacific Coast.

Lonicera (Honeysuckle)
The honeysuckles are also highly popular flowering climbers, and one good reason for this is their sweet fragrance.

Although many climbing honeysuckles are planted against houses, they tend to look better scrambling over arches, sheds and trellises.

These climbers like conditions similar to those for clematis, though they do not need the full sunshine that clematis require to flower well.

Hydrangea petiolaris is a very useful and attractive wall shrub.

Clematis X *jackmanii* is one of the most widely planted large-flowered varieties, flowering from July to September.

Clematis 'Nelly Moser' is a striking variety and will flower from May to September.

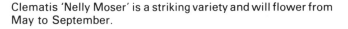

One of the better honeysuckles, *Lonicera periclymenum* 'Belgica'.

The wild plant that grows so rampantly in woods and along country roads is the Japanese honeysuckle, *L. japonica,* which long ago escaped from cultivation. The fragrance of its early summer blooms is stirring, but otherwise it is a weed. *L. japonica* 'Aureo-reticulata' is grown primarily for its mottled foliage, which is popular with flower arrangers.

Less rampant and so more suitable are the simi-evergreen *L.* ×*brownii* 'Fuchsoides', which flowers from June to September, and *L. heckrotii* which flowers for a similar period.

Regular pruning may be necessary, and mulching with peat or leafmold is definitely beneficial.

Parthenocissus (Virginia creeper)
A wall covered with Virginia creeper as autumn tints suffuse the plant is a very spectacular sight. They are self-clinging and need no help in their efforts to cover walls or fences.

The only problems come with the names, which have become very confused over the years. The true Virginia creeper is *Parthenocissus quinquefolia,* and this has deeply cut five-lobed leaves. But the species best known and most widely planted, especially against old suburban houses, is *P. tricuspidata,* the Boston ivy, occasionally listed as *Ampelopsis. P. t.* 'Lowii' has smaller leaves and the young growth is tinged purple.

Parthenocissus showing the different shape of adult and juvenile leaves.

The most colorful species is *P. henryana,* which has dark bronze-green leaves. If grown in the shade these show white and pink variegation.

Satisfactory results can be obtained in most garden soils that have been enriched with organic matter before planting, but the best growth will come from a rich loam with plenty of moisture.

Pruning is no more than removing unwanted shoots in summer.

Polygonum baldschuanicum, popularly known as mile-a-minute vine, is a rampant grower, useful for covering sheds and garages.

Passiflora (Passion Flower)
A more refined climber is the passion flower, *Passiflora caerulea,* though it is best reserved for more sheltered gardens and preferably given a warm south or westerly facing site.

Given a warm and well-drained site, the passion flower will grow rapidly to 20—30 ft (6—9 m) high, supporting itself with tendrils, and giving a magnificent show of its exotic flowers from June to September.

Cold winters will damage the upper growth, but if this is pruned away in the spring, when the plant is cut back to limit size, new growth will sprout after all but the hardest winters.

Polygonum baldschuanicum
(Russian Vine)
Another rampant grower is the mile-a-minute or Russian vine, *Polygonum baldschuanicam* — an established plant can grow 16 ft (5 m) in a year. It is similar to silver lace vine, *P. aubertii* which has small creamy white flowers. Both vines are perfect subjects for rapidly covering eye-sores such as oil tanks, sheds and garages.

Any site and soil will be adequate, but it is worth paying a little attention to soil if you want it to become established rapidly.

There is little to match a well-grown wisteria in May, when the long trusses of fragrant mauve flowers cascade in profusion.

Pruning is more a case of hacking back if the plant is allowed to get out of control.

Wisteria

The real aristocrat of wall climbers must surely be the wisteria, which is an absolute joy in May when the great trusses of fragrant mauve flowers, 8 in. (20 cm) or more long, hang from the leafless branches.

The two most popular species are *Wisteria floribunda* and *W. sinensis*, the stems of the first twining clockwise and those of the second twining anti-clockwise. Both have a white-flowered form.

Perhaps most spectacular of all is *W. f.* 'Macrobotrys', which has the longest racemes of flowers.

Wisteria will grow in anything from heavy clay to quite light soils. Seed-raised *W. sinenis* may take many years to flower, but grafted plants of named cultivars are more free-flowering.

As these plants do not take kindly to root disturbance, container-grown plants are to be recommended. But do not despair if newly transplanted specimens are slow to break into growth, an occasional spray with water will help things along.

A sheltered site is preferable, ideally a south or west facing wall, to avoid damage to the flowers from late frosts.

Pruning can be done in two bites. All lateral side growths from the main branches can be cut back to within 1—1½ in. (2—4 cm) of the flowering spurs in early spring, then on vigorous plants the current season's lateral growths can be shortened in August.

Conifers

There is a very wide and interesting range of conifers for use in the garden, whatever its size or shape. And although most people believe that all conifers are evergreen and do not shed their leaves each autumn, there are a few that do cast their leaves as the winter months approach. For instance, the common larch, with its beautiful light green shoots in spring when the leaves are unfolding, is a magnificent sight. Also, there is the maidenhair tree, *Ginkgo biloba,* with its distinguished and uniquely shaped leaves which are brilliant yellow in the autumn.

Such is the diversity of their size, form and color that entire gardens can be formed by using just conifers. There are excellent types for every purpose, from the Scot's pine grouped in a copse to provide shelter, Leylands and western red cedars for evergreen hedges, stately cedars for specimen planting, different cultivars of Lawson's cypress for year-round color in large borders, prostrate junipers for ground cover and to replace lawns, to the miniatures for troughs, tubs and rock gardens.

Vigorous young plants set carefully in reasonable soil conditions really do give attractive gardens with the very minimum of work. It is, perhaps, the labor-saving value of these plants, coupled with the different leaf color of the cultivars, which accounts for their increasing popularity.

While every conifer has its place in the garden and a number have several places and uses, the speed of growth and ultimate size are of great importance. Generally, garden catalogues list conifers under two headings *conifers* and *dwarf and slow- or low-growing conifers.*

There is no problem with the ordinary stronger-growing conifers. Space can be given for them to develop over the years, especially where single

Chamaecyparis lawsoniana 'Ellwoods Gold' is one of the larger dwarf conifers attaining up to 20 feet in height.

Juniperus scopulorum 'Blue Heaven' is an attractive juniper for any garden, with its year round blue foliage.

plants are grown as specimens. It is the dwarf and slow-growing kinds which cause the difficulties, especially as some are not as slow-growing as others! Even worse, some of the dwarfs are so dwarf that it takes too long to see their beauty in maturity.

Nurserymen often sell the different kinds of Lawson's cultivars and other tall growers in very small sizes. These are often one- and two-year-old cuttings at 5—6 in. (12—15 cm) high in $3^1/_2$ in. (9 cm) pots, and they look very attractive and appear ideal for rock gardens and troughs. Once established, however, they put on 15—18 in. (40—45 cm) of growth a year and quickly outgrow the space available to them.

There is no harm in using these attractive young plants of large conifers in restricted places, just so long as space is allowed for their future increase in size. Alternatively, they could be transplanted to a larger space in a few years.

When using young plants of stronger-growing kinds as fillers for gardens, we get a better appearance immediately after planting, and they also give protection to the very tiny true dwarfs which develop slowly and will eventually fill the allotted area.

DWARF AND SLOW-GROWING CONIFERS

It may generally be assumed that conifers classified as dwarf and slow-growing will reach no more than 10 ft (3 m) in ten years. Nurserymen have difficulty in classifying plants such as *Chamaecyparis lawsoniana* 'Ellwoodii' and 'Ellwood's Gold', which are very attractive for one to four years, when they are 6—24 in. (15—60 cm) high and set in tubs or in the rock garden. However, they eventually reach 14—20 ft (4—6 m) and, like most conifers, broaden at the base, taking them well outside the dwarf catergory.

Ideally, we would like plants which grow quickly to the size we want and

Conifers are versatile plants, and as well as making good specimen plants they are equally at home in a mixed border.

then just stop growing. The fascination of gardening, however, is the continual development and changing scene through the years. one of the most attractive features of plants is the rich color of new growth, and vigorously growing young conifers invariably look better than tired, old and starved specimens.

Make sure all conifers, especially the evergreen types, do not grow into one another or trespass on the territory of other plants. The foliage will go brown and die completely if shaded from light, and once a browned patch has been formed it is very difficult and often impossible to encourage new growth to replace it. It should be pruned off.

GOOD SOIL PREPARATION

All conifers will thrive in well-cultivated garden soils. Where the soil is especially difficult, choosing the right kind of plant can help, as will thorough preparation, such as adding plenty of peat moss, leafmold and well-rotted compost to heavy and sandy soils. On alkaline soils you may have to add peat moss and sulfur to make a moderate to slightly acid soil.

Thorough preparation of the site before planting is essential. Once planted, conifers are likely to remain undisturbed for many years. In the case of cedars it may be several centuries. While the extremes of acidity and alkalinity may cause problems, the main aim must be to provide a rooting area which is free draining, especially in the winter, yet remains moist in the summer.

Evergreen foliage forms a canopy over the soil and, while the leaves absorb some moisture, they prevent it reaching the roots. Dry roots will mean poor and slow growth. A thorough soaking in mid-summer, especially in hot and dry weather in drier parts of the country, will give strong new growth which improves the appearance and enriches the color of plants.

Mixing plenty of damp peat into the soil before planting is the easiest way to get a moisture-retentive soil. A mulch of either bark chips or wood chips spread over the surface in spring will help retain the accumulated winter moisture.

Matching Plants to Soil

The following list of plants is a general guide to soil requirements. The firs *(Abies)*, will not thrive in dry, shallow, limey soils. *Picea omorika*, Serbian spruce, will be better in these areas. *Chamaecyparis*, the false cypress, is best in neutral to acid soils, while *Juniperus*, the junipers, and *Taxus*, the yews, thrive in all soils.

Larix, the larches, and *Thuja* are not happy in wet, poorly drained soils; *Taxodium*, swamp cypress, is better here. *Pinus sylvestris*, Scot's pine, is not so successful in wet acid and dry limey soils, while *Pinus nigra*, the Austrian pine, will have better growth in alkaline areas.

Given sufficient moisture, most of the dwarf and slow-growing kinds are successful in poor, thin soils—a factor which can be used to retain size.

Selecting the Site

An open and sunny site is needed to get the best color on cream- and yellow-leaved conifers. Several of the yellows

Individual specimen conifers add stature and impact to a garden scene.

tend to scorch in cold winds and in very hot and strong sunlight. The best conditions are found in a protected sheltered garden.

It is often said the blue- and silver-foliaged conifers are best in partial shade. Although they will grow under these conditions, the best color is produced in the open on fertile soils.

The accommodating × *Cupressocyparis leylandii* will grow vigorously and give shelter in all soils and sites, including exposed coastal areas. One of its less hardy parents, *Cupressus macrocarpa*, the Monterey cypress, also grows well in coastal areas, where hardy, as will *Pinus nigra*.

Chamaecyparis lawsoniana, Lawson's cypress, and its many cultivars is not happy in very exposed sites and tends to brown if exposed to cold and drying northerly and easterly winds.

The prostrate and semi-prostrate junipers grow well in most sites, even north-facing slopes. They are ideal to retain the soil on steep banks.

Cedars make magnificent specimen plants where space allows. *C. atlantica* 'Glauca' (right) can be transplanted as a quite large specimen.

TRANSPLANTING CONIFERS

Quite large specimens of many conifers can be transplanted from the open ground and it is not uncommon to see 15—20 ft (4—6 m) high *Cedrus atlantica* 'Glauca' being transplanted successfully. The best time to move conifers is either March and April or September and October. At this time the sun is not too hot and new root growth is quickly made to establish the plant before the onset of summer or winter respectively.

To ensure that the conifer transplants well, cut the soil to a spade's depth in a circle about 2—3 ft (60—90 cm) from the plant's trunk. This should be done about 6—12 months before actually moving it. We need to move as large a soil-ball with the roots as possible. Cutting around the plant with a spade 6—12 months ahead of lifting cuts the main side roots and encourages the production of fibrous roots.

The new site must be well prepared by digging the soil thoroughly to one or two spade's depths and mixing in peat moss or garden compost. Dig out a large hole before digging around the conifer to be moved.

When the conifer is more than 2 ft (60 cm) high it will probably take two or more people to lift and transplant it. Ensure that the soil is well moistened and dig a trench around the plant 9—24 in (23—60 cm) out from the trunk. The larger the conifer, the greater the size of root-ball there is to be moved.

Having dug around the plant, cut underneath with a spade, as deep as is practical, remembering the soil-ball will be heavy. Roll up half of a large piece of burlap or plastic and, once you have cut halfway under the plant, push the rolled sheet under the root-ball. Cut through the other side, pushing towards the sheet. Eventually, roll the sheet around the root-ball.

Where the move is no great distance, it is easy to lift the four corners of the sheet and to carry the plant. Where distance and weight prevent carrying in this way, tie the sheet tightly around the soil-ball. This is best done by tying opposite corners, like the ends of a head scarf, against the trunk at soil level. As an added precaution, one or two pieces of strong string can be tied around the root-ball.

Once moved into the prepared hole the sheet is rolled back and removed. Well-moistened and crumbly soil is then firmed around the roots.

You should spray the foliage with an

Conifers are often sold with a root-ball wrapped in burlap. Provided the wrap is not a plastic material, plant with it on, and firm the soil well.

Chamaecyparis lawsoniana 'Minima Aurea' makes a golden dwarf pyramid.

anti-desiccant to reduce the loss of moisture from the leaves while new roots are made. Syringing over the foliage several times a day in hot, windy and dry weather also helps conifers survive the move.

Another method of protecting the plants from wind damage is to drive three or four stakes into the soil around the plant and fix burlap to them. Plastic can also be used, but ensure that the top is open and the plastic well out from the tree to prevent excessive heat and drying in hot sun. When using plastic it is better to erect the plastic around the windward side of the plant only.

Large conifers will also need secure staking to hold them until new roots are formed.

Sometimes, when moving conifers, the soil-ball breaks away. This occurs especially with heavy soils and where the soil is dry. Should this happen, I find it advisable to remove the soil and pack well moistened peat moss around the roots in its place. New roots are soon made into the damp peat and then out into the soil. If the air pockets and lumps of loose, dry soil are left in place, the roots dry out and the plant will go brown.

Where soil does break away extra care is needed in spraying with water and protecting from drying winds. I have successfully moved 3—4 ft (1—1.3m) Lawson cultivars in dry conditions in mid-summer, but the roots were packed around with wet peat and the foliage sprayed over several times a day for a week or two. If this can be done you should have no trouble at the correct transplanting times, except with *Cupressus* species, which do not take kindly to root damage.

While there may be some risk of damaging roots when lifting and transplanting from the open ground, all these problems are removed when container-grown plants are purchased from the nursery or garden center. Container plants can, of course, be planted at any time of year as long as the soil is not frozen or waterlogged. If the roots seem pot-bound, prune or loosen some from ball.

What to buy

Conifers purchased with their roots balled in plastic and burlap must look fresh and in no way dull, a sure sign that they have been allowed to dry out. The root-ball needs to be tightly held

This illustration proves that conifers are not only for large gardens. Dwarf conifer collections can be made to look very attractive in small front gardens.

around the roots. Good nurserymen will see that the balled plants are regularly sprayed over with water, the root-ball buried in damp peat or similar materials to keep plants fresh and upright. It is advisable to remove all root wraps when planting, although the burlap wraps which rot in a few months in the soil can be left in place when planting.

Container-grown conifers should be able to be lifted by the stem without coming out of the soil. Recently potted specimens which start to come up out of the compost as you lift by the stem should be avoided.

Look for shapely specimens, nicely covered with foliage down to soil or compost level and without patches of brown on the outer surface. It is quite natural to find some inner browning in dense foliage types like *Chamaecyparis pisifera* 'Boulevard'.

Lighter, brighter colored tips to the foliage are a good sign of strong, vigorous new growth.

After-planting Care

Once established conifers require little further attention. Specimens in grass and lawns need a circular bed, 2—3 ft (60—90 cm) out from the stem, of cultivated soil. Grass will compete for water in dry weather and where the grass is allowed to grow the lower branches of the conifer will go brown with the lack of light.

Conifers growing into one another and into other plants will also go brown at the point where they merge and careful thinning of plants or trimming back is needed to avoid this.

While fertilizer is not essential the application of a *little* general fertilizer in spring will give stronger new growth and richer colors.

Heathers associate well with dwarf conifers, as this picture of *Juniperus scopulorum* 'Sky Rocket' shows. Most dwarfs are equally suitable.

USING CONIFERS FOR EFFECT

Stately cedars in rolling acres of lawn give a relaxing atmosphere and the soaring tips of giant Californian redwoods, *Sequoia sempervirens*, 300 ft (100 m) up in the air can be quite breathtaking where hardy.

While not everyone has room for these stately trees, there are different types with size and shape to suit every garden situation. Even the Californian redwood, where hardy, could be planted in the local park to provide generations of children with fun punching the spongy-reddish brown bark. Who knows, your planting may outlive the 2200 years of the oldest recorded specimen.

Picea glauca 'Albertiana Conica' makes an attractively shaped tree.

If you want the romance of this great tree in your own small garden, then *Sequoia sempervirens* 'Adpressa' is the answer. Very slow growing, it has rich creamy white branch tips in summer. Once it gets its roots down and starts to produce strong lead branches, it must be pruned back to retain the dwarf habit and prevent it attempting to emulate its much more vigorous near relative.

Specimen Conifers

Gardens 30—40 ft (10—12 m) wide and 60 ft (20 m) or so long provide scope for one or several specimen conifers, especially when set in lawns and among low-growing plants.

The different colored Lawson cultivars, the juniper 'Blue Heaven' and Servian spruce are good examples for this kind of use.

A border of mixed conifers can provide year-round color and form.

Dwarf conifers can add much interest to a small garden.

Take the space down even further and the very neat column-like growth of juniper 'Skyrocket' or fastigiate yews then come into their own. They can even be planted in a double line to give a colonnade leading to a formal rose garden.

Semi-prostrate plants like the golden Pfitzer juniper can also be used as specimens, either jutting out from walls and fences like buttresses or spreading out from paved areas.

Mixed Conifer Borders

Planting a collection of evergreen conifers in one bed or border is by far the most satisfactory way to use these plants. Each one can be positioned to contrast with and to show off its neighbor. More upright kinds at the back can be graded in height to prostrate types in the foreground.

Once again space limitations are no problem, provided you select stronger growing kinds for large areas and the dwarf and slow growing types for small beds. These can be rearranged to fit in your favorites or similar types more freely available and suited to your area. Ensure that the different colors contrast to get the brightest year-round effect, and that the different foliage shapes contrast with one another.

Chamaecyparis lawsoniana 'Blue Nantais' is a striking blue color year round and especially in early autumn. It is seen here in association with potentilla and heathers.

Rock Garden Conifers

Very slow growing conifers can be positioned among rocks to give a miniature mountainside appearance. Lack of space really is no problem with the smallest species growing satisfactorily in sink and trough gardens.

Conifers can be grown alone and mixed with other alpine plants, according to taste. *Juniperus communis* 'Compressa' is a favorite, with an upright cigar shape, and the neat rounded shape of green *Chamaecyparis pisifera* 'Nana' and steel-blue *Picea mariana* 'Nana' are other popular choices.

Some of the stronger prostrate kinds like *Juniperus procumbens* 'Nana' look attractive over rocks but will need cutting back to retain their spread.

Specimens for Tubs

Two shapely evergreens each side of a door or path are popular with gardeners, and conifers can fit the bill. Attention first and foremost must be given to soil and watering. A good, rich loam-based soil is ideal and a deep pot or tub is essential. I like to see the tub as deep as one-third, and certainly one-quarter, the height of tall upright conifers.

Once potted the tub conifer will require regular watering, especially in hot weather. A most popular plant for tubs is *Chamaecyparis lawsoniana* 'Ellwoodii' and a 3—4 ft (1—1.2 m) specimen will take up to 2 gallons (10 liters) of water a day in very hot weather. Other Lawson cultivars, *Chamaecyparis pisifera* types (especially 'Boulavard'), and *Thuja orientalis* 'Aurea Nana' are attractive in tubs.

Where the tub has good drainage holes in the base, over-watering is unlikely but giving sufficient water to tubs filled with root in very hot weather is not easy. Remember, dense evergreen foliage sheds water and even in showery weather it will be necessary to water the tub. Drying winds in autumn, winter and spring can be especially deceptive and if the conifer is allowed to become really dry and the foliage starts to brown it is very difficult to get the attractive new growth desired.

Half lifting the tub off the ground is the quick way to check moisture of soil. When wet the tub will be heavy, and as it dries it gets noticeably lighter. Once the tub feels light, water till moisture runs from the base, check then to see just how heavy the tub has become. Water again when the tub has lost weight.

Thuja orientalis 'Aurea Nana' is an attractive dwarf of neat shape.

Chamaecyparis lawsoniana 'Allumii' used for screening.

SCREENS AND WINDBREAKS

While close-clipped conifers for formal hedging are described in the chapter on hedges, mention must be made here of the usefulness of conifers for forming a natural screen, especially the taller and faster-growing kinds. Shelter from wind is desirable in most gardens, and on exposed and coastal sites it is vital.

A natural-looking belt of shelter can quickly be achieved in the larger garden with ×*Cupressocyparis leylandii, Picea omorika, Tsuga canadensis* and *P. pungens* and *Thuja plicata.* Mix a few larch and pine in to give added variety, and where there is ample space plant a clump of birch in the foreground — the white bark will show particularly well against dark evergreens in winter.

Ground Covers

Prostrate junipers offer the best opportunity of all for work-free gardening. Closely planted they give complete ground cover and weed smothering. Even better, on banks they not only provide an attractive appearance but the strong root growth helps to retain soil and prevent rain-washed erosion.

The different colored forms of juniper are best for this. Fortunately they grow well on virtually all soil types, including shallow rocky soils, partially shaded sites and in exposed positions.

The dark green leaf types like *Juniperus communis* 'Repanda', *J. procumbens* 'Nana' and *J. chinensis* 'Parsonnii' are best on really tough soils and sites. Choose different habits and plant these in groups to get the most attractive combination. Place the taller

As an alternative to grass, consider *Juniperus squamata* 'Blue Carpet'.

One of the merits of conifers is their variety of form as well as color. *Juniperus X media* 'Mint Julep' holds its branches at an attractive angle.

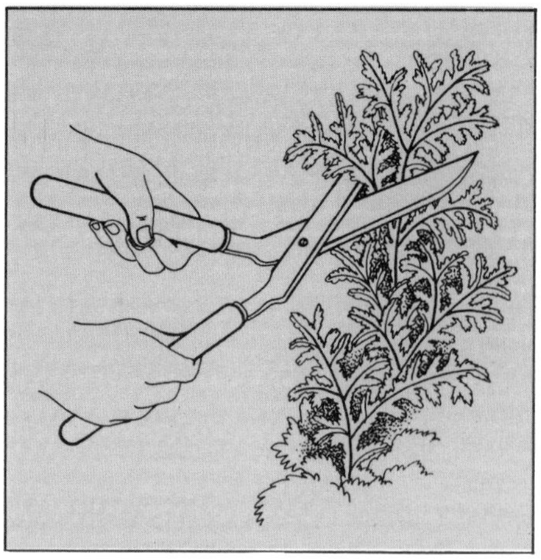

It is often sufficient to trim conifers to shape with shears.

growing junipers with their branches jutting out at 45 degrees from the ground towards the top or back of the bank. Grade down to lower types like *J. horizontalis* 'Wiltoni' and *J. virginiana* 'Prostrata' in the middle, and very low types in the foreground.

Growth quite as attractive as short grass but without the need to mow can be achieved with *J. horizontalis* 'Repens'. Extra color can be added in the foreground with such types as *J. communis* 'Depressa Aurea', bright yellow in early summer turning red-bronze in winter, and the bright silver-blue *J. squamata* 'Blue Star'.

The perfect replacement for a well clipped grass is the quite flat growing *J. horizontalis* 'Glauca', commonly and quite aptly called the "carpet juniper". It smothers the ground no more than 4 in. (10 cm) high and will spread 5 ft (1.5 m) in 8—10 years.

Where good-sized, 10—12 in (25—30 cm) diameter, pot-grown plants are used a spacing of three plants per square yard (square meter) will give ground cover in two years. Very attractive combinations can also be achieved by using the taller types as specimens surrounded by very prostrate junipers or ground cover plants like *Euonymus fortunei* 'Variegatus'.

TRIMMING AND PRUNING

Formal hedges of cypresses, *thuja* and yew will need regular clipping, and July is a good time for this. The first spring flush of growth has been made and the secondary late summer growth will cover the cuts and give a well-furnished appearance in winter.

Wherever possible use pruners to prune out the unwanted branch tips neatly. While arbovitaes *(Thuja)* and yew will grow again, even when cut hard back, most other evergreen conifers are best cut no farther back than the young green branches. Cut back hard into the brown hardened wood of hemlocks and you will have a permanent empty hole back to the trunk.

Juniperus communis depressa 'Aurea', yellow in spring, red in winter.

Most young conifers can have their shape improved by a light trimming in April or May. The skill here is to shave off no more than the tips with hedge trimmers. The side branches will soon produce two or more shoots behind every cut to give a more bushy and well branched plant. If you give this treatment to flat-sided Lawson cultivars the plants will soon develop into neat cone shapes.

Do not cut the top main growth of any upright conifers, save those which develop more than one central leader, in which case it is best to reduce to one if the straight conical shape is to be maintained.

Some prostrate conifers like *Picea pungens* 'Prostrata' will suddenly produce a strong upward-growing branch. Where this happens the upward branch must be cut out completely to prevent the plant losing its horizontal growth. habit. Big cuts on *Picea* are best covered with a bitumen paint to reduce resin loss, and subsequent damage.

PROPAGATION

Many of the forest and larger conifers are raised from seed. It is not difficult and seeds of types like larch, spruce and pine can be sown in the open garden in March and in two years seedlings a few inches high will be ready to transplant. These seedlings are slow-growing in their early years, however, and it is usually preferable to buy young plants.

The many cultivars with special color or shape will not come true from seed and these have to be reproduced either from cuttings or, for those which do not root readily such as cedar, pine and spruce, by grafting.

Young shoots 3—4 in. (7—10 cm) long, torn from the branch with a heel — a piece of the older bark at the base of the shoot — in August or September will root in sandy soil in a cold-frame. Once again the growth is slow and it will often take a year to get a small rooted plant.

Many false-cypress types and similar kinds will root more quickly given some bottom heat in propagating frames in a greenhouse. Dipping the base of cuttings in a rooting hormone chemical will help to speed rooting.

Quite different branch and plant shape is produced by different cuttings taken from the same plant. What is known as juvenile growth on a number of conifers is quite different from the mature growth. Take strong lead shoots from the top of *Thuja occidentalis* 'Rheingold', for example and it will quickly grow into a tallish conical shape. Take cuttings from the base of a more juvenile form and the growth will be more feathered and the growth will be more feathered and the shape nearer a mound than pointed. Eventually these juvenile cuttings will grow out into the mature form.

The garden plant *Cryptomeria japonica* 'Elegans' is a permanent juvenile form of *C. japonica* and the soft, much more "frothy" growth is unrecognizable against the mature adult foliage.

Completely new cultivars of conifers can be secured by rooting cuttings which have "sported", that is suddenly changed in appearance. The dwarf forms of Canada hemlock are examples.

Congested and fasciated growth also occurs on some types, especially the "witches broom" out-growth on pines

Picea pungens 'Prostrata' is a low-growing form of Colorado spruce.

A beautiful golden conifer that deepens in shade by autumn, *Thuja occidentalis* 'Rheingold'. It grows slowly to about 6 ft (1.8 m).

and spruce. Cuttings rooted from these can give completely new cultivars.

PESTS AND OTHER PROBLEMS

Pests: Aphids and mealybugs (sap sucking insects related to aphis and producing tufts of white waxy wool around them) can be a problem, especially on pine and spruce. Spray with malathion in late spring or early summer to control the pest. A penetrating forceful spray is needed to get through the waxy covering.

Red spider mite can also affect *Picea* and attack is most likely in hot dry weather. Regular syringing with water reduces the chance of attack.

Diseases: Honey fungus can affect many conifers and *Thuja plicata* appears to be particularly susceptible to this disease. Remove and destroy infected plants and sterilize the soil with formaldehyde.

Phytophthora on *chamaecyparis* can be a problem and it spreads in warm, damp conditions. The first symptoms are dull appearance, with a loss of color on certain branches, followed by browning. Infected plants are best destroyed and the site used for plants other than conifers, rhododendrons and heathers for a few years.

Browning of evergreens: There are several causes of browning, not least of which is the attention of dogs in suburban areas. Apart from fencing, the use of deterrent sprays and planting back from pavements, there is little that can be done about this.

Cold, drying winds will burn back evergreens in the winter, and newly planted *Chamaecyparis* cultivars can be especially susceptible. Protecting young plants and the planting of a surround of tougher plants are the means of avoiding this.

Sudden browning of shoots on *Juniperus sabina* 'Tamariscifolia' is caused by wilt and is best pruned out.

CONIFERS: DWARF, SLOW GROWING AND PROSTRATE KINDS

Name	Common Name	Height 10 years	Ultimate Likely Height in Gardens	Ultimate Likely Spread	Soil Preference
Abies balsamea 'Hudsonia'	Balsam Fir	8 in. (20 cm)	30 in. (75 cm)	30 in. (75 cm)	Moist, pH 6-7
Cedrus libani 'Sargentii'	—	2 ft (60 cm)	3 ft (90 cm)	10–13 ft (3–4 m)	Most
Chamaecyparis lawsoniana 'Minima Aurea'	—	10 in. (25 cm)	4 ft (1:2 m)	30 in. (75 cm)	Free draining, pH 5.5-7
C.l. 'Minima Glauca'	—	12 in. (30 cm)	3 ft (90 cm)	3 ft (90 cm)	"
Chamaecyparis obtusa 'Nana Gracilis'	—	20 in. (50 cm)	13 ft (4 m)	6:5 ft (2 m)	"
C.o. 'Nana Lutea'	—	10 in. (24 cm)	30 in. (75 cm)	2 ft (60 cm)	"
C.o. 'Pygmaea'	—	8 in. (20 cm)	3 ft (90 cm)	3 ft (90 cm)	"
Chamaecyparis pisifera 'Boulevard'	—	3 ft (90 cm)	10 ft (3 m)	6½ ft (2 m)	Moist, pH 5.5-6.5
C.p. 'Filifera Aurea'	—	30 in. (75 cm)	10 ft (3 m)	10 ft (3 m)	Moist, pH 5.5-6.5
C.p. 'Nana'	—	6 in. (15 cm)	2 ft (60 cm)	3 ft (90 cm)	Moist, pH 5.5-6.5
C.p. 'Plumosa Auea'	—	3 ft (90 cm)	16 ft (5 m)	10 ft (3 m)	Moist (not clay), pH 5.5-6.5
Juniperus chinensis 'Pyramidalis'	—	6½ ft (2 m)	13 ft (4 m)	8 ft (2.5 m)	Most, pH 6.8
Juniperus communis 'Compressa'	—	1 ft (30 cm)	3 ft (90 cm)	8 in. (20 cm)	Most, pH 6.8
J.c. 'Hibernica'	Irish Juniper	6½ ft (2 m)	16 ft (5 m)	12 in. (30 cm)	Most, pH 6.8
J.c. 'Depressa Aurea'	—	10 in. (25 cm)	20 in. (50 cm)	10–13 ft (3–4 m)	Most, pH 6.8
J.c. 'Repanda'	—	5 in. (12.5 cm)	6 in. (15 cm)	10–13 ft (3–4 m)	Most, pH 6.8
Juniperus horizontalis 'Bar Harbor'	Creeping Juniper	4 in. (10 cm)	5 in. (12.5 cm)	13–16 ft (4–5 m)	Most, pH 6.8
Juniperus sabina 'Tamariscifolia'	—	10 in (25 cm)	20 in. (50 cm)	10 ft (3 m)	Most, pH 6.8
Juniperus squamata 'Blue Star'	—	12 in. (30 cm)	3 ft (90 cm)	3 ft (90 cm)	Most, pH 6.8
J.s. 'Meyeri'	—	4 ft (1.2 m)	8 ft (2.5 m)	3 ft (90 cm)	Most, pH 6.8
Juniperus virginiana 'Gray Owl'	—	12 in. (30 cm)	3 ft (90 cm)	13 ft (4 m)	Most, pH 6-8
Picea abies 'Nidiformis'	—	1 ft (30 cm)	3 ft (90 cm)	3 ft (90 cm)	Most, pH 6-8
Picea glauca 'Albertiana Conica'	—	28 in. (70 cm)	6½ ft (2 m)	3 ft (90 cm)	Most, pH 6-8
Picea mariana 'Nana'	—	4 in. (10 cm)	12 in. (30 cm)	20 in. (50 cm)	Most, pH 6-8
Pinus mugo 'Compacta'	Dwarf Mugo	2 ft (60 cm)	5 ft (1.5 m)	5 ft (1.5 m)	Most, pH 6-8
Pinus strobus 'Nana'	Dwf. White Pine	20 in. (50 cm)	6½ ft (2 m)	10 ft (3 m)	Most, pH 6-8
Pinus sylvestris 'Watereri'	Dwf. Scots Pine	5 ft (1.5 m)	16 ft (5 m)	13 ft (4 m)	Most, pH 6-8
Thuja occidentalis 'Lutea Nana'	Dwf. Aborvitae	3 ft (90 cm)	10 ft (3 m)	3 ft (90 cm)	Most, pH 6-8
T.o. 'Rheingold'	Dwf. Aborvitae	3 ft (90 cm)	10 ft (3 m)	6½ ft (2 m)	Most, pH 6-8
T.o. 'Conspicua'	Dwf. Arborvitae	6½ ft (2 m)	13 ft (4 m)	3 ft (90 cm)	Most, pH 5.5-8
Thuja orientalis 'Aurea Nana'	Dwf. Arborvitae	2 ft (60 cm)	6½ ft (2 m)	3 ft (90 cm)	Most, pH 5.5-8
Tsuga canadensis 'Hussii'	Dwf. Hemlock	10 in (25 cm)	2 ft (60 cm)	2 ft (60 cm)	Most, pH 5-5.5
T.c. 'Pendula'	Sargent's Hemlock	5 ft (1.5 m)	15 ft (4 m)	30 ft (9 m)	Most, pH 5-5.5

Leaf Color	Purpose	Special Features
Dark glossy green	Rock garden	Forms a neat rounded hummock of growth
Blue green	Rock garden	Most attractive trained down a low retaining wall
Golden yellow	Rock garden, heather garden	Flat shoots packed tightly together in neat rounded growth
Rich green	Rock garden, heather garden	Neat, semi-globular shape
Bright green	Specimen, heather garden	Neat rounded branchlets, C.o. 'Nana is slower growing and more rounded
Golden yellow	Rock garden, sink and heather garden	One of the best dwarf golden conifers
Green	Rock garden and sink garden	Reddish branches contrast with green foliage
Steel blue	Tubs, rock and heather garden	One of the most popular dwarf conifers
Golden yellow	Heather garden, mixed conifer border	Finely cut foliage similar to Japanese maples
Dark green	Sink and rock garden	Compact with tightly packed shoots
Golden green	Tubs, heather garden and mixed border	Feathery foliage which darkens in winter
Steel Blue	Heather garden, mixed border	Beautiful color, needs space to remain well-furnished with new growth
Light gray-green	Pots, rock garden and sink garden	The finest cigar-shaped dwarf conifer
Light green	Specimen, heather garden	A superb columnar shape
Bright yellow, turning bronze	Ground cover, heather garden	Brilliant color in full sun in spring
Dull green	Ground cover	One of the best and toughest ground covers
Steel blue	Ground cover	Quite as flat as grass
Gray green	Ground and bank cover	Fast-growing ground cover
Silver blue	Specimen, heather and rock garden	One of the brightest foliage junipers
Steel blue	Specimen, heather garden	Best as a young plant, trim in spring to retain attractive young shoots
Gray blue	Ground cover, heather garden	Very easy, low shrubby ground covering
Glossy, dark green	Rock garden, specimen	Tiers of branches form flat-topped "nest"
Bright green	Tubs, rock and heather garden	Perfect cone shape, very attractive spring shoots
Blue gray	Rock and sink garden	Neat bun shape of attractive foliage
Dark green	Rock garden	A small cultivar of the mountain pine
Light blue-green	Rock garden	A very attractive cultivar of white pine
Blue green	Heather garden, specimen	New growth forms attractive brown candles
Yellow green	Heather garden, mixed border	Color deepens with the approach of winter
Old gold	Heather garden, tubs	Dense globose ground-covering shape, reddish in winter
Rich yellow	Tubs, specimen, heather garden	T.o. 'Elegantissima' is similar but slower growing
Yellow to bronze	Tubs, specimen, heather garden	Dense growth in globe shape; one of the best
Dark green	Rock garden	Short, twiggy growth, very dwarf
Dark green	Specimen	Wide spreading, pendulous habit, but slow growing

YOUR GUIDE TO CONIFERS: TALL KINDS

Name	Common Name	Height in 10 Years	Likely Ultimate Height	Soil Preference
Abies grandis	Vancouver	10 ft (3 m)	260–300 ft (80–100 m)	Moist, pH 6-7
A. homolepis	Nikko Fir	10 ft (3 m)	100 ft (30 m)	Moist, pH 5-5.5
Araucaria araucana	Monkey Puzzle	5 ft (1.5 m)	80 ft (25 m)	Moist, loamy
Cedrus atlantica	Atlas Cedar	10 ft (3 m)	80 ft (25 m)	Moist soils — even to
Cedrus deodara	The Deodar	13 ft (4 m)	65 ft (20 m)	heavy clay provided it is not waterlogged
Cedrus libani	Cedar of Lebanon	10 ft (3 m)	60 ft (18 m)	"
Chamaecyparis lawsoniana	Lawson Cypress	10 ft (3 m)	100 ft (30 m)	Free draining, pH 6.5–7
C.l. 'Allumii'	—	6½ ft (2 m)	50 ft (15 m)	"
C.l. 'Columnaris'	—	6½ ft (2 m)	30 ft (9 m)	"
C.l. 'Ellwoodii'	—	5 ft (1.5 m)	20 ft (6 m)	"
C.l. 'Fletcheri'	—	6½ ft (2 m)	23 ft (7 m)	"
C.l. Pottenii'	—	6½ ft (2 m)	33 ft (10 m)	"
Chamaecyparis nootkatensis	Nootka Cypress	10 ft (3 m)	100 ft (30 m)	Most soils
Cryptomeria japonica 'Elegans'	—	5 ft (1.5 m)	20 ft (6 m)	Moist
X Cupressocyparis leylandii	Leylands	33 ft (10 m)	100 ft (30 m)	Moist soils, pH 5.5–8
Cupressus macrocarpa	Monterey Cypress	16 ft (5 m)	65 ft (20 m)	Most soils
Gingko biloba	Maidenhair Tree	10 ft (3 m)	60 ft (18 m)	Most soils
Juniperus chinensis 'Pfitzeriana'	Pfitzer Juniper	Spread to 13 ft (4 m)	6½–10 ft (2–3 m)	All soils, pH 5.5–8
Juniperus scopulorum 'Blue Haven'	—	6½ ft (2 m)	20 ft (6 m)	Most soils
J.s. 'Skyrocket'	—	6½ ft (2 m)	23 ft (7 m)	Most soils
Larix decidua	Common Larch	16 ft (5 m)	100 ft (30 m)	Not too wet or dry, pH 5.5–7
Picea omorika	Serbian Spruce	10 ft (3 m)	70 ft (22 m)	Most soils, pH 5.5–8
P. pungens	Colorado Spruce	10 ft (3 m)	100 ft (30 m)	Most, pH 5–7.5
Pinus nigra	Austrian Pine	13 ft (4 m)	100 ft (30 m)	Most soils, pH 5.5–8
P. strobus	White Pine	13 ft (4 m)	200 ft (61 m)	Most, pH 5–5.5
Pinus sylvestris	Scots Pinus	13 ft (4 m)	80 ft (25 m)	Most soils, pH 5.5–7
Pseudotsuga menziesii	Douglas Fir	100 ft (4 m)	200 ft (61 m)	Most, pH 5–5.5
Sciadopitys verticillata	Jap. Umbrella Pine	6½ ft (2 m)	40 ft (12 m)	Moist, humus-rich
Taxus baccata	Common Yew	6½ ft (2 m)	20 ft (6 m)	Moist, pH 5.5–8
T.b. 'Fastigiata'	Irish Yew	6½ ft (2 m)	16 ft (5 m)	Most, pH 5.5–8
Thuja plicata 'Zebrina'	—	13 ft (4 m)	65 ft (20 m)	Most, pH 5.5–8
Tsuga canadensis	Canada Hemlock	10 ft (3 m)	80 ft (25 m)	Most, pH 5–5.5

Leaf Color	Purpose	Special Features
Glossy green	Specimen, achieves great size	Leaves fragrant when crushed. For Pacific North West
Glossy, dark green	Specimen	Hardy. Does well in East
Dark green	Specimen	Resists wind, unusual overlapping leaves. Mild climates
Gray green	Specimen	C.a. 'Glauca' is beautiful silver blue
Silver to green	Specimen	
Dark green	Specimen	Heavy snow may break branches
Green	Hedge, screens	Better not clipped hard
Bluish green	Specimen, hedge	Columnar habit
Rich blue-green	Specimen, mixed borders	Very neat columnar habit
Blue green to light green	Specimen, tub and large rock garden	'Ellwood's Gold' has yellow tips
Gray green	Specimen, tub	A larger 'Ellwood'
Light green	Specimen, mixed border	Elliptical, crowded feathery growth
Dull green	Specimen	Hardy, the golden C.n. 'Lutea' and weeping C.n. 'Pendula' are very attractive
Green, red bronze in winter	Specimen, mixed border	Attractive spring and winter color
Rich green	Hedges, screens	The best fast growing screen
Bright green	Screening	Good by the sea in mild climates
Light green	Specimen and avenues	Deciduous, golden autumn leaves
Rich green	Ground cover	A very adaptable and useful plant. J.m. 'P. Aurea' and J.m. 'P. Old Gold' are good golden forms
Silver blue	Specimen, mixed border	Outstanding color
Gray green	Specimen, tubs	Slender columnar growth, also called J. virginiana 'Skyrocket'
Light green	Open woods, specimen	Beautiful light green spring leaves and deciduous golden autumn foliage
Dark green above, silver beneath	Specimen	More decorative alternative to Christmas tree
Green to silver blue	Specimen	Hardy and adaptable
Dark green	Wind breaks and shelter belts	One of the easiest and best pines
Blue green	Specimen, screens	Hardy and adaptable, beautiful form
Blue green	Specimen	Reddish branches attractive on established trees
Dark green to blue green	Specimen	Fairly adaptable, graceful pyramidal habit
Glossy, dark green	Specimen	Graceful, slow-growing pyramid
Dark green	Hedges and topiary	Easy to grow even in shade, hardy
Dark green	Specimen and tubs	Very neat columnar growth, T.b. 'Fastigiata Aurea' is a golden form
Green and creamy-yellow	Specimen	A good, conical shaped, variegated conifer
Dark green	Hedges, specimen	Very hardy, shade tolerant

Garden Flowers

Some gardeners, and especially exhibitors at flower shows, are fascinated by one group of plants, and traveling the countryside I see gardens filled with just dahlias or summer bedding plants or roses. Most of us, however, prefer a happy mixture of flowering subjects and to my mind mixing the different groups gives the best effect and helps achieve a long season of color in the garden.

Bare patches in herbaceous beds and borders can be temporarily filled with either seed-raised annuals or summer-flowering plants grown from corms and tubers. Spring-flowering bulbs associate well with seed-raised biennial flowers and help to decorate rock gardens.

Most of the groups provide flowers for cutting and space must be found in the vegetable plot if a good supply of cut material is needed for indoors without plundering the ornamental garden.

Flower growing can be very inexpensive with many kinds quite easily raised from seed. As one's knowledge of gardening and eye for quality becomes more refined then selected named varieties, vegetatively propagated, become more significant.

When starting from seed don't begrudge a little extra money for the better quality packet. It will be money well spent. Generally speaking it is good advice to go for the better quality stock whether seed, bulb or plant, always allowing for the year's latest novelty introduction. If you want the interest and excitement of growing the latest introduction then by all means pay the premium. If you are looking for the best possible value for money then let your neighbors make the first-year trial and then pick out obvious winners when prices ease back.

I see nothing wrong with buying smaller and cheaper *vigorous* young plants; they will soon grow, given the right treatment. Older cut-price stock at the end of a planting season is usually not such a good buy, especially as we go into the hotter, drier summer weather.

Many different kinds of plants can be used to bring color to the garden.

The secret of success in all gardening, let alone flower growing, is to get the job done in good time. If you happen to have forgotton or over-looked one sowing or planting job then it is better to wait . . . the next season will come round all too quickly! If you happen to be the forgetful type, buying foil-packed seeds would be a wise precaution to take. Seeds packed in this way will hold their germination for a year or longer.

Color and fragrance

I have no fears about mixing flower colors; very few natural colors clash in the way man-made dyes will. A very pleasing effect can be achieved, however, by planting a harmonious group of colors in one garden or one section of the garden.

Silvers and pinks through to purple are a classic example. Silver and pink alone looks very fresh, as does green, deep blue and white. Rich copper foliage contrasting with scarlets and yellows to gold makes a bright, eye-catching combination.

Fragrance does need remembering and a few clumps of strongly-scented plants will bring a new breath of life to the garden air.

Good examples are hyacinths and wallflowers in spring, day-lilies and lilies in summer, and nicotiana and stocks in the autumn.

SEED-SOWING TIME	Sept Oct	Nov Jan	Feb	Mar	Apr	May	June	July	Aug
Hardy Annuals to flower in 6-8 months	●●	■	■■	■●	●●	●●			
Half-hardy Annuals to flower in 3-6 months		■	■■	■■	■■	■			
Biennials to flower next year				●	●●	●●	●●	●●	●
Perennials to flower next year and in successive years		■	■■	■●	●●	●●	●●	●	
Dahlias				■	■■	●			
PLANTING OUT TIME									
Annuals						●	●●	●	
Biennials	●●	●			●●	●●		●	●●
Perennials	●●	●			●●	●●	●	●	●●
Gladiolus				●●	●●	●●	●●		
Fuchsias and Dahlias						●	●●	●	
Lily-hardy	●●	●							

■■ indoors ●● outdoors

Meter-square patches of hardy annuals grown from an early spring sowing.

Nasturtiums are always bright and colorful, but 'Alaska' has the added attraction of brightly variegated leaves.

HARDY ANNUALS

No group of flowers can challenge the hardy annuals for speed of growth from sowing to flowering, ease of cultivation and value for money. One packet of seed, under a dollar, will more than fill a square meter of garden. There are plants of varying height, from the neat low edging provided by linaria (toadflax or bunny rabbits) which comes in mixed colors, the yellow and white tipped *Limnanthes douglasii* and *Nemophila insignis,* both grown on the West Coast, to the 5—6½ ft (1.5—2 m) larkspur and lavatera, the pink mallow.

The smaller-growing kinds are usually very quick to flower and are popular for children's gardens. Where the period from sowing to flowering is short it is worth making two or three sowings at three-week intervals in the same soil to provide a succession of growth and flower. Kinds like Virginian stock will grow, flower, self-seed and grow again in the one season to give double value for money in cool, moist climates.

Several kinds provide a strong fragrance, with the low edging plant mignonette and taller night-scented stock good examples. Neither have brightly colored flowers and it is worth mixing the stocks with a bright flower like viscaria to provide both color and fragrance.

Many hardy annuals are excellent subjects to cut and arrange in water. Obvious examples include: annual poppy, *Chrysanthemum tricolor* calendula, cornflower, clary, *Gypsophila elegans,* larkspur, nigella and sweet pea. The more flowers you cut, the more new growth and additional flowers will be produced.

All kinds listed can be sown outside in open ground in the fall or in coldframes in colder regions, to produce earlier flowering next summer. In most cases the autumn sowing will produce bigger plants and better flowers than normal spring-sown plants.

When selecting a number of hardy annuals for a flower border, as well as heights, fragrance and cutting, remember the flowering season. A number flower quite late in the summer and into early autumn and these help to maintain color. Useful in this respect are calliopsis, Californian poppy, love-lies-bleeding (red and green kinds), and annual chrysanthemums.

Planning a border

If you haven't grown hardy annuals before I suggest drawing drills across the plot 3 ft (1 m) apart in both directions. This gives yard or meter squares, and then parallel drills are drawn with a pointed label within each square.

The straight rows of annuals soon merge into one another as they grow. Straight rows make it easier to identify the emerging seedlings and it is quite easy to hoe between the rows to kill weeds. Space the rows 6 in. (15 cm) apart for the dwarf growers and up to 18 in. (45 cm) for tall ones.

Some annuals will take several weeks to germinate and with these and varieties you have not grown before, which makes seedling identification difficult, mix a little radish seed in the row. The radish will germinate in a very short time and clearly indicate the rows for hoeing. The line of seedlings will also be seen as they grow a week or two later. Just pull out the radish once they

The ever-popular candytuft is very easy to grow and very free flowering.

have done their indicating job. Often the annuals can be thinned then.

Where the seed is not sown too thickly there is no need to thin, unless you want really large individual plants with bigger single flower stems for cutting. Thin seedlings to stand a similar distance down the row as between rows, and up to half the eventual height is a good spacing.

Generally speaking rich garden soil is not required. Overfed annuals produce an excess of foliage which in extreme cases masks the flowers. Tall lank growth will tend to flop when heavy with rain and spoil the graded height effect.

Hot, sunny banks and light quick-drying soils are good for eschscholzia (Californian poppy) and nasturtiums. They revel in the sunshine and thrive in poor soil. Once sown both will self seed and cover the soil for several years with brilliantly colored flowers.

The nasturtium is especially valuable, the more recent cultivars like 'Red Roulette' carrying flowers well above the leaves. Their bright flowers can be used to color and give a peppery flavor to salads. Excellent subjects for windowboxes, tubs, hanging baskets and all containers, they are better sown in April or May; earlier sowings can be damaged by cold.

Once germinated and thinned little further cultural treatment is needed. The taller-growing types, reaching over 2 ft (60 cm), may need some support. Twiggy branches, such as prunings from apple trees, should be pushed into the soil as the young plants grow. Flowers and foliage will quickly cover the sticks.

Most plants can be left to self seed if the seedlings will cause no nuisance the following year. The seed pods of some plants, such as nigella, commonly called love-in-a-mist, and poppies, are very useful in dried arrangements.

A number of hardy annuals can also be dried for permanent use. One of the brightest is helichrysum, commonly and aptly called strawflower because the flowers are brittle like straw. Cut the flowers to dry before the yellow center shows. Other drying candidates are pink and purple bracts of clary, rose-pink larkspur and rose-purple xeranthemum, which is best cut when just fully open.

All these flowers to be dried are best cut, bunched and hung in a nice drying atmosphere out of strong sunlight. Once dry and brittle they are ready for arrangement.

Godetia deserves to be grown more widely, as it is a colorful plant, and besides being easy to grow it is good for cutting and for filling the flower border.

Love-in-a-mist is another easily grown annual that comes in a variety of colors.

Finally a suggestion for the rock and alpine garden. Many of the perennial alpine plants are spring flowering and a sprinkling of seeds of *Brachycome iberidifolia,* the Swan River daisy, in shades of blue, and leptosiphon, commonly called stardust because the tiny plants are covered in star-shaped flowers, will bring an extra splash of color in summer.

Bulbs are useful for filling gaps in the rock garden. Here hyacinths have been planted with the multi-headed *Tulipa praestans* 'Fusilier'.

BULBS AND CORMS

Many of the spring-flowering bulbs we plant in the autumn, such as hyacinths, daffodils and tulips, have all the leaves and every minute detail of the flower formed within the dry bulbs.

Once established in reasonable garden conditions many of the bulbs and corms increase in number and flower year after year, without special attention. There are many of the smaller-flowering kinds, from aconites, and cyclamen to anemones and scillas, which naturalize under trees. Daffodils are the best to naturalize in grass, while muscari will come up year after year in flower and shrub borders.

The spring-flowering bulbs are excellent partners to late spring and early summer biennials. Combinations such as pansies and Double Early tulips, wallflowers and Darwin tulips, bellis and muscari are good examples.

Bulbs can be used more extravagantly in small gardens, and a massed bed of hyacinths close to the house will fill rooms with their fragrance. Masses of crocus edging paths and a stately clump of crown imperials will bring flashes of color.

Most of the spring-flowering subjects up to 18 in. (45 cm) in height are good subjects for pots, tubs, window-boxes and patio plant containers. A strawberry pot filled with crocus, *Iris reticulata* and dwarf narcissi can be a real eye-catcher.

Special bulb mixes in plastic bags can also be used for bulb culture where space is strictly limited. Choose dwarf kinds because the shallow peat does not provide support for the taller flowers, which are best planted deeper in soil.

Sunny banks are ideal for planting groups of spring-flowering bulbs, which seem to appreciate the free-draining site and warm position.

While spring bulbs are in full flower it is wise to think of planting the summer flowering kinds. These include large-flowering gladioli, the fragrant near relative acidanthera, galtonia, ismene, lilies, montbretia and tigridia. The lilies are included here because bulbs are often sold in spring, but for best results most will grow much better from an autumn transplanting.

Most true bulbs are not demanding when it comes to soil. Tulips are better in lighter, free-draining soils because slugs can cause damage by eating bulbs in wet, heavy clay. Daffodils (*Narcissus*) grow better in heavier soils.

A sunny site is best for most bulbs, but for part shade choose aconites, tuberous begonias, hardy cyclamen, erythroniums, scillas and snowdrops. The protection of a south-facing wall is advisable for *Amaryllis belladonna* (not to be confused with the indoor large-flowered amaryllis), ixia, nerine, and sparaxis.

Where crocus and narcissi are planted in grass, remember it will be

Crocus and hyacinths growing in plastic planters filled with soilless mix.

necessary to leave the grass uncut until the bulb foliage yellows if the bulbs are to multiply and flower for many years.

Spring-flowering bulbs are planted from August to November. The sooner the small bulbs are planted the better. Left out of the ground they shrivel and the small food reserves are lost. Snowdrops are best moved immediately after flowering while the leaves are still green. Daffodils can be planted as late as Christmas and tulips even into the New Year if the soil remains unfrozen. Planting as late as this means very short flower stems and not the best of flowers for two seasons.

Summer-flowering bulbs are planted from March to May, with the more tender kinds better planted in April or May, especially in heavy soils. Fertilizers are not really needed as long as the soil has been well dug and well-rotted compost or peat moss added over a season or two.

Where small numbers of bulbs are planted be sure to group them. It is better to buy a few more bulbs of fewer varieties, then really concentrate the planting to get the best effect. Bulbs for naturalizing are best scattered at random and planted where they drop. When planting among biennial plants, such as wallflowers, plant these first and then set out the bulbs.

A row or two of daffodils, iris, gladioli and tulips can be planted in the vegetable garden for cutting. Leave as many leaves as possible when cutting the flowers if the bulbs are wanted for flowering in future years.

Dead-heading

Where possible the removal of dead flower heads will prevent seedpod formation and help to build up the bulbs or corms. You can leave the heads on crocus, chinodaxas, muscari, scillas, snowdrops and tigridia, because these plants will increase from the falling seeds. Tulip flower heads must be snapped off and removed as the petals start to fall. Left to fall naturally the falling flower parts stick to the leaves and encourage entry of a disease known as tulip fire. Take just the bells from hyacinths, leaving the plump stalk to help nourish the bulb.

Tidy gardeners sometimes feel tempted to tie the ageing leaves of crocus and daffodils in knots. This is better *not* done, for once the leaves have cracked near soil level, as happens in the tying process, little food will pass to the bulb and the foliage might as well be cut off.

Lifting, Drying and Storing

Try to leave the bulbs and corms until the foliage has died down naturally before lifting, cleaning off old roots and storing in a cool, and for tender subjects, frost-free place before re-planting. Where bulbs like daffodils and tulips need lifting to make way for summer bedding plants leave them as long as possible. Then lift carefully, retaining the foliage and as much root as possible. These lifted bulbs should then be covered with damp peat or fine soil in a cool spot to dry off naturally.

While most bulbs are best dried slowly and naturally, gladioli are different. Once the leaves start to yellow lift the plants and cut the stems off just $1/2$ in. (1 cm) above the corm. Place in a very warm spot, even over a radiator, and dry quickly. In two or three weeks the husk will be dry and the old shrivelled corm can be twisted off. Then dry again for a week or two before storing in trays and paper bags. Where gladioli are lifted, the stems left on and tied in bunches to dry, the possibility of storage rots developing is much increased.

Small bulbs and cormlets surrounding larger specimens are best discarded unless you are prepared to grow the little ones on separately to flowering size for two or three years.

Some Popular Bulbs

Allium species, the flowering onions are easy to grow and are rapidly increasing in popularity. Their mauve-blue flower heads and subsequent

Smaller hyacinth bulbs give the right flower size for outdoors. Tall tulips and daffodils in plastic planters need a sheltered site so they won't tip over.

Anemone blanda flowers very early and can be naturalized in woodlands.

seed heads are popular with flower arrangers. All soils are suitable.

Anemone blanda is a lovely early spring-flowering plant for rock gardens and shady spots. It mixes well with aconites, and snowdrops. Plant the strange-shaped corms in early autumn.

Do not confuse this with the *Anemone coronaria*, so popular as a cut flower in the double 'St. Brigid' and single 'De Caen' form. Cut-flower anemones can be planted in the autumn to flower in winter in greenhouses or outdoors in mild regions in early spring. Or corms 1 in. (2—3 cm) in diameter planted 5 in. (12.5 cm) apart in May give the most flowers. Soak the corms in water for several hours before planting.

Caladium is grown in summer for its richly colored, arrow-shaped leaves. The tubers are started into growth indoors in flats of damp peat moss in late winter, about the same time as are tuberous begonias (see page 98). When the weather warms (late spring), they can be put in large pots or set in the open ground or in planters to decorate terraces. Grow in humus-rich soil in part shade.

Colchicum autumnale, commonly called the autumn crocus with its big crocus-like flowers, produces large, broad shiny leaves in spring. The autumn flowers will come from bulbs if placed on the windowsill without soil or water. This bulb is best planted among shrubs to give a splash of autumn color.

Crocus fall into three main groups, and all are planted in the autumn. The true autumn-flowering varieties have small autumn flowers ahead of the spring growth of foliage. Next are the winter-flowering (in mild climates) or early spring species with small daintily marked flowers. Last are the large-flowered Dutch type in shades of white, blue and yellow as well as bicolors.

Eranthis hyemalis, the winter aconite, is one of the earliest spring flowers. It will spread well under trees once it has become established.

Cyclamen come in a range of species to give small delicate flowers from July to March. Very popular are *neapolitanum,* flowering in the autumn followed by green marbled silver leaves in spring, and *C. coum,* flowering from January to March.

Established plants self-seed and it is easier to establish pot-grown plants rather than dry corms. This plant will thrive in quite dry conditions such as under trees.

Galanthus nivalis, the snowdrop, also grows well under trees.

Eranthis hyemalis, commonly called winter aconite, is one of the earliest plants to flower in spring. Plant in August or September and see that the tubers are kept moist until well established.

Fritillaria are unusual plants. Two quite different types are grown. *F. meleagris,* the snake's-head fritillary, 12 in. (30 cm) high, is a good subject to naturalize under trees and in grass. *F. imperialis,* the crown imperial, grows to a stately 2—3 ft (60—90 cm) high and bears yellow or orange flower heads in April.

This is the plant which supposedly hung its head after Christ passed by in the garden of Gethsemane, and each flower holds "tear-drops" in the base.

Hyacinthus are always popular, and the large-flowered Dutch hybrid hyacinths are available in colors from white, yellow, orange, red, mauve, to light and dark blue. Choose small bulbs with a 5—6 in. (13—14 cm) circumference for outdoor use in exposed situations. The smaller flower heads from smaller bulbs stand up better to the wind. Roman hyacinths are very early flowering and are therefore best grown indoors in pots.

Iris come in four groups. The earliest to flower are the small species like *I. danfordiae,* yellow, and various blue shades of the sweetly scented *I. reticulata.* These are ideal for rock gardens and windowboxes. Then there are Dutch, Spanish and English iris. The Dutch flower in late May and each flower stem produces two flower buds, one opening after the other, which gives a long cut-flower life. Next to flower are the more slender Spanish iris and then finally the larger flowering English iris open in June and July.

Lilium species and hybrids need planting while the bulbs are fresh and plump. Virus diseases are carried by aphids and reduce the vigor of lilies so remove any ailing specimens. New hybrids free of virus will grow vigorously in most garden soils. Many are stem rooting, so plant 6—10 in. (15—25 cm) deep and mulch with leaf mold, as they come through the soil in spring. New plants can be propagated from bulb scales and from seed. The seed is best sown outside or in frames exposed to frost. Seedlings will develop in the spring and reach flowering size in about three years.

Many lilies grow well in pots, but choose good-sized bulbs and plant one to a 6—8 in. (15—20 cm) pot. Half fill the pot and plant the bulb in good potting mixture. Plunge in peat and once shoots 1 in. (2—3 cm) high have formed remove the peat and fill the pots up with more good soil. *L.* 'Destiny', *L.* 'Enchantment', and *L. regale* are good for pots and can be planted in the garden after flowering. Lilies associate well with azaleas and rhododendrons.

Muscari, commonly called grape hyacinth, is a very showy blue spring-flowering bulb. Once established it can become almost invasive. There is no better sight, however, than a bold patch of this bright blue flower. It mixes well with dwarf early-flowering tulips and daffodils.

Lilies can be propogated from the scales. A small bulb forms at the base.

Lilies are attractive plants in the garden as well as grown in pots. 'Destiny' is one of the many good hybrids.

Narcissi come in many different flower types forming separate groups, but I would like to make a plea for more miniature species in the rock garden. Watch for the *N. cyclamineus* hybrids like 'Peeping Tom', which is an early yellow.

Large trumpet daffodils generally flower first and the smaller the cup the later the flowering. Plant breeders are changing this by introducing later-flowering big trumpets, but the general rule remains. The bigger the bulb the more flowers it will produce for all varieties.

Choose the 'Pheasant Eye' types for the best fragrance.

Where narcissi have grown for years in grass but stop flowering, lift the clumps in late summer, split them up and replant. This allows the bulbs to build up their size to flower again. Soft, rotten bulbs which contain white maggots will be infested with narcissus fly and must be destroyed. Work lindane dust around the dying foliage to prevent further narcissus fly attack.

Scilla has two popular types, the early and small *Scilla siberica,* which has bright blue flowers carried on stems 6 in. (15 cm) high in March and April, and the giant wood hyacinth (Endymion hispanicus syn. *S. campanulata* with pink, blue and white kinds. The latter is best planted under trees and among shrubs where the bulbs will multiply rapidly if they are simply left undisturbed.

Tulipa is another genus containing many groups, which helps to provide a succession of flowering. The dwarf hybrids of *T. greigii* and *T. kaufmanniana* come first, and are followed by single earlies, double earlies, the triumphs (which are good to force for cut flowers), the Darwin hybrids, lily-flowered, Darwins, cottage and then finally parrot and fringed tulips.

Tremendous advances have been made with the dwarf hybrids and many have attractive chocolate markings on the leaves.

Flower size is also increasing, with huge flowers on such Darwin hybrids as 'Gudoshnik', creamy peach and red, 'Apeldoorn', vivid scarlet, and 'Jewel of Spring', yellow.

If you like the fringed and curled edges of the parrot tulips be sure to plant them where strong winds will not snap off the brittle stems.

The flagon-shaped flowers of the lily-flowered kinds are especially good for cutting.

Massed summer color is easily achieved from seed-raised summer bedding plants. Plan the scheme carefully before planting.

Geraniums, fuchsias and annuals are ideal for all plant containers.

SUMMER BEDDING PLANTS

Seed catalogs and seed packets are scattered with such initials as H.A. (hardy annual), H.H.A. (half-hardy annual), H.B. (hardy biennial), H.P. (hardy perennial) and H.H.P. (half-hardy perennial). If you compare several catalogs there will be contradictions because the lines between these different groups of plants are somewhat blurred.

The lovely blue brachycome (Swan River daisy) can be sown outside in spring in warmer regions, and yet it needs raising indoors as a half-hardy annual in colder areas. The continuous flowering *Begonia semperflorens* is raised and bedded out for one season as a half-hardy annual when in fact it is perennial and, protected from frost, will flower for several years. Lobelia, salvias, verbena and some stocks can also be grown as perennials, but the half-hardy annual treatment is much more common.

Summer bedding plants is the term I prefer to use to describe all those plants which are raised from seed indoors in early spring. The seedlings are transplanted into seedboxes or pots and then slowly hardened to outdoor conditions before planting out in early summer to fill the garden with color.

They are most striking grouped in formal bedding schemes and surrounded either by neatly mown lawn or cleanly swept paving. While a useful means of filling gaps in mixed borders, their other main use is in plant containers. Tubs, troughs, window-boxes and every kind of outdoor planter can be filled with them.

The cost of raising the slower-growing kinds which need sowing very early in spring in quite high temperatures, 60-70°F (15-21°C), means they are often best left to commercial growers. However, if you have a sunny windowsill, a fluorescent light set-up or, of course, a warm greenhouse, you can sow begonias, impatiens, lobelia, petunia, salvia, snapdragons and others.

Faster-growing types like alyssum, aster, marigold and zinnia can be sown later in the open ground, about mid-May in much of the North or earlier in the South.

Whether growing your own or buying plants it is worth remembering bigger plants spaced more wisely will give the best show. Some nurserymen cram up to 60 seedlings in a small tray. While these might look cheaper at the outset they will not give the value for money achieved when a lesser number of larger plants are brought for the same or slightly higher price.

A sure indication of well-grown bedding plants is uniform height, and nice bushy plants with strong dark green leaves. Plants grown too quickly, in temperatures that are too high will have soft growth and a pale green, "drawn up" appearance. Soft plants like this will not take kindly to being planted outdoors.

Should you wish to raise your own bedding plants and not have indoor growing conditions then hardier plants like alyssum, pansies and stocks can raised under cold-frames from an April sowing. Another possibility is to sow in early autumn when the soil is warm and overwinter under frames or simply sow in the open ground in late fall for spring germination.

Where you have broad windowsills it is also worth overwintering *Begonia semperflorens*. Before the autumn frost, water the beds of begonias well and lift good plants with a fair ball of soil — about the size of a fist. Pot these plants up in 5 in. (13 cm) half-pots (the sort year-round pot chrysanthemums are grown in). Either a good loam-based potting mixture or a purchased soilless mix are suitable for this. Cut back the top growth by about half and bring the potted plants indoors. In a few weeks new growth will be flowering.

The varieties with red flowers make good Christmas flowering plants. These overwintered plants can be put out in the garden again the following May or June.

Once we have well-grown young plants, whether in boxes or singly in pots, the critical time is transplanting outside. Even where the soil is well prepared, planting too soon can mean destruction by frost, and planting too late can mean shrivelling up in the heat of the sun. Single pot-grown subjects will have a bigger root-ball and are therefore better able to withstand late planting.

Generally I prefer to plant on the early side, with frost less of a problem in sheltered city and suburban gardens and in coastal areas. If your garden is in a hollow where cold frosty air gathers, and in cold areas, it is wiser to delay and to use more pot-grown plants.

Water all plants well before planting out. I like to add liquid fertilizer before transplanting to give the bedding a flying start. All plants will flower better with the dead flower heads removed. This is important for dahlias, Swan River daisies, marigolds, nicotiana, petunias, salvias, stocks and zinnias, but not really practical with alyssum, ageratum and lobelia. The F_1 hybrid *Begonia semperflorens* never sets seed and is perfect for sun and part shade.

Sunny spots are ideal for petunias and all the marigolds, whereas snapdragons, ageratum and begonias will withstand the rain. Watch for slugs in wet weather, especially just after planting out. Aphids can be a problem with nicotiana and petunias in dry weather, but one spray will soon clear this pest.

Hoeing through the beds early in the season will be necessary to control weeds but once the bedding plants cover the ground they need little attention. Where spring bulbs and bedding such as pansies are slow to finish flowering, summer bedding can be planted in between. The French marigolds do a good cover-up job in

Hybrid African marigolds have huge yellow and orange flower heads. Also in the picture are alyssum, ageratum, China asters and French marigolds.

The perennial gloriosa daisy is usually treated as a half-hardy annual.

BEDDING PLANT CHART

Plant	Height	Space	When to plant outside	Flower from
Ageratum	low	6-8 in.†	from late May	June
Alyssum (F)	low	6-8 in.	from mid April	May
Antirrhinum	low-tall	10-14 in.	from mid April	June
*Aster	med.	8-10 in.	from early May	Aug.
Begonia, Wax	low	6-10 in.	from late May	June
Coleus	med.	10-14 in.	from mid May	Aug.
*Dahlia	med.-tall	12-15 in.	from late May	Aug.
Lobelia	low	6-8 in.	from early May	June
*Marigold African	med.-tall	8-12 in.	from late May	July
Marigold French	low-med.	6-12 in.	from late May	July
Nasturtium	low	8-10 in.	from early May	June
Nemesia	low-med.	8-12 in.	from early May	July
Nicotiana (F)	med.-tall	12-15 in.	from mid April	July
Pansy	low	8-12 in.	from late March	April
Petunia	med.	10-12 in.	from mid May	July
Phlox drummondii	low-med.	8-10 in.	from late April	July
Salvia	med.	10-12 in.	from mid May	July
*Stock Ten Week (F)	med.	10-12 in.	from early April	June
*Zinnia	low-tall	10-12 in.	from late May	July

*Provide flowers to cut (F) fragrant.
Space – larger plants spread wider when transplanted.
When to plant – hardiness guide for average northern conditions. In frost-free and mild climates, plant in fall for winter-spring bloom.
† *8 in. = 20.3 cm*

Sempervivums and sedums grow well in sink gardens, troughs and other planters.

Tumbling masses of *Alyssum saxatile*, which is easily raised from seed, dwarf phlox and aubrieta cover terrace walling most effectively.

this case. Spring-flowering daffodils covered with summer-flowering seed-raised 'Peter Pan' zinnias is also effective.

ALPINE AND ROCK PLANTS

Where lack of space curtails your gardening activities the small-growing alpine and rock plants really come into their own. Large gardens, too, can accommodate them in more grandiose schemes with carefully designed rock faces that give a mountainside feel. Big rock gardens can take a lot of maintaining, however, so be careful not to construct more than is easily weeded.

A modest raised rock garden up to 15 ft (5 m) across is one possibility and small raised gardens within dry stone walling another. The narrow cracks between paving slabs and stone sink gardens, either on the flat or raised 2 ft (60 cm) or so from the ground are other possibilities. Even three or four tiers of cement blocks make an acceptable rock garden when planted.

Where the situation is somewhat shaded then gardens built with logs or railroad ties or the lighter landscape ties can be made and planted with ferns and wildflowers.

Excepting wildflowers, all alpine planting needs to be on free-draining soil. Add plenty of coarse gritty material to heavy soil. Ideally make up a mix of two parts good soil, one part peat moss and one part coarse sand or fine gravel — rather like a good seed mixture — for rock plants.

You will need a good heap of soil even for the 15 ft (5 m) rock garden and it is best to prepare this in advance of construction. See that the rocks are placed in position first, working the soil mixture into the crevices as the rock garden is being constructed.

Even when planting sink gardens, after putting some coarse material at the base for drainage, position rocks first and then infill. Remember to place the sink in its final position before filling — the empty sink can be heavy enough without rocks and soil!

Quite small rocks are heavy and when building even a small feature in a suburban garden several tons of natural stone are needed. For most of us a small raised bed supported by a dry stone wall is the easiest to handle and, set at the right height, the edge makes a

Even where space is limited, there is room for a few rock plants. Sink gardens and other containers offer one very attractive solution to this problem.

good and convenient place to sit.

It is important to have soil back up to the wall for satisfactory growth. Just removing the odd brick in a wall and attempting to fill it with compost is not satisfactory. Many alpines have fine searching roots which penetrate some depth in hot, sunny weather.

Seedlings often develop in the tiny crevices between paving. Take advantage of this natural occurrence and brush alyssum, thyme and similar seeds into crevices where you want plants to grow.

Natural stone sinks and old troughs have become expensive and are not easy to obtain. One possible alternative is to put a rough veneer over a discarded glazed sink. Scratch over the surface first if possible, then apply one of the weatherproof, all-purpose glues. Once the glue is tacky cover with a $\frac{1}{2}$—$\frac{3}{4}$ in. (1.5 cm) layer of cement mix. This needs to be one part cement, one part sand, and one part peat moss mixed with water to a doughy consistency.

A sink garden substitute resembling stone can be made from 1 part cement, $1\frac{1}{2}$ parts peat moss and $1\frac{1}{2}$ parts perlite, reinforced by chicken wire. Use sand or cardboard boxes as molds. Make drainage holes with nails, removed before the mix hardens.

Where the sink is very shallow and in other planting sites with very little soil, include different kinds of sedum and sempervivum, commonly called house leeks. Another name for sempervivum is hen and chicken because one larger plant is surrounded by young offspring. They have a special place in the rock garden because of their neat rosette shape, the many different colored forms and large flower heads. A strawberry pot planted with a collection of these plants can look most attractive.

The drumstick primula, *P. denticulata*, is easily raised from seed or root cuttings. It needs a bold rock to provide sensible proportions.

The rich blue lithospermum flowers for weeks in the rock garden.

Select and plant your rock feature over a whole season to get the longest flowering period. Spring is the time when many different types flower but there are the summer-flowering pinks, the continuously-flowering blue lithospermum and autumn-flowering *Gentiana sino-ornata,* the last two best grown in the cool, moist Pacific Northwest.

Where the chosen rock and/or soils are alkaline, then aubrieta, arabis, *Alyssum saxatile,* dianthus and saxifraga are safe bets. On acid soils then gentiana, lithospermum and even the prostrate heaths like the late winter-flowering *Erica carnea* 'Springwood White' come into their own.

Many gardens have banks and terrace walls to divide split-level gardens. All too often these are peppered with reject concrete and sundry stone. Where such material has been used then good plant growth can cover a multitude of unsightly objects.

Aubrieta, alyssum, helianthemum (rock rose) and arabis will do a good cover-up job in spring and early summer. Remember to trim these subjects back after flowering to keep the growth neat and vigorous. Aubrieta cut back really hard after flowering produces a beautiful mound of new growth which will be smothered in flower the following spring.

Good-value-for-money plants are aethionemas, which flower for weeks, and the tough ajuga with several different colored leaf forms. Choose campanulas for good blue coloring and an easy nature almost regardless of soil type. Then there are the masses of white flowers on iberis, interesting edelweiss (leontopodium), the bright mimulus, and lovely pink rock phlox with carpets of flower. There are so many delights in this group of plants.

Don't be put off by lack of space. A collection of 40 or more can be grown in less than a square meter surface area. Even between paving slabs it is possible to build a collection with *Thymus* species, which are good in this situation because their crushed leaves are nicely fragrant. Try to keep the planting from areas which are very heavily trodden, however, as there is a

Early summer gardens just would not be the same without the flower and fragrance of stocks, which can be grown as annuals or biennials.

limit to the punishment plants will take. The very flat platinum-colored growth of *Raoulia australis* is also attractive in paving.

There are dwarf shrubs like daphnes and potentillas, deciduous and evergreen dwarf trees to give height and scale to the garden. Where these woody subjects are used a reasonable depth of compost and sufficient summer moisture for attractive growth is needed.

Do not overlook conifers, for there are many suitable true dwarfs that will add much in the form of shape and texture to a rock site. The chapter on conifers will provide ideas.

BIENNIALS

Much of the early summer flower color comes from seed-raised biennials. All too often we are so busy in late spring and early summer that these plants, which are sown one year to flower and die the next, are forgotten.

It might be rather a long time to wait from sowing to flowering in comparison with annuals, but if you need convincing that these plants are worth growing just think of double daisies, honesty, forget-me-nots, pansies, sweet William and wallflowers. Even in those bitterly cold areas where leafy plants will not overwinter unprotected, biennials are worth carrying over in a cold frame.

The most common use of this group of plants is as spring bedding in association with spring-flowering bulbs. Wallflowers and forget-me-nots with tulips, English daisies (Bellis) and pansies with muscari are some of the popular combinations.

Several are worth growing to fill gaps in the herbaceous and mixed flower borders. Good examples for this are Iceland poppy, honesty and verbascum. It is also worth growing a few Canterbury bells, Iceland poppies, stocks and sweet William separately for cutting.

Sowing

All the biennials mentioned can be sown outside in the open ground during May or June. Sowing at this time needs a little care because hot sun can shrivel up tiny seedlings. Find a partially shaded site and see that the soil is thoroughly moistened before allowing the surface to dry and starting to sow.

It may well be necessary to give several really good waterings in hot weather to get the seedlings properly established.

Very fine seed like Iceland poppy and foxglove are safer sown in pots of seed mixture but see that the pots are kept cool and moist.

Stock and wallflower seedlings are likely to be attacked by flea beetle, which eats neat round holes in the young leaves. Dust the seedlings when damp with carbaryl or rotenone to prevent damage.

Nicely established seedlings can be spaced out either in seedboxes like bedding plants, or outside in nursery rows possibly on the vegetable plot. They are probably easier to look after in nursery rows and need final transplanting to the flowering position in early autumn.

Leafy plants like stocks and wallflowers will need a little protection from cold drying winds in exposed gardens. A few bushy twigs or low netting will give protection.

In early spring go round and refirm plants which have been rocked about by the wind and lifted by frost. Then hoe a little general fertilizer in around them.

After flowering the plants are usually pulled up and rotted down on the compost heap.

If the dead flowers are cut off stocks, especially East Lothian Stocks, they will often produce a second flush of flower. The same can be said for foxgloves and if the heads are cut off before the seed falls millions of self-sown seedlings will be avoided.

If you keep pinching off the dead flower heads from pansies they will flower all summer in moist, cool climates.

Polyanthus primroses produce large fragrant flowers in a good color range.

Pyramids of pink, blue and white flowers of Canterbury bells in early summer.

It could be argued that pansies, violas and hollyhocks should be grouped under the perennial heading but they seem to do best if treated as biennials.

Some Good Biennials

Bellis perennis, commonly called English daisy, has a massed small-flowered type and a large-flowered one. For the best plants sow in a frame in March or April. One of the earlier spring flowers, it shows color from March onwards. It is a good edging plant.

Campanula calycanthema, Canterbury bell, has lovely shades of blue, pink and white. There is a double and a cup-and-saucer form; the latter has a flower shape just like a cup and saucer. Space the taller growing kinds at least 12 in. (30 cm) apart.

Dianthus barbatus, the common sweet William is a very prolific plant, perfect to grow for cut flowers. There are self colors and the bicolored 'Auricula-eyed' varieties. When grown for cutting just sow thinly where you want the plants to flower. Space rows at least 12 in. (30 cm) apart.

Digitalis, the foxglove, can hardly be called common with modern strains of *D.* 'Excelsior Hybrids' having huge spikes, and the stems are encircled with flowers, unlike the single row up the stems of the wild plant. Lovely colors from white and cream to deep pink and purple.

Erysimum asperum, or Siberian wallflower has bright orange, fragrant flowers on rounded plants with prostrate foliage. It can be sown August or September, and the smaller plants can be transplanted more easily.

Hollyhock, *Althea rosea,* is one of the tallest biennials and in the 'Chater's Double' strain easily reaches 6 ft (1.82 m). More acceptable for today's gardens are the lower-growing 'Silver Puffs' and 'Majorette' strains, which, if sown in early spring, bloom in summer. Hollyhocks can act as perennials.

Lunaria or honesty has simple pale purple or white flowers but when the seed pods split they leave silver heads popular in dried flower arrangements. Watch out for the strain with attractive cream and green variegated leaves. A good plant to grow under trees and in shade.

Myosotis, the forget-me-not, is so free seeding you are hardly likely to overlook it. All soils and sites are suitable and the dwarf forms make good pot plants.

Pansies and **violas** are really perennials, but are also treated as annuals from an early spring sowing. By far the best results, however are obtained from sowing outside in a shady spot in late July. Set the plants outside in their flowering position in early autumn and the size and quality of flower the next year will be unsurpassed.

Papaver nudicaule, the Iceland poppy, is one of the most productive cut flowers. Cutting just as the bud splits to show the petal color and burning the cut ends, either in boiling water or a flame, to prevent milky white sap flow, is the key to longer life once cut. It is easiest to sow the seed and raise in boxes to plant out in the flowering site in the autumn. In very cold areas overwinter in the boxes in frames and plant out in early spring.

Bellis perennis or double daisies make excellent spring-edging plants.

Stocks are often treated as annuals, but the Brompton kind are best treated as biennials. While some kinds of stock can have the double-flowered plants selected by their pale green seedling leaf color, the Bromptons are not easily selected in this way. They have a good color range and fragrance.

Wallflowers, *Cheiranthus cheiri.* The tip here is to get dwarf bushy plants.

Tulips and wallflowers give color and fragrance to early summer flower borders. The purple shrub is *Berberis thunbergii* 'Atropurpurea Nana'.

Sow seeds of or buy dwarf kinds and pinch out the growing tip once seedlings are 4—5 in. (10—12 cm) high, to encourage bushiness.

Try to plan your herbaceous border to provide good contrasts. Here astilbe in the foreground contrasts with the flower and foliage of a polygonum.

HERBACEOUS PLANTS

Whether you know these plants as perennials, hardy border flowers or herbaceous plants is not important, but their value for color, for cutting and garden use is undisputed. Stately gardens in the past had borders 12—20 ft (4—7 m) wide and 300 ft (100 m) long, banked by hedges.

Smaller gardens demand less extravagant uses, and island beds and much smaller borders are the order today. Many modern cultivars have shorter, stronger stems and compact growth.

The term herbaceous describes perennial plants which grow, flower and seed in a season but do not die. The rootstock is hardy and perennial, producing new shoots in spring and new foliage and flowers every year.

While herbaceous borders are carefully planned and planted in new gardens, for most people it is more a continuing process. A mixed flower border is inherited, old and unwanted types are removed and new plants introduced. Both ways, soil preparation is important.

Thoroughly dig the soil before planting, removing all perennial weeds. Where perennial grass and stubborn weed roots run through the soil it is better to plant annuals for a season or two until the soil is clean. Let these weeds get among phlox, asters and the like at your peril. Be careful that a "friendly neighbor" doesn't give you a helping of weeds in with some hardy plant divisions!

Hosta ventricosa 'Variegata' (top), *Filipendula ulmaria* 'Aurea' and ajuga.

Mix plenty of well-rooted compost or peat moss in soil when digging. Some plants, like peonies, will flower for years without transplanting, so once again there is only one chance to get the soil foundation right.

Position vigorous plants together to avoid the slower growing and finer specimens being smothered. Arrange taller plants carefully to the back, the center or to one side of the bed. Try to get a sequence of flowers, from spring doronicum to autumn aster. Try also to achieve contrasts in foliage, the rounded green leaves of euphorbia against silver artemisia and purple *Sedum maximum* 'Atropurpureum'.

Most of these plants are at their best in the second and third summer. It is for this reason that regular splitting up of old stock and propagation of new is recommended.

The process can go on almost the whole year round. Some plants, like peonies, are best split in early autumn, others, like asters in April. Root cuttings of anchusa and phlox need to be made in late fall, and *Iris germinica* and pyrethrum are best split after flowering in summer.

A whole range of varieties can be raised from seed sown indoors in spring and in the open ground in early summer. The Christmas rose grows easily from seed sown outside in the autumn to germinate in spring.

Young plants not only grow better but they divide better and provide more free-rooting cuttings. If you're producing low-cost plants from seed, grow a good number of seedlings, select the best forms and propagate these vegetatively.

It is worth increasing really good forms of delphinium for example. Take cuttings in early spring when the shoots are 3 in. (7.5 cm) high. See that there is a piece of the old hard root on the base of each cutting. Put $^1/_2$ in. (12 mm) of sharp sand in the base of a glass jar, add 1—2 in. (3—5 cm) of water and put the cutting in this. If placed on a north-facing windowsill roots will form in a few weeks and the cutting can be potted up in any potting mixture and planted out once established.

Bright contrast between white and yellow. *Chrysanthemum maximum* and copper helenium. The 'day-lilies' (*Hemerocallis* right) have a long flowering season.

Stately spikes of yellow verbascum and steel-blue eryngium against a background of conifers.

When propagating new plants by division always select vigorous young shoots from the outer edge of each clump. The best way is to tease one or two such divisions off with a fork or trowel. Plant them, then when they are well established the old parent plant can be dug up and discarded.

Michaelmas daisies are colorful autumn plants that attract butterflies.

A good dressing of general fertilizer hoed into the surface each spring will give much better growth and flowers. Where big single spikes are wanted on plants like delphiniums, lupines and phlox, reduce the shoots in spring.

Space plants at least 12—15 in. (30—38 cm) apart in groups with the groups of different kinds 18—24 in. (45—60 cm) apart. Five plants per square meter is a good average density, the small kinds closer, the larger more widely spaced. Work out group plantings to keep filling gaps — for example when the lupines go over and dead heads are cut off, adjacent salvia flowers can provide continuity. Really good value plants give months of flower and *Sythrum virgatum, Anemone japonica* and potentilla are but three candidates.

Plants growing over 18—24 in. (45—60 cm) high will need some form of support, especially in windswept gardens. There are several methods, with either single stakes or groups of three canes for each clump being the most common. Larger beds can be supported by erecting large mesh net horizontally over the plants. Drive two stout stakes, the width of the net apart, every 10 ft (3 m) along the border, shorter stake to the front, taller to the back or center. As the plants develop so the net can be raised, securing the sides of the net to the stakes. There are proprietary circular mesh supports on three wire legs which do a similar job for single plants.

Another good system is the use of bushy branches. These are pushed in around each plant and the tops broken over and inwards to help support the stems which grow through the twigs.

Most herbaceous plants grow well in a wide variety of soils. Where the site is open and sunny, growth will be strong and the need for support less. There are a number suited to more difficult soils.

Damp shaded soils are suitable for astilbe, dicentra, epimedium, hosta (especially the variegated leaf forms) and lythrum.

Hot sunny soils are suited to hemerocallis, *Iris germanica,* nepeta and sedum.

A number will give good ground cover and once established smother out weed. Early spring flowering *Bergenia,* the taller *Geranium* 'Johnson's Blue' and silver-leaved *Stachys byzantinus* are examples.

Flowers to cut are provided week after week by pyrethrum, *Chrysanthemum maximum* and *scabiosa.* Several can be cut in flower and dried for winter arrangement; the yellow *Achillea filipendulina* and steel-blue *Echinops ritro* are popular for this use.

Begonia X*tuberhybrida*, especially the smaller multiflora cultivars, are useful for bedding outside. The tubers can be stored for another year.

Where the roots are thick and succulent a little winter protection may be needed, especially on wet, heavy soils. Wrap straw around the leaves of newly planted kniphofia in the autumn to provide frost protection.

SPECIALIST FLOWERS

Some gardeners are especially attracted to certain plants and where the specialist enthusiasm is common groups and societies are operated to further the cultivation of that genera. The following flowers are just a few of many that have their devotees and are worth including in the average garden.

Begonias and Gloxinias

The large, fully double-flowered begonias grown from tubers dominate this group, though other kinds are grown as bedding plants and houseplants. The trailing tuberous begonias are attractive in hanging baskets. They are good subjects for part shade. Warmth and moisture are needed to start the tubers into growth in spring. One method is to put the tubers in a flat of damp peat moss in a warm room. Once roots and shoots are seen, pot up singly in a humus-rich potting compost.

Large tubers with more than one shoot can be cut in half. Alternatively cut off stout shoots to root as cuttings but retain a piece of the old corm on the cutting.

The gloxinias, which are botanically known as *Sinningia,* require the same treatment to start them into growth, and when sprouted before potting are less likely to be planted upside down. They do best in pots.

Carnations and other Dianthus

The genus *Dianthus* has something for every gardener it is so varied, although not all kinds grow well in every region, especially where summers are very hot and humid.

Sweet William *(D. barbatus)*, a biennial, is one of the easiest as it blooms in early summer before excessive heat arrives (see page 95).

Then there are many new hybrid dianthus forms that are grown as annuals and provide masses of bright color. Although these hybrids bloom best where summers are cool and moist from early-spring-sown seeds, they have also proved successful where summers are warmer. They can be sown in late summer in mild climates for winter and spring displays. Some worthwhile kinds are the heat-resistant 'Lace' hybrids, the 'Charm' series, only 6 in. (15 cm) high, and the red and white 'Snowfire'.

Among perennial dianthus are the cottage pinks *(D. plumarius)* which are quite tolerant of average garden conditions. They and the so-called perpetual or hardy border carnations are smaller versions of the florist's carnation *(D. caryophyllus)*, an important commercial cut-flower. Hardy border carnations do well outdoors in regions of the Pacific, but elsewhere most summers are too hot and winters too cold for them.

The florist's carnation can be grown in pots in a cool home greenhouse at temperatures between 45—60°F (7—16°C), the lower night temperatures being preferable. Cuttings are made in winter and rooted in peat moss and sand, then potted into $3^1/_2$ in. (9 cm) pots. Add a 4 in. (10 cm) pot of lime to a bushel of soil. Pinch off new growth to induce bushiness until fall. Final pot size should be 8 in. (20 cm).

Chrysanthemums

Hardy early-flowering chrysanthemums can be left in the soil overwinter to produce autumn flowers,

Lovely fragrant carnations can be grown successfully in a cool greenhouse.

grown much the same as Michaelmas daisies. Much better results will be obtained, however, where cuttings are taken from new basal shoots each spring. Certainly cuttings need to be taken annually for large single blooms and plants to flower in greenhouses.

The cultural sequence starts in autumn and early winter when chrysanthemums have finished flowering and dormancy has started. Single plants are cut back and lifted from the soil or pot. Most of the soil is then shaken off and all green shoots cut off at soil level. If you leave 2—3 in. (5—7 cm) of woody stem on each root, really a division or clump, it can be handled more easily.

Place the roots in flats 3—4 in. (8—10 cm) deep, pack potting compost around the roots and water them in. Place these flats in a cold-frame overwinter and bring into warmer conditions in early spring. Once new green shoots 3 in. (8 cm) long develop take softwood cuttings. Rooted cuttings are potted on into $3^1/_2$ in. (9 cm) pots. If you have no heat to root cuttings, then using new shoots with roots already attached will give passable results.

Early-flowering varieties are planted outdoors in spring and those kinds to be flowered under glass repotted in sequence to 5 $^1/_2$ in. (13 $^1/_2$ cm) and ultimately 8—10 in. (25—30 cm) pots.

Once well established, young plants have the growing tip pinched out to increase the number of flowering shoots. If the tip is cut off when plants are 10—12 in. (25—30 cm) in height an average of six to eight flower stems are likely. If you want to grow really big single exhibition flowers then reduce the number of flower stems to two or three.

Potted, later-flowering varieties are taken outside, once in their largest pot. Standing the pot on sand or ashes helps to reduce the amount of watering.

Each plant will need one or more canes and several ties to support the flowering stems as they develop. Where a number of flowers are required on each stem, for a cut spray perhaps, little disbudding is necessary. Some spray varieties will flower more uniformly if just the lead center bud is removed. All but the top lead bud must be pinched out where one large flower on each stem is required.

Quite a number of the outdoor early-flowering cultivars will produce good disbudded single blooms and, if fed and watered after they are cut, will

Late-flowering spray and single bloom chrysanthemums in pots under glass. Choose hardy, early flowering varieties for growing in the garden.

produce a second flush of attractive spray flowers.

Mid and late flowering varieties grown in pots need to be taken under

Dahlias are equally attractive as cut flowers or as garden plants.

glass in the autumn before the chance of severe frost. Ventilate the greenhouse as much as possible after housing to reduce the chance of mildew fungus forming on the leaves and botrytis wet rots forming on the flowers.

Commercial growers root cuttings quite late into July and plant these cuttings staight into the border soil to run one or two flowers per cutting.

Dahlias

Dahlias are one of the most prolific of summer and early autumn flowers. Plant either tubers in spring or well rooted cuttings after the chance of frost in early summer.

They grow rapidly and need good reserves of moisture and plant food, so prepare the soil well before planting. Many grow quite tall and produce heavy leafy plants. Allocating one stout stake with at least 3 ft (1 m) out of the ground is necessary if late summer and early autumn damage from wind is to be avoided.

Lower growing, bedding types are

Fuchsias are good plants for tubs, either mixed with other plants or used alone. Plant pendula varieties to trail over the side of a container or in hanging baskets.

raised from seed but the better cut flower kinds, whether cactus, decorative, pompon, anemone-flowered or collerette are better propagated vegetatively.

Once frost has cut back flowers and leaves lift the whole plant and cut off the top, leaving 6 in. (15 cm) of stem. Some of the stems are so thick they need cutting with a saw. Where a good long growing season has occurred, plump tuberous roots will be found.

Shake the soil from these and stack them upside down to dry out in a dry, airy garage. They will take a week or two to dry so keep the lifted tubers warm and free from frost.

Once dry when all the soil has been shaken from the roots, I like to store them in dry peat moss.

In early spring the tubers can be flatted like chrysanthemum roots to produce cuttings, or they can be replanted. Big tubers, with several stems, will often divide up before planting to increase the numbers.

Dahlia cuttings need to be taken young; once the cuttings get large and the stems hollow they are more difficult to root. If you can cut off the cutting in such a way that you leave behind two immature leaves more cuttings will come from the axils of the two leaves.

Cuttings rooted in late spring and early summer can be kept in $3\frac{1}{2}$ in. (9 cm) pots all summer to produce pot tubers. The root restriction produces neat plump tubers rather like those bought in plastic prepacks in spring. Pot tubers dried off naturally in the autumn are easier to overwinter than those grown in open ground.

Fuchsias

There are few plants to equal the fuchsia for pot, tub and hanging basket cultivation. Many, in mild regions, will overwinter if given a little protection. The top growth dies right back rather like herbaceous plants and new shoots come from the base in spring.

Plants in containers should be dried off somewhat in the autumn. If the compost is kept slightly moist and the plants given the shelter of a cool basement or garage at 40°F (4°C) overwinter, they will often survive.

The best way to replace stock is to root softwood cuttings in summer and overwinter young plants. Where a temperature of 50°F (10°C) can be maintained the young plants will continue to grow. More softwood cuttings can then be taken in spring to increase the stock of each variety.

Standard forms with the head grown on a 2—3 ft (60—90 cm) trunk are best grown from cuttings taken July to August. If you can find cuttings with leaves in threes rather than pairs up the stem, they will make more freely branched and bushier plants. Keep these cuttings growing right through the winter. Pinch out all the side shoots to push the growth upright, and tie the single stem to a cane. Once the growing tip has reached the length of stem you require, pinch out the growing tip to develop a bushy head.

All young plants will need the growing tip pinched out twice to produce shapely plants. This is especially the case for pendulous varieties grown in hanging baskets.

Gladioli

While there are early and late flowering varieties, the best way to get a

Plant gladioli fairly deep to help support the heavy flower stems.

Houseplants

The sight of plants indoors brings pleasure to everyone, and most of us get satisfaction from seeing a living plant in our care thrive and increase in size and beauty. To achieve success, however, calls for a careful choice of subjects.

Many of the plants we choose to grow indoors are far from their natural habitat and climate, but if you choose with care and select the right plant for the right conditions, the risk of failure is considerably reduced.

One of the most common and most popular indoor foliage plants is the rubber plant, *Ficus elastica*, a native of tropical jungles. It does well in the average temperatures of our homes, tolerating even the dry atmospheres so different from its jungle habitat. Good light, even filtered sunlight is essential, though. Given these conditions, eventually it will outgrow the space available.

Modern, well-lighted, air-conditioned offices provide ideal conditions for the rubber plant and other similar foliage plants that in nature would have tropical conditions. And such plants bring life to what can otherwise be stark surroundings. Indoor plants can, in fact, contribute more than beauty. They trap dust and give off moisture, which can improve the dry atmosphere created by central heating. And they make excellent natural screens in open-plan offices and showrooms.

Windows overlooked by neighbors can be screened effectively with light foliage plants in pots on the sill and with climbing or trailing subjects hanging from rods at the top of the window.

Where a tall free-standing plant display is needed there are various pole and cane supports which hold both 3½ in. (9 cm) and 4½ in. (11 cm) pots. It is often cheaper to use several plants in this way rather than to buy one large and expensive specimen.

The Grape Ivy *Cissus rhombifolia* is a robust houseplant, easy to grow.

Pot covers almost always enhance the appearance of a plant. A variety of antique containers can be used, from copper kettles to small, timber, half barrels, as well as the wide variety of modern containers.

Don't be afraid to use flowering plants as attractive centerpieces. Many such plants raised from seed die after flowering and it makes sense to place them in full view rather than to extend their life for a few days but not see them to such full effect. Good flowering pot plants are often cheaper than cut flowers, and give excellent value for money in comparison.

LOOKING AFTER YOUR PLANTS

Plants have six basic requirements, whether grown indoors or out — light, air, warmth, moisture, a rooting medium, and food. Light is by far the most critical of these for houseplants.

Light

During the winter, both the length of day and the brightness of daylight are insufficient for ideal growth. That is why many foliage plants benefit from being moved close to a window during the winter.

The stronger and brighter light of summer allows many plants to grow adequately even when positioned quite well into the room. This is because the light penetrates well into the room and is reflected off light surfaces such as white ceilings and walls. Some plants are naturally able to withstand shady conditions better than others. As a general rule, the variegated forms with less chlorophyll in the leaf tend to need more light.

Although light is good, there can be too much, and on occasions sunlight on south-facing windows in high summer can cause leaf scorch. This only happens where net curtains trap the heat, where plants are given insufficient water, or where particularly susceptible, fleshy-leaved subjects like African violets are put in these positions. Generally, lack of light is a far more serious problem.

Symptoms of insufficient light are long, thin stems with wide spaces between leaves, yellowing of older leaves, and pale green young leaves and growing tips. When the temperature is high, encouraging fast growth in poor light, these symptoms are worse.

Where plants like geraniums are being overwintered on a windowsill and the lack of light gives thin, pale green growth, a back reflector of kitchen foil will improve things.

Almost any plant grown in a really shady position (where it is almost too dark to read, will need to be given periods in the light to recuperate. The growth of some plants in dark sites can also be improved with artificial light from bulbs and tubes. The African violet, for example, can be grown very successfully in artificial light. It is important to remember, however, that with some plants artificial light can cause problems if it upsets the natural length of day; the production of flowers on christmas cactus and of the red bracts on poinsettia will be inhibited.

Air

Plants absorb carbon dioxide from the air in daylight to convert into plant food, and release oxygen, and in this way they make a significant contribution to our environment. In the past we were concerned with fumes from town gas fires and stoves damaging houseplants, but today natural gas releases more carbon dioxide, and this helps to improve growth. In fact, it has been suggested that any improvement in growth that comes from speaking to your plants each day results from the extra carbon dioxide exhaled while talking!

Generally, however, we have no need to worry about *air,* as there is plenty in every situation. It is only cold drafts that cause concern, or a dry atmosphere. Both can be overcome.

Warmth

With regard to temperature, it is a matter of finding plants suited to the room—extra heat or less heat is unlikely to be provided just for the plants. Fortunately, there is a wide choice, from hardy items like ivies and azaleas, which withstand frost, to dieffenbachia and cacti, which relish hot, arid conditions.

It is easier to get plants which need warmth settled in the home position in late spring or early summer. Then by reducing the water in winter they can be kept just ticking over through the dark cold months. They start to grow again quickly when light and temperatures increase.

By using special hydroculture techniques it is possible to grow plants without soil. Watering and feeding become much easier with this system.

Weighing is an accurate method of determining water need (see text).

Watering

This is the one area where we exert total control. There is little we can do if the sun doesn't shine, but when it comes to watering everything is in our hands. And it is important to remember that it is not only water at the roots that is vital. Air moisture, or humidity, is also extremely important. Plants grouped together will provide humidity for one another. Syringing the foliage occasionally will also help to improve humidity around the plants. Standing the plants on pebbles on water-filled trays is even better. Hot air rising continuously from radiators and heaters is of great comfort to the pest red spider, but of little benefit to plants. To see for yourself watch the leaves of plants tremble continuously if placed over a radiator.

Most water is, of course, absorbed through the roots, and the best way to check water requirements for pot plants is to pick them up and feel the weight. Wet plants will be heavy, then as the water dries up the pots will become lighter. To convert this to foolproof terms, seek the advice of an experienced grower; if he says a plant is just nicely damp, pop it on scales, make a note of the weight, and water whenever weight loss is recorded. Just add water until the original weight is gained.

Most plants grow best by drying out somewhat and then being watered. This is better than keeping plants constantly wet.

Capillary watering is another useful method. One way to achieve this is with a saucer of fine silver sand. Wet the sand, place the pot firmly on this, water once from the top and then just keep the sand damp. The plant will then draw up the water it needs.

Pot plant wicks are a variation on this theme, with the water needed by the plant being drawn up through a wick which goes through the drainage hole in the base of the pot and up into the compost.

When watering remember less is needed when growth is slower in winter, and if you water by weight it means a weightwatcher's diet through the winter months.

Hydroculture is a special method of growing plants without soil, and with this system all the rules about watering are broken. The plants are grown in sand or heat-expanded clay granules and the pot stands in a constant depth of about 1 in (2.5 cm) of water.

Potting Mixtures

The days when gardeners made up potting composts or mixtures (the two terms are interchangeable but American gardeners usually say mixture or mix) to suit the tastes of each individual plant have long since gone. Most plants simply are not fussy about what they grow in so long as the medium is well drained and the proper nutrients are supplied.

However, many fine-rooted indoor plants prefer a humusy soil, readily made with peat moss or leaf mold. Ferns, begonias, African violets and most foliage plants prefer such a humusy mixture and also do well in the peat moss-based soilless mixtures. These last can be a little light in weight.

Groups of houseplants usually look better than isolated plants.

Adding sand to peat mixes gives extra weight. Sand and peat moss in equal parts is an ideal mix for rooting cuttings. Cacti and many succulents need a sandy growing medium.

While most gardeners prefer to buy packaged potting mixes, either soilless or soil-based, garden soil can be used (see Indoor Sowing, page 15), often "as is", or it can be improved by adding peat moss and/or sand. Soil-based mixtures contain nutrients so feeding is less critical, as is watering. The soilless mixes in plastic pots can become waterlogged.

Plants can be grown without any compost, but this is a special technique known as hydroculture, which was mentioned previously. In this case the sand or granules serve primarily to anchor the plant.

Feeding

It must be remembered that the compost in a small pot cannot contain sufficient food to keep a plant growing healthily for very long — it must be supplemented with a liquid fertilizer.

It is best to use one of the plant foods sold specially for houseplants, as it is much easier to mix small quantities.

It is difficult to give rule-of-thumb instructions on frequency of feeding. First read the instructions carefully on houseplant food containers. Do not exceed the dosage rates and remember that in winter when many plants' growth rate slows and nearly stops, little if any feeding is required.

Plants growing rapidly will need more regular feeding and large plants in small pots may need a dilute liquid feed at very nearly every watering. The response to fertilizer is quite rapid when needed, and with careful observation and experience you will soon get the measure of each plant's needs. Brown tips to the leaves is a common sign of excessive feeding and lack of moisture increases the concentration of plant food to aggravate the situation still further.

Where flowering plants make masses of leaves to the point of covering the flowers, reduce the fertilizer. Very slow growth, and small leaves which are lighter green than normal probably indicates insufficient plant food.

MATCHING PLANT TO PLACE

If a houseplant is positioned in a situation that doesn't suit it, there is bound to be an uphill struggle to keep it healthy. Success is far more certain if you decide the kind of environment you can offer your plants and choose accordingly.

The sections below have been arranged to help you select those plants that will suit the various conditions you may be able to provide.

Plants Which Need Warmth

Many of today's popular houseplants come from subtropical and tropical regions. Introducing these plants to our homes in late spring, summer or early autumn gives them a chance to become acclimatized before the onset of shorter days and colder nights.

Varieties grown for their attractive foiage such as *Begonia rex, Codiaeum* (Croton), *Dieffenbachia, Ficus, Maranta* and *Monstera* are good examples. Flowering kinds include *Aphelandra* (which also has attractive striped leaves), *Columnea,* (African-violet), and *Saintpaulia.*

Ivies can make an interesting collection with their different leaf forms.

Campanula isophylla is a delightful plant if kept in a cool room in good light to prevent it becoming too straggly. There is also a white form, *C.i.* 'Alba'.

Plants to Withstand the Cold

A number of hardy garden plants can be grown indoors in pots. Ivies are the perfect example, with many variegated leaf forms of *Hedera helix,* the small-leaved English ivy, and *Hedera canariensis* the Canary Island ivy. If you have ivies which have become drawn up, woody and leafless at the base they will often recover completely if planted outside.

It will be appreciated that their total hardiness means they will survive indoors when the heating goes off at night in winter. There are several other plants in this category, from aucuba with cream spotted leaves to fatsia, sometimes called aralia.

The bigeneric cross between *Fatsia* and *Hedera,* × *Fatshedera,* makes a good indoor plant. If you really want to have fun, try running a stem of × *Fatshedera* up and then bud ivy on to the top to form an attractive indoor weeping tree.

Flowering shrubs also come into this hardy category with evergreen azalea, camellias, citrus, fuchsias and hydrangeas being good examples.

Where these plants have been forced into early flower with heat, be sure to expose them slowly to the cooler temperatures before returning them to the garden.

Although camellias are quite tough be careful when you bring them indoors. If the air is too hot and too dry there will inevitably be premature flower bud drop. These plants are perfect to bring color into an unheated sun lounge, porch or cold greenhouse in winter or spring.

Easy Plants

If indoor plants have the habit of dying in your care start with the easy-to-grow types first. Ivies, chlorophytums (th spider plant), cissus, *Philodendron scandens,* grape-ivy and tradescantia can be reccommended. All these are not only easy to grow but they are easy to propagate as well — the spider plant from runners, the rest from cuttings. Several will root from soft young shoots placed in a glass of water on a light windowsill.

Plants for a Dry Atmosphere

Central heating and the dry atmosphere in large office blocks and stores requires special plants. Some plants are much beter equipped than others The bromeliads, which include the pineapple, will stand the dry air but require light. Several, like *Neoregelia carolinae* retain a pool of moisture in the central brightly colored vase of leaves. Keep this topped up to keep them happy in dry conditions.

Aechmea, the Greek vase or urn plant, is another bromelaid; it is one of the longest flowering plants and has attractive silver leaves. Other plants which tolerate arid conditions are sansevieria (mother-in-law's tongue), which eventually produces fragrant white flowers, and the almost indestructible aspidistra.

Plants for Wet Soil

As a general rule plants should be allowed to dry out somewhat before watering again, and it is not good practice to leave them standing in saucers of water. There are, however, a few plants which will quite happily stand in water all the time.

These exceptions are baby's tears *(Soleirolia soleirolii)* with its many small green leaves on creeping stems, *Astilbe* and *Cyperus,* commonly called umbrella grass. These will come to no harm if stood in a saucer of water.

Plants for Bottle Gardens

A small sealed world within a bottle can be ideal for some plants. Even if the top is left uncorked the need to water will be much reduced. Plants, especially ferns and the small-leaved ivy and snake-skin fittonia, will thrive even in

Try experimenting with containers. This fittonia is in a wine bottle.

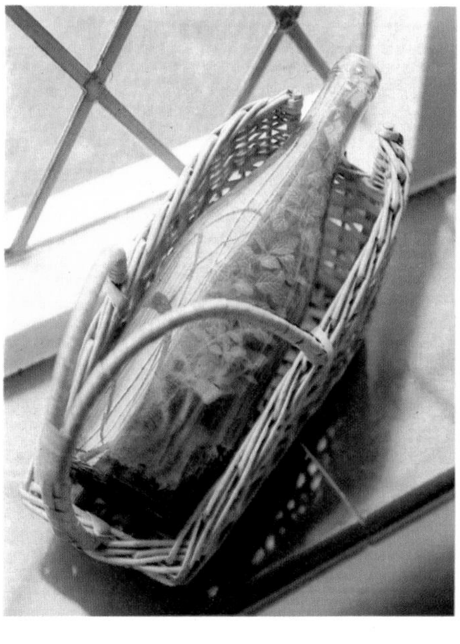

green glass bottles, but remember darker glass means less light.

Avoid placing planted and sealed bottles in full sun in midsummer because this can cause leaf scorch. While flowering plants like saintpaulia, African violet, can be grown in glass jars it is difficult to remove dead flowers which if left start to rot in the humid atmosphere.

Choose a peat-based compost or a weak sterilized loam-based potting compost for bottles. Too rich a compost and too much fertilizer will produce excessive growth which just overfills the container.

See that the compost is just nicely moist and fill into the jar through a paper funnel. Once planted just water round the glass to clean it and dampen the plants down.

Where condensation forms on the inside of the glass remove the stopper and leave the bottle to dry for a few days before resealing. You may need to do this several times before the glass clears.

Use small rooted cuttings and watch them grow like the proverbial ship in a bottle. Goldfish bowls and large brandy glasses also help to provide the humid conditions saintpaulias appreciate. Planted in these it is easy to remove dying flowers.

Other plants suitable for all bottle gardens and terrariums include *Asplenium nidus, Begonia rex, Cryptanthus bivittatus, Ficus pumila,* miniature sinningias and scindapsus.

AN A–Z OF PLANT CARE

Achimines A very free-flowering plant in summer, it requires treatment similar to tuberous begonias and sinningia (gloxinia). Warmth in spring is required to start the tubers into growth, and during the growing season the compost should be kept nicely damp.

The plants are better kept out of strong, hot sunshine, especially as water droplets on the leaves would cause brown spots to appear.

Anthurium The scarlet bract on this plant lasts very well in water if cut. It is difficult to grow conventionally, demanding an open orchid-like potting mixture of fir bark and coarse sphagnum moss.

Aphelandra If you let this plant become dry and wilt the shiny white and green leaves will not come up again. It is grown for the yellow flower bracts as well as for its attractive leaves.

Araucaria (Norfolk Island Pine). This very elegant houseplant is quite easy to grow, being virtually hardy. It will stand some shade and eventually grows 6 ft (2 m) tall.

Azalea These Indian, evergreen azaleas are hardy in mild climates and used in the North for winter color. The tip for watering is to see that a 1 in. (2.5 cm) high damp mark exists up the stem from compost level. No damp mark means the plant needs watering. More than 1 in. (2.5 cm) means the compost is plenty wet enough.

To keep the plant for another year, plunge the pots outside throughout the summer and keep watered, then bring indoors in winter to flower again in a cool room.

Begonia This is a large group of plants. The fibrous-rooted wax begonias are raised from seed and the F_1 hybrids continue to flower the year round.

Plants used outside for summer bedding can be lifted in the autumn before the frost and will continue to flower in pots right through the winter. If outdoor and indoor plants have become rather tall just prune them back to a few inches (5—10 centimeters) above the pot.

The new Reiger types have masses of flowers, either large singles with yellow stamens or double flowers. Scarlet 'Fireglow' is very popular and looks well under artificial light. Use a systemic fungicide to control mildew which is more of a problem where the growing conditions are too cold. Tall plants can be cut back and they will soon grow away again and continue flowering.

Beloperone (Shrimp Plant). Trim this easy-to-grow plant back by half, preferably in late spring or during the summer if the branches get leggy and short of leaves at the base.

Capsicum Easily raised from seed, the plant has colorful fruits in winter.

See that plants are well fed as the fruits swell and color in order to prevent leaf fall.

Chrysanthemum The year-round pot varieties are of little use once they have flowered. Plants bought in flower in spring may flower again in the autumn if planted in the garden but this is very much a gamble. When purchasing flowering plants in winter see that the flowers are fairly well open. In the bright days of summer, plants purchased in bud will last longer.

Cyclamen Light cool conditions and a humid atmosphere are ideal for

This magnificent specimen of the bird's nest fern, *Asplenium nidus,* is growing and thriving in the author's home.

cyclamen. The bathroom and kitchen are often good spots.

If you want to flower the corm a second year, keep watered and fed until May, then place the pot on its side to dry out. In early autumn stand the pot upright and start watering. When new growth starts, a little old compost can be scraped from round the top of the pot and replaced with new. Water and feed as normal and the plant should flower indoors in late winter.

Plants grown the second and subsequent years often prove easier to keep.

Euphorbia (Poinsettia). Where the cyclamen requires cool conditions and leaves yellow and wilt in too much heat, the popular scarlet, pink or white-bracted poinsettia requires warmth. If you keep the plant on a light warm windowsill, and the compost just damp, the colored bracts will stay on the plant for months.

While it is not possible to equal the nurseryman's quality a second year, it is still worth trying to flower them again. Dry the plant in late spring by leaving the pot on its side. In early autumn cut the branches back to 2—3 in. (5—7.5 cm) above the pot. Burn the cuts with a match to stem the loss of white sap. Then water and feed as for other houseplants.

If you keep your specimen out of artificial light red bracts will form again in late winter.

Ferns There are obviously many ferns to grow, but those below are among the most attractive and reliable. True ferns will stand shady sites and some withstand cold.

A well-grown spider plant in a macrame hanger in the author's home.

Asparagus setaceus (asparagus-fern), not a true fern, is raised from seed best sown in April. A very popular and easy houseplant with long trailing stems once well established.

Cyrtomium falcatum, the Japanese holly fern, is one of the toughest ferns to grow, and will withstand drafts and smoke better than most other kinds. Water well in summer, but only sparingly in winter.

Pteris types are easy and very attractive, with divided leaves which are variegated in some species.

Asplenium nidus (bird's nest fern) and *Adiantum* (maidenhair) are better given slightly warmer conditions. Old leaves and leaves on plants subject to checks from cold temperature produce masses of brown spores on the underside in early spring. New leaves soon grow to replace the older ones.

Fuchsia Best grown as a summer flowering plant on terrace or porch. Bud drop is usually caused by a shortage of water. Keep the plants well watered with dilute liquid feed and new flower buds will soon form.

Hibiscus Do not be afraid to prune this indoor flowering shrub back hard in spring. New flowering shoots will soon form.

Hydrangea Plants forced into early flower will survive subsequently in the garden in a mild climate. Do not take forced plants outside until the chance of frost has passed. Some pink varieties produce blue flowers in acid soil.

Palms There are several types suitable for indoors, from the small parlour palm, *Neanthe bella,* to the taller kentias *(Howea forsterana),* and the eventually tree-like *Phoenix canariensis.* All will survive shaded positions but need warmth and a damp compost. Sponge the leaves and see that they get some light, especially in winter.

Pelargonium The zonal pelargonium, commonly called geranium, is a most popular houseplant. Easy to root from cuttings in summer it is best kept a bit on the dry side. Prune long leggy plants back hard in early spring.

Pelargonium ×domesticum is the regal pelargonium, a big showy early summer-flowering plant. Take cuttings of new shoots after the main flush of flower in early summer.

To repot a plant, first knock it out of the old pot and tease out a few roots. Use the old pot as a mold and pack fresh mixture between the two pots. Firm the root-ball, ensuring there are no air pockets, then water thoroughly.

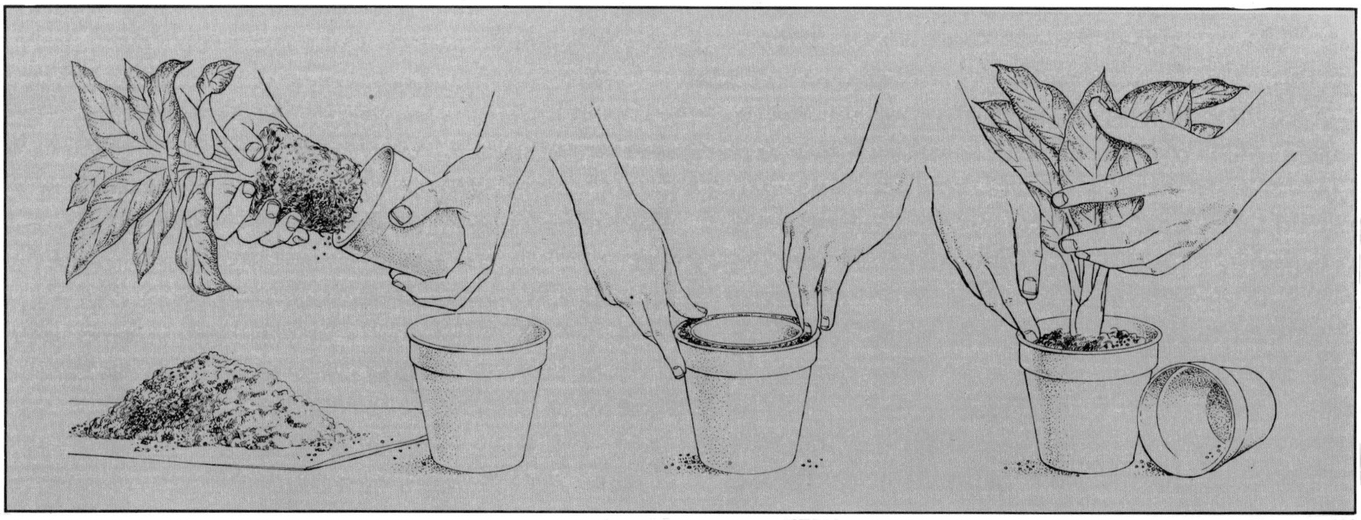

Saintpaulia (African Violet). A very popular plant which grows and flowers well under artificial light. If you have plants which produce plenty of leaves but no flowers, let the compost dry out somewhat for 3—4 weeks. Flower buds will soom form and routine feeding and watering can be continued.

Solanum (Christmas Cherry). An attractive member of the tomato family but definitely *not* edible.

Stephanotis A sweetly scented white-flowering but tender climber. Grow on a trellis or keep in bush form by pinching back trailers.

FLOWERS FROM BULBS

A number of our spring-flowering bulbs grow well in pots and, given a little warmth once well rooted, can be forced into early flower. The secret of success is to pot up early and keep outside and cool until well rooted. Most of the potting composts are suitable or you can use the soil from your garden.

Crocus, hyacinths, *Iris reticulata*, narcissi, snowdrops and tulips need 2—3 in. (5—7.5 cm) shoots above the pot before bringing indoors. I like to leave crocus, iris and snowdrops outside until the flower buds are visible. Give these three bulbs too much heat too soon and they produce all leaves and no flowers.

Amaryllis is a very popular bulb and the large flowers, often coming before the leaves, are very dramatic. Pot up the bulb in any good potting compost, then give bottom warmth of about 68°F (20°C), a good place being over a radiator or hot water tank.

Once growth starts the temperature can be lowered to 55—60°F (13—15°C) and the plant can be moved to a light windowsill.

After flowering keep watering and feed occasionally to build up the bulb. Although the bulbs can be kept growing I like to put the pot on its side in late summer to dry the plant off. Start into growth again in winter. Do not be in a hurry to repot: once every three years is usually sufficient. Root-bound plants flower well given a liquid feed in spring.

Cacti and succulents are popular, trouble-free plants. They usually look best grouped together in the home.

Crocus look best indoors if special crocus bowls are used for planting.

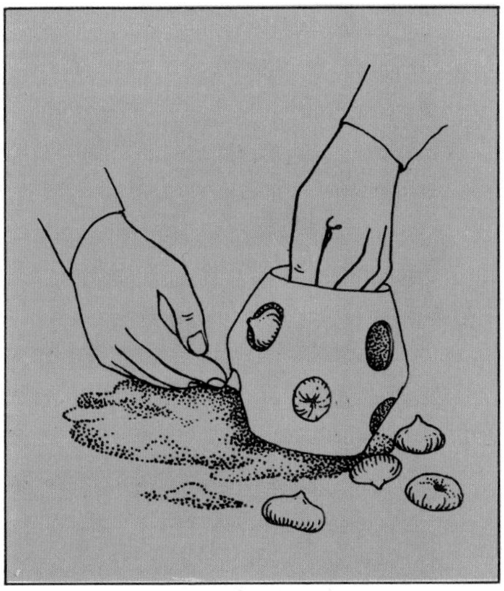

Cacti and succulents

This group of plants is said to be popular the world over, perhaps because the true cacti do manage pretty well on neglect. Most will stand the cold of winter indoors as long as compost and air are dry.

Water in spring and they swell up, flower and grow at an alarming rate. Quite modest rooting, they do not need repeated repotting and grow satisfactorily in pots seemingly too small.

Succulents need treatment more akin to general houseplant care but drying off a little helps flower bud formation.

Very popular are the jungle or leaf cacti — Easter cactus (*Rhipsalidopsis gaertneri*), the crabclaw or Thanksgiving cactus (*Schlumbergera* ×*buckleyi*) and Christmas cactus (*S. trucata*).

Getting the last two to flower around the holidays can be a problem. However, if the plants are summered outdoors in part shade, watered as needed, then in the fall given short day treatment with no artificial light at night, buds should form. Keeping the plants cool through autumn also helps induce flowering. After flowering, rest the plants for a month or so by easing off on water.

PROPAGATION

The majority of indoor ornamental plants can be raised from either seed or soft tip cuttings. The methods used for this are identical to all indoor seed and softwood cutting raising, from vegetable and bedding plants to shrubby subjects. Even cacti can easily be raised from seed if sown fresh, ideally within two years of gathering.

Aerial layering

Extra-large houseplants like *Ficus elastica*, (the rubber plant) and *Monstera deliciosa*, (the swiss cheese plant) can be propagated by an aerial layer. Here the top 9—15 in. (23—38 cm) is rooted on specimens which have outgrown the space available for them. There is the added bonus that once the top has been

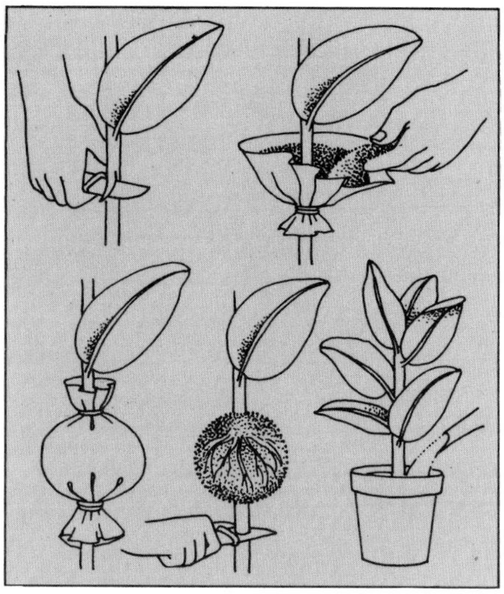

The rubber plant is suitable for aerial layering. The method is described below.

taken out, the original plant will often shoot out below the cut to produce new branches.

Choose the warm months of the year when plants are growing well and there is good light for aerial layering. Select a clean piece of stem and make a slanting cut about 2 in. (5 cm) long up the stem and a little less then half way through. Tuck damp sphagnum moss or peat moss into and around the cut. Hold this in place with a sheet of plastic.

Cutting the base of a plastic bag open and slipping the tube over the plant is the easy way to wrap the cut. Tie the bottom of the tube around the stem of the plant, put the moss in place and then secure the plastic tube at the top, twisting and wrapping to hold the rooting medium in place.

Once roots are well formed the rooted tip can be cut right off and potted up into potting compost, but keep the leaves well syringed for several days. It is advisable to keep the potted cutting out of hot sun and covered with a plastic bag for several days until well established.

Milky sap will flow from the cut rubber plant stem but this will dry and seal in time.

Leaf and Stem Cuttings

The beginner to indoor gardening can start propagating by placing the young growing tips of plants like coleus, fuchsia, grape ivy and tradescantia in a glass with 1 in. (2.5 cm) of water. The shoots should be 2—3 in. (5—7.5 cm) long. If placed on a light, warm windowsill roots will soon form and the rooted cuttings can then be potted up singly.

If you require a greater challenge then mature leaves with 1—2 in. (2.5—5 cm) of sound stem taken from an African violet will root in damp peat. Warmth and covering with a plastic bag will speed rooting. It is advisable to remove the bag for half an hour or so each day to let the rather hairy leaf dry off and reduce the chance of soft rots causing damage.

Even more skill is needed to root the 1 in. (2.5 cm) square sections cut from leaves of *Begonia rex* and the 1 in. (2.5 cm) wide sections of sansevieria and streptocarpus leaves. Lay the begonia pieces like postage stamps flat on the compost and the streptocarpus end up slightly in the compost for best results. Light, warmth and humidity are all that are required to grow new plants from such small pieces of plant.

Pips, Stones and Tops to Grow

Try growing indoor plants from citrus pips, date stones, avocado pear seed, fresh peanuts and even pineapple tops. While it is possible to get the peanuts to produce a few nuts, and after several years 3 ft (1 m) wide pineapple plants will fruit, the chances of other plants cropping is remote.

Where the citrus are kept in small pots and the roots restricted, some seedlings will flower and very occasionally plants will set fruit.

All these plants need plenty of warmth to get them growing. Once roots start to form they can be moved to a light warm windowsill and treated like other houseplants.

An easy way with pineapple is to take a fresh fruit with all the leafy top intact and just snap the top out. Remove a few smaller lower leaves and place the top in a jamjar. The base of the leafy shoot

Orange and lemon trees are easily grown from pips, kept in a warm place.

must be just covered with water. If placed over a radiator or boiler for warmth, roots soon form and the top can then be potted up and grown on.

Mature plants can be encouraged to flower by placing them close to ripe fruit. The ethylene gas given off by all ripe and rotting fruits, for instance apples, speeds the formation of the pineapple fruit spike.

Roots and Tubers

Begonias and gloxinias grown from tubers, and the swollen roots of climbing lily — *Gloriosa rothschildiana* - and caladium, need plenty of warmth to start them into growth. I like to place these in damp peat in a plastic bag in a very warm place but not in full sunshine, then pot them up once shoots and roots start to form.

Division

A few plants like the aspidistra and sansevieria can be propagated by division. It is best to wait until the mother plant is well grown and the pot full of roots before cutting off a shoot with roots from the outside edge.

PRUNING

Many houseplants need no pruning, but the more rampant growers will need the tips pinched out and branches cut back to restrict their size and encourage long spindly stems to branch out.

All the young ivies, cissus and rhoicissus, for example, are better with the growing tips pinched out to produce more bushy specimens. Where these growing tips are 2—3 in. (5—7.5 cm) long they can be used as cuttings to produce more plants.

Woody plants like hibiscus and hydrangea can be pruned back hard in spring — the hydrangea after flowering — and strong new growths will develop from the stump. Azalea, on the other hand, needs no more than a very gentle trim after flowering to retain shape.

Yellowing and browning leaves are best removed. In the case of cyclamen and similar succulent plants be sure to remove the leaf stalk cleanly. Old pieces of stalk can rot back and damage the whole plant.

Cyclamen leaves are cleanly removed by rolling leaf stem between finger and thumb through 180° and then plucking it away from the corm.

Miniaturized trees, usually called bonsai — which translated from the Japanese means tray-grown — can be kept small by pruning the roots. Once tree seedlings are established in pots the old, gnarled appearance is obtained by root restriction.

Keeping the plant rootbound in a small container, and twisting and shaping the young branches achieves the aged look. The branches can be wired to hold the desired branch shape until the wood hardens and stays in position naturally.

Cleaning

All plants grow better and look more attractive with clean leaves. Regular syringing with water keeps plants fresh and helps wash off dust. Occasionally, however, it is necessary to wipe all shiny leaves over with a damp cloth. A rather tedious job with small-leaved ivies but well worth the effort.

Extra shine can be brought to glossy leaves either by sponging over with milk and water or spraying with proprietary leaf-shine oils. Give this cosmetic treatment very occasionaly to prevent the leaf shine materials building up on the leaf too much.

PESTS AND DISEASES

The best way to limit pest and disease problems is a strong, healthy plant. Ailing specimens are the first to become infected.

Aphids are everywhere and sooner or later every home is likely to attract this pest. There are many sprays that can be used to control all aphids; and the systemic kinds which are taken up in the plant sap and remain effective for several weeks are best.

Cyclamen mites, too minute for the naked eye, cause distorted foliage and crown growth of African violets cyclamen, fuchsias, etc. Dip in or spray with Kelthane.

Insecticides based on resmethrin are quick-acting and safe to use in the home. This chemical will also control *whitefly* if four sprays at three-day intervals are given. If whiteflies are sprayed just once, more eggs hatch and quickly reinfest the plant. Fuchsias, impatiens and pelargoniums are all very susceptible to whitefly. Cineraria and calceolaria attract aphids.

Hot, dry conditions are ideal for *red spider* to increase. The symptoms are yellowish-bronzed leaves. Severe attacks have cobwebbing over the leaves and myriads of the tiny red mites. A moist atmosphere, which means syringing regularly with water, reduces the chance of attack. Rotenone sprays will help control, although badly infested plants are difficult to clean even with

Leaves yellowing and falling prematurely can be due to too much or too little water. Brown leaf edges are often caused by too much fertilizer or lack of humidity.

diazinon and systemic insecticides. Ivies, roses and crotons are susceptible to red spider attack in hot, dry conditions.

Mealy bugs, insects rather like tiny woodlice covered with waxy-white hair, occur on cacti and a number of houseplants. These are best removed with Q Tips or cotton from the medicine chest on the end of a match dipped in either alcohol or dilute malathion.

Scale is a small brown or grayish brown limpet-like creature found on the undersides of leaves, usually against the mid-rib and under branches close to the main stem. It can be removed with the point of a knife and controlled by spraying with malathion and systemic insecticides.

Two diseases — the soft brown rot caused by botrytis and the white felty growth of mildew — are the most likely to be encountered indoors. Systemic fungicides containing benomyl will give control on many plants. Begonias are especially susceptible to mildew.

Be sure to read the instructions carefully on all proprietary chemicals. Some plants are damaged by certain materials, ferns being especially susceptible to burn from malathion.

When applying dilute sprays to remove scale and mealy bug, wear rubber gloves, and with obnoxious-smelling insecticides take the plant outside to spray. Better control will often be achieved where the plant is placed inside a large plastic bag during spraying. The plant should be kept sealed in the bag for a few hours to achieve a complete kill.

Keep sprayed plants out of hot sunshine for a few hours.

YOUR GUIDE TO HOUSEPLANTS

Name		Recommended Min Temp indoors	Flowering Period	Description	Cultural Tips
Achimenes	M	18°C (65°F)	June–Oct.	Upright or trailing plants with purple pink or white flowers.	Keep in a light place, but shade from hot sun. Needs warmth and humidity. Likes a peat compost.
Adiantum Maidenhair Fern	M	10°C (50°F)		Delicate soft green fronds on wiry stems.	Requires atmospheric moisture. Keep on pebbles in water-filled trays.
Ananas Pineapple	M	18°C (65°F)	Fruits late summer	Grown for their attractive, strap-like foliage.	A light position is required. Spray leaves with water occasionally.
Anthurium Flamingo Flower	D	10°C (50°F)	Most of the year	Unusual red flowers rather like an opened-up arum.	Grows best in all-peat compost. Surround pot with damp peat.
Aphelandra Zebra Plant	M	13°C (55°F)	July–Sept.	The green leaves are boldly striped with white. Flowers yellow.	Warmth and evenly moist, not wet, compost are important. Once leaves wilt they they stay down.
Araucaria Norfolk Island Pine	E	5°C (41°F)		An easy houseplant, with pine-like branches	Will withstand some shade, and most room conditions.
Aspidistra Cast Iron Plant	E	10°C (50°F)		A tough foliage plant. There is a cream and green variety.	Will tolerate shade and a dry air, but best in light shade.
Asparagus Asparagus Fern	E	7°C (45°F)		These ferns have dainty foliage. Easy to grow.	Will tolerate shade. Needs plenty of water; regular feeding helps.
Asplenium Birds Nest Fern	M	13°C (55°F)		Rich green blade-like leaves that grow in a rosette.	Requires a light position out of direct sunshine. Use a peat compost.
Azalea Evergreen Azalea	M	13°C (55°F)	Nov.–April (forced)	Popular gift plants. Very floriferous.	Keep in a light position and always well watered. Needs humusy, acid soil.
Begonia Rhizomatous	M	15°C (60°F)		Most popular are the *B. rex* and Iron Cross foliage begonias.	A light position out of direct sunshine is required.
Tuberous	M	15°C (60°F)	Summer	Large camellia-like flowers. There are trailing kinds with smaller flowers.	A temperature of 21°C (70°F) is required to start the tubers. Remove single female flowers.
Fibrous	E	18°C (65°F)	May–Jan.	Often used for bedding, but are also excellent pot plants.	An occasional liquid feed keeps them growing vigorously. Do not overwater.
Beloperone Shrimp Plant	E	7°C (45°F)	March–Nov.	Pinky-orange shrimp-shaped flowers over a long period.	Thrives on a sunny windowsill. Cut back straggly plants in spring.
Calceolaria Slipper Flower	M	7°C (45°F)	Feb.–May	Soft velvety pouched flowers, in red, yellow or orange.	Avoid high temperatures. Give a position on a light windowsill. Buy flowering plants, then discard.
Camellia	M	5°C (41°F)	Jan.–April	Exotic waxy flowers, in shades of red, white and pink.	Plunge pots outdoors during the summer in part shade. Keep well watered indoors.
Campanula isophylla Star of Bethlehem	M	10°C (50°F)	July–Oct.	A plant of trailing habit, with masses of pretty blue or white flowers.	Pinch out growing tips in spring to produce compact plants. Root soft green shoots.
Capsicum Pepper	M	10°C (50°F)		Grown for attractive winter yellow to purple fruits.	Keep well fed and moist. Discard once fruits shrivel.
Chamaedorea Parlor Palm	M	13°C (55°F)		A small palm, growing to 3 ft (1 m).	Best in indirect light. Sponge leaves occasionally with water.
Chlorophytum Spider Plant	E	7°C (45°F)		Long narrow leaves and plantlets produced on the ends of stems.	Grows best with good light and with plenty of water.
Chrysanthemum	E	10°C (50°F)	All year	Well-known dwarfed versions of the garden chrysanthemum.	A light position and cool temperature will keep them flowering.
Cissus Kangaroo Vine	E	7°C (45°F)		A climber with glossy green leaves.	Will survive in subdued light but grows better in good light.
Codiaeum Croton	D	15°C (60°F)		Foliage plants, usually with red, yellow, orange and green variegation.	Avoid fluctuating temperatures. Keep in good light. Syringe in summer.
Coleus Flame Nettle	M	15°C (60°F)		Popular foliage plants, with leaves in many varied colors.	Good light is needed for well-balanced growth.
Cryptanthus Earth Star	M	13°C (55°F)		A star-shaped rosette of variegated leaves.	Very easy to grow. Keep on dry side in winter.
Cyperus Umbrella Grass	M	13°C (55°F)		Grass-like leaves arranged like umbrella spokes on a long stalk.	Place in good light and keep constantly moist.
Cyclamen	M	10°C (50°F)	Aug.–May	Well-known flowering pot plants popular as gifts.	Needs a steady cool temperature and water supply and light position.
Dieffenbachia Dumb Cane	M/D	13°C (55°F)		Striking foliage plants with variegated leaves, usually cream and green.	Feed monthly through summer. Keep out of direct sun in summer but place in light position in winter.
Dracaena Dragon Plant	D	13°C (55°F)		Variegated strap-like leaves.	A light position is required for strong leaf color. Feed every two weeks in summer.
Episcia Flame-violet	M	18°C (65°F)	Spr.–Fall	White, pink, red flowers and handsome foliage	Needs humusy soil, good light. Relative of saintpaulia.

Name		Recommended Min Temp indoors	Flowering Period	Description	Cultural Tips
Eurphorbia pulcherrima Poinsettia	M	13°C (55°)	Nov.–Feb.	Bright red bracts, though there are pink and white forms.	Keep moist but not over-wet, and keep in a light position
X Fatshedera	E	4°C (40°F)		Glossy hand-shaped green leaves. Perfect foliage for a cool situation.	Will thrive in light or more shaded conditions. Plants that have grown too tall can be cut back in March.
Ficus Rubber Plant	E/M	15°C (60°F)		Besides *F. elastica,* there are species with foliage of different shape.	Variegated kinds need good light, but not direct summer sun.
Grevillea Silk Oak	M	7°C (45°F)		Feathery light green foliage.	Keep well watered while growing actively. Provide light conditions.
Hedera Ivy	E	2°C (35°F)		Besides the common ivy, there are kinds with attractively shaped and variegated foliage.	Will grow well in shade, but variegated kinds need brighter conditions.
Hippeastrum Amaryllis	E	13°C (55°F)	Dec.–Aug.	Massive, spectacular flowers, carried on a strong stem.	A bottom heat of 21°C (70°F) advisable to start growth.
Kalanchoe	E	5°C (41°F)	Feb.–March	Heads of small bright red flowers, contrasting against glossy green foliage.	Feed occasionally. Best stood outdoors for the summer, but do not allow to dry out.
Maranta Prayer Plant	M	15°C (60°F)		Striking, variegated leaves, those of *M. leuconeura* folding together at night.	Keep in quite shady conditions. A moist atmosphere is required.
Monstera Swiss Cheese Plant	M	13°C (55°F)		Large shiny green foliage; big holes and gashes develop in older leaves.	Direct aerial roots into the compost or moss-wrapped supporting stakes. to improve growth
Peperomia	M	13°C (55°F)		Compact houseplants with a variety of leaf shapes, forms, and textures.	Moist, warm conditions are best. Position in good light but out of direct summer sun.
Philodendron	M	13°C (55°F)		A group of foliage plants with a variety of interesting leaf shapes.	Sponge leaves occasionally. Climbing forms should have a piece of cork bark or a moss-filled cylinder to take the aerial roots.
Pilea cadierei Aluminium Plant	E	10°C (50°F)		Green leaves with silvery markings.	Kept moist this is one of the easiest plants to grow.
Platycerium Stag's-horn Fern	M	10°C (50°F)		A most dramatic fern, with broad forked leaves shaped like a stag's horn.	Grows well in a peat-based compost Syringe or sponge occasionally. Keep atmosphere moist.
Primula	E	7°C (45°F)	Jan.–May	Pretty spring-flowering plants, the popular species being *P. obconica* and *P. malacoides.*	Keep damp at all times. It is best in cool conditions. Buy blooming plants, then discard.
Rhipsalidopsis Easter Cactus	M	10°C (50°F)	April–May	A 'leaf cactus' with leaf-like stems and bright red or pink flowers.	Put outside during the summer. Commence watering when the red buds are seen at the stem tips.
Saintpaulia African Violet	M/D	13°C (55°F)	Almost year round	Profusion of flowers carried over neat, hairy leaves for a long period.	Warmth and a light position are both important. While the plants are flowering keep compost nicely moist.
Sansevieria Mother-in-law's Tongue	E	10°C (50°F)	Very occasionally	Large, variegated tongue-like leaves.	Best in full sun. Be careful not to overwater in winter.
Saxifraga stolonifera Mother of Thousands	E	7°C (45°F)		Small variegated rounded leaves, and tiny plantlets produced on runners.	Keep well watered throughout the year. Place in good light out of direct summer sunshine. Feed occasionally.
Schlumbergera Thanskgiving and Christmas Cacti	M			"Leaf" cacti similar to Easter cactus but bloom in winter. Showy red flowers.	Summer outdoors in part shade. Short-day plants so keep from artificial light in fall to force flowers by holidays. Reduce water after flowering.
Senecio cruentus Cineraria	M	7°C (45°F)	Dec.–May	Daisy-like flowers in a wide range of colors. A valuable winter-flowering plant.	A light, cool position is required. Water carefully. Buy flowering plants, then discard.
Sinningia Gloxinia	M	18°C (65°F)	June–Sept.	Large trumpet-shaped flowers and thick velvety leaves.	A temperature of 21°C (70°F) is required to start the tubers. Use an all-peat compost.
Solanum Winter Cherry	E	7°C (45°F)		Bright red berries in December and January.	Spray flowers with water to help set the fruit. Once set, feed biweekly.
Tradescantia	M	7°C (45°F)		Popular foliage plants, with striped leaves	Pinch out all green shoots to preserve variegation. Provide a light position.
Vriesia Flaming Sword	D	13°C (55°F)	May–July	Attractive banded leaves and long-lasting red bracts.	Use an all-peat compost and water freely in summer. Need warm damp atmosphere.
Zebrina	M	13°C (55°F)		Trailing plant with silver. purple and green leaves.	Keep pinched back to avoid straggly plants. Feed biweekly during summer months.

Key E easy to grow
M medium-difficult to grow
D demanding to grow

Roses

Modern roses provide one of the cheapest and easiest forms of flower gardening. Even where space is limited, there are dwarf kinds and miniatures to be grown and enjoyed. And vigorous young plants set out carefully will give from 20 to 50 years of flowering in moderate climates.

While to the purist roses are best seen on their own, quite satisfactory plant partnerships can be made. Planting daffodil bulbs among the stronger-growing yellow bush roses works well. Many yellow roses have fresh green leaves which go nicely with the daffodil flowers, and as they go by, the rose foliage covers the drying bulb leaves. Bright red tulips contrast with the copper shoots of many red roses.

Shrub roses and climbers supported by poles can be planted among other shrubs to very good effect.

TYPES OF ROSES

Although there are thousands of different varieties of roses, they can be easily classified into five main groups: hybrid tea and grandiflora; floribunda; miniature; climber; and shrub roses.

The first three groups above can be budded or grafted on to a tall single stem to produce a standard, or what Americans quite aptly call a tree rose. Where you need to bring added height to a bed or to displays of roses, then standards fill the bill.

Weeping standard roses are produced by budding rambler varieties on to tall stems.

Hybrid Tea and Grandiflora Roses

Most popular of all are the bush hybrid tea roses, which have large shapely flowers borne either singly or in twos and threes on a long single stem. Keen rosarians growing for exhibition and flower arrangers growing blooms to cut will disbud (remove any smaller buds below the one main flower) to get perfect single flowers.

The best-known hybrid tea is 'Peace', a large yellow, edged pink, with rich dark, glossy green leaves. Popular for many years, it is now being superseded by less spreading bushes like the rich yellow 'King's Ransom'. When we think of roses we usually have fragrant red varieties in mind and 'Alec's Red', 'Ernest H. Morse' and 'Fragrant Cloud' are popular in this category.

Vigor of growth, disease resistance and number of flowers are being increased with the continual introduction of new varieties, and the white 'Pascali' is a good indication of these developments. Unusual colors from near brown to the silver-lilac and fragrant 'Blue Moon' add to the variety.

A fairly recent class of roses is the grandiflora, a class that combines characteristics of hybrid teas in flower form and of floribunda in the number of flowers to a stem. Grandifloras tend to grow tall and are very vigorous. The best-known variety is the tall, rich pink 'Queen Elizabeth'.

There are roses which grow from 12 in. (30 cm) to several meters high. Some vigorous climbing roses such as 'New Dawn' grow 15 - 20 ft (4 - 6 m) in height and spread. Others like 'Golden Showers' make nice 6 ft (2 m) high pillars of growth.

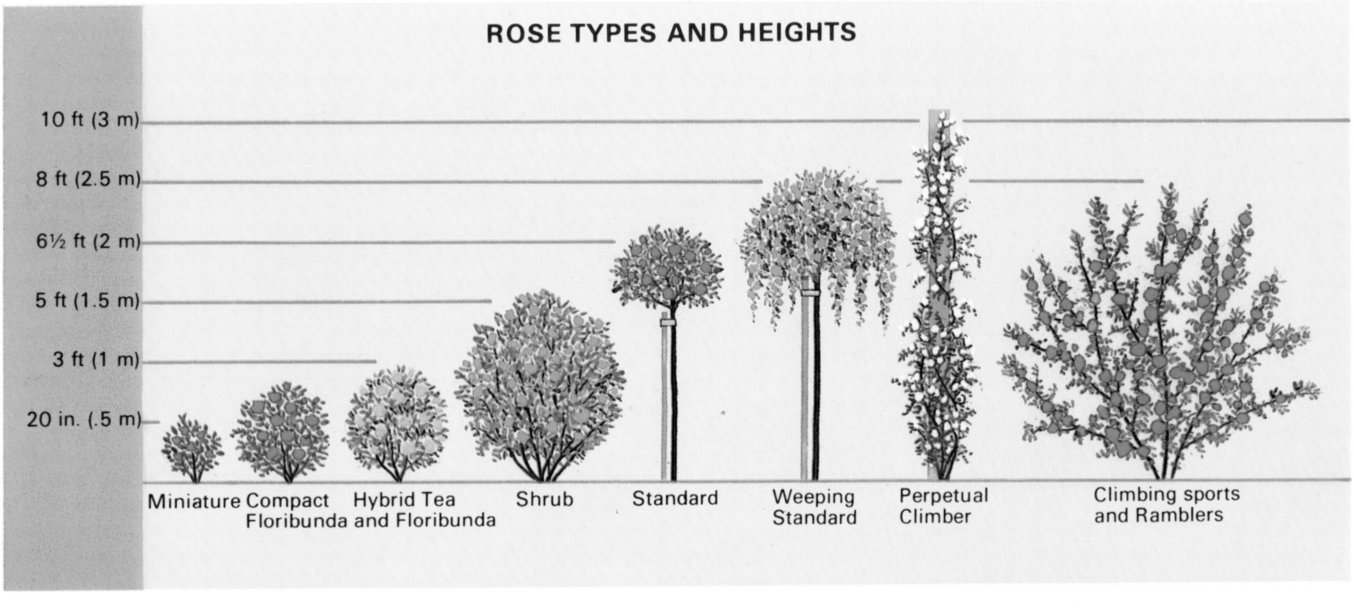

Prune the occasional old branch right out at the base of climbing roses.

Floribunda and Polyantha Roses

Where a mass of color rather than single bloom quality is the requirement, then the floribunda varieties should be chosen. Sometimes we come across the name polyantha rose within the group and this refers to small rounded flowers of polyantha pompons (these were the forerunners of hybrid polyanthas and then the modern floribunda hybrids).

Large single hybrid tea blooms remain popular in gardens and for cutting.

It was the famous rose breeder Poulsen of Denmark who introduced the hybrid tea-polyantha rose cross in 1924 to bring us the modern floribundas of today. Two polyantha roses still widely planted are 'The Fairy' and 'Margo Koster'.

Good examples of varieties with shapely flower buds massed on a strong stem are the white 'Iceberg', the scented 'Apricot Nectar', and the vivid red-gold 'Charisma'. Colors, flower shape and plant habit are continually changed by the introduction of new varieties, yet the two-tone pink-red single-flower floribundas like 'Betty Prior' remain popular.

The majority of varieties in these two groups will grow 2—3 ft (60—90 cm) and more high, the taller growth occurring in mild regions.

Miniatures

Even smaller are the true miniature rose, growing eventually to 10—15 in. (25—38 cm) high. Purchasing these can be somewhat confusing because plants of the same variety grown from rooted cuttings are smaller and take longer to reach their ultimate size than bushes which have been propagated by grafting or budding the variety on to a more vigorous rootstock.

Today we have varieties with very neat, shapely flowers in great profusion in a good range of color. Some of the most popular kinds include orange-red 'Starina' 'Gold Coin', coral-pink 'Chipper, white 'Cinderella' and red 'Red Imp'.

Climbers and Ramblers

There are three divisions within this group although once again the dividing lines are merged by continual crosses made by plant breeders.

Ramblers, as a general rule, have long arching branches which are smothered with clusters of small single and semi-double flowers in early summer. One terrific flush of color and they are finished. A typical rambler is the old 'Dorothy Perkins' which produces an abundance of pink flowers in late spring. The pale pink 'New Dawn' is more perpetual flowering than other varieties and has larger flowers.

It is the continuous flowering habit we seek, and modern climbing roses will flower from early summer to the frost. Many climbers used in the past were sports (a sudden freak growth from H.T. and floribunda varieties)

Miniature roses are ideal for raised beds and windowboxes.

Modern floribundas, such as 'Orange Sensation' generate a mass of color.

Shrub roses are at their best in June and July. They blend well into a mixed border of other shrubs and herbaceous plants.

spotted by nurserymen and reproduced by budding.

Climbing sports of vigorous varieties like 'Peace' flower well in June and once established flower again in fall. The climbing form of the rich copper 'Mrs Sam McGredy' is more vigorous than its bush form and performs well in the garden.

Generally speaking, however, the modern truly perpetual flowering climbers are best in today's gardens. Masses of beautiful flowers are produced by 'Red Fountain', scarlet; 'Golden Showers', pale gold; 'Rhonda', pink; 'Handel', a cream and pink; and salmon-pink 'America'.

A special note should be made of the well-proved 'Blaze', with its many clusters of large double scarlet flowers, slightly fragrant. It grows very well on walls and is vigorous and trouble-free.

Shrub Roses

Once again two clear divisions can be seen — the true species roses with Latin names, and the modern shrub roses with more ordinary names. Most of these roses need room and are at their flowering best at early summer.

Rosa moyesii reaches over $6^1/_2$ ft (2 m) and is grown for the early blood-red flowers and large orange-red hips. *Rosa rubrifolia* has pale pink flowers and red hips but its great beauty is the blue-gray over rich copper foliage. It needs pruning back regularly to get the best leaf color on new growth. *Rosa* 'Frau Dagmar Hastrup' is often seen along the German main roads and as a dense ground cover planting in Holland. It has large single carmine-pink flowers followed by masses of scarlet hips.

The old cottage garden feel can be brought to your shrub border with the sweetbrier rose, *Rosa rubiginosa,* with scented leaves, yellow *Rosa* 'Fruhlingsgold', and repeat-flowering white *Rosa* 'Nevada'.

Alternatives to Formal Beds

While the formal rose beds with bush and standard forms are most popular, there are many alternatives. Miniature roses are fine grown on the windowsill in pots, in windowboxes, troughs and tubs, as well as in the open garden.

The more vigorous ramblers and climbers are attractive sprawling up through old trees, over tree stumps, trellis and unsightly sheds and garages, walls and fences. Perpetual-flowering climbers are best up poles and over pergolas, especially when mixed with large-flowering clematis. They are ideal to train against walls and the stronger growing kinds can be widely spaced and trained horizontally on wires to form a low hedge or boundary.

A large well-grown standard rose can become quite a feature in small gardens where there is no space for trees.

Shrub roses will produce a good screen with the more fiercely thorned keeping out unwanted trespassers. Tall upright varieties of roses like 'Queen Elizabeth' make good informal hedges and screens.

Site and Soil

Roses grow well in very nearly every garden. On very light sandy soils, on limestone or alkaline ones and on heavy clay, the incorporation of well-rotted compost and peat moss in quantity will considerably increase growth.

A few rose diseases such as crown gall can persist in the soil and attack a new rose unless the soil is treated with a fumigant. Or where an ailing rose in a group needs replacing introduce some fresh soil to the planting area. Any other plant will follow roses without any problem, so soil can be exchanged with another part of the garden, such as the vegetable plot, where a rose replant is unavoidable.

Where the planting site is very heavily overshadowed by trees rose growth will be drawn and thin. It is best to use shade-tolerant ground covers in such situations.

On most garden soils digging the area over to one full spade's depth and mixing in organic material as you go will be sufficient for 20 to 30 years' strong growth. If you want the very best roses, try to dig some peat and compost into the sub-soil. Where the sub-soil is very heavy clay, be sure to leave this in position, just improve it

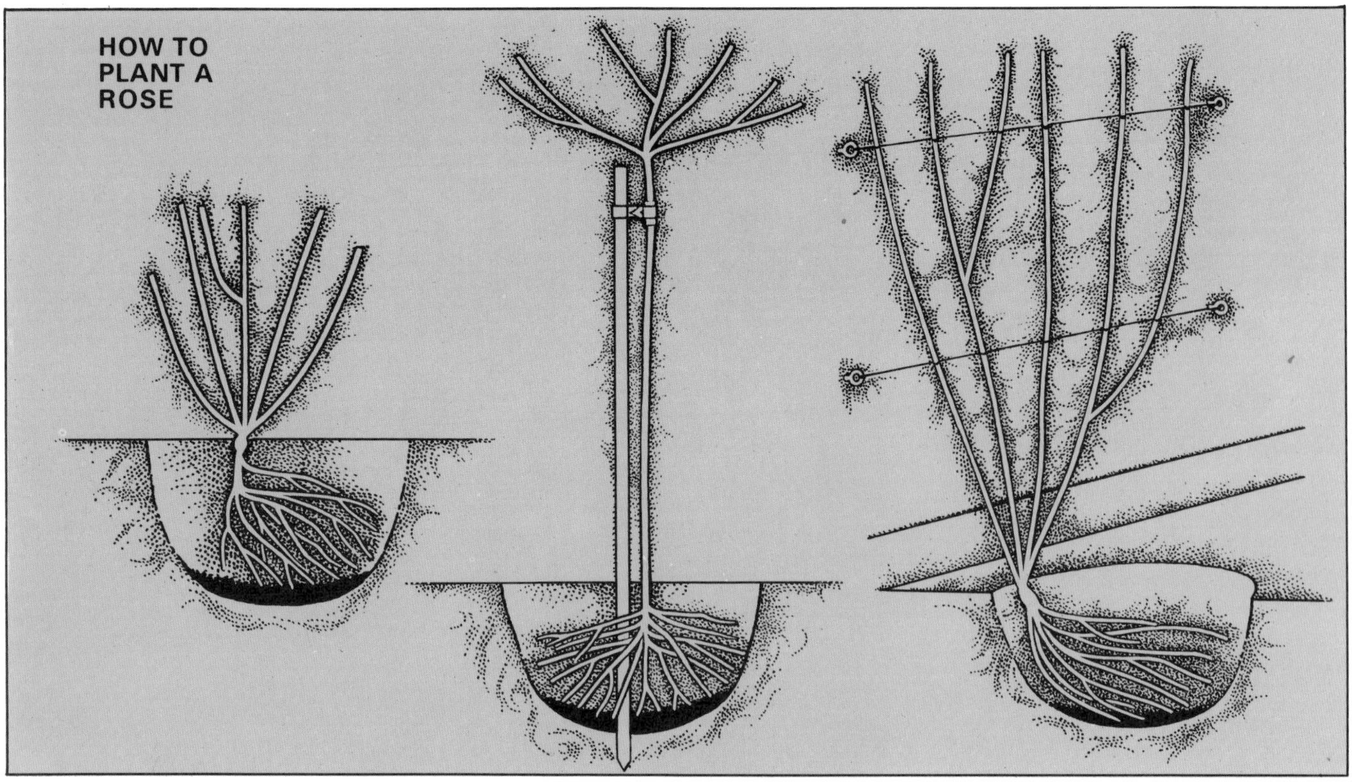

Plant with the rounded, swollen part of stem just below or at soil level. Secure the *top* of a standard rose to a stout stake. Some form of wire support will be needed to train climbing roses against walls or fences.

somewhat by adding plenty of organic material.

It is advisable to cultivate two spades' depth against walls before planting climbers. See that plenty of water-retaining organic matter is worked into the lower soil to provide moisture in summer. Climbers against walls which are dry at the roots become susceptible to mildew and red spiders.

I prefer planting in groups of one variety for the best effect. Where different varieties are mixed be sure to arrange the taller and stronger growing types either to the center or back of the group. The spacing between plants will depend on the type and vigor of the variety.

Pot-grown roses can be planted at any time except winter in the North. Be especially careful when transplanting freshly potted container roses in spring. For these, it is best to cut the base off the container, place in position and then cut off the container side, filling in with soil as you go to keep root disturbance to a minimum.

Plants well rooted in the container and growing strongly are sure to take hold quickly. All containers need watering well before planting. Equally, "bare root" roses which can be planted in frost-free soil any time from October to March inclusive need damp roots when being planted.

Where roses arrive with roots looking dry, soak the root and up the stem as far as is practical in water for an hour or two before planting. Very shrivelled rose bushes can often be plumped up again by totally burying in the soil for a week or two.

Should "bare root" bushes be delivered before you are ready to plant and when soil conditions are too wet or too frosty, either pack damp peat round the roots or dig a trench and bury the roots in soil until everything is ready.

MINIMUM PLANTING DISTANCES BETWEEN PLANTS

Miniature Roses	1 ft*
Hybrid Tea Bush Roses	2-4 ft
Floribunda Bush Roses	2-2½ ft
Grandiflora Bush Roses	2-4 ft
Low Growing Shrub Roses	3 ft
Standard Roses	3-4½ ft
Weeping Standard Roses	4½-6 ft
Strong Growing Shrub Roses	6 ft
Perpetual Climbing	8 ft
Climbing Sports and Ramblers	10 ft

Bush roses should not be planted closer than ½ their planting distance from the edge of bed or border. Greater planting distances apply to mild climates.
* *1 ft* = 0.3 m

Prune off any damaged roots when planting, and with "bare root" bushes I like to reduce the top growth down to 12—15 in. (30—38 cm). Full pruning can then be undertaken later.

While it is not to be generally recommended, bush roses will often survive lifting and transplanting outside the recommended season. It is, of course, necessary to cut off all flowers and buds and keep the plants well watered. Very good establishment will also come from transplanting in late September, stripping off all leaves and cutting the bushes back by at least one-third. New roots are made before winter and the plants grow away very strongly the following spring.

PRUNING

While heated discussion continues on the best time to prune roses, experience has taught me a simple code which works. The once-flowering ramblers are best with old, flowered wood removed in summer after flowering. Shrub roses can be given similar treatment, although the cutting need not generally be so harsh. The perpetual-flowering shrub roses need only careful thinning in spring.

All other roses need pruning in early spring as buds swell. The only qualification to this is reducing the top growth of bush and standard roses by

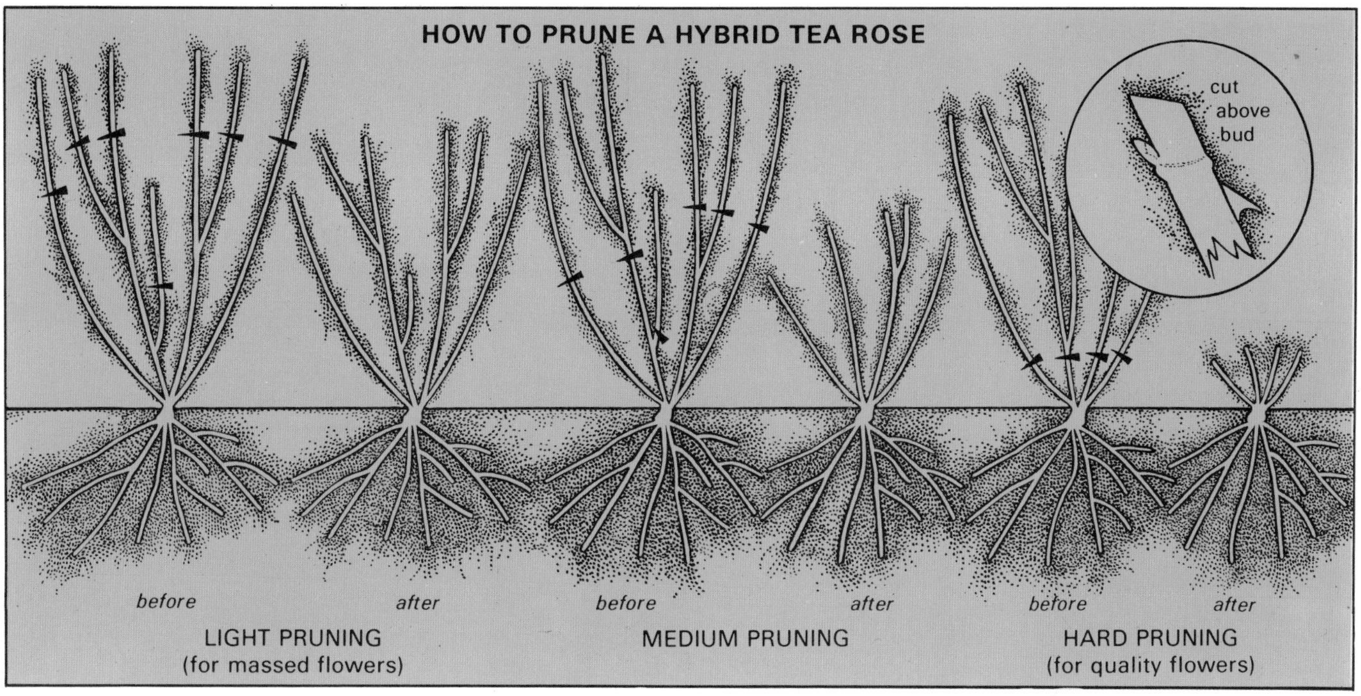

up to one-third in the late autumn to reduce resistance to strong winter winds. If all the top is left on, the plants rock in high winds and this opens a hole in the soil round the base of each plant. This hole can fill with water, and the waterlogged conditions can damage roots, in an extreme case killing the plant.

The early spring pruning is one of the most important and one of the easiest and most satisfying of cultural operations. You can certainly see where the job has been done and it gives a really tidy appearance to the garden. New growth and flowers are so much better as a result of the pruning.

Taking the job in stages, the autumn cut-back coupled with a complete rake up and removal of leaves does much to reduce disease attack. Then in spring prune out all thin, old and diseased branches.

It is easy to do this with a good sharp pair of pruners and gloves. The good strong young branches can then be cut back from 15 in. (38 cm) to 8 in. (20 cm). Newly planted roses are cut back harder than established roses, usually to 4—5 in. (10—12 cm).

Remember, the harder you prune the stronger the new growth will be. Very hard cutting back means less flowers but each one will be so much bigger. Lighter pruning means more flowers but each flower somewhat smaller.

It is best to prune back to a few branches 8 in. (20 cm) above ground for big exhibition hybrid tea blooms and 15 in. (38 cm) for floribundas to produce the desired mass of flowers.

Do not be afraid to cut bush roses — invariably a skilled gardener would cut out more, however hard you feel you have pruned. Try to leave straight single branches sticking up from the crown of the bush. Where the branch ends in a series of short stumpy branches it seldom produces worth-while flowers.

The perpetual-flowering climbers are pruned in much the same way except we keep the main branches, and cut all the side shoots coming from them, back to 2—4 in. (5—10 cm). Every now and then an old branch can be cut right back to encourage new branches to shoot out from the base.

Where new, supple branches are tied over horizontally it encourages the development of a flowering side shoot from the bud at the base of every leaf. Once these flowering shoots have started to grow, the branch can be tied up vertically again if necessary.

Spray with lime-sulfur or oil emulsion in spring if you have any left from fruit trees.

New growth will sprout from the oldest, blackest, hard barky-looking wood. Ideally cut just above the line caused when a leaf falls. If you can't see this then prune virtually blind and cut off the old snags as soon as the new shoots are seen sprouting out.

The only other pruning needed is to cut out any badly diseased foliage and old flower heads as the petals fall. Dead-heading is most important if more flowers are to be encouraged. When you remove the dead blooms don't just snap them out. Look down the stem to a good leaf with plump bud between leaf and stem. Cut above this and a flowering shoot will develop.

FEEDING ROSES

Where masses of wood are being cut out annually, roses will need feeding to encourage strong renewal growth. Ideally work a good dressing of proprietary rose fertilizer into the surrounding soil after pruning. It is well worth giving all perpetual-flowering roses another top-dressing of fertilizer after the first summer flush in July to help maintain good flower production. Water this fertilizer in well if the soil and weather are dry.

A light dressing in early autumn will also see that the plants are well nourished ready for the burst of growth next spring. Small, poorly colored leaves, weak spindly growth, and small flowers with few petals are sure signs of insufficient plant food.

WINTER PROTECTION

In most northern regions, roses need winter protection. This can vary from straw, evergreen boughs and other litter mounded over the bush (but what a cosy nest for mice!) to compost and leaves held in place by a chicken wire cylinder. A nuisance, but a reliable method is to mound soil, carted from elsewhere, over the plants. Tree roses (and climbers tied together) can be wrapped in straw and burlap or, after loosening the root ball, tipped over and buried in the soil.

SUMMER CARE

After pruning and feeding in March, it is wise to apply a 2—3 in. (5—7.5 cm) mulch of peat, compost or similar material to retain moisture and help smother weeds during the summer. This is especially valuable on light, quick drying soils.

Where these mulches are used be sure that burning cigarette ends are not carelessly dropped because if the mulch smoulders around roses it can kill them.

Watering

Watering is necessary during droughts when the soil should be given a thorough soaking. Adding plenty of organic matter and maintaining a mulch will help to conserve soil moisture. Try to avoid wetting the leaves.

Coping with Suckers

Most roses today are propagated by budding (occasionally miniature roses are grafted) on to specially selected vigorous rootstocks. The old *Rosa canina* stock, while producing roses of very long life, tended to throw up many suckers from below ground.

Modern stocks like *R. laxa* do not have the same suckering weakness but occasional suckers will occur.

There is no absolutely foolproof means of identifying suckers, but they do come from below the nobbly point where the budded variety joins the rootstock.

Usually they are much lighter green and smaller leaved than the cultivated variety. Once you are sure it is a sucker — and not a lovely new branch growing up from the base — pull it away. Get hold of the sucker as low as possible and then tear it out. If possible put your foot against the bush to support it while pulling the sucker away.

Some common rose pests: *a* rose leafhopper; *b* leaf cutter bee damage; *c* rose chafer (this gray-tan beetle also attacks buds and flowers); *d* tortrix moth damage; *e* spittle bug; *f* thrips damage; *g* red spider mite attack; *h* typical caterpillar damage.

Propagation

The more vigorous varieties of roses, especially ramblers and floribundas, can be propagated by taking hardwood cuttings. Select shoots of the current year's growth as it starts to harden in autumn. Insert these outside in sandy soil and they will be rooted and ready to transplant in 14 months' time.

More reliable results will be obtained where the required variety is budded on specially selected rootstocks in June or July, but this is a job for the nurseryman or very keen amateur.

Miniature roses can be grown from seed, but not special varieties.

ROSE TROUBLES

There are three diseases of roses which occur quite commonly and chemical sprays are needed to control their spread. Most widespread is powdery mildew, a fungus which produces grayish-white spots on the leaves and flower buds, eventually spreading so as to cover completely shoots and branches.

Mildew is spread by the wind and is worse in humid weather. Avoid wetting the entire bush. Some varieties like the rambler 'Dorothy Perkins' and the glorious red floribunda 'Europeana' are more susceptible than others. Mildewed shoots are best pruned out, especially early in the season. Apply sprays weekly.

Black-spot is the most aptly named fungus disease and under mild, damp or rainy conditions spread can be very rapid. The first sign of attack is small black spots on the leaf, the spots being edged yellow. The spots gradually enlarge and increase in number, causing leaf fall.

Some varieties are more susceptible

than others; those with hard, shiny leaves are usually more resistant. Try to space bushes properly and avoid wetting the foliage.

See that all old leaves are cleared up and burned in winter where infection has occurred. Spray over the bushes and ground in early spring with lime-sulfur. Mulching will also help prevent reinfection from overwintered spores in the soil.

Spray the plants during growth with either protective or systemic fungicides to prevent infection of the new growth or kill germinating spores as they grow into the leaf.

Rose rust is most serious on the Pacific Coast and severe attacks will cause the death of bushes. The first signs are small clusters of orange pustules on the underside of the leaves. These eventually turn black in autumn, then the leaves fall. Sprays of maneb and zineb will protect leaves from further infection by rust and also blackspot.

Biweekly sprays with chemical combinations like maneb and dinocap will control all three diseases. New systemic fungicides which are taken up in the plant sap and actually kill these diseases are now available to amateurs. Benomyl, sold under such trade names as Benlate and Tersan, is a fungicide with systemic action.

The main pest of roses is green aphid, severe attacks covering the leaves with a black sooty mold. There are many suitable insecticides to control them; those based on pirimicarb will leave beneficial insects such as lacewings and ladybirds unharmed. Spray twice at 3—4 day intervals to get a complete kill.

There are a number of other minor pests of roses which we see from time to

Prune out shoots severely infected with mildew and spray with a systemic fungicide to clean up such infections.

time. In some regions the destruction from mice is anything but minor. Since the mice work underground, control is difficult. Contact your county extension agent for regional controls.

Caterpillars of several kinds of moth are best killed by pinching them when seen, or by using sprays based on carbaryl.

The same spray will control leaf-rolling sawfly, rose slug-worm, spittlebug and leaf hopper (small yellowish insects which leave behind tell-tale empty white skins).

Leaf cutter bees will remove quite a large part of leaves from roses and beech but this creature is worth the damage it does for the interest it causes. If found the nests can be destroyed to prevent further damage but control is not usually necessary.

The various beetles that infest rose bushes can be controlled by hand picking and cabaryl.

While this may appear a formidable array of pests and diseases, in practice roses will grow and flourish for years without sprays and regardless of the many pests.

An occasional combined fungicide and pesticide spray will help produce the perfect blooms all keen gardeners desire.

Orange pustules on the undersides of leaves are typical symptoms of rust.

Black-spot usually brings early leaf fall on infected plants

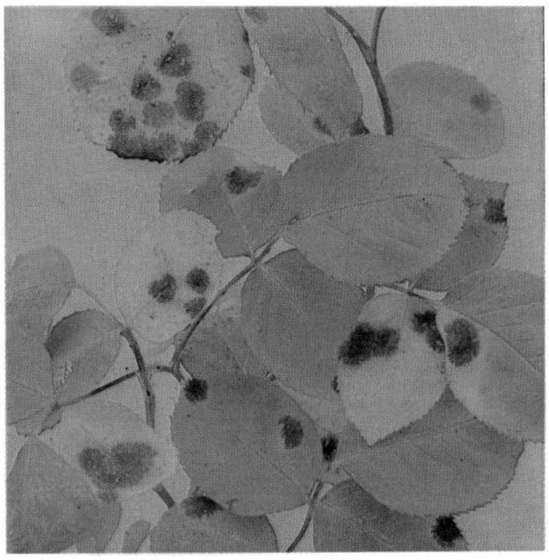

Choosing Roses

There are so many really good roses it is very difficult to choose the best for our gardens. I cannot recommend enough visits to public gardens and garden centers at the time when the roses are in flower in order to be sure the growth, color and fragrance meets with your approval.

Fruit

Contrary to widespread belief you do not need a lot of space to grow a selection of fruit crops. Even an area as small as 12 ft × 7 ft (3.5m × 2.3m) can support a surprising amount.

Planting in a small area naturally calls for careful planning, but a plot the size mentioned can support two rows of strawberries, three rhubarb plants, three rows of raspberries, a couple of blueberries, a redcurrant and a gooseberry, a few blackberry hybrids and an apple tree. It will be necessary to thin out some of the soft fruit as the different kinds grow and demand more space, but this is no more than is often done commercially.

The growing plan shown on the following page is only one of countless fruit combinations which can be used, but it offers a framework from which to start. The tree is best placed to the north of the plot, and although it could be a plum or pear, an apple on dwarfing roots is likely to be easier to handle.

In some respects a small garden has advantages for fruit growing. Where the plot is fenced on one or two sides it is an advantage when it comes to netting for protection against birds.

Vines, cane and cordon fruits can also be planted against fences. Grapes, however, require patience during the three to four years before they start fruiting, and careful pruning.

Strong cold winds in spring can be a real problem for fruit growers, and again suburban gardens fenced and hedged provide protection.

Fruit trees and bushes do not need much regular attention, apart from some pruning and the occasional spraying.

When replanting do not plant another apple where there was one before. Rotate with pear and stone fruits. Crop rotation is not practiced to the same extent with fruit as it is with vegetables, but on an intensively cropped plot it will be necessary to scrap strawberry plants after three or four years. The area cleared of strawberries could either be taken up by the increasing size of soft fruit bushes or be replanted with rhubarb. It may be possible to replant a few strawberries where rhubarb crowns were lifted to force.

Raspberries growing in part of the author's 12 ft × 7 ft (4 m × 2 m) fruit plot, showing how even a small area can produce worthwhile yields.

Light is important on densely planted plots. Raspberries and soft fruits would need to be kept well pruned and canes tied in to allow light to get through to the strawberries.

Growing the redcurrant and gooseberry bushes on a stem 2—2½ ft (60—75 cm) high would provide more space for strawberries and rhubarb.

BUYING FRUIT TREES

It is vital to start off with healthy stock. Trouble will soon spread in an intensively cropped area, and virus diseases in unhealthy plants will considerably reduce yields and cannot be cured by garden sprays.

All the advice given on buying shrubs applies to fruit bushes too, but additionally pay attention to the leaves of soft fruit such as raspberries and strawberries — avoid any that are showing unnaturally yellow, mottled, contorted or stunted leaves.

Rootstocks

Rootstocks are a vital consideration when buying top fruit such as apples or pears. An apple variety can have a spread of 16 ft (5 m) or 30 ft (9 m), depending on the rootstock.

All stone fruits (cherries, plums etc.), and apples and pears are better grafted on to special roots rather than produced as plants on their own roots. A suitable rootstock can significantly affect ultimate tree size, and also induce

Dwarfing rootstocks keep apple trees small and easily managed but need secure stakes.

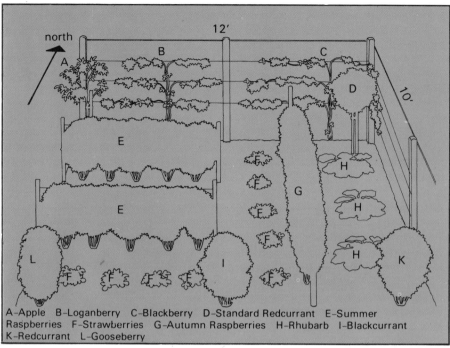

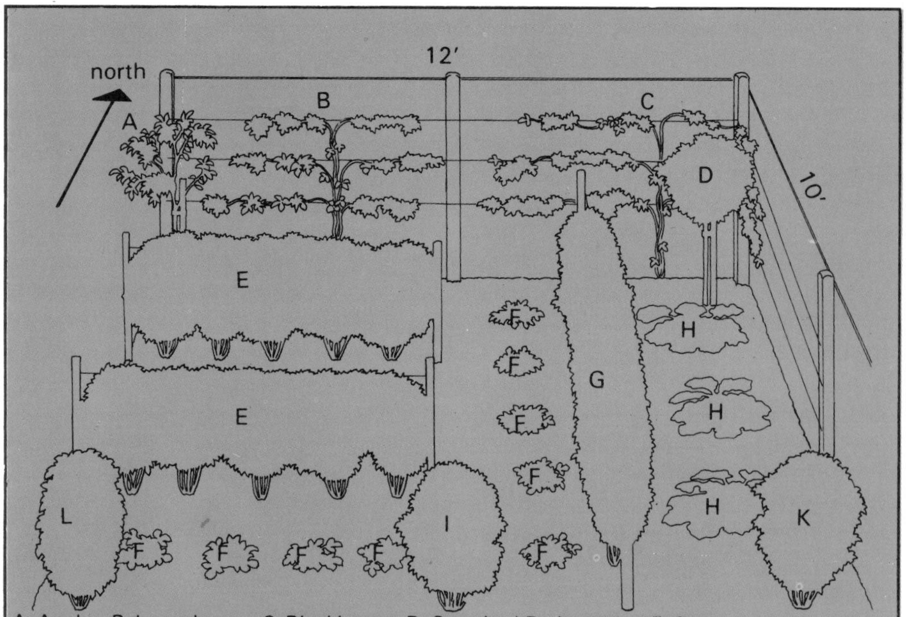

One possible cropping plan for a 12 ft × 10 ft (4 m × 3 m) fruit plot.

earlier fruiting. There are other factors such as disease resistance with certain cherry and grape stocks, and pest resistance in some apple stocks.

Research is under way to find suitable dwarfing rootstocks for cherries. A sweet cherry can take up 30 ft (9 m) and is also self-sterile.

Apple Rootstocks

Thanks to the work at East Malling and Long Ashton research stations in England, there is a range of good rootstocks available for apples.

M 9 (Malling 9) is a very dwarfing stock suitable for good soils. It is essential to keep trees on this stock *securely staked* for the *whole* of their life.

M 26 (Malling 26) is a more recent introduction and is slightly stronger growing than M 9. It will need secure staking in poor sandy soils but like M 9 will start fruiting in the second and third year from grafting.

MM 106 (Malling Merton 106) is described as semi-dwarfing because on good soils it provides medium-sized trees and on poor soils dwarf trees. MM 106 is the best all-round stock for gardens.

MM 111 (Malling Merton 111) is vigorous, producing excellent bush trees. It is resistant to drought and is the best for really poor soils.

Trees on MM 111 stock will fruit several years later than the dwarfing stocks, but will produce heavier yields.

M 9 and M 26 are ideal for cordons and dwarf pyramid apples, while MM 111 is most suitable for bush and standard trees.

A recent addition is M 27, which is comparable to M 9 in its dwarfing effect.

The chart (right) provides a guide to planting distances for rootstocks.

Pear Rootstocks

The stock recommended for general garden use is EM Quince A (East Malling Quince A). This stock produces trees 12 ft (3.6 m) across.

EM Quince C has a more dwarfing effect but it needs to be used with a vigorous variety and on good soil.

Plum Rootstocks

Dwarfing stock Pixie, which is a new kind, requires good soil. The one best suited to the average garden is 'St. Julien A'. 'Brompton' is more vigorous and should be used where heavy bearing varieties are grown well for maximum yield.

'St Julien' will produce trees 12—15 ft (3.6—4.6 m) across, while 'Brompton' produces trees 18—20 ft (5.5—6.1 m) in diameter.

APPLES

Dwarf trees are usually the most practical for limited properties. Many nurseries, though, sell semi-dwarf trees (on M 7) that will eventually require a ladder.

Dependable Varieties

Most of the following can be obtained as dwarf or semi-dwarf as well as standard-size trees. Remember that apples are self-unfruitful and two or more varieties that bloom at the same time or whose blooming periods overlap are necessary for cross pollination. If you do not have space for more than one tree, select a "family" or 5-on-1 tree — five different varieties grafted on one tree that will pollinate each other.

Before making a final decision, check with your county extension agent (listed in the telephone book under the county government) to be sure the varieties are suited to your region.

'Beacon'. An early apple for cold regions. Heavy bearer; keeps well.

'Cortland'. Red-striped skin and white flesh. Dessert and cooking.

Approximate guide to diameter of some typical trees on selected rootstocks.

SELECTED ROOTSTOCK			
Rootstock	Strong growing varieties	Medium varieties	Less vigorous varieties
M 9	16 ft (5 m)	12 ft (3.6 m)	10 ft (3 m)
M 26	20 ft (6.1 m)	15 ft (4.6 m)	11 ft (3.3 m)
MM 106	25 ft (7.5 m)	16 ft (5 m)	12 ft (3.6 m)
MM 111	30 ft (9 m)	20 ft (6.1 m)	15 ft (4.6 m)

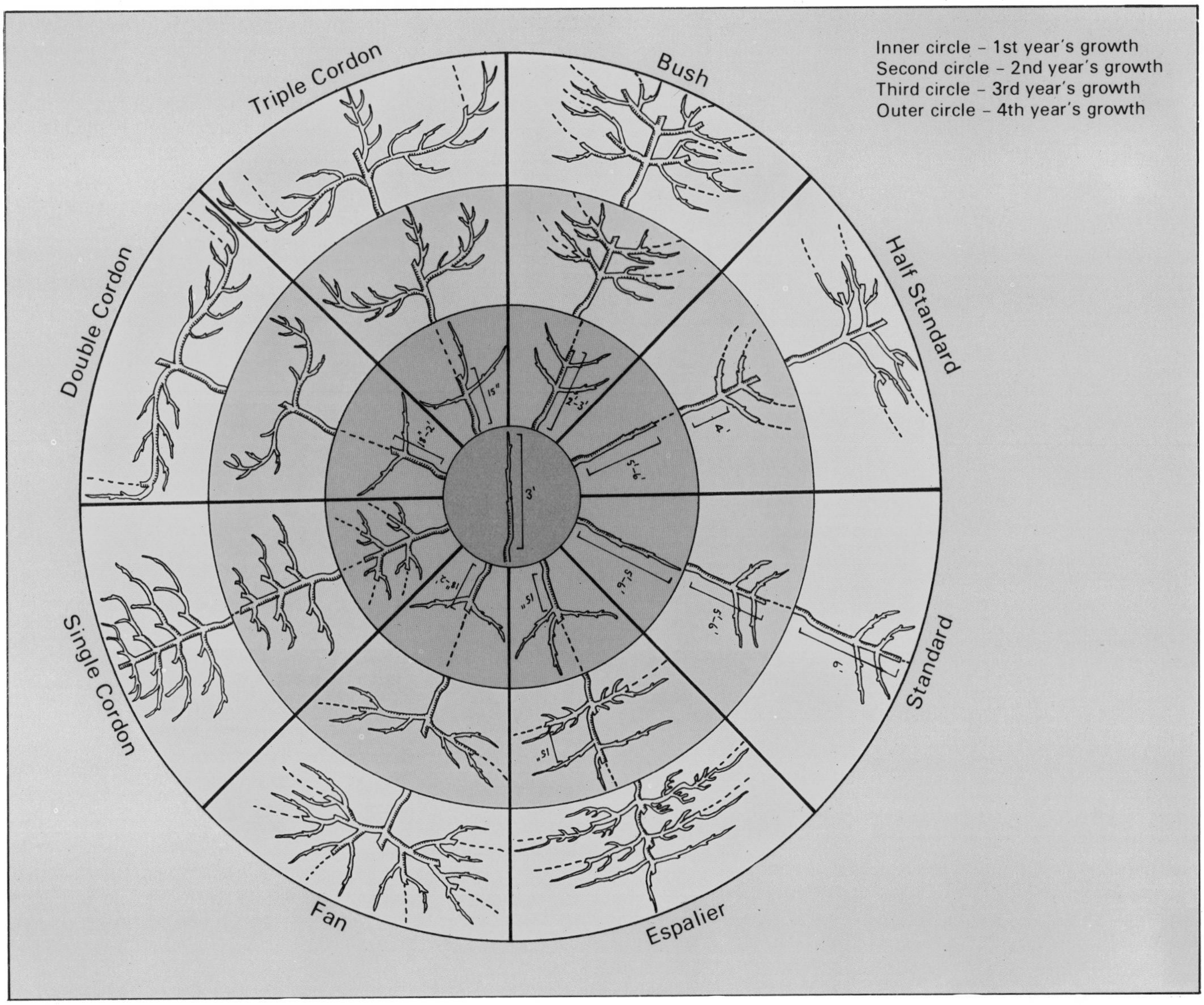

Starting with a maiden tree (center), it is possible to produce many different tree shapes by careful pruning and training. Each ring of the circle represents one year's growth.

YEAR ROUND FRESH FRUIT												
Fruit	Jan	Feb	Mar	April	May	June	July	Aug	Sept	Oct	Nov	Dec
Apricot								●●	●			
Apple ('Julyred', 'Red Astrachan', 'Lodi')							●	●●●	●●●	●		
Apple (mid-season, 'Macoun', 'Cartland')									●	●●●	●●●	●
Apple (late, e.g. 'Idared', 'Mutsu')	●●	●●●	●●●	●●●	●●●	●				●	●●●	●
Blackberry							●	●●●	●●●	●●		
Cherries							●●●	●●●				
Currants						●●	●●					
Gooseberries					●●	●●●	●●					
Grapes									●●	●●●	●	
Loganberries							●●	●●				
Peaches								●●	●●			
Pears (early)								●●	●●			
Pears (late)										●●	●●●	●●
Plums							●●	●●●	●●			
Raspberries						●●	●●●					
Raspberries (everbearing)									●●●	●●●		
Rhubarb		●●FORCED		●●●	●●●	●●●	●●●	●				
Strawberries						●●●	●					
Strawberries (everbearing)								●	●●●			
NOTE: Bearing times may differ according to climate												

'Spartan' is a useful late dessert apple for a small garden. It also tends to be hardy and disease resistant.

Cordons[1] may be used alongside a path where space is limited. Dwarf pyramids[2] give the heaviest crops in the quickest time and take up little room. Standards[3] produce the heaviest crops over a long period but take several years before bearing heavily. Semi-dwarf trees[4] are somewhere between the pyramid and standard forms, have a long life and bear heavily.

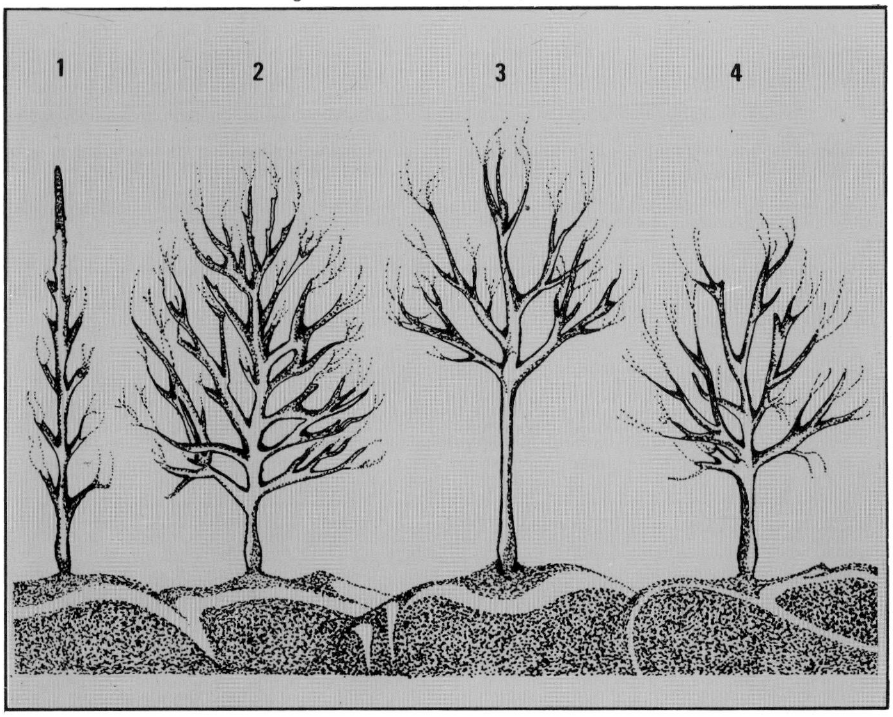

'Cox Orange Pippin'. High dessert quality. Susceptible to frost injury and diseases. (Offered by Miller Nurseries, Canandaigua, N.Y. 14424.)

'Criterion'. Large, red-blushed fruits in mid-fall. For dessert and cooking. Stores until spring.

'Empire'. Fine dessert apple that stores better than 'McIntosh'.

'Fireside'. Large red fruits that store for three months. For coldest regions such as North Dakota.

'Golden Delicious'. Fine dessert apple; retains quality under long storage.

'Granny Smith'. New green variety from Australia. Ripens very late.

'Haralson'.Late variety that stores well. For coldest regions.

'Idared'. Handsome red fruit of dessert quality. Precocious bearer. Ripens late and stores well.

'Jonagold'. Yellow skin with scarlet stripe. Fine dessert apple that stores well. A triploid so cannot pollinate other varieties.

'Julyred'. Early variety with blush-colored skin with stripes.

'Macoun'. Small-to-medium red apples similar to McIntosh. Good dessert quality. Well suited to Northeast.

'McIntosh'. Remains a favorite dessert apple because of flavor, color and crisp white flesh.

'Mutsu'. Huge yellow fruits in late fall. High quality for dessert and cooking. Disease resistant; stores well. Triploid; can't pollinate other apples.

'Spartan'. Handsome McIntosh-quality fruits but later. Stores well.

'Spigold'. Large red-striped fruit in late October. Vigorous growth as semi-dwarf. Another triploid.

'Summer Red'. Early variety from British Columbia. Dessert quality.

'Yellow Transparent'. Attractive fruits in early August. Dessert.

'Wealthy'. Very hardy old variety with bright red fruits. Dessert and cooking quality.

'Winter Banana'. Large, yellow fruits with pink blush and banana aroma. Dessert quality. Keeps well. Grows well generally but also does well in cooler West Coast areas.

Cultivation

Any well-cultivated garden soil suits apples. Study catalog descriptions carefully to be sure you are getting the right variety and size for your purposes.

It is important when planting to see that the knobbly section of stem above soil level (the graft) is clear of the earth. If you cover the graft with soil the variety will produce its own roots and the effect of the rootstock will be lost. However, if the graft has been made well above the soil line, it is worth planting deeper — provided the graft is not covered — as this will reduce the need to stake and encourage earlier and heavier fruiting.

Do not plant apples in hollows where cold spring frosts are likely. Choose late-flowering varieties for cold frosty areas.

Keep soil around newly planted trees free of weeds. Competition from weeds in the first year can reduce growth by 50 per cent, and this effect can be continued well into the tree's life.

Most apple trees, once established, will overbear. Thin after June drop so fruits are 2—8 in, (5—20 cm) apart.

'Grenadier' is a prolific and disease-resistant early apple. A cooker, it is picked green but ripens to yellow. 'R.I. Greening' and 'Granny Smith' are also green.

Harvesting

To pick an apple, hold it and lift up through 90° from the branch. It will come away easily if it is ready to pick. Do not snatch the fruit from the tree as this can break off a spur and remove the next season's flower bud.

The fruit can be stored in trays in a cool, slightly damp atmosphere. Remove the ripe fruits, otherwise these will speed the ripening process of the remaining apples.

Pruning

Many fruit nurseries make a point of shipping properly pruned fruit trees. Otherwise instructions are usually included for pruning the newly planted tree. The age of the tree also has a bearing on the amount of necessary pruning. For instance, a one-year dwarf tree should be cut back to a height of about 30 in. (76 cm). Older trees with branch growth should have it shortened by about half. A pyramidal-shaped dwarf should have its main leader taller than any side branches. Retain only wide-angled branches as the more horizontal the branches, the more compact the tree will be. Generally a 5-year-old dwarf will have developed 5 to 7 side branches from the main trunk. Dwarf trees often need little later pruning.

With spur pruning, wood formed in the summer is cut back to four buds.

Pests and Diseases

Aphids cause leaves to curl, shoots to distort and feel sticky. Use a tar oil winter wash and prune off distorted twigs with overwintering eggs.

Birds sometimes take ripe fruit, but one of the advantages of dwarf trees is that a net can be thrown over the tree to prevent this.

Canker causes dark hollows in the bark which spread. The wood around it then swells, and if girdled the piece of branch above dies. Pare away diseased wood, burn the pieces and paint the wound.

Caterpillars such as cankerworms, leaf rollers and others, can be handpicked from small trees, controlled to some degree by grease bands such as Tanglefoot. However, a multipurpose fruit spray is most efficient.

Maggots which have entered leaving one neat hole are from the *codling moth*. Trap by wrapping sacking or corrugated cardboard around fairly smooth bark in June. Remove and burn in October. Maggots which eat the surface of fruit before burrowing belong to the *sawfly*.

The fruits drop before they ripen, and these should be picked up and destroyed. Also use a multi-purpose spray every 10 days.

Mildew looks like a grayish growth over shoots and leaves. Multipurpose fruit spray should control it.

Scab causes brown and blackish spots to appear on the leaves and fruits. Light green patches also develop on the leaves. Rake up and burn all diseased leaves, especially any which fall early.

Woolly aphis have a waxy white covering; dormant oil spray should kill eggs and natural predators kill adults.

A warm sunny position and a long growing season are needed for quality grapes as well as attention and dedication from the gardener.

GRAPES

Grapes require more effort and skill than most home garden fruits. There is also the matter of patience because it may take from 3—5 years from planting for a good harvest. There are grape varieties for most American climates. Contact your county extension agent and state agricultural experiment stations for information on regional grape culture and suitable varieties.

In the South, varieties of the native Muscadine grape are grown. In California and a few other Western areas, European grapes are cultivated while in the colder regions of the USA, hybrids from the native fox grape and European varieties are grown.

Cultivation

Grapes are long lived and very hardy. They are also deep rooting and require a free-draining soil that is not too rich. Even though the roots are very hardy when dormant, avoid frost pockets as young spring growth can be damaged by late frosts.

Prepare the soil by digging two spades' depth or by cultivating with a power tiller. Plant 2-year vines in spring from 6—10 ft (1.8—3 m) apart.

Mulch to retain moisture, especially near walls.

'Black Hamburg' is an old European grape variety renouned for its sweet and juicy fruits.

Harvesting

Before gathering grape bunches, taste a grape to be sure they are ripe. Unripe grapes do not ripen off the vine.

Pruning

Southern grapes are usually grown on arbors and require little pruning or training beyond that needed to restrict their growth.

While American grape varieties can be grown over arbors or a fence with pruning limited to removal of older canes, serious growers prefer the 4-cane Kniffen system in which the single-stem vine's four canes (two on each side) are tied on two wires between posts at 10 ft. (3 m) intervals. Grapes are produced on one-year canes that are cut off after bearing with four more canes retained to take their place.

The same system is used for some European grapes such as 'Thompson Seedless' but more often head or spur pruning and cane pruning are the systems. Still a third method is cordon training which uses a two-wire fence. In head or spur pruning, the 1—3 ft (30—91 cm) vine is topped by ahead of short branches or spurs.

Pests and Diseases

While grapes have their share of pests and troubles, the trend is toward disease-resistant varieties like the early blue 'Buffalo'.

PEACHES

In warm sheltered gardens in favorable areas peaches can be grown outdoors quite satisfactorily as bush trees. If trained as fans against south or west facing walls, they will thrive and fruit even in some of the less favorable

Although peaches are really only suitable for warm and sheltered sites, they can be very successful if given the right location and are quite easy to grow.

areas. There are natural dwarfs, such as Bonanza, which take up little space or can grow in tubs.

Dependable Varieties

Trees grown from pips will sometimes fruit satisfactorily, but it is best to grow named varieties grafted on to the dwarfing 'St. Julien A' rootstock.

All the 'Haven' varieties are especially hardy. Consult local authorities for regional varieties.

Cultivation

Trees with bare roots are best planted in October or November, or early spring; container grown peaches can be planted at any time.

Choose a well-cultivated soil that is moderate to slightly acid and free draining but also water retentive in summer. Add plenty of well-rotted compost before planting, especially near walls or fences.

Peaches must be watered well in very dry weather and it is wise to aid pollination by dusting the open flowers midday with a feather or soft paintbrush when dry and sunny. Gently misting with water on sunny days also helps. After the "June drop" has naturally thinned the fruits, thin them out again about 6—8 in. (15—20 cm) apart for final development.

Harvesting

When fruits start to ripen, tie the leaves back to expose the fruits to sun. Once the flesh is soft to touch around the stalk, gather the fruits. Spaced on tissue in a cool place, they will store for a week or two.

Pruning

Established bush peaches require little pruning apart from cutting out any diseased and dead wood in spring. An occasional branch can be pruned back at the same time to encourage new growth from the center of the tree.

Fan trees are perhaps best purchased from the nursery with the basic branch framework formed. Then it is a matter of pruning the lead shoots of each branch back in early spring. It is best to cut back to a cluster of three buds at one point in order to get two or three new branches radiating out from the cut.

When the branches have extended to the area available, prune to achieve fruiting. Fruit is produced on the previous year's wood. The plump rounded buds are flower buds, the longer, thinner ones produce growth. Any shoots that grow toward the wall or at 90° away from it should be rubbed out in April when young, soft and green.

Select shoots on top and beneath each branch, and about every 6 in. (15 cm) along and tie to the horizontal support wires, placed 9 in. (23 cm) apart. Pinch out the tip of side shoots when 18 in. (45 cm) long. Each year a strong new shoot should be trained from the base of the lateral and alongside it as a replacement. The fruited branch is cut out in late summer. Surplus shoots can be pinched back to four leaves or rubbed out.

Pests and Diseases

Aphids can be controlled with dormant oil sprays in winter or with proprietary multipurpose sprays in summer.
Mildew is usually the result of dry soils. If the disease appears, sulfur sprays at 14-day intervals will afford control.
Peach leaf curl causes curled leaves with red blisters. Spray with Bordeaux mixture or ferbam before the buds begin to swell. Repeat 10 days later and again before the flower buds open and once more as the leaves fall in the autumn.

PEARS

Although pears need similar treatment and conditions to apples, they generally need a warmer climate.

The vigorous young shoots and leaves are soft and all too easily damaged by strong cold winds in spring. Because they benefit from the

Peach leaf curl is a very disfiguring disease; spray early to control it.

Pears can grow into very large trees on seedling rootstocks but on 'Quince A' stock make compact, early-flowering trees.

protection offered they are often grown as wall trees.

A well-cultivated garden soil should give good results, but avoid alkaline soils.

Dependable Varieties

Pears are self-sterile so two or more different pears must be planted for proper pollination. If space is lacking, plant a three-on-one dwarf tree in which the three pollinate each other. Dwarf pears are usually grown on quince and 'Old Home' pear stock. 'Bartlett' is an early pear famous for quality. Not resistant to fire-blight.

'Beurre d'Anjou' is a fine dessert pear, late, that stores well.

'Clapp's Favorite' is early, hardy and productive, a good pollinator and resistant to fire blight.

'Colette' has large yellow fruits blushed pink that ripen from mid-August to midfall. Not resistant to fire blight.

'Doyenne du Comice', an outstanding variety for Pacific Northwest.

'Magness' has green-yellow fruits of good quality. Fire-blight resistant but its pollen is sterile.

'Parker' is similar to 'Bartlett' and hardy enough for Minnesota.

'Seckel' has small pears of high dessert quality. Resistant to fire blight.

Cultivation

Spacing between plants will depend not only on rootstock but also vareity and pruning. A moderate variety on 'Quince A' can be spaced 12 ft (3.5 m) apart with hard pruning. A vigorous variety on the same stock on good soil but lightly pruned will need 15 ft (4.5 m) between trees.

Pears will grow best where the soil under them is in grass. The grass prevents the tree from growing too vigorously and being susceptible to fire blight. Keep pear trees a little under-nourished! However, bearing-age trees competing with grass can benefit from 1 oz per sq yd (30 g per sq m) of sulfate of ammonia in spring.

Where pear trees flourish but fail to set fruit, inadequate pollination or spring frosts are usually the cause.

Harvesting

Pears should be picked when they are ripe but *before* they soften. The fruits should separate easily from the tree when lifted through 90° in the hand.

Both flavor and smell develop better if the fruit is stored in single layers in trays or boxes in a cool damp atmosphere.

Pruning

Pears are pruned in a similar way to apples, although too much hard pruning can lead to fire blight disease. Lead shoots of established trees can be cut back to 2 in. (5 cm) each winter and all laterals to 1 in. (2.5 cm).

The number of fruiting spurs may have to be reduced on established trees if they are not to carry too many small fruits which also must be thinned.

You should aim for between seven and ten main branches for closely planted bush trees.

Pests and Diseases

Aphids, including green and black ones, may cause a black sticky mold over leaves and shoots. A dormant oil spray followed by multipurpose spray after the petals have fallen, will bring control.

Fireblight is a serious disease. Symptoms are a sudden total blackening of young shoots as if burned by fire; and liquid streaks running down the bark of branches is another sign.

All infected wood must be cut out and burned, and the tools used must be sterilized. Cotoneaster, mountain ash, apple and pyracantha are also affected by fireblight.

Pear leaf blister causes pale green or pink blisters, turning brown on the leaves from April onwards. Lime sulfur — which also controls scab — can be applied in spring as the buds begin to open, but it must not be used on the variety 'Comice'. A small

Fruit buds are plumper than the rather triangular vegetative buds.

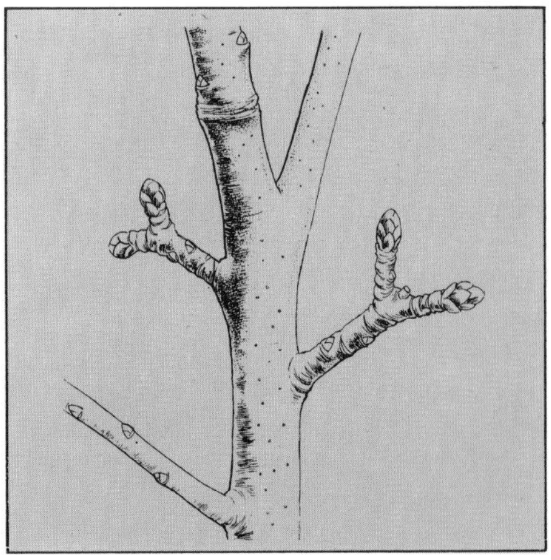

attack can be controlled by burning infected leaves. Mites are the cause.
Pear midge is an occasional pest that once present will reappear year after year until sprayed. Small fruits fail to develop, turn black and fall. White maggots will be found inside fruits. Spray when the petals fall with dimethoate or malathion.
Pear scab shows itself as black scabs and cracks on fruit. Other symptoms are light green spots on the leaves which turn brown, and blistered and spotted young shoots. Collect and burn diseased leaves and prune out diseased shoots. Spray with captan.

PLUMS

After a "family" (5-on-1) dwarf apple tree, a European dwarf plum such as 'Yellow Egg' or a gage type such as 'Early Transparent' would be my next choice for a small garden.

Plum trees require less pruning than most fruit trees and even some standard-size trees remain compact. There's a plum for nearly every region and American gardeners can choose from among Japanese and European types as well as native plums.

Plums can make good fruit trees for small gardens, especially if grown on a suitable dwarfing rootstock such as 'St. Julien A'.

Dependable Varieties

Check with county extension agents for the best varieties for your region. Many plums are self-fertile but bear more heavily if another variety is present.

'DeMonfort' is a purple European plum, sweet and juicy, that ripens in late summer.

'Early Transparent Gage' forms a dwarf tree and ripens its sweet plums early over a long period.

'French Damson' is a tart European plum used for preserves.

'Green Gage' ('Reine Claude') is a well-known European dessert plum that bears even more heavily when pollinated by another European plum.

'Ozark Premier' is a Japanese plum for the Midwest. Needs another Japanese variety for pollination.

'Santa Rosa' is a large dark red Japanese plum. Requires pollination.

'Sapalta' is a hybrid cherry-plum for preserves. Plant 'Compass', another hybrid with it.

'Shiro' has beautiful gold plums on a small tree but needs another Japanese plum to pollinate it.

'Stanley' has blue plums for dessert or preserves in early fall.

'Superior' is a hardy early plum that pollinates other Japanese plums.

'Yellow Egg' is a European plum that ripens in early fall.

Many fruits can be trained neatly as space-saving cordons.

Space can also be saved by growing fan-trained trees against a fence.

Cultivation

Trees on a 'St. Julien A' stock should be spaced 12 ft (3.5 m) apart, those on more vigorous stocks further than this.

A heavy mulch of manure and well-rotted compost will improve the performance of these fruits.

Avoid placing the trees in frost pockets where the early blossoms can be injured by a freeze.

Thin fruits in June or July, if necessary, to leave one every 2 in. (5 cm) along the branch. Do not thin 'Damson' varieties.

Harvesting

For eating fresh the fruit is best picked over several times, selecting only fully ripe fruit. Earlier gathering is acceptable for cooking purposes.

FRUIT TREES: PEST AND DISEASE CONTROL			
Problem	**Fruit**	**Control and Timing**	**Notes**
Pests			
Aphids	Apple, Pear Plum, Cherry	*Multiple purpose fruit sprays (can be purchased from garden centers, mail-order nurseries) containing methoxychlor and malathion. Apply at pink bud stage.	Dormant oil sprays kill eggs
Caterpillars, Cankerworms, Sawfly (larvae)	Apple	Multiple purpose fruit spray (as above) after petals fall.	Pick up fruits as they fall and destroy
Codling Moth (larvae)	Apple, Pear, Plum	Multiple purpose fruit spray (or carbaryl) applied 3 times at 10-day intervals after petals fall.	Same as above
Plum Curculio	Apple, Pear, Plum, Cherry, Peach	Multiple-purpose fruit spray (or carbaryl) after petals fall and repeated twice thereafter at 10-day intervals.	Same as above
Apple Maggot	Apple	Multiple purpose fruit spray every 10-14 days, starting after petals fall.	Same as above.
Leaf Roller	Apple, Peach	Multiple purpose fruit spray after petals fall, repeated 10 days later and again in midsummer.	
Pear Psylla	Pear	Delayed dormant spray when buds show green tips. Then multiple purpose sprays when buds show pink, and again after petals fall.	
Peach Borer	Peach, Cherry	Sap oozes from tunnels in trunk and congeals into jelly consistency. Dig out larvae with wire. Spray bark with carbaryl or methoxchlor in late spring and early summer. Repeat twice at 3-week intervals. Consult county extension agents.	
Diseases			
Scab	Apple, Pear	Spray with a fungicide (captan, maneb, benomyl, or ferbam) at green tip bud stage and every 7 days through bloom** stage.	Collect and destroy fallen leaves.
Brown Rot	Peach, Plum	Spray with fungicide (captan, ferbam or sulfur) before blossoms open, after they fall and twice thereafter at 7-day intervals.	Collect and destroy mummied fruits in winter.
Mildew	Apple, Pear Peach	Add maneb or ferbam to multiple purpose spray in late spring.	Collect and destroy fallen leaves.
Peach Leaf Curl	Peach	Spray with Bordeaux mixture, ferbam or lime-sulfur in early spring and repeat before buds begin to swell.	

* A typical multiple purpose spray contains malathion, methoxychlor and captan. Follow manufacturer's instructions for time between spray and harvest and other precautions.

** Never spray insecticides on blooms as this can kill bees. Consult county extension agents for regional spraying information.

Pruning
Nurserymen usually supply trees which have the basic branch framework established. Leave unpruned in the first year or just tip tree's transplanted bare root, and in the second spring (the first spring for container-grown trees) cut the lead shoots which will grow to form main branches back by half.

Subsequently it will only be necessary to shorten back the lead shoots of strong growing varieties like the Japanese varieties in spring to avoid producing long weeping branches.

Much of the training of fan trees will probably have been done by the nursery. Side shoots growing at right angles to the wall should be rubbed out while young and green. Other laterals are tied in to the horizontal support wires and surplus shoots stopped by pinching out the tip after seven leaves have formed. After fruiting prune back the seven-leaf-long shoots by half and cut out any thin and unwanted branches. Very strong upward growing shoots from the center of the fan should be removed.

Pests and Diseases
Aphids can cause a black sooty mold on leaves and fruit and also distort growth of leaves and young fruits. Use multiple-purpose fruit spray.
Birds can be a major problem but most plums are compact enough to be protected by light nets.
Maggots (apple) can infest fruits. Multiple-purpose spray with methoxychlor or carbaryl applied from early to mid-summer is control.
Plum curculio larvae can spoil fruits. Spray as above as petals fall and at 7—10 day intervals.

BLACKBERRIES
Cultivated blackberries are not to be compared with the wild forms found in our hedgerows. Named varieties are adaptable to virtually all garden situations, bear freely over a long period, and have the advantage of big berries and luscious flavor.

Dependable Varieties
'Bailey' produces large berries that begin ripening in early summer.

'Darrow' fruits early and is hardy and very productive. It is widely grown in the North.

'Oregon Thornless' is also called 'Evergreen Thornless'. This variety is late and is grown in the Pacific Northwest. The huge succulent berries have a delicious bramble flavor. Medium vigor; it needs plenty of water to achieve maximum berry size.

Cultivation
Even a shaded site or north-facing wall are acceptable though the yield will be less than in more open and sunny sites. The biggest, juiciest fruits will come from good soil to which manure and compost have been added.

Avoid digging around blackberry roots. It is much better to hoe the surface lightly to control weeds, and to mulch each spring with well-rotted compost.

Blackberries are ideal trained on

wires stretched between stout posts against a shed, wall or fence. The wires should be approximately 2, 3, 4 and 5 ft from the ground.

Plant the less-vigorous varieties 6 ft (2 m) apart, vigorous kinds 12 ft (4 m) apart.

Harvesting
If the stems have been tied in to the wires regularly, picking should be no problem.

Pruning
At the end of the season cut out at ground level all the stems which have borne fruit. Tie in new stems as they develop, keeping them away from fruiting stems (see page 134). When the fruited stems have been pruned out, the new branches that will produce the next season's crop can be tied in. Bare root plants transplanted in spring or in fall should be cut back to 9 in. (23 cm) above the soil.

Pests
Aphids are easily controlled by spraying with malathion.
Raspberry beetle, which causes small maggots in the fruit, can also be controlled satisfactorily with malathion or rotenone as buds appear and as fruits turn pink.

Cultivated blackberries are far removed from the wild bramble, having larger, more succulent berries. This variety is 'Oregon'. It is not hardy in most northern regions.

Loganberries are well worth a place in the fruit garden in mild climates.

LOGANBERRIES
The loganberry was raised by Judge J. H. Logan in his garden at Santa Cruz, California, in 1881.

It has achieved more attention in Britain in recent years than here, where as a blackberry hybrid, it is usually grouped with the boysenberry ('Boysen'), dewberry ('Lucretia'), youngberry ('Young') and others. Most of these are grown in the South, Pacific Northwest or parts of the West Coast where winters are mild.

Dependable Varieties
'Logan' and 'Thornless Logan' are the major available varieties.

Cultivation
Practically all soils and sites are suitable, though slightly acid soil conditions are best. Add plenty of well-rotted compost and manure to limy soils. Well-rotted compost is also needed on heavy soils to improve drainage, and on sandy soils to retain moisture in summer.

Loganberries require a slightly warmer site than blackberries.

Keep loganberries well watered once

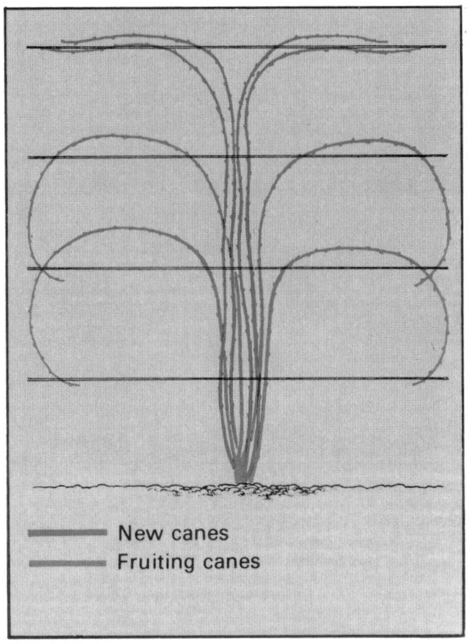

A recommended method of training blackberries and its hybrids.

the fruits have set to get the largest and most succulent berries.

Harvesting
Once the fruit is ripe, in July and August, hold it between the thumb and first two fingers and gently twist from the stem. It will come away easily.

Pruning
As for blackberries.

Pests and Diseases
Cane spot causes circular purple spots on the stems, leaves and flower stalks in May and June. These spots become larger and the centers turn gray. Cut out diseased stems and spray with a copper fungicide before flowering and again once fruit has set.
Raspberry beetle. It is the small reddish maggots of this beetle that are found in the fruits. Spray with rotenone or malathion as buds form and again just before they open.
Spur blight symptoms are dark purple blotches which turn silvery gray where leaf joins the stem.

Spray the emerging canes with benomyl, followed by two or three successive sprays at 10—14-day intervals. Destroy canes after pruning.

BLUEBERRIES
Hybrid blueberries are borne from early to late summer, depending on variety and climate. Surplus berries freeze well but fresh home-grown berries, fully ripe, are a special treat. The twiggy shrubs are ornamental in all seasons, make an attractive hedge and are trouble-free.

Dependable Varieties
Varieties of the highbush blueberry are grown in the North while the rabbiteye blueberry is grown in the South.

'Tifblue', 'Delite', 'Bright Blue', 'Southland', 'Bluebelle', 'Climax', 'Homebell' and 'Woodard' are rabbit-eye varieties. Three different varieties should be planted as rabbiteye bushes are self-sterile.

'Berkley', 'Bluecrop', 'Blueray', 'Coville', 'Darrow', 'Earliblue', 'Elizabeth', 'Herbert' and 'Patriot' are among the highbush hybrids. For bigger crops, plant two or more varieties which will also extend the ripening season.

Cultivation
Plant highbush blueberries about 4—6 ft (1—1.8 m) apart in rows 8 ft (2 m) apart. As a hedge, closer planting is possible but the crop will be diminished.

Plant rabbiteye bushes 5—6 ft (1.5—1.8 m) apart with 10 ft (3 m) between rows. For hedges, set them 3 ft (91 cm) apart.

Blueberries require a humusy, acid soil. A pH rating of 4.5 is ideal. Mix a good amount of peat moss and rotted compost in the planting holes. Set the plants 1—2 in (2.5—5 cm) deeper than their former depth to encourage new sucker growth.

Water well and mulch with rotted sawdust, oak leaves or garden compost and as the mulch is decomposed, add more. Fertilize once a year with a complete fertilizer, such as 5-10-5, or any fertilizer formulated for rhododendrons and camellias, as buds start to open at rate of 1 oz. (28 g) per year of the plant's age but no more than 8 oz (226 g) per plant. Some extra nitrogen may be given to speed decomposition of the mulch.

Pruning
No pruning is needed until about the third year. Thereafter in early spring, remove some old canes and shorten long shoots. Reduce heavily budded shoots by a third.

Harvesting
As berries color, protect them from birds with a plastic net. Pick only fully ripe fruits as once picked, the ripening process stops.

This is the fabled black currant of Europe and Britain.

One of the most popular red currants is 'Red Lake', which bears large fruit on long trusses.

White currants are like small white grapes and are delicious in a dessert or eaten fresh.

RED AND WHITE CURRANTS

White currants are like small white grapes, delicious eaten fresh as a dessert. Red currants, on the other hand, are eaten as jelly with meat, used with other fruits like raspberries in pies, in tarts, and in preserves.

Dependable Varieties

'Red Lake' has large fruit on long trusses.

'Wilder' is popular in the Midwest. Its berries are very large.

'White Imperial' is the major white currant.

Cultivation

Currants are tolerant of varying soils from acid to neutral.

Plant 4—5 ft (1.2—1.5 m) apart, allowing the wider spacing for more vigorous varieties.

Incorporate plenty of well-rotted compost into the soil before planting, and mulch each spring. Add a high potash fertilizer (possibly one for roses or tomatoes) each spring at $1^1/_2$—2 oz per sq yd (40—60 g per sq m).

Harvesting

For jelly, pick just before ripe. 4—5 lb (1.8—2.3 kg) can be expected from an established bush in July.

Pruning

A young bush which has grown for two summers should have the current year's main branch tips cut back by half.

The side shoots on both young and established plants can be cut back to 1 in. (2.5 cm) to form fruiting spurs.

Established plants can have an occasional old branch cut out completely to be replaced by new growth. Once branches have reached the required height each season's new lead growth can also be cut back to 1 in. (2.5 cm).

Pests and Diseases

Birds can be a problem as berries show color. Net to protect the bushes. *Coral spot* shows as red spots on the wood. Prune back to disease-free wood. Spray with Bordeaux after pruning. Check soil drainage.

Currant aphids cause leaves to pucker and reddish blisters to appear. Spray with malathion.

GOOSEBERRIES

Gooseberries provide some of the season's earliest soft fruit. They bear over a period of 12 weeks and are useful for many summer desserts. They are also excellent for sauces, making jams and are suitable for freezing.

Gooseberries prefer a sunny site, but partial shade will give acceptable yields. They are exceptionally hardy and along with currants can be grown in the coldest regions. Gooseberries are long lived and can bear well for over 20 years.

Gooseberries and currants should not be grown within 1,000 ft (300 m) of white pines because they are alternate hosts of the white pine blister rust.

Dependable Varieties

'Fredonia' has late red berries on vigorous and productive bushes.

'Pixwell' has large, pink-colored berries that are reputed to hang well below the thorns.

'Poorman' has red berries in abundance from very vigorous bushes. Highly recommended for the home garden.

'Welcome' has pink berries on near-thornless bushes.

Cultivation

Improve the soil before planting by adding plenty of well-rotted compost.

A high-potash fertilizer should be worked into the soil before planting, and a spring application made at 1—2oz per sq yd (30—60 g per sq m).

A spring mulch of well-rotted compost will help to smother weeds, and also retain moisture to increase the berry size.

Plant gooseberries 4—6 ft (1.2—1.8 m) apart, the wider distances for the more vigorous varieties. Space single cordons 1 ft (30 cm) apart, double cordons 2 ft (60 cm) apart, and triple cordons 3 ft (1 m).

Gooseberries are a useful summer fruit. As berries begin to ripen and change color, use a net to protect them from birds.

When berries begin to form, make certain that the bushes do not suffer from lack of water. A mulch will conserve soil moisture.

It makes cultivation and picking easier if gooseberries are grown on a short stem, 6—9 in. (15—23 cm) high. It may be necessary to remove one or two roots and a couple of low branches when planting to achieve this.

Harvesting
Thin the fruits to leave the berries 1 in. (2.5 cm) apart on the stem as soon as the thinnings are large enough to cook, about early summer. Later every-other berry can be picked to provide more culinary fruit, the remainder left to grow on the bush until ripe. An established plant on reasonable soil should yield from 5—15 lb (2.3—6.8 kg) per bush.

Pruning
Little pruning is needed during the first few years, then cut back the lead shoots by half the summer's growth in winter.

Prune drooping branches back to an upward growing bud to encourage more upright branches.

Once the branches have reached the required height and length, cut the lead shoots back to 1 in. (2.5 cm) or so each winter.

Side shoots can be pruned back to six or seven leaves in July, and cut further back to 1 in. (2.5 cm) in winter. Pruning these side shoots into short fruiting spurs gives larger single fruits of better quality.

Where yield rather than quality is the aim, however, encourage strong growth from the center of the bush and cut out the occasional older branch to make space.

Pests and Diseases
Powdery mildew sometimes coats shoots, leaves and fruit with a powdery white growth which turns felty and brown.

Burn diseased shoots in late August. Spray with a systemic fungicide two or three times at 7—14 day intervals.

Gooseberry sawfly caterpillars can cause problems. These are green with black spots, and they eat all the leaves to the leaf ribs during late spring. Control this pest by either picking off the caterpillars or by spraying.

RASPBERRIES
Raspberries are the most rewarding fruit for gardens. Excellent for dessert and culinary purposes, as well as freezing.

Raspberries will grow satisfactorily on all well-cultivated soils, and on most sites, including partially shaded ones, though waterlogged ground must be avoided.

Dependable Varieties
There are two kinds of raspberries — the early or summer-fruiting that start to bear as strawberry harvests end and

Gooseberries and red and white currants can be grown as cordons against fences, walls or wires, illustrated are single (left), double (center) and triple (right) cordons.

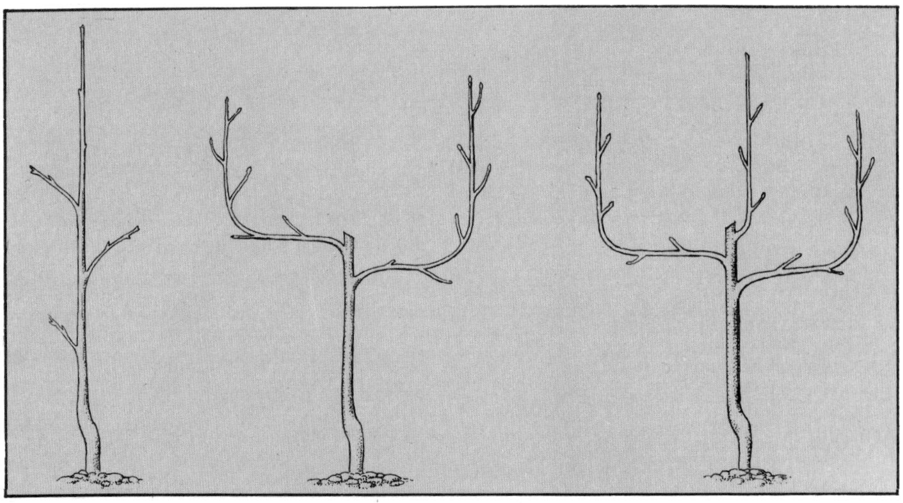

the autumn-fruiting, also called everbearers, that fruit from late summer up to freezing weather.

'Black Hawk' ripens in midseason.

'Bristol' is another black with glossy berries of excellent quality.

'Clyde' is a purple-fruited variety that ripens late-mid-July in N.Y.

'Fall Gold' bears in early July and again in fall.

'Fall Red' bears an early crop and another in late summer.

'Heritage' is an outstanding everbearer with berries of high quality.

'September' is a reliable everbearer with medium-sized red fruits.

'Sodus' has purple fruits that ripen over several weeks.

'Taylor' has early red berries that ripen over a three week period.

Cultivation

When preparing the ground for raspberries, dig in plenty of well-rotted compost or peat moss.

Be sure the soil is clear of perennial weeds before planting, which should ideally be in late fall for bare root canes, though any time the ground is not frozen to spring is all right.

Always plant 'certified' disease-free stock, and plant firmly 2—3 ft (60—91 cm) apart, and if more than one row is planted allow 4—6 ft (1.2—1.8 m) between rows.

When transplanting do not allow the roots to become dry.

A heavy mulching with well-rotted manure or compost each spring will help to control weeds. Try not to dig close to surface-rooting raspberries.

Autumn-fruiting varieties are virtually self-supporting, but summer-fruiting kinds may need support. Tie new growth to wires placed 3 ft (1 m) and 5 ft (1.5 m) high, secured to stakes.

Plenty of water and liquid fertilizer as fruits start to swell will increase the yield and strengthen canes for next season's crops.

Harvesting

When ripe a gentle pull should part the fruit from the 'plug' which stays behind on the cane, though some varieties come away quite easily.

Pruning

After setting out bare-root canes of summer and autumn (everbearers) raspberries in either fall or spring, cut them back to 6—9 in. (15—23 cm) above soil level.

The summer kinds, which bear on previous year's canes, will bear the following summer, but the autumn varieties will bear a crop the first year on the tips of the canes.

Prune out all canes of the summer varieties after they have fruited and tie new canes to the wires every 3—4 in. (7.5—10 cm). Cut out small surplus canes.

Autumn varieties will bear a second summer crop on previous fall canes, which should be headed back in early spring to cause branching. After bearing, cut them off at ground level. The new canes that follow will bear the fall crop on the canes' tips.

The early crop of autumn bearers can then be eliminated by cutting back the canes to the ground in late winter or early spring.

Raspberries, strawberries, black and red currants growing in the author's garden, showing netting protection. The net is supported on plastic containers on canes.

Pests and Diseases

Raspberry beetle causes small maggots in ripe fruit. To control, spray or dust with rotenone or malathion when the first pink fruit is seen.

Cane spot may be seen in May or June as purple spots which turn grey with a purple edge. Spray with benomyl.

Spur blight shows itself as purple blotches in August. These turn silver and cause die-back. Spray with benomyl.

This disease tends to affect young overcrowded canes worst.

STRAWBERRIES

If the only space you have is a foot or two of windowsill, it is possible to have succulent red strawberries in late April or early May. Outside they can be grown on a paved area in pots, boxes, various hanging containers and in tubs or barrels. The smallest plot should be able to accommodate a row to produce fruit either in summer or from August to the frost.

There are three main types of strawberry — the ordinary summer-fruiting cultivars, the everbearers and much smaller alpine strawberries.

Dependable Varieties

Always buy certified virus-free stock and beware of runners offered by friends who may be unaware that their plants are diseased. In fact, it is best to buy new plants every three years. The following are some well-known varieties that are not necessarily suitable for every region or climate. Consult your county extension agent for local suggestions.

'Fairfax' has early, sweet berries; 'Fortune', midseason and large; 'New Empire', huge, late fruits; 'Ogalla', large, everbearing; 'Ozark Beauty' is everbearing.

Restrict runners to two or three: 'Premier', early, adaptable; 'Sparkle', a late variety popular throughout the Northeast.

'Surecrop' has early, sweet berries and is widely planted.

'Suwannee' is an old variety, considered by the N.Y.S. Fruit Testing Coop at Geneva to be the best flavored of all strawberries. Fruits are of medium size, ripen in mid-season.

Alpine Strawberries

These are sometimes listed under perpetual fruiters. Varieties like 'Baron Solemacher' carry finger-nail-sized berries from June to the frost. The small fruit has rather large woody seeds. Sown in spring it bears the same year.

Cultivation

All well-cultivated soils are suitable, especially if enriched with well-rotted compost. A sunny position is best but they will bear in some shade. Spring planting is best in the North. These spring planted bare root plants will benefit from having the blooms removed in May to build strength for future seasons' crops. Pot-grown runners can be planted later than mid-August and because they suffer no root disturbance will fruit well the following June. Set the plants 12—18 in. (30—45 cm) apart in rows 2 ft (60 cm) apart.

An easy way with strawberries is to plant a single row fairly closely, crop it the first summer, then take at least one good runner from each plant to form a new row, digging the fruited row in afterwards. This prevents perennial weeds becoming established, and masses of runners rooting everywhere. The strawberry then becomes a one-year rotation in the vegetable plot.

Where space is ample, the hill and matted row systems are two common ways of growing strawberries. Ask your county agent for instructions as well as for strawberry varieties recommended for your region.

Mulching with black plastic is a simple method of cultivation. Strips 2 ft (60 cm) wide are placed down the row. Make two drills in the soil 9 in. (23 cm) each side of where the strawberry plants will go, as if you were sowing seeds, and put the edge of the plastic in the drill and pull back soil to bury the edges. This will give an 18 in. (45 cm) strip, in which you cut crosses where the runners are to be planted.

The strawberries will grow well through the plastic, which suppresses weeds, keeps the fruit clean, stops runners rooting everwhere and gives up to five years of work-free strawberry harvests.

Do not plant strawberries too deeply or too shallowly, but do plant firmly.

Runners on summer-fruiting kinds should be pinched off as soon as they appear unless you intend saving one or two for a new planting. Runners on everbearing varieties are left to flower and fruit.

It is beneficial to apply a liquid tomato ferilizer as the berries start to swell to increase fruit size and help build the plant's reserves.

Straw is traditionally used to cover the soil and keep the fruit clean, but plastic sheeting is easier.

Windowsill growing

If you want to grow strawberries on the windowsill, half-pots of 6 in. (15 cm)

Strawberries are always popular, and heavy crops are easily achieved. The berries need the protection of black plastic or straw.

diameter are ideal. Use an all-peat potting compost, and pot up runners in early August. Leave the plants outdoors until February, then bring them in and grow like houseplants. Tickle the flowers with a feather when in full bloom to pollinate, then by late April you can be picking ripe berries.

Growing in tubs

Good crops can be obtained by planting in tubs used by cider and vinegar makers. They need drilling with drainage holes at the base, and also round the side at intervals of about 15 in (37 cm). Place a layer of broken-up pieces from clay pots or pebbles at the bottom, to cover the drainage holes and to permit surplus moisture to escape. Over these pieces, place some coarse compost, then fill up to within 1 in (2.5 cm) of the top with prepared loam, peat and decayed manure. Also, give a handful of superphosphate to each tub.

Plant 6 in (15 cm) apart in a tub and, from spring, keep the plants well supplied with moisture, for they will obtain only limited amounts naturally.

Strawberries are easily propagated from runners, pegged into pots to root. Once rooted and established, the runners can be severed from the parent plant.

Pests and Diseases

Aphids stunt and yellow leaves.

Botrytis or 'gray mold' causes the fruit to go brown and rotten, the brown subsequently being covered with a furry gray mold. Fungicides like benomyl will achieve control.

Root weevils and grubs can be destructive. White grubs are often a problem when strawberry plants are set in former sod areas. Methoxychlor applied to soil will control.

SMALL FRUITS: PEST AND DISEASE CONTROL

Problem	Fruit	Control and Timing	Notes
Pests			
Aphids	Currant, Gooseberry, Raspberry, Strawberry	Malathion (as in multiple purpose fruit spray — see Fruit Tree Chart on page 132) as leaf buds are opening. Or use rotenone.	
Cyclamen and Two-spotted Mites	Strawberry, also Blackberry, Raspberry, Currant, Gooseberry	Use Kelthane when damage is noticed (except during blooming and fruit formation and ripening).	
White Grub	Strawberry	Apply diazinon or chlordane* to soil before planting.	Avoid planting in former sod areas.
Root Weevil	Strawberry	Apply methoxychlor to soil before planting.	
Caterpillars and Sawfly (larvae)	Raspberry, Strawberry	Spray with carbaryl** or rotenone when pests are seen. Or just as blossom buds appear.	
Japanese Beetles, Rose Chafers	Grape, Raspberry	Spray with carbaryl or methoxychlor in early summer as beetles appear. Repeat at 10-14 day intervals as needed. Handpick in small plantings and if infestations are light.	
Grape Berry Moth (larvae)	Grape	Spray as above.	
Tarnished Plant Bug	Blackberry, Strawberry, Raspberry	Spray with malathion just before buds open.	
Diseases			
Botrytis Fruit Rot (Gray Mold)	Blackberry, Raspberry, Strawberry	Spray with benomyl or captan just before bloom and at weekly intervals though harvest.	Remove and destroy dead leaves. Pick often to remove ripe, rotting fruits.
Black Rot	Grape	Spray with captan just before bloom, just after and at 10-14 day intervals thereafter until early fall.	Remove mummied berries and infected canes destroy.
Mildew (Downy and Powdery)	Grape, Strawberry	Downy mildew on grapes, spray as above; powdery mildew on grapes, as above, or use benomyl. On strawberries, same timing as above but use dinocap or lime sulfur and repeat at 10-14 day intervals until 1-2 weeks before harvest.	
Spur Blight	Blackberry, Raspberry	Apply captan at green tip bud stage, when new canes are 6-8 in. (15-20 cm) high, when 12-15 in. (30-40 cm) high and just before bloom.	After harvest, cut and destroy infected canes.

*State and federal regulations regarding use of chlordane and other pesticides differ.
Check with county extension agent for advice and latest information.
**Do not spray blooms with insecticides which can kill bees.
Follow manufacturer's instructions for time between spray and harvest and other precautions.

Vegetables

The rewards of growing flowers and shrubs are clear to anyone — their beauty and fragrance are enough. Yet vegetables are no less satisfying to grow — a neat, well-kept vegetable plot can do credit to any garden. Many vegetables are attractive enough in their own right, and would not look amiss in a flower border.

The reason most gardeners grow vegetables is, of course, because they prefer the better taste of home-grown vegetables picked fresh from the garden. The financial gain must be a bonus.

The wide range of different varieties of vegetable now available to gardeners has also added a great deal to the fun of vegetable growing.

Grow new varieties alongside well-proven kinds so that you can gradually assess what best suits your garden conditions and taste.

Few gardeners have perfect site and soil conditions for growing every kind of vegetable, although repeated cultivation and the addition of organic material will do much to improve them.

When sowing seed, try to avoid the temptation to sow it too thickly and deeply. Most seeds need no more than a light covering of soil, particularly if the soil is good and moist. In dry conditions, it is worth running some water along the base of the drill before sowing, especially if you are using pelleted seed.

Germination depends to some extent on weather conditions and the vegetable in question, but in most cases it takes two or three weeks — longer, of course, in cold weather.

No gardener should be deterred purely on grounds of space from attempting to grow vegetables — it's quite feasible to grow a selection of vegetables and herbs in tubs, window-boxes and other containers. It is possible to grow a suprisingly wide range of crops that will contribute significantly to the family budget in a plot only 10 ft × 12 ft (3m × 4m).

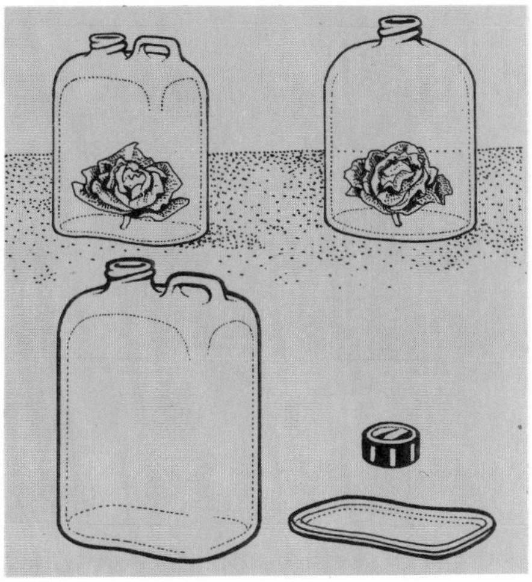

Inexpensive clochelike protection can be provided by removing the base from plastic containers.

For best use of space and protection (cloches, polyethylene tunnels, etc.), grow several suitable crops together.

Protection from the elements

Because the greatest saving is achieved by having your own crops ready for picking while the prices in the shops are still high, it is well worth giving some of your plants the benefit of some protection. Cutting your own lettuce for most of the year and harvesting your first beans a few weeks before everyone else also brings its own sense of satisfaction.

Providing suitable protection need not involve much expenditure either — even discarded white and clear plastic containers can make an extremely useful contribution (simply cut out the base, as shown above) but make sure you screw the cut edge into the soil for $^1/_2$ in. (1 cm) or so to prevent the wind blowing the container away.

See the section that begins on page 167 for other ways to protect plants.

Planning

When starting to grow vegetables for the first time and at the beginning of each new year it is a help to measure up the plot available and work out where all the different kinds of vegetables you would like to grow will fit. Remember you should rotate the crops, to avoid having one crop in the same position for several years.

Study seed catalogs and packets for information on crop maturity dates so you can plan on having a succession of the same as well as different vegetables all season. For instance, peas are sown very early in spring (for how early in your region, see pages 142-143) and after they are harvested, such warm weather crops as snap beans and summer squash can follow. To keep the garden productive into fall and even into early winter in some regions, consult the map on page 144 for dates of the first killing frost in your area, then check the table below for the crop you wish to grow and when it must be planted to mature before freezes arrive. In both tables, the earlier date or as close as possible to it gives the best results. In much of the North, most long-maturing, warm weather crops can only be planted once.

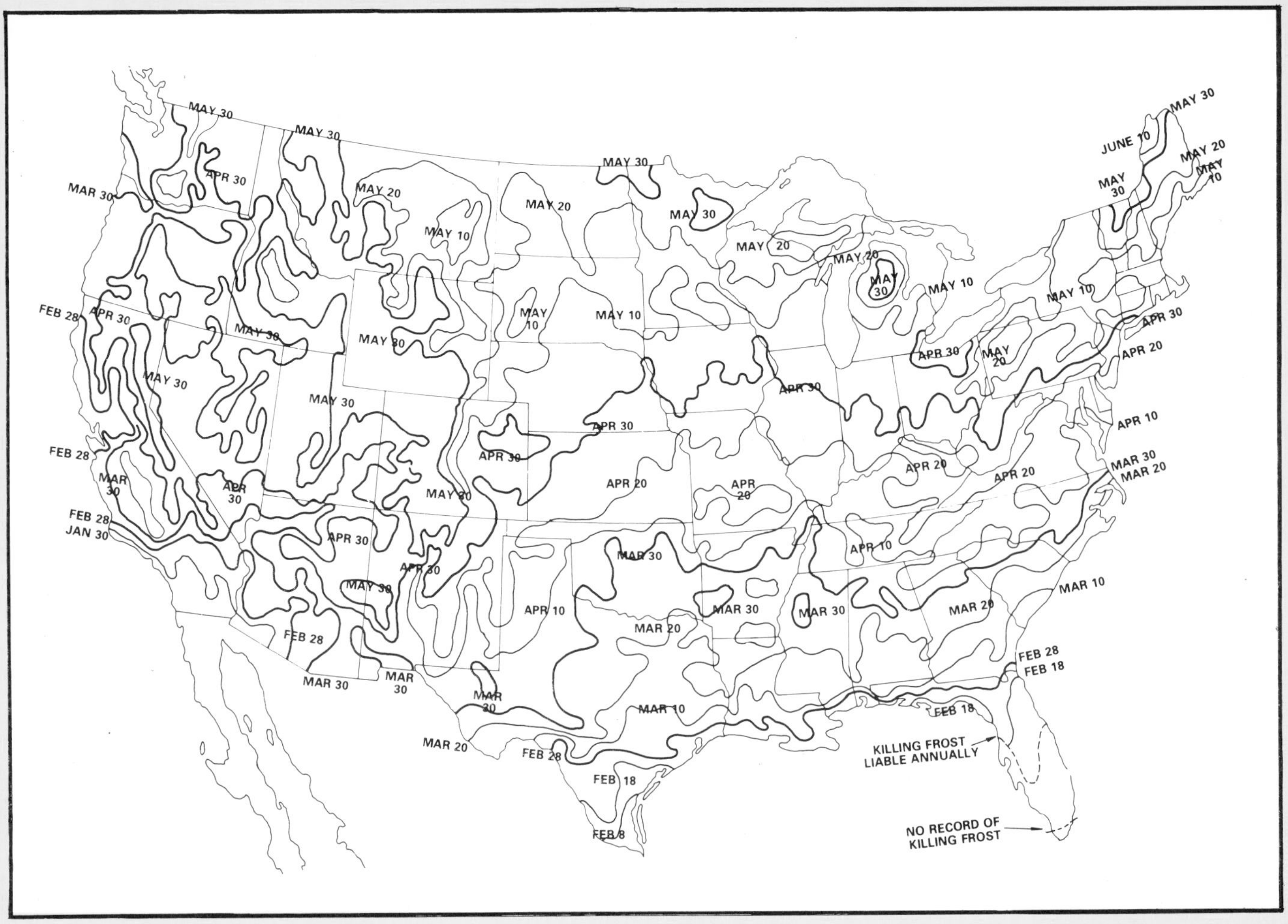

Map to show average dates of last killing frost in spring.

EARLIEST DATES, AND RANGE OF DATES, FOR SAFE SPRING PLANTING OF VEGETABLES IN THE OPEN

Crop	Planting dates for localities in which average date of last freeze is—						
	Jan 30	Feb 8	Feb 18	Feb 28	Mar 10	Mar 20	Mar 30
Asparagus[1]					Jan 1–Mar 1	Feb 1–Mar 10	Feb 15–Mar 20
Beans, lima	Feb 1–Apr 15	Feb 10–May 1	Mar 1–May 1	Mar 15–June 1	Mar 20–June 1	Apr 1–June 15	Apr 15–June 20
Beans, snap	Feb 1–Apr 1	Feb 1–May 1	Mar 1–May 1	Mar 10–May 15	Mar 15–May 15	Mar 15–May 25	Apr 1–June 1
Beet	Jan 1–Mar 15	Jan 10–Mar 15	Jan 20–Apr 1	Feb 1–Apr 15	Feb 15–June 1	Feb 15–May 15	Mar 1–June 1
Broccoli,[1]	Jan 1–30	Jan 1–30	Jan 15–Feb 15	Feb 1–Mar 1	Feb 15–Mar 15	Feb 15–Mar 15	Mar 1–20
Brussels sprouts[1]	Jan 1–30	Jan 1–30	Jan 15–Feb 15	Feb 1–Mar 1	Feb 15–Mar 15	Feb 15–Mar 15	Mar 1–20
Cabbage[1]	Jan 1–15	Jan 1–Feb 10	Jan 1–Feb 25	Jan 15–Feb 25	Jan 25–Mar 1	Feb 1–Mar 1	Feb 15–Mar 10
Cabbage, Chinese	([2])	([2])	([2])	([2])	([2])	([2])	([2])
Carrot	Jan 1–Mar 1	Jan 1–Mar 1	Jan 15–Mar 1	Feb 1–Mar 1	Feb 10–Mar 15	Feb 15–Mar 20	Mar 1–Apr 10
Cauliflower[1]	Jan 1–Feb 1	Jan 1–Feb 1	Jan 10–Feb 10	Jan 20–Feb 20	Feb 1–Mar 1	Feb 10–Mar 10	Feb 20–Mar 20
Celery and celeriac	Jan 1–Feb 1	Jan 10–Feb 10	Jan 20–Feb 20	Feb 1–Mar 1	Feb 20–Mar 20	Mar 1–Apr 1	Mar 15–Apr 15
Chard	Jan 1–Apr 1	Jan 10–Apr 1	Jan 20–Apr 15	Feb 1–May 1	Feb 15–May 15	Feb 20–May 15	Mar 1–May 25
Chervil and chives	Jan 1–Feb 1	Jan 1–Feb 1	Jan 1–Feb 1	Jan 15–Feb 15	Feb 1–Mar 1	Feb 10–Mar 10	Feb 15–Mar 15
Chicory, witloof					June 1–July 1	June 1–July 1	June 1–July 1
Corn salad	Jan 1–Feb 15	Jan 1–Feb 15	Jan 1–Mar 15	Jan 1–Mar 1	Jan 1–Mar 15	Jan 1–Mar 15	Jan 15–Mar 15
Corn, sweet	Feb 1–Mar 15	Feb 10–Apr 1	Feb 20–Apr 15	Mar 1–Apr 15	Mar 10–Apr 15	Mar 15–May 1	Mar 25–May 15
Cress, upland	Jan 1–Feb 1	Jan 1–Feb 15	Jan 15–Feb 15	Feb 1–Mar 1	Feb 10–Mar 15	Feb 20–Mar 15	Mar 1–Apr 1
Cucumber	Feb 15–Mar 15	Feb 15–Apr 1	Feb 15–Apr 15	Mar 1–Apr 15	Mar 15–Apr 15	Apr 1–May 1	Apr 10–May 15
Eggplant[1]	Feb 1–Mar 1	Feb 10–Mar 15	Feb 20–Apr 1	Mar 10–Apr 15	Mar 15–Apr 15	Apr 1–May 1	Apr 15–May 15
Endive	Jan 1–Mar 1	Jan 1–Mar 1	Jan 15–Mar 1	Feb 1–Mar 1	Feb 15–Mar 15	Mar 1–Apr 1	Mar 10–Apr 10
Fennel, Florence	Jan 1–Mar 1	Jan 1–Mar 1	Jan 15–Mar 1	Feb 1–Mar 1	Feb 15–Mar 15	Mar 1–Apr 1	Mar 10–Apr 10
Garlic	([2])	([2])	([2])	([2])	([2])	Feb 1–Mar 1	Feb 10–Mar 10
Horseradish[1]							Mar 1–Apr 1
Kale	Jan 1–Feb 1	Jan 10–Feb 1	Jan 20–Feb 10	Feb 1–20	Feb 10–Mar 1	Feb 20–Mar 10	Mar 1–20
Kohlrabi	Jan 1–Feb 1	Jan 10–Feb 1	Jan 20–Feb 10	Feb 1–20	Feb 10–Mar 1	Feb 20–Mar 10	Mar 1–Apr 1
Leek	Jan 1–Feb 1	Jan 1–Feb 1	Jan 1–Feb 15	Jan 15–Feb 15	Jan 25–Mar 1	Feb 1–Mar 1	Feb 15–Mar 15
Lettuce, head[1]	Jan 1–Feb 1	Jan 1–Feb 1	Jan 1–Feb 1	Jan 15–Feb 15	Feb 1–20	Feb 15–Mar 10	Mar 1–20
Lettuce, leaf	Jan 1–Feb 1	Jan 1–Feb 1	Jan 1–Mar 15	Jan 1–Mar 15	Jan 15–Apr 1	Feb 1–Apr 1	Feb 15–Apr 15
Muskmelon	Feb 15–Mar 15	Feb 15–Apr 1	Feb 15–Apr 15	Mar 1–Apr 15	Mar 15–Apr 15	Apr 1–May 1	Apr 10–May 15
Mustard	Jan 1–Mar 1	Jan 1–Mar 1	Feb 15–Apr 15	Feb 1–Mar 1	Feb 10–Mar 15	Feb 20–Apr 1	Mar 1–Apr 15
Okra	Feb 15–Apr 1	Feb 15–Apr 15	Mar 1–June 1	Mar 10–June 1	Mar 20–June 1	Apr 1–June 15	Apr 10–June 15

Crop	Planting dates for localities in which average date of last freeze is—						
	Jan 30	Feb 8	Feb 18	Feb 28	Mar 10	Mar 20	Mar 30
Onion[1]	Jan 1–15	Jan 1–15	Jan 1–15	Jan 1–Feb 1	Jan 15–Feb 15	Feb 10–Mar 10	Feb 15–Mar 15
Onion, seed	Jan 1–15	Jan 1–15	Jan 1–15	Jan 1–Feb 15	Feb 1–Mar 1	Feb 10–Mar 10	Feb 20–Mar 15
Onion, sets	Jan 1–15	Jan 1–15	Jan 1–15	Jan 1–Mar 1	Jan 15–Mar 10	Feb 1–Mar 20	Feb 15–Mar 20
Parsley	Jan 1–30	Jan 1–30	Jan 1–30	Jan 15–Mar 1	Feb 1–Mar 10	Feb 15–Mar 15	Mar 1–Apr 1
Parsnip			Jan 1–Feb 1	Jan 15–Feb 15	Jan 15–Mar 1	Feb 15–Mar 15	Mar 1–Apr 1
Peas, garden	Jan 1–Feb 15	Jan 1–Feb 15	Jan 1–Mar 1	Jan 15–Mar 1	Jan 15–Mar 15	Feb 1–Mar 15	Feb 10–Mar 20
Pepper[1]	Feb 1–Apr 1	Feb 15–Apr 15	Mar 1–May 1	Mar 15–May 1	Apr 1–June 1	Apr 10–June 1	Apr 15–June 1
Potato	Jan 1–Feb 15	Jan 1–Feb 15	Jan 15–Mar 1	Jan 15–Mar 1	Feb 1–Mar 1	Feb 10–Mar 15	Feb 20–Mar 20
Radish	Jan 1–Apr 1	Jan 1–Apr 1	Jan 1–Apr 1	Jan 1–Apr 1	Jan 1–Apr 15	Jan 20–May 1	Feb 15–May 1
Rhubarb[1]							
Rutabaga				Jan 1–Feb 1	Jan 15–Feb 15	Jan 15–Mar 1	Feb 1–Mar 1
Salsify	Jan 1–Feb 1	Jan 10–Feb 10	Jan 15–Feb 20	Jan 15–Mar 1	Feb 1–Mar 1	Feb 15–Mar 1	Mar 1–15
Shallot	Jan 1–Feb 1	Jan 1–Feb 10	Jan 1–Feb 20	Jan 1–Mar 1	Jan 15–Mar 1	Feb 1–Mar 10	Feb 15–Mar 15
Sorrel	Jan 1–Mar 1	Jan 1–Mar 1	Jan 15–Mar 1	Feb 1–Mar 10	Feb 10–Mar 15	Feb 10–Mar 20	Feb 20–Apr 1
Spinach	Jan 1–Feb 15	Jan 1–Feb 15	Jan 1–Mar 1	Jan 1–Mar 1	Jan 15–Mar 10	Jan 15–Mar 15	Feb 1–Mar 20
Spinach, New Zealand	Feb 1–Apr 15	Feb 15–Apr 15	Mar 1–Apr 15	Mar 15–May 15	Mar 20–May 15	Apr 1–May 15	Apr 10–June 1
Squash, summer	Feb 1–Apr 15	Feb 15–Apr 15	Mar 1–Apr 15	Mar 15–May 15	Mar 15–May 1	Apr 1–May 15	Apr 10–June 1
Tomato	Feb 1–Apr 1	Feb 20–Apr 10	Mar 1–Apr 20	Mar 10–May 1	Mar 20–May 10	Apr 1–May 20	Apr 10–June 1
Turnip	Jan 1–Mar 1	Jan 1–Mar 1	Jan 10–Mar 1	Jan 20–Mar 1	Feb 1–Mar 1	Feb 10–Mar 10	Feb 20–Mar 20
Watermelon	Feb 15–Mar 15	Feb 15–Apr 1	Feb 15–Apr 15	Mar 1–Apr 15	Mar 15–Apr 15	Apr 1–May 1	Apr 10–May 15

Crop	Planting dates for localities in which average date of last freeze is—						
	Apr 10	Apr 20	Apr 30	May 10	May 20	May 30	June 10
Asparagus[1]	Mar 10–Apr 10	Mar 15–Apr 15	Mar 20–Apr 15	Mar 10–Apr 30	Apr 20–May 15	May 1–June 1	May 15–June 1
Beans, lima	Apr 1–June 30	May 1–June 20	May 15–June 15	May 25–June 15			
Beans, snap	Apr 10–June 30	Apr 25–June 30	May 10–June 30	May 10–June 30	May 15–June 30	May 25–June 15	
Beet	Mar 10–June 1	Mar 20–June 1	Apr 1–June 15	Apr 15–June 15	Apr 25–June 15	May 1–June 15	May 15–June 15
Broccoli[1]	Mar 15–Apr 15	Mar 25–Apr 20	Apr 1–May 1	Apr 15–June 1	May 1–June 15	May 10–June 10	May 20–June 10
Brussels sprouts[1]	Mar 15–Apr 15	Mar 25–Apr 20	Apr 1–May 1	Apr 15–June 1	May 1–June 15	May 10–June 10	May 20–June 10
Cabbage[1]	Mar 1–Apr 1	Mar 10–Apr 1	Mar 15–Apr 10	Apr 1–May 15	May 1–June 15	May 10–June 15	May 20–June 1
Cabbage, Chinese	(2)	(2)	(2)	Apr 1–May 15	May 1–June 15	May 10–June 15	May 20–June 1
Carrot	Mar 10–Apr 20	Apr 1–May 15	Apr 10–June 1	Apr 20–June 15	May 1–June 1	May 10–June 1	May 20–June 1
Cauliflower[1]	Mar 1–Mar 20	Mar 15–Apr 20	Apr 10–May 10	Apr 15–May 15	May 10–June 15	May 20–June 1	June 1–June 15
Celery and celeriac	Apr 1–Apr 20	Apr 10–May 1	Apr 15–May 1	Apr 20–June 15	May 10–June 15	May 20–June 1	June 1–June 15
Chard	Mar 15–June 15	Apr 1–June 15	Apr 15–June 15	Apr 20–June 15	May 10–June 15	May 20–June 1	June 1–June 15
Chervil and chives	Mar 1–Apr 1	Mar 10–Apr 10	Mar 20–Apr 20	Apr 1–May 1	Apr 15–May 15	May 1–June 1	May 15–June 1
Chicory, witloof	June 10–July 1	June 15–July 1	June 15–July 1	June 1–20	June 1–15	June 1–15	June 1–15
Corn salad	Feb 1–Apr 1	Feb 15–Apr 15	Mar 1–May 1	Apr 1–June 1	Apr 15–June 1	May 1–June 15	May 15–June 15
Corn, sweet	Apr 10–June 1	Apr 25–June 15	May 10–June 15	May 10–June 1	May 15–June 1	May 20–June 1	
Cress, upland	Mar 10–Apr 15	Mar 20–May 1	Apr 10–May 10	Apr 20–May 20	May 1–June 1	May 15–June 1	May 15–June 15
Cucumber	Apr 20–June 1	May 1–June 15	May 15–June 15	May 20–June 15	June 1–15		
Eggplant[1]	May 1–June 1	May 10–June 1	May 15–June 10	May 20–June 15	June 1–15		
Endive	Mar 15–Apr 15	Mar 25–Apr 15	Apr 1–May 1	Apr 15–May 15	May 1–30	May 1–30	May 15–June 1
Fennel, Florence	Mar 15–Apr 15	Mar 25–Apr 15	Apr 1–May 1	Apr 15–May 15	May 1–30	May 1–30	May 15–June 1
Garlic	Feb 20–Mar 20	Mar 10–Apr 1	Mar 15–Apr 15	Apr 1–May 1	Apr 15–May 15	May 1–30	May 15–June 1
Horseradish[1]	Mar 10–Apr 10	Mar 20–Apr 20	Apr 1–30	Apr 15–May 15	Apr 20–May 20	May 1–30	May 15–June 1
Kale	Mar 10–Apr 1	Mar 20–Apr 10	Apr 1–20	Apr 10–May 1	Apr 20–May 10	May 1–30	May 15–June 1
Kohlrabi	Mar 10–Apr 10	Mar 20–May 1	Apr 1–May 10	Apr 10–May 15	Apr 20–May 20	May 1–30	May 15–June 1
Leek	Mar 1–Apr 1	Mar 15–Apr 15	Apr 1–May 1	Apr 15–May 15	May 1–May 20	May 1–15	May 1–15
Lettuce, head[1]	Mar 10–Apr 1	Mar 20–Apr 15	Apr 1–May 1	Apr 15–May 15	May 1–June 30	May 10–June 30	May 20–June 30
Lettuce, leaf	Mar 15–May 15	Mar 20–May 15	Apr 1–June 1	Apr 15–June 15	May 1–June 30	May 10–June 30	May 20–June 30
Muskmelon	Apr 20–June 1	May 1–June 15	May 15–June 15	June 1–June 15			
Mustard	Mar 10–Apr 20	Mar 20–May 1	Apr 1–May 10	Apr 15–June 1	May 1–June 30	May 10–June 30	May 20–June 30
Okra	Apr 20–June 15	May 1–June 1	May 10–June 1	May 20–June 10	June 1–20		
Onion[1]	Mar 1–Apr 1	Mar 15–Apr 10	Apr 1–May 1	Apr 10–May 1	Apr 20–May 15	May 1–30	May 10–June 10
Onion, seed	Mar 1–Apr 1	Mar 15–Apr 1	Mar 15–Apr 15	Apr 1–May 1	Apr 20–May 15	May 1–30	May 10–June 10
Onion, sets	Mar 1–Apr 1	Mar 10–Apr 1	Mar 10–Apr 10	Apr 10–May 1	Apr 20–May 15	May 1–30	May 10–June 10
Parsley	Mar 10–Apr 10	Mar 20–Apr 20	Apr 1–May 1	Apr 15–May 15	May 1–20	May 10–June 1	May 20–June 10
Parsnip	Mar 10–Apr 10	Mar 20–Apr 20	Apr 1–May 1	Apr 15–May 15	May 1–20	May 10–June 1	May 20–June 10
Peas, garden	Feb 20–Mar 20	Mar 10–Apr 10	Mar 20–May 1	Apr 1–May 15	Apr 15–June 1	May 1–June 15	May 10–June 15
Peas, black-eye	May 1–July 1	May 10–June 15	May 15–June 1				
Pepper[1]	May 1–June 1	May 10–June 1	May 15–June 10	May 20–June 10	May 25–June 15	June 1–15	
Potato	Mar 10–Apr 1	Mar 15–Apr 10	Mar 20–May 10	Apr 1–June 1	Apr 15–June 15	May 1–June 15	May 15–June 1
Radish	Mar 1–May 1	Mar 10–May 10	Mar 20–May 10	Apr 1–June 1	Apr 15–June 15	May 1–June 15	May 15–June 1
Rhubarb[1]	Mar 1–Apr 1	Mar 10–Apr 10	Mar 20–Apr 15	Apr 1–May 1	Apr 15–May 10	May 1–20	May 15–June 1
Rutabaga			May 1–June 1	May 1–June 1	May 1–20	May 10–20	May 20–June 1
Salsify	Mar 10–Apr 15	Mar 20–May 1	Apr 1–May 15	Apr 15–June 1	May 1–June 1	May 10–June 1	May 20–June 1
Shallot	Mar 1–Apr 1	Mar 15–Apr 15	Apr 1–May 1	Apr 10–May 1	Apr 20–May 10	May 1–June 1	May 10–June 1
Sorrel	Mar 1–Apr 15	Mar 15–May 1	Apr 1–May 15	Apr 15–June 1	May 1–June 1	May 10–June 10	May 20–June 10
Soybean	May 1–June 30	May 10–June 20	May 15–June 15	May 25–June 10			
Spinach	Feb 15–Apr 1	Mar 1–Apr 15	Mar 20–Apr 20	Apr 1–June 15	Apr 10–June 15	Apr 20–June 15	May 1–June 15
Spinach, New Zealand	Apr 20–June 1	May 1–June 15	May 1–June 15	May 10–June 15	May 20–June 15	June 1–15	
Squash, summer	Apr 20–June 1	May 1–June 15	May 1–30	May 10–June 10	May 20–June 15	June 1–20	June 10–20
Sweetpotato	May 1–June 1	May 10–June 10	May 20–June 10				
Tomato	Apr 20–June 1	May 5–June 10	May 10–June 15	May 15–June 10	May 25–June 15	June 5–20	June 15–30
Turnip	Mar 1–Apr 1	Mar 10–Apr 1	Mar 20–May 1	Apr 1–June 1	Apr 15–June 1	May 1–June 15	May 15–June 15
Watermelon	Apr 20–June 1	May 1–June 15	May 15–June 15	June 1–June 15	June 15–July 1		

[1] Plants.
[2] Generally fall-planted

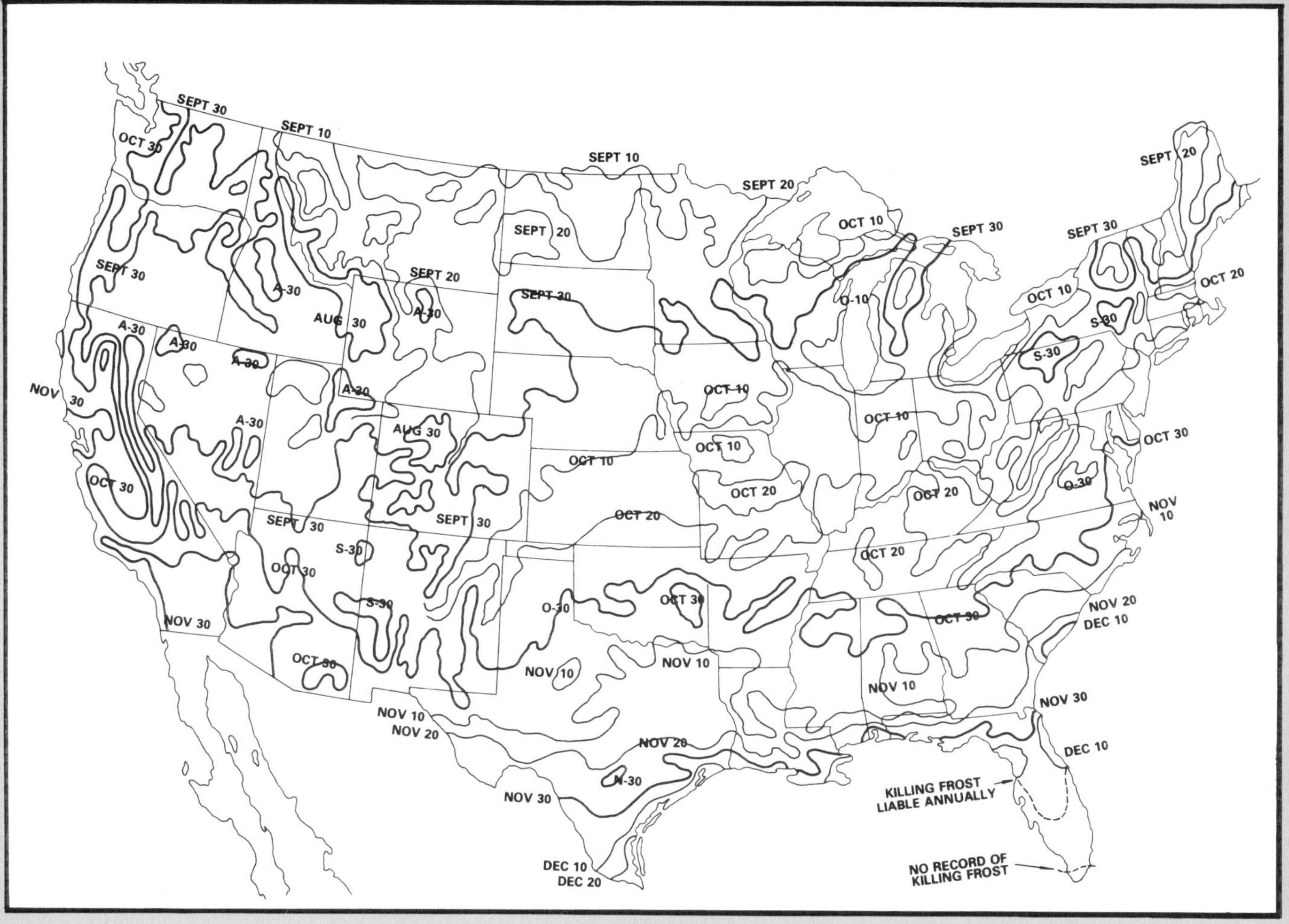

Map to show average dates of first killing frost in fall.

LATEST DATES, AND RANGE OF DATES, FOR SAFE FALL PLANTING OF VEGETABLES IN THE OPEN

Crop	Planting dates for localities in which average dates of first freeze is—					
	Aug 30	Sept 10	Sept 20	Sept 30	Oct 10	Oct 20
Asparagus[1]					Oct 20–Nov 15	Nov 1–Dec 15
Beans, lima				June 1–15	June 1–15	June 15–30
Beans, snap		May 15–June 15	June 1–July 1	June 1–July 10	June 15–July 20	July 1–Aug 1
Beet	May 15–June 15	May 15–June 15	June 1–July 1	June 1–July 10	June 15–July 25	July 1–Aug 5
Broccoli	May 1–June 1	May 1–June 1	May 1–June 15	June 1–30	June 15–July 15	July 1–Aug 1
Brussels sprouts	May 1–June 1	May 1–June 1	May 1–June 15	June 1–30	June 15–July 15	July 1–Aug 1
Cabbage[1]	May 1–June 1	May 1–June 1	May 1–June 15	June 1–July 10	June 1–July 15	July 1–20
Cabbage, Chinese	May 15–June 15	May 15–June 15	June 1–July 1	June 1–July 15	June 15–Aug 1	July 15–Aug 15
Carrot	May 15–June 15	May 15–June 15	June 1–July 1	June 1–July 10	June 1–July 20	June 15–Aug 1
Cauliflower[1]	May 1–June 1	May 1–July 1	May 1–July 1	May 10–July 15	June 1–July 25	July 1–Aug 5
Celery[1] and celeriac	May 1–June 1	May 15–June 15	May 15–July 1	June 1–July 5	June 1–July 15	June 1–Aug. 1
Chard, Swiss	May 15–June 15	May 15–July 1	June 1–July 1	June 1–July 5	June 1–July 20	June 1–Aug 1
Chervil and chives	May 10–June 10	May 1–June 15	May 15–June 15	([2])	([2])	([2])
Chicory, Witloof	May 15–June 15	May 15–June 15	May 15–June 15	June 1–July 1	June 1–July 1	June 15–July 15
Corn salad	May 15–June 15	May 15–July 1	June 15–Aug 1	July 15–Sept 1	Aug 15–Sept 15	Sept 1–Oct 15
Corn, sweet			June 1–July 1	June 1–July 1	June 1–July 10	June 1–July 20
Cress, upland	May 15–June 15	May 15–July 1	June 15–Aug 1	July 15–Sept 1	Aug 15–Sept 15	Sept 1–Oct 15
Cucumber			June 1–15	June 1–July 1	June 1–July 1	June 1–July 15
Eggplant[1]				May 20–June 10	May 15–June 15	June 1–July 1
Endive	June 1–July 1	June 1–July 1	June 15–July 15	June 15–Aug 1	July 1–Aug 15	July 15–Sept 1
Fennel, Florence	May 15–June 15	May 15–July 15	June 1–July 1	June 1–July 1	June 15–July 15	June 15–Aug 1
Garlic	([2])	([2])	([2])	([2])	([2])	([2])
Horseradish[1]	([2])	([2])	([2])	([2])	([2])	([2])
Kale	May 15–June 15	May 15–June 15	June 1–July 1	June 15–July 15	July 1–Aug 1	July 15–Aug 15
Kohlrabi	May 15–June 15	June 1–July 1	June 1–July 15	June 15–July 15	July 1–Aug 1	July 15–Aug 15
Leek	May 1–June 1	May 1–June 1	([2])	([2])	([2])	([2])
Lettuce, head[1]	May 15–July 1	May 15–July 1	June 1–July 15	June 15–Aug 1	July 15–Aug 15	Aug 1–30
Lettuce, leaf	May 15–July 15	May 15–July 15	June 1–Aug 1	June 1–Aug 1	July 15–Sept 1	July 15–Sept 1
Muskmelon			May 1–June 15	May 15–June 1	June 1–June 15	June 15–July 20
Mustard	May 15–July 15	May 15–July 15	June 1–Aug 1	June 15–Aug 1	July 15–Aug 15	Aug 1–Sept 1

Crop	Planting dates for localities in which average dates of first freeze is—					
	Aug 30	Sept 10	Sept 20	Sept 30	Oct 10	Oct 20
Okra			June 1–20	June 1–July 1	June 1–July 15	June 1–Aug 1
Onion[1]	May 1–June 10	May 1–June 10	([2])	([2])	([2])	([2])
Onion, seed	May 1–June 1	May 1–June 10	([2])	([2])	([2])	([2])
Onion, sets	May 1–June 1	May 1–June 10	([2])	([2])	([2])	([2])
Parsley	May 15–June 15	May 1–June 15	June 1–July 1	June 1–July 15	June 15–Aug 1	July 15–Aug 15
Parsnip	May 15–June 1	May 1–June 15	May 15–June 15	June 1–July 1	June 1–July 10	([2])
Peas, garden	May 10–June 15	May 1–July 1	June 1–July 15	June 1–Aug 1	([2])	([2])
Pepper[1]			June 1–June 20	June 1–July 1	June 1–July 1	June 1–July 10
Potato	May 15–June 1	May 1–June 15	May 1–June 15	May 1–June 15	May 15–June 15	June 15–July 15
Radish	May 1–July 15	May 1–Aug 1	June 1–Aug 15	July 1–Sept 1	July 15–Sept 15	Aug 1–Oct 1
Rhubarb[1]	Sept 1–Oct 1	Sept 15–Oct 15	Sept 15–Nov 1	Oct 1–Nov 1	Oct 15–Nov 15	Oct 15–Dec. 1
Rutabaga	May 15–June 15	May 1–June 15	June 1–July 1	June 1–July 1	June 15–July 15	July 10–20
Salsify	May 15–June 1	May 10–June 10	May 20–June 20	June 1–20	June 1–July 1	June 1–July 1
Shallot	([2])	([2])	([2])	([2])	([2])	([2])
Sorrel	May 15–June 15	May 1–June 15	June 1–July 1	June 1–July 15	July 1–Aug 1	July 15–Aug 15
Spinach	May 15–July 1	June 1–July 15	June 1–Aug 1	July 1–Aug 15	Aug 1–Sept 1	Aug 20–Sept 10
Spinach, New Zealand				May 15–July 1	June 1–July 15	June 1–Aug 1
Squash, summer	June 10–20	June 1–20	May 15–July 1	June 1–July 1	June 1–July 15	June 1–July 20
Squash, winter			May 20–June 10	June 1–15	June 1–July 1	June 1–July 1
Tomato	June 20–30	June 10–20	June 1–20	June 1–20	June 1–20	June 1–July 1
Turnip	May 15–June 15	June 1–July 1	June 1–July 15	June 1–Aug 1	July 1–Aug 1	July 15–Aug 15
Watermelon			May 1–June 15	May 15–June 1	June 1–June 15	June 15–July 20

Crop	Planting dates for localities in which average date of first freeze is—					
	Oct 30	Nov 10	Nov 20	Nov 30	Dec 10	Dec 20
Asparagus[1]	Nov 15–Jan 1	Dec 1–Jan 1				
Beans, lima	July 1–Aug 1	July 1–Aug 15	July 15–Sept 1	Aug 1–Sept 15	Sept 1–30	Sept 1–Oct 1
Beans, snap	July 1–Aug 15	July 1–Sept 1	July 1–Sept 10	Aug 15–Sept 20	Sept 1–30	Sept 1–Nov 1
Beet	Aug 1–Sept 1	Aug 1–Oct 1	Sept 1–Dec 1	Sept 1–Dec 15	Sept 1–Dec 31	Sept 1–Dec 31
Broccoli	July 1–Aug 15	Aug 1–Sept 1	Aug 1–Sept 15	Aug 1–Oct 1	Aug 1–Nov 1	Sept 1–Dec 31
Brussels sprouts	July 1–Aug 15	Aug 1–Sept 1	Aug 1–Sept 15	Aug 1–Oct 1	Aug 1–Nov 1	Sept 1–Dec 31
Cabbage[1]	Aug 1–Sept 1	Sept 1–15	Sept 1–Dec 1	Sept 1–Dec 31	Sept 1–Dec 31	Sept 1–Dec 31
Cabbage, Chinese	Aug 1–Sept 15	Aug 15–Oct 1	Sept 1–Oct 15	Sept 1–Nov 1	Sept 1–Nov 15	Sept 1–Dec 1
Carrot	July 1–Aug 15	Aug 1–Sept 1	Sept 1–Nov 1	Sept 15–Dec 1	Sept 15–Dec 1	Sept 15–Dec 1
Cauliflower[1]	July 15–Aug 15	Aug 1–Sept 1	Aug 1–Sept 15	Aug 15–Oct 10	Sept 1–Oct 20	Sept 15–Nov 1
Celery[1] and celeriac	June 15–Aug 15	July 1–Aug 15	July 15–Sept 1	Aug 1–Dec 1	Sept 1–Dec 31	Oct 1–Dec 31
Chard, Swiss	June 1–Sept 10	June 1–Sept 15	June 1–Oct 1	June 1–Nov 1	June 1–Dec 1	June 1–Dec 31
Chervil and chives	([2])	([2])	Nov 1–Dec 31	Nov 1–Dec 31	Nov 1–Dec 31	Nov 1–Dec 31
Chicory, Witloof	July 1–Aug 10	July 10–Aug 20	July 20–Sept 1	Aug 15–Sept 30	Aug 15–Oct 15	Aug 15–Oct 15
Corn salad	Sept 15–Nov 1	Oct 1–Dec 1	Oct 1–Dec 1	Oct 1–Dec 31	Oct 1–Dec 31	Oct 1–Dec 31
Corn, sweet	June 1–Aug 1	June 1–Aug 15	June 1–Sept 1			
Cress, upland	Sept 15–Nov 1	Oct 1–Dec 1	Oct 1–Dec 1	Oct 1–Dec 31	Oct 1–Dec 31	Oct 1–Dec 31
Cucumber	June 1–Aug 1	June 1–Aug 15	June 1–Aug 15	July 15–Sept 15	Aug 15–Oct 1	Aug 15–Oct 1
Eggplant[1]	June 1–July 1	June 1–July 15	June 1–Aug 1	July 1–Sept 1	Aug 1–Sept 30	Aug 1–Sept 30
Endive	July 15–Aug 15	Aug 1–Sept 1	Sept 1–Oct 1	Sept 1–Nov 15	Sept 1–Dec 31	Sept 1–Dec 31
Fennel, Florence	July 1–Aug 1	July 15–Aug 15	Aug 15–Sept 15	Sept 1–Nov 15	Sept 1–Dec 1	Sept 1–Dec 1
Garlic	([2])	Aug 1–Oct 1	Aug 15–Oct 1	Sept 1–Nov 15	Sept 15–Nov 15	Sept 15–Nov 15
Horseradish[1]	([2])	([2])	([2])	([2])	([2])	([2])
Kale	July 15–Sept 1	Aug 1–Sept 15	Aug 15–Oct 15	Sept 1–Dec 1	Sept 1–Dec 31	Sept 1–Dec 31
Kohlrabi	Aug 1–Sept 1	Aug 15–Sept 15	Sept 1–Oct 15	Sept 1–Dec 1	Sept 15–Dec 31	Sept 1–Dec 31
Leek	([2])	([2])	Sept 1–Nov 1	Sept 1–Nov 1	Sept 1–Nov 1	Sept 15–Nov 1
Lettuce, head[1]	Aug 1–Sept 15	Aug 15–Oct 15	Sept 1–Nov 1	Sept 1–Dec 1	Sept 15–Dec 31	Sept 15–Dec 31
Lettuce, leaf	Aug 15–Oct 1	Aug 25–Oct 1	Sept 1–Nov 1	Sept 1–Dec 1	Sept 15–Dec 31	Sept 15–Dec 31
Muskmelon	July 1–July 15	July 15–July 30				
Mustard	Aug 15–Oct 15	Aug 15–Nov 1	Sept 1–Dec 1	Sept 1–Dec 1	Sept 1–Dec 1	Sept 15–Dec 1
Okra	June 1–Aug 10	June 1–Aug 20	June 1–Sept 10	June 1–Sept 20	Aug 1–Oct 1	Aug 1–Oct 1
Onion[1]		Sept 1–Oct 15	Oct 1–Dec 31	Oct 1–Dec 31	Oct 1–Dec 31	Oct 1–Dec 31
Onion, seed			Sept 1–Nov 1	Sept 1–Nov 1	Sept 1–Nov 1	Sept 15–Nov 1
Onion, sets		Oct 1–Dec 1	Nov 1–Dec 31	Nov 1–Dec 31	Nov 1–Dec 31	Nov 1–Dec 31
Parsley	Aug 1–Sept 15	Sept 1–Nov 15	Sept 1–Dec 31	Sept 1–Dec 31	Sept 1–Dec 31	Sept 1–Dec 31
Parsnip	([2])	([2])	Aug 1–Sept 1	Sept 1–Nov 15	Sept 1–Dec 1	Sept 1–Dec 1
Peas, garden	Aug 1–Sept 15	Sept 1–Nov 1	Oct 1–Dec 1	Oct 1–Dec 31	Oct 1–Dec 31	Oct 1–Dec 31
Pepper[1]	June 1–July 20	June 1–Aug 1	June 1–Aug 15	June 15–Sept 1	Aug 15–Oct 1	Aug 15–Oct 1
Potato	July 20–Aug 10	July 25–Aug 20	Aug 10–Sept 15	Aug 1–Sept 15	Aug 1–Sept 15	Aug 1–Sept 15
Radish	Aug 15–Oct 15	Sept 1–Nov 15	Sept 1–Dec 1	Sept 1–Dec 31	Aug 1–Sept 15	Oct 1–Dec 31
Rhubarb[1]	Nov 15–Dec 1					
Rutabaga	July 15–Aug 1	July 15–Aug 15	Aug 1–Sept 1	Sept 1–Nov 15	Oct 1–Nov 15	Oct 15–Nov 15
Salsify	June 1–July 10	June 15–July 20	July 15–Aug 15	Aug 15–Sept 30	Aug 15–Oct 15	Sept 1–Oct 31
Shallot	([2])	Aug 1–Oct 1	Aug 15–Oct 1	Aug 15–Oct 15	Sept 15–Nov 1	Sept 15–Nov 1
Sorrel	Aug 1–Sept 15	Aug 15–Oct 1	Aug 15–Oct 15	Sept 1–Nov 15	Sept 1–Dec 15	Sept 1–Dec 31
Spinach	Sept 1–Oct 1	Sept 15–Nov 1	Oct 1–Dec 1	Oct 1–Dec 31	Oct 1–Dec 31	Oct 1–Dec 31
Spinach, New Zealand	June 1–Aug 1	June 1–Aug 15	June 1–Aug 15			
Squash, summer	June 1–Aug 1	June 1–Aug 10	June 1–Aug 20	June 1–Sept 1	June 1–Sept 15	June 1–Oct 1
Squash, winter	June 10–July 10	June 20–July 20	July 1–Aug 1	July 15–Aug 15	Aug 1–Sept 1	Aug 1–Sept 1
Tomato	June 1–July 1	June 1–July 15	June 1–Aug 1	Aug 1–Sept 1	Aug 15–Oct 1	Sept 1–Nov 1
Turnip	Aug 1–Sept 15	Sept 1–Oct 15	Sept 1–Nov 15	Sept 1–Nov 15	Oct 1–Dec 1	Oct 1–Dec 31
Watermelon	July 1–July 15	July 15–July 30				

[1] Plants.
[2] Generally spring-planted.

The large central flower bud of globe artichokes should be cut first, using pruners. Cut when the buds are plump and fully swollen.

ARTICHOKE

Apart from sharing a name and the fact that they are both perennial vegetables the globe and Jerusalem artichokes have little in common and are best considered separately.

Globe Artichoke

The large globe-shaped flower buds produced by these plants are cut to provide a delectable vegetable. The plant produces very attractively divided silvery-gray leaves.

To grow this crop well, choose a sheltered sunny site, dig the soil well, and add well-rotted compost and/or manure. It is best to avoid heavy, wet soils.

Plant young suckers (the side shoots growing around the main stem) or seedlings in spring, 2—2$^1/_2$ ft (60—75 cm) apart. Firm in well.

Give the newly planted offsets plenty of water in dry weather until they are well established. In early winter, when the leaves start to die down, cut away the old flower stems and tie the younger leaves up together before drawing soil up round the stems.

Apply a general fertilizer in spring at the rate of 2—3 oz per sq yd (60—85 g per sq m) and mulch with well-rotted manure or compost to improve growth.

Harvest from established plants in July, when the flower buds are plump and fully swollen and before the scales have hard brown tips.

In the USA, globe artichokes are grown commercially in the cool, coastal areas of California — around San Francisco. The plants rarely survive winter in cold climates — even with careful protection.

Lift tubers of Jerusalem artichokes as they are required.

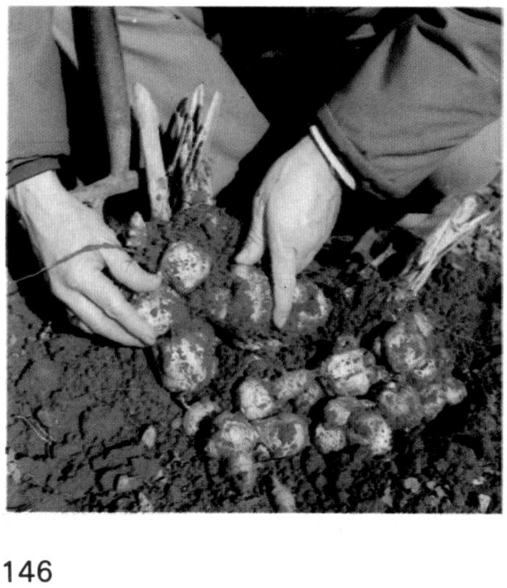

Jerusalem Artichoke

This plant is grown for its tubers, which are like knobbly potatoes. The stems grow 6—8 ft (1.8—2.5 m) high and are perfect for a quick summer screen.

Full sun or sun and partial shade provide suitable sites for this crop, and any soil will yield tubers, although better soils produce heavier crops.

Plant the tubers in spring or fall, 3—6 in. (7.5—15 m) deep, 15 in. (38 cm) apart.

During the season, hoe to eliminate weeds and pinch out tips to prevent flower buds developing.

ASPARAGUS

Select an open sunny site and well-drained soil for asparagus. Light soils tending to be sandy are ideal; add sand to very heavy soils to improve drainage. Dig the soil very thoroughly in the fall and mix in well-rotted garden compost and manure. Add limestone if pH is lower than 6.5.

You can raise plants from seed, but it is more common to buy one- or two-year-old seedlings (called one-year and two-year "asparagus crowns") in April. If you have to delay planting them for a few days, store in damp peat.

Dig out a trench 8—10 in. (20—25 cm) deep and 12 in. (30 cm) wide. Then form a shallow ridge 3 in. (7.5 cm) high at the base. Space the crowns 15—18 in. (38—45 cm) apart with the string-like roots spread over both sides of the ridge. Then cover them with about 2—3 in. (5—7.5 cm) of soil and subsequently, when hoeing to control weeds, slowly fill up the trench with soil. You should space the rows 4—5 ft (1.2—1.5 m) apart if you are growing more than one row.

Each autumn and spring, earth up the rows by drawing 1—2 in. (2.5—

Asparagus crowns should be planted on a slight ridge in a prepared trench.

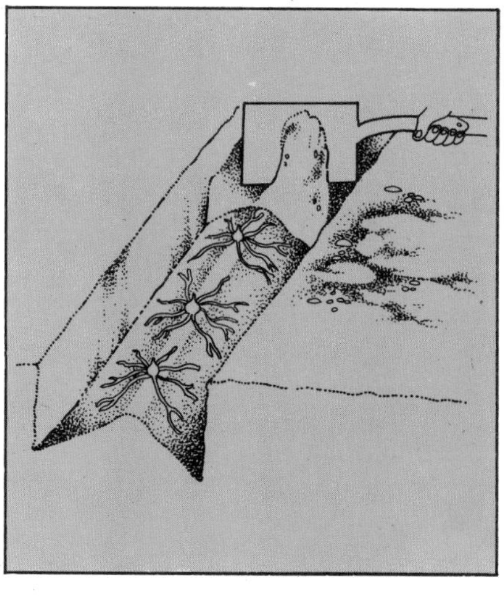

5 cm) of soil each side of the row.

Sprinkle general fertilizer along the row in spring at the rate of 2—3 oz. per sq yd (60—85 g per sq m). Mulch with well-rotted compost after mid-June.

If the grayish grubs of the asparagus beetle are a problem dust or spray with rotenone.

A year after planting out, one spear can be cut from each crown. The following year all the spears can be cut over a four-week period, and in the third year (when plants are four to five years old) spears can be cut for six weeks. Stop all cutting by mid-June.

Cut the spears when they are 4—6 in. (10—15 cm) above the soil, and always

Broad beans, as hardy as peas, must be sown very early.

Snap beans are popular vegetables that yield a heavy crop — but the beans must be picked regularly to avoid tough pods developing.

cut before the tip starts to open into foliage-producing shoots. Cut about 2—4 in. (5—10 cm) below the surface.

BEANS

Snap Beans

Any well-cultivated garden soil and an open sunny site suit the nutritious snap bean. If space is lacking, grow the climbing or pole varieties. Bush varieties of snap bean will grow in tubs, planters and window boxes on terraces, balconies and roof gardens.

The seeds may rot in cold wet soil and the tender young shoots are not frost-tolerant so wait until mid- to late spring before sowing. In most northern regions, two successive sowings can be made each season.

Sow the seeds 2—3 in. (5—7 cm) apart in rows 2 in. deep (5 cm), allowing about 18—30 in. (45—76 cm) between rows. Thin the seedlings to about 4—6 in. (10—15 cm) apart. Pick the beans frequently to prolong the harvest — freeze the surplus.

There are many varieties of either green-or yellow-podded (wax) types. For a change, try 'Roma', a buttery flat-podded type, or its pole counter-part 'Romano'.

Lima Beans

Unlike snap beans, the lima bean must be shelled. A tasty treat awaits those who eat their first home garden-grown limas! The beans can also be dried for later use.

Lima beans, also available in bush or pole varieties, require a longer growing time (65—90 days) than snap beans and revel in hot weather, making them especially popular in the South and other mild climate regions. Northerners can grow these beans successfully if they plan properly and have the garden space to devote to a single crop for most of one season.

Lima bean seeds vary in size but most varieties can be sown 3—4 in. (7—10 cm) apart and finally thinned to 6—10 in. (15—25 cm) apart.

Other Beans

The soybean, well known for its distinctive flavor and nutritious qualities, can be grown in the home garden but is most successful where the growing season is long. However, a recent introduction named 'Frost-beater' matures within 78 days, making it an excellent choice for most northern gardens.

Sow the seeds when the soil has warmed (same time as snap and lima beans) about 2 in. (5 cm) deep and 3—4 in. (7—10 cm) apart. Soybean pods, which must be removed, are tough. Pour boiling water over the pods and let them soak for about 5 minutes. Then the beans can be squeezed out for further cooking or drying. Or cook the pods longer in salted water and squeeze out the beans at the table, as the Japanese do.

The broad or fava bean is a staple crop in Europe and Britain, but is hardly known here. This is a pity because broad beans, also shell beans, are uniquely flavorful, and are as easy to grow as peas, having the same growing requirements. They are another good crop for northern gardens.

Sow in early spring in the North (in the fall in the South) 2 in. (5 cm) deep, allowing 9—12 in. (23—30 cm) between plants which grow tall and bushy. Black

Broccoli is a prolific vegetable, harvested over a long period. Once the central head has been harvested smaller heads develop.

aphids may cluster on the growing tips which can be pinched off to discourage them.

Runner beans are very popular abroad but are known mainly here in the form of the ornamental scarlet runner bean. Start the seeds indoors in peat pots about 5 weeks before last frost date since it takes about 120 days from seed to harvest of the edible 10 in. (25 cm) pods.

Runner beans grown here in peat-filled bags with supports needs a long season.

BEETS AND SWISS CHARD

Any site, except those which are heavily shaded, and all well-dug garden soils are suitable for growing beet. It really thrives best, however, in warm, light soils. Add humus-forming compost and peat moss to light sandy soils to retain moisture.

Each knobbly piece from the seed packet is in fact a cluster of seeds and not just one seed. Space these clusters 2—3 in. (5—7.5 cm) apart down the row, 1 in. (2.5 cm) deep with 9—15 in. (23—38 cm) between the rows. Make the first sowing as soon as the frost is out of the ground. Sow at regular intervals till early July to provide a succession of young roots.

Single out the seedlings if more than one grows at each station. Cook young beets and their leafy tops together for a delicious dish.

Swiss chard is also a beet but it is grown for its succulent stalks and large leaves which are usually steamed or cooked in a little water.

One variety 'Rhubarb' has red stalks and attractive red-tinged foliage.

Sow the seeds where they are to remain in early to late spring in rows about ½ in. (1 cm) deep. Thin the seedlings to stand about 6 in. (15 cm) apart with 12-24 in. (30—60 cm) between rows. Take off the outer leaves as you need them, leaving the inner leaves to develop.

The leafy tops of beet can be cooked like spinach.

BROCCOLI AND KALE

While broccoli and kale require similar cultural treatment, it is the green sprouting broccoli commercially sold in frozen form as broccoli spears), which starts off the harvesting from midsummer to winter. In the South and in other mild climate regions the kales then take over and survive the toughest weather to provide fresh green vegetables through the winter and spring, to be followed by the white, the early purple and the late purple sprouting broccoli, which may be picked from early spring to early summer.

When looking for kale in the seed catalogs, also look out for its other name — borecole.

The kales will stand very exposed conditions but choose a more sheltered site for the broccolis, and remember they form very large plants.

Sow in shallow drills ½—1 in. (1—2.5 cm) deep, 6—9 in. (15—23 cm) apart in April and May. Plant out the resulting seedlings in the cropping site when they are big enough to handle, 20—30 in. (50—75 cm) apart. You can plant out calabrese more closely if you want to produce an abundance of small spears for freezing.

Stout growth is needed to withstand winter weather, so be sure the plants are well firmed to achieve this. When setting out, put the plant stems well down in the soil — this will improve the plant's anchorage and help it to withstand strong winds. The only other cultural treatment necessary is occasional hoeing to control weeds if you don't mulch, and watering in dry weather.

All these plants are very easy to grow and are generally trouble-free, but club root and cabbage root maggots can be problems. You can achieve chemical control of these by pouring one cup of Terrachlor solution in planting hole for club-root and by soaking the soil with diazinon for root maggots. Pick off by hand the green caterpillars of cabbage white butterfly should they occur, or spray the plants with rotenone or *Bacillus thuringiensis*.

BRUSSELS SPROUTS

The key to producing quality crops of this fall or winter vegetable is to select hybrid varieties to grow on fertile soils, from which you pick sprouts while they are small and firm.

Brussels sprouts takes from 80—90 days to maturity. It is a fall crop in the North, a winter one in the South and other mild climates. Sow in spring in the North for September harvests, later for winter harvests elsewhere. Sow seed in shallow drills 1 in. (2.5 cm) deep and 6 in. (15 cm) apart.

Water the seedlings well before lifting and transplanting into the growing site from May to early July. Hoe occasionally to destroy weeds until the leaves cover the soil and naturally smother weed growth. During very dry weather help growth by watering well and giving liquid fertilizer.

For control of club-root and root maggots of cabbage fly, see Cabbages below. Pick off the green caterpillars of cabbage white butterflies or spray with rotenone.

Perfect stems packed with sprouts are normal on F^1 hybrid varieties of Brussels sprouts. Such varieties require fertile soils and plenty of water.

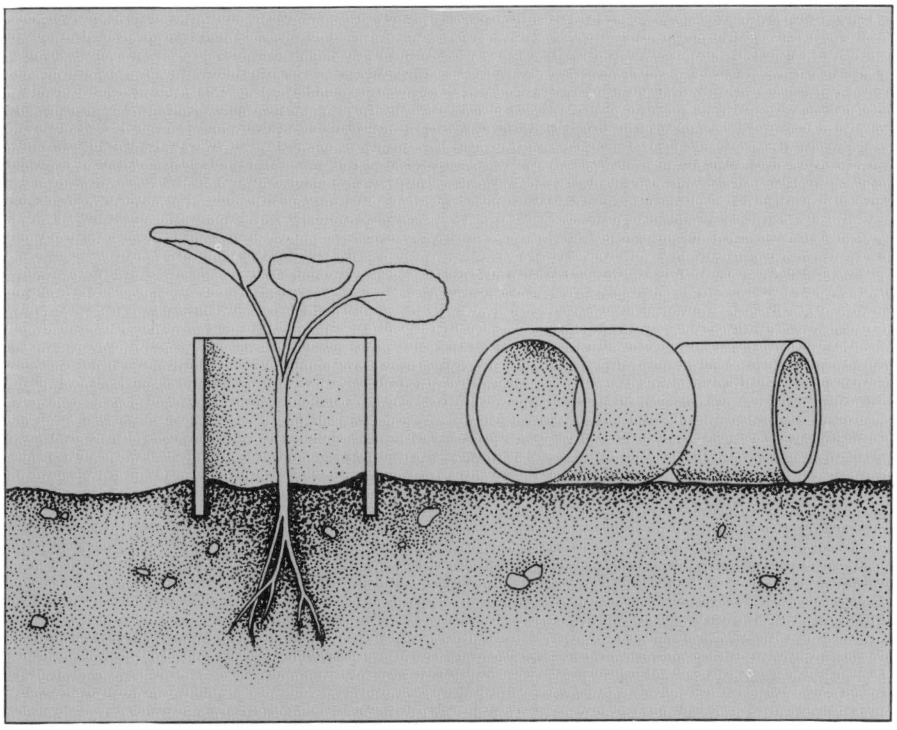

Cardboard tubes pushed into soil protect young plants from cutworms.

CABBAGES

Common cabbages and the fancy-leaved Savoy types (for Chinese cabbage, see page 152) are easy crops to grow but have never attained the popularity among home gardeners here they hold in Britain and Europe. This is a pity for the cabbage is nutritious and high in vitamins and minerals. It stores well and is very hardy and can endure some freezing. It can be grown and harvested all winter in much of the South and Pacific regions. In the North it does best in spring and early summer and in the fall.

Most sites and just about all soils are suitable but sandy, lean soils will need improving with ample organic matter — well-rotted compost and animal manures. In very acid soils, mix in limestone as cabbage prefers a slightly acid to slightly alkaline soil condition.

The chart on the next page lists some recommended varieties of early, mid-season and late cabbage varieties and gives an idea of the differences in maturing times. Planting two or three different varieties of cabbage at different seasons can stretch out the harvest and provide heads for storage.

For the earliest cabbages to mature before hot weather arrives, sow seeds of early varieties indoors or in a greenhouse in March in the North, from January to February in mild climates (or about five to eight weeks before date

Work a little fertilizer into the soil around spring-maturing cabbage plants.

of the last spring frost — see pages 142 and 143). Sow the seeds thinly in shallow drills $^1/_2$ in. (1 cm) deep in flats of soilless mix. If a greenhouse isn't available, grow in a sunny window or under fluorescent lights.

The young plants can be set out from four to six weeks later, first being hardened off in a cold frame or gradually exposed to outdoor conditions for about a week. In the open ground space them about 18—24 in. (38—60 cm) apart. Start harvesting as the centers harden.

Midseason and late varieties can be sown directly in the garden in mid to late spring for harvest in late fall.

Do not let the soil dry out and fertilizing these later-maturing cabbages once or twice with a high nitrogen fertilizer will pay off.

Pests are the same as for broccoli. Green worms can be especially troublesome. If rotenone does not check them, try sprinkling the plants with salt.

CARROTS

Only very heavily shaded sites cause difficulties in growing carrots and all garden soils will yield reasonable crops, although ideally the soil should be light and sandy for the straightest roots.

Sow as soon as soil conditions are suitable. It is better to delay sowing than to sow when the soil is cold, wet and too sticky. Sow in shallow drills $^1/_2$—1 in. (1—2.5 cm) deep and just cover the seeds with soil. Space the rows 9—12 in. (23—30 cm) apart. Make several regular sowings from spring to early summer, to give a succession.

The main problem for beginners with carrots is that the seeds are fine. Do not sow too deep and do not let the soil dry out before germination has started.

CABBAGE CHART

Variety	Days to Maturity	Remarks
Copenhagen Market (early)	72	Well-rounded heads, 6½ in (16.5 cm) across.
Dwarf Morden (very early)	55	Miniature Canadian variety especially suited to small gardens. Round, split-proof heads, 4 in (10 cm) across.
Early Dark Green Savoy (early)	72	Small for Savoy type, with heads 5½–6 in (14–15 cm) across. Recommended for home plots.
Early Jersy Wakefield (early)	63	Yellows resistant. Small pointed heads, 7 in (18.5 cm) deep. Mild flavor.
Emerald Cross Hybrid (early)	63	Round compact heads, 6–9 in (15.5–23 cm) across. Resistant to splitting.
Penn State Ballhead (late-winter)	110	Improved Danish Ballhead variety. Recommended for storing. Heads 7–8 in (17.5–20.5 cm) across.
Red Acre (midseason)	86	Deep red, compact variety resistant to splitting.
Savoy King (midseason-late)	90	Large heads. Heat-resistant. Can be harvested at early as well as mature stage, making it desirable for home gardeners who don't want to eat cabbage every day.
Stonehead Hybrid (early)	70	Yellows resistant. Compact 6 in (15 cm) spread. Recommended especially for home vegetable plots.

Quick-germinating radish seeds are often sown with carrot seeds to mark the rows and space out the carrots.

Thin the seedlings to stand 1 in. (2.5 cm) or so apart. When they are large enough to handle, this will allow you to pull either every other, or every two-in-three, carrots from the stage when they reach finger thickness. Leave the remaining carrots to reach maincrop size. Hoe regularly between plants and rows. If your carrots do not grow as quickly as you would like, water the foliage with a foliar feed.

If your garden space is limited, then look through catalogs for some of the miniature varieties such as the "golf-ball".

CAULIFLOWER

Success with this vegetable depends on working backward from the date of maturity, so the plants begin to mature in cool weather. In most regions this means fall. Unless you live in a cool moist climate and have really fertile soil, cauliflower will probably present more problems than broccoli, kale or

Carrot shapes — read the catalog descriptions and choose the varieties whose shapes suit your soil. Shorter, stubbier varieties are best in rocky soil.

cabbage. Seedlings can be set out as soon as the danger of frost is past to secure rapid growth before hot weather. However, it is best grown as a late fall crop in most of the North. In the South and much of the Pacific region, it is a winter and spring crop.

Select an open sunny site. Cauliflower grows best in well-cultivated soils which you can further improve by adding plenty of very well-rotted organic matter. this gives rapid growth and good-sized curds (the name given to the white cauliflower heads). If the soil is acid give it a dusting of lime.

For summer harvest sow indoors in peat pots eight to ten weeks before average date of last frost. After the third leaf (two round seed leaves will be followed by the third, which is rough-edged and the first true leaf) appears, the potted seedlings need cold frame or Hotkap protection to produce sturdy plants. Plant out in the growing site 18 in. (45 cm) apart after danger of frost is past.

For fall harvest in the North, sow outdoors in a seed bed in early summer, the seed just covered, in rows 9 in. (23 cm) apart. Water the plants well before transplanting into the growing site. Leave 20—24 in. (50—60 cm) between. plants and between rows. As the curds (heads) begin to develop break the midrib of a few large leaves and fold these outer leaves over the cauliflower head. This keeps the head beautifully white. The purple and green varieties do not require blanching.

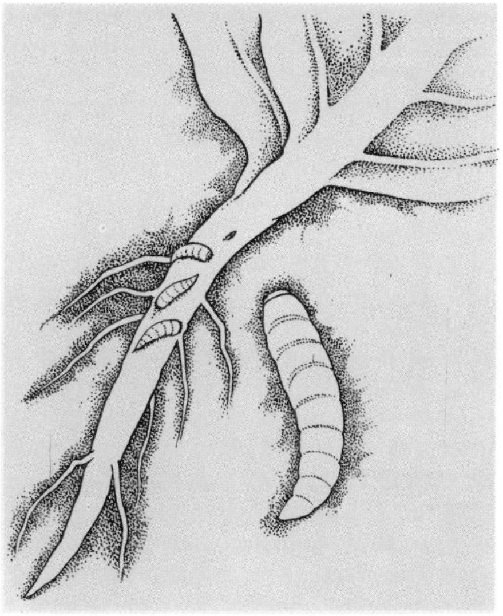

Maggots of cabbage root fly cause brassica crops to wilt and die.

Rotate the growing site each year. For pests, see broccoli.

CELERY

Most garden sites are suitable for celery, but a deeply dug, rich soil is needed for the best results. Cultivate plenty of well-rotted organic matter into the soil ahead of sowing celery. This is especially necessary for blanched types; the self-blanching types are not quite so demanding.

Ideally all types should be sown under glass in spring, preferably in mid-March or April. Make two sowings, one early and one late, to extend the harvesting period.

Sow in soilless mix, in a temperature of at least 50ºF (10ºC). When seedlings are just large enough to handle transplant them into flats filled with potting compost. Once established you can grow them in a frame, for transplanting into the growing site in mid to late spring.

All self-blanching kinds can be planted in a square block of several rows. The inner plants will become more blanched and better to eat than those growing in the outside and in single rows. The smaller plants are when transplanted the less likely they are to run prematurely to seed. Set out plants 9—12 in. (23—30 cm) apart in both directions. Once established, mix in a general fertilizer at 1 oz per sq yd (30 g per sq m), and water well in dry weather.

Varieties which need blanching should be planted in trenches, setting the plants 6 in. (15 cm) apart in the base of the trench.

Celery varieties which need blanching can also be grown on the surface of the soil without trenching, either by earthing-up like potatoes or by placing a wooden board on each side of the row and filling with peat moss.

You can begin blanching when the leaves are 12—15 in. (30—38 cm) high. Always leave the green leaves exposed and increase the height of blanching up the stem in stages over several weeks.

Brown spots on the leaves are caused by celery leaf spot fungus, which can be controlled with sprays of Bordeaux mixture of maneb or zineb.

Celery fly or leaf miner may cause trouble and you can identify these by brown blisters which appear on the leaves from spring on. Pick off infested leaves or pinch to destroy the small larvae which tunnel between the two surfaces of the leaves. Where attacks persist spray with malathion.

CELERIAC

Celeriac, or "turnip-rooted celery", considerably extends the fresh celery season as it may be lifted and stored well into the winter.

Sow as for celery, or alternatively

Control maggots of root fly by using cardboard disks.

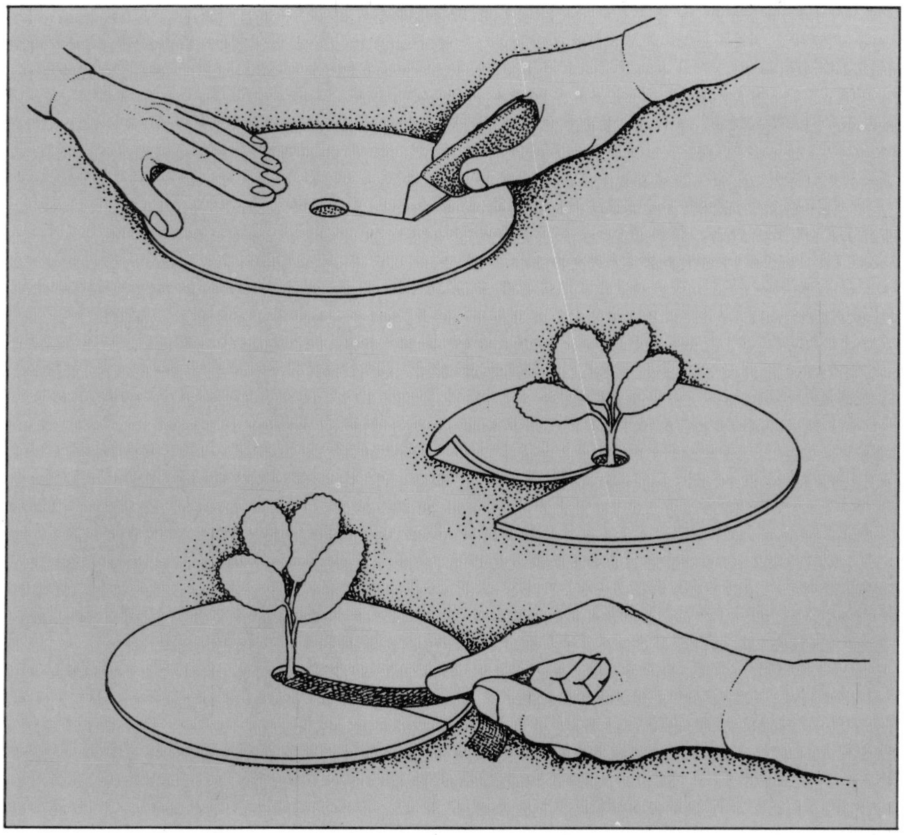

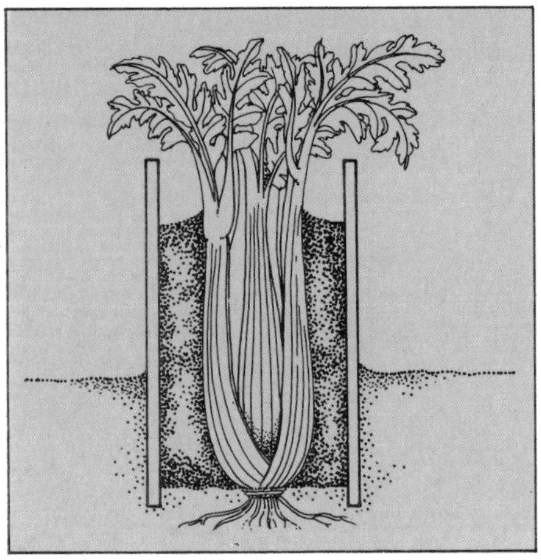

Blanching celery by filling between boards with peat keeps stems clean.

plants may be bought in spring.

Draw out a deep drill and plant out in the base 9—12 in. (23—30 cm) apart. The drill makes subsequent watering easier as growth and succulence is dependent on ample moisture. Space the rows 15—18 in. (38—45 cm) apart. Hoe to control weeds, and remove side shoots which may develop.

CHICORY

The plump, cream and white forced shoots of chicory, called "chicons", sites to other cabbage crops, and a soil It is also called Witloof chicory and Belgian endive. The roots require a long growing season (about 110 days) to reach good size for forcing. The tops can be cooked as greens or used in salads when young and tender.

Any site is suitable provided it is not in heavy shade, and any well cultivated soil will grow chicory.

Sow in rows in the garden in April or May, just covering the seed with soil. Single out the seedlings to 6 in. (15 cm) for 'Witloof', as soon as they are large enough to separate easily. Space the rows 15—18 in. (38—45 cm) apart.

Hoe occasionally to kill weeds and in very dry weather give a few heavy waterings to help to swell the roots.

When the leaves start to turn yellow in October or November and before there is a hard frost, lift the roots. Holding the root in one hand twist off the leaves with the other and cut or snap off the thin root end to give plump roots 6 in. (15 cm) long. Store these in a box of dry peat moss or sand in a cool, frost-free place.

From December to March put five or six roots upright in an 8 in. (20 cm) diameter flower pot, packing damp sand, light soil or peat around the roots. Invert a size larger pot and cover the holes. Keep the soil moist, and in a temperature of 50°F (10°C) every root will form a chicon in approximately three to four weeks.

A deep box, about 12 in. (30 cm) deep, works better than a pot since the tops of the roots should be well covered.

The forced shoots of chicory are known as chicons. The roots before forcing can be seen in the foreground. Chicons are produced in three or four weeks.

Celeriac is also known as turnip-rooted celery. It can be stored for use throughout the winter.

CHINESE CABBAGE

Chinese cabbage flourishes in similar sites to other cabbage crops, and a soil improved by the addition of well-rotted organic matter is essential to retain moisture.

Sow direct in the growing site in early July, just covering the seed with soil. Thin the seedlings to 9—12 in. (23—30 cm) apart, in rows spaced 12—15 in. (30—38 cm) apart.

Make sure the plants do not lack moisture at the roots during hot weather. Otherwise just hoe occasionally to control weeds. This crop grows well in polyethylene-covered greenhouses for late fall harvest.

Good firm heads will be ready in the late autumn. The heads may be boiled in the same way as cabbage, but they have a much milder flavor.

Alternatively, the leaf ribs of outer leaves may be cooked or steamed and the hearts may be shredded and used raw for salads.

CUCUMBER

Even the smallest garden has space for a few cucumber vines, especially when compact varieties like 'Spacemaster' and 'Patio Pik' are chosen. Space can be saved with standard vining varieties by training them upwards against a wire fence or string trellis.

Cucumber seeds can be sown in the garden, where they are to remain rather than transplanted, as soon as the soil warms and about the time frosts cease. For an earlier crop, sow the seeds indoors, about four weeks before frosts

Chinese cabbage is becoming better known. It has a milder flavor than cabbage.

Indoor varieties of cucumber can be grown in pots on the windowsill. Choose short-jointed all female varieties, like 'Fembaby' F[1], for this.

end in Jiffy 7 peat pellets or other peat pots so there will be no disturbance of the roots when they are set out.

Plant in a sunny site and in soil which you have improved by adding plenty of organic matter from the compost pile. Plant seeds about $^1/_2$ in. (1.27 cm) deep and thin seedlings to 12 in. (30 cm) apart in the row. Trellis-trained vines can be spaced closer together, about 4—6 in. (10—15 cm) apart. Side-dressing with 5-10-5 or a liquid fertilizer after the plants begin to flower and bear is beneficial. Although not essential, it is a good idea to pinch off the main stem at six to eight leaves, thus encouraging the side shoots to develop. Pick maturing fruits promptly to maintain production. If space permits, make a second sowing a few weeks after the first.

ENDIVE

There are two main types of endive — the Batavian type, which resembles a cos lettuce, and the curled type, which has divided and curled leaves. It is a member of the same genus as chicory.

All garden sites and any well-cultivated garden soils are suitable.

Take a chance on sowing in April to provide a summer crop, but choose one of the curled-leaf varieties. You will, however, be more successful from sowings of both types in late June to early August to mature in fall or winter. Sow in rows 12—15 in. (30—38 cm) apart. Use a cold frame or polyethylene house in cold regions.

Thin the seedlings to stand 12—15 in. (30—38 cm) apart. Hoe occasionally to control weeds and apply a top dressing of nitrogenous fertilizer or liquid feed if you want to encourage rapid growth.

When the plants are well developed either cover with an upturned flower pot or place a square of light board over the center of the plant. This blanches the leaves over a period of three to six weeks according to speed of growth and makes them more succulent and less bitter to taste.

KOHL-RABI

Pretty well any site is suitable for kohl-rabi, as long as it is not too over-shadowed or dry. Any well-cultivated garden soil will suit.

Sow in the North from early to mid-spring, and for a succession of crops sow two or three batches over this period.

Dust acid soils with lime before sowing. Other than this just hoe occasionally to destroy weeds and water well, ideally with some liquid fertilizer, in very dry weather.

Club-root can attack these crops and control is the same as for broccoli.

LEEKS

Most sites, except those which are heavily shaded, and all well-cultivated soils are suitable for leeks.

Sow early in the year, in February or

Endive 'Green Curled' does best where autumn is long and cool.

Leeks are a useful winter vegetable and are quite easy to grow. The fibrous roots also help to break up heavy soil.

March, under cover to get the earliest and largest blanched stems. An outdoor sowing in March or April will provide adequate crops, however. Transplant early seedlings into the growing site in May, and the outdoor raised plants in June. Space plants 9 in. (23 cm) apart in the row, and the rows 12—15 in. (30—38 cm) apart.

When transplanting, use dibber to make a good hole 1 in. (2.5 cm) or more in diameter and 6—8 in. (15—20 cm) deep, drop the young plant into this and water it in. There is no need to fill back any soil.

Water with a dilute liquid fertilizer in dry weather. When hoeing, draw soil up round the stem a little at a time to lengthen the blanched stem. Cut back big old leaves by half to encourage a greater length of blanched stem.

Leeks are very hardy and can be left in the soil all winter. Mulch to prevent freezing so plants can be dug as needed.

The attractive swollen stems of kohl-rabi are best eaten while still small.

LETTUCE

There are four main groups of lettuce varieties — the rounded cabbage types which are further subdivided into soft leaved or butterhead; the curly crisp types; romaine or cos lettuce; and finally the open-hearted cut-leaved or oak-leaved types. All require similar cultural conditions although some varieties have specific seasons for sowing and harvesting which are best followed for assured crops.

Seed catalogues will list many varieties, which may appear bewildering. However, the good catalogues guide the home gardener toward heat-resistant varieties such as 'Ruby'.

Whichever kind you grow, dig all the organic matter you can obtain into the soil. As they are shallow-rooted plants it is not necessary to dig the compost deep into the ground. Where summers are excessively hot, light shade may help lettuce crops.

By careful selection of varieties and sowing at suitable times, and with some protection available, it is possible to harvest lettuce for most of the year. In the north, try growing lettuce in a cold frame or polyethylene house for late fall and winter harvests.

It is important to sow summer varieties little and often. Try to avoid transplanting lettuce in mid-summer.

Final spacing depends to some extent on variety, but 6—12 in. (15—30 cm) apart is about right for most kinds.

Thin cos type so that they are 9 in. (23 cm) apart and with 12 in. (30 cm) between the rows.

Water the plants well in dry weather, giving them an occasional good soaking, rather than repeated light waterings. Give liquid fertilizer in dry weather to speed growth.

Most cos lettuces need no special treatment. In fact about the only variety offered here is 'Paris White' and it is self-blanching.

Slugs can be a major problem at certain times — use slug pellets strictly according to directions on the container. Or sink saucers of beer in the ground in which the slugs will drown.

MARROWS AND SQUASH

One of the earliest and perhaps one of the fastest growing of our garden vegetables is summer squash. Since all summer squash varieties are borne on the bush rather than trailing plants,

Butterhead lettuce (top), cos lettuce (center), oak-leaf lettuce (bottom).

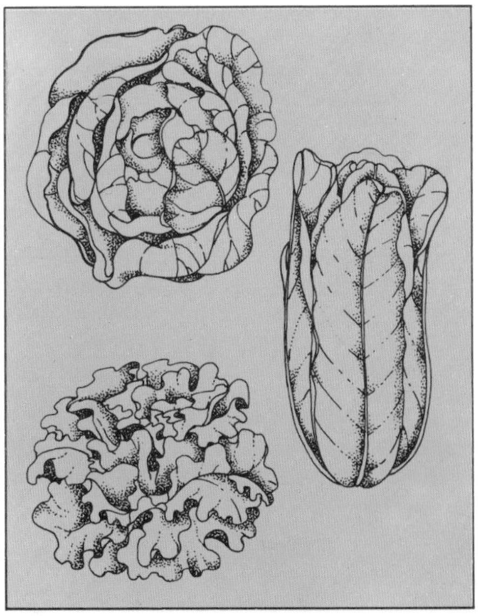

Cut young cos lettuce leaving a stump. A second lettuce will then grow.

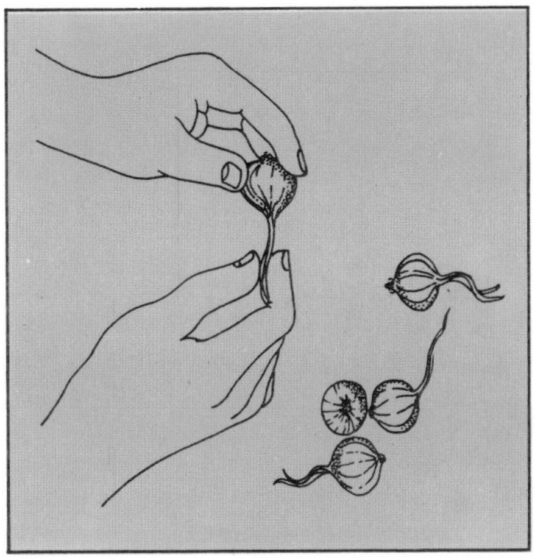

Twist off the strawy tip before planting onion sets to stop birds pulling them up.

even the smallest garden can accommodate a few plants.

Less common in small gardens are the fall 'Butternut' and 'Acorn' and winter 'Hubbard' varieties, simply because they are vines that take up a lot of space and require a long growing season. Included as summer squash are zucchini varieties (similar to marrows and courgettes of English and Continental gardens) and patty pan varieties that bear the white disklike fruits with scalloped edges.

Sunny sites are best and a soil with plenty of well-rotted compost and manure to retain moisture. Sow seed in Jiffy 7 or peat pots in early May in the North. Transplant the young plants to the growing site in late spring when there is no more likelihood of frost. Remember, these plants are tender — one frost will kill them and you will have to start again.

The more usual method is to sow three seeds direct in each growing site in late spring, so they are timed to emerge soon after any possibility of frost.

Cut all summer squash when the fruits are 4—5 ins (10—12.5 cm) long. Nearly all varieties are best harvested while still young.

Exceptions to cutting young are fall and winter squash which need a long, warm summer to fully mature. When cut, store by hanging in nets in a dry cool place. Remember that winter squash won't keep unless the fruits have fully matured on the vines.

The squash vine borer is a common, persistent pest of all kinds of squash, both bush and vine types. Spray or dust plants with methoxychlor in late spring and repeat two more times at ten-day intervals. Wait one day before harvesting. Always follow container directions carefully.

Zucchini squash is prolific. Harvest when fruits are 6 in. (15 cm) long.

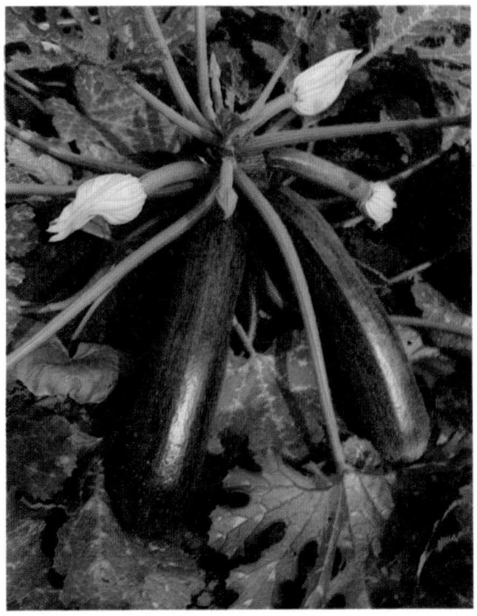

ONIONS AND SHALLOTS

The easiest way to make sure you have an early supply of onions is to plant sets. These are young onion bulbs that were grown from seed and are always available from garden centers and seed houses. Just push these small bulbs into cultivated soil in early spring — from February to May according to climate. control weeds and begin harvesting after three months or as needed.

Shallots are much larger than onion sets but require the same treatment. Each shallot will grow and multiply to produce four to eight new shallots.

Both crops require a fertile soil rich in organic matter. Applying a sprinkling of 5-10-5 fertilizer along each side of the row and then watering in well will give the plants a boost after they are about 8 in. (20 cm) tall.

All varieties of onions may be sown from seed to pull when young as salad onions but if you want them specifically for this purpose, select bunching varieties such as 'White Lisbon' and others. The usual globe onions grown from seed require a long growing season to reach good size in the North. In mild climates, of course, they grow well all winter. In the North, seeds can be sown indoors in late winter in soilless mix and grown in a sunny window or under fluorescent lights. Plant out in spring, after hardening off plants, about 2—3 in. (5—7 cm) apart in rows 1—2 ft. (30—60 cm) apart. Salad onions can be sown in shallow drills in the open ground in early to late spring and again in late summer and fall. In mild climates sow globe onion seeds in fall for spring harvest.

PARSNIPS

All ordinary garden soils will produce worthwhile parsnips, but those which have been well dug in the fall and have had rotted organic matter added for previous crops are best.

Sow any time from late February to April, when the soil surface is reasonably dry and crumbly. Get good germination by starting the seed into growth indoors on damp tissue. Be sure to sow outside as soon as the tiny roots start to show. Space the rows so that they are 12—15 in. (30—38 cm) apart.

Thin the seedlings in two stages, firstly to 2—3 in. (5—7.5 cm) apart and then, when these are well established, to the final spacing distance of 4—6 in. (10—15 cm). If you want large roots space the rows 15—18 in. (38—45 cm) apart. The roots are very hardy and can be left in the ground all winter.

PEAS

All garden sites and soils will produce acceptable pea yields. This crop invariably grows well in soil not previously cultivated for vegetables.

Sow as early as the soil can be worked, usually around St. Patrick's Day. In the deep South and much of the Pacific regions, sow seed in fall and winter. After these sowings, sow successionally in the growing site through the spring at 10-day intervals and again in midsummer for fall harvests.

Sow seeds in a V-shape drill 2—3 in. (5—7.5 cm) deep. Sow dwarf varieties to give 16 plants per 12 in. (30 cm) of row, spacing the rows the same distance apart as the height of the plant (see seed packet). Or sow seeds in double rows about 3 in. (7 cm) apart with 30 in (76 cm) between the double rows. When the seedlings are 2—3 in. (5—7.5 cm) high they will need some form of support. The old and quite satisfactory method was to insert twiggy sticks up both sides of the row.

Tall peas, like the new 'Sugar Snap' which has a very succulent edible pod as well as peas will need nets or sticks 4 ft (1.2 m) high for support. Most garden centers and mail-order seed houses sell special netting that can be strung between a double row of peas for the tendrils to cling to. A good watering in dry weather after pod formation improves the yield.

PEPPERS

There is a distinct difference between the sweet pepper, *Capsicum annuum,* and the very hot chili or cayenne pepper, variety *frutescens.* The fruits of the sweet pepper are large and rather square lobed and they may be cooked as

Lift parsnips in spring before new growth and store them in dry peat.

a vegetable or used fresh in salads. The much smaller, more pointed fruits of the cayenne pepper are used fresh for flavoring or they may be dried and ground up to provide chili powder. They are more tender than sweet peppers in their growing state and need slightly warmer conditions.

There are not, as is often believed, red and green varieties of sweet pepper. They all start off green, like tomatoes, and turn red as they ripen. If you want the maximum yield from each plant it is advisable to gather the sweet peppers while they are still green. If left on the plant until they turn red, the total number of fruits yielded by the plant is reduced.

The pepper is a relative of the tomato (also eggplant) and is as easy to grow, requiring very similar treatment. It is one of the major home garden vegetables and even the smallest plot has space for a few bushes.

All well-cultivated garden soils will give reasonable results, but those containing plenty of organic matter will give the heaviest yields as they encourage root development.

A sunny site is essential to provide the warmth and exposure needed for the best pepper harvests. Peppers are also suitable for the home greenhouse where they will thrive under the same conditions as required by tomato plants.

In addition to the greenhouse and sunny gardens, peppers are attractive plants to grow in large pots on patios, terraces and balconies. They are even worth a try in window boxes.

Except in the South and other mild climate regions, pepper seeds are always sown indoors about two months before thoroughly warm weather has arrived outdoors, at which time it it safe to set them in the open ground. Young

Peas must be sown in early spring so they grow during cool weather and bear before summer heat arrives.

plants can be set out-doors a few weeks sooner if they are placed under Hotkaps. The quickest way to grow them indoors is in Jiffy 7 pellets, the peat disks that swell into little fertilized pots when wet. Sow two seeds per pot, pinching off the weaker one after germination. Grow in a warm, sunny window, in a greenhouse if you have one or under fluorescent lights. A second transplanting from the Jiffy 7 pots is usually unnecessary. Pinch out growing tips on young plants for a bushy habit of growth.

POTATOES

All gardens are suitable for potatoes, although crops will be light if grown in heavily shaded spots or where the soil is very light. You will get the heaviest yields from well-cultivated soil with plenty of well-rotted organic matter dug into it.

"Seed potatoes" are not seeds as such, but tubers from the previous year's crop. Ideally they should be about the size of an egg.

If your seed potatoes are larger than the ideal you can cut them to make two or more planting pieces as long as every piece has its own shoot.

A good way to increase the yield and get slightly earlier crops is to place the seed potatoes in trays in a temperature of 50°F (10°C) in a light position for six to eight weeks before planting, to produce short dark green shoots. This pre-planting sprouting is called chitting. Whether chitted or not, plant the tubers in rows with a trowel 4—5 in. (10—12.5 cm) deep, 12—15 in. (30—38 cm) apart, with 24 in. (60 cm) between the rows. Begin planting outdoors in late March or early April — or four to five weeks before the last frost is likely to occur.

When the young shoots appear above the ground, draw up soil from between the rows around the stems. This is called "earthing up". If young shoots have come through and frosts are still likely, pull the soil right over them to give protection. Alternatively you can protect against frost by covering the rows with Hotkaps or polyethylene tunnels, but this is rarely necessary, or just covering with sacking on nights when frost is forecast.

Repeat the earthing-up process several times as the crop grows. This operation increases the roots made by the potato stem and increases yield. It also prevents the tubers turning green and becoming inedible.

In very damp conditions in the fall potato blight can be troublesome. This causes dark spots on the leaves and premature yellowing. You can prevent this by growing early varieties and lifting them early. Alternatively, use a protective copper-based spray in early June.

RADISH

There are two kinds of radish: the ordinary spring radish, which can be harvested throughout the spring and the winter radish (black or red skinned and much larger than the ordinary radish).

Radishes will grow in all reasonably well-cultivated soils from early to late spring or so long as the weather remains cool. The crispest and best flavored radishes are those grown quickly on fertile soil in a sunny position.

Start sowing the ordinary radish as soon as soil conditions allow. You should be able to sow very early in the North — just as soon as the soil is workable. Draw shallow drills 6 in. (15 cm) apart and sow the seed thinly down the row. Sow in succession every ten to fourteen days from early to late spring.

Sow winter radish in July, *not* before, in rows 12 in. (30 cm) apart. Thin out the seedlings as they develop to stand 6—8 in (15—20 cm) apart in the row.

Cabbage root maggots can infest the

Large seed potatoes can be cut into smaller sections, each with a shoot.

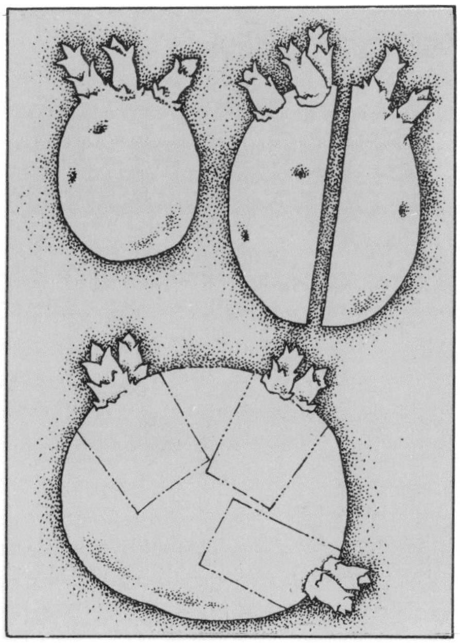

Potatoes will yield the heaviest crops on well-cultivated soil that contains plenty of organic matter.

Part of a display of over 40 varieties of radish grown by the author and staged at the Chelsea flower show in 1976.

roots but are most severe on early sowings, decreasing with successive sowings. So ignore — or dust diazinon over the rows after sowing.

RHUBARB

Rhubarb thrives in any site — however bad — and all reasonably cultivated garden soil will give good results. It is one of the easiest plants to grow and very productive.

Succulent pink stems of forced rhubarb make a good winter sweet. But remember, it is only the stems of the plant which are eaten — the green leaves contain poisonous oxalic acid.

Rhubarb is best propagated from plants of named varieties. Dependable varieties are 'Cherry Red', 'Ruby', 'McDonald' and 'Valentine', all of which have red stems. You can order roots from nurseries in spring or fall.

Use plants that are three to five years old, lift them during the dormant period and chop them with a spade to produce five or six planting pieces.

Each piece, or 'set', must have one rounded pink bud and a fair share of root system.

Dig the soil well and clear it of perennial weeds before planting the sets $2^1/_2$ ft (75 cm) apart (October and March are good times to divide established clumps or plant new ones from a nursery).

Do not attempt to harvest a crop the first year. A few stems can be pulled the second year before cropping more heavily and forcing in successive years.

Always try to leave about four good leaves on each plant to continue building up the strength of the plant.

One strong crown should yield 6 lb (3 kg) a year from February to August.

Plants to be forced indoors should be lifted and left on the surface exposed to cold temperatures or packed in bushel baskets surrounded with soil to prevent the roots from drying out until they are brought indoors to force.

Be careful when lifting not to break off too many thongy roots. Pack damp peat, soil or similar material around the roots, keep them dark and warm, 50—55°F (10—13°C), then forced stems will be ready to pull in about a month.

An alternative method is to place the crowns indoors in a black polyethylene bag with damp peat moss.

Forced stems are ready when the pale lemon leaf color starts to darken. Try to pull just before this darkening occurs and the leaf edges go brown. Discard the roots after forcing.

A popular way to force the rhubarb is to cover with straw and an old bucket.

An alternative method is to put lifted crowns in a black plastic bag.

SALSIFY AND SCORZONERA

These two less common root vegetables are quite easy to grow. They require similar treatment both in the garden and the kitchen, but it is easy to distinguish between the two. Scorzonera roots have a black skin which can be removed by scalding and scraping. Salsify is a similar shape, but the roots are brown, not black.

Sow from mid to late spring in rows 12—15 in. (30—38 cm) apart. A long growing season is needed.

Thin the seedlings to stand 6—9 in. (15—23 cm) apart in the row when they

Salsify (left) and scorzonera (right) are quite distinct vegetables.

are big enough to handle. Hoe occasionally to control weeds and water the plants well in dry weather.

SPINACH AND NEW ZEALAND SPINACH

True spinach is one of the fastest maturing leaf vegetables and is ideal to grow as an intercrop between slower-maturing vegetables such as celery and leaks.

Since in most regions of the North (in the South it can usually be grown all winter), spinach only thrives in cool weather, such as in fall or spring, some care should be taken in choosing varieties. 'Bloomsdale Long-Standing' is slow to bolt while 'Hybrid No. 7' is resistant to downy mildew. 'Winter Bloomsdale' (45 days) is recommended for fall and winter growing in mild climates.

Full sun or partial shade are both acceptable and the best soil is a rich, humusy moisture-retaining type. Light, dry soils and hot weather make plants run prematurely to seed. To get continuous spring harvests, sow spinach succesionally every 14 days from early to mid spring and again in August and September. Sow the seed thinly in drills 1 in. (2.5 cm) deep and 12—15 in (30—38 cm) apart. Thin the seedlings to 5—6 in. (12—15 cm). As soon as leaves are large enough start to gather them, picking the largest ones first. Don't strip the plant, in fact harvest no more than half the leaves at a time, leaving smaller leaves to develop, (although don't leave them too long, or the leaves will be old and tough and will soon be invaded by leafminers. These pests appear as the weather warms and in home plots the season for spinach is so short control is hardly worth the trouble, but malathion at 10-day intervals is the cure).

New Zealand Spinach

The spreading plants of New Zealand spinach are often called 'cut-and-come-again' because they provide a continuous supply of leafy shoots.

Most garden sites and soils will give acceptable results but sunny positions and light well-drained soils are best.

Sow the seeds in early spring as they require cool soil to trigger germination outside in early May. Space the rows 2—2½ ft (60—75 cm) apart and the plants 18—24 in. (45—60 cm) down the row.

Maintain rapid growth by constant watering in dry weather. Pinch out the growing tips, especially those that form early in the season, to encourage the development of side shoots.

Malabar spinach

Malabar spinach *(Basella alba)* is another spinach substitute and like New Zealand spinach does not mind summer heat. It is a vine-like plant and in the small garden may take up too much space unless trained on a trellis. Seeds can be sown in spring after the ground warms and harvesting of the foliage can start in about 70 days from sowing. Malabar spinach is a good subject for a city terrace or roof garden where it could serve a decorative function as well as culinary use.

New Zealand spinach is a real pick-and-come-again vegetable.

Tampala

Tampala *(Amaranthus gangeticus)* is not a true spinach either, and is related to a genus that is more familiar to flower gardeners. Seeds can be sown in the open ground after both soil and weather have warmed and the leaves are ready for harvesting from six to eight weeks later. They can be steamed or used raw in salads and their flavor is slightly reminiscent of that of the globe

Spinach is an annual vegetable with a rapid rate of growth. This makes it ideal to crop between slower-growing vegetables.

Rutabagas have been rather neglected but if harvested before they become too big are tender and delicious. They are undemanding in their requirements.

artichoke. With any new vegetable, it is best to plant a small patch only the first year until the family has had a chance to decide whether the vegetable is to its taste.

SWEDE OR RUTABAGA

Swedes are rather neglected vegetables but are becoming more appreciated now that smaller roots tend to be sold for home use instead of those more suited to cattle food.

Any land that's suitable for turnips will also be right for swedes. Avoid soil infested with club-root or select the disease-resistant variety 'York'.

Sow swede in early to midsummer so most of the growing season is in cool temperatures of fall. Swedes do not grow well in warm weather or in the South. Space seed rows 15 in. (38 cm) apart and thin seedlings to stand 6—9 in (15—23 cm) apart in the row. The smaller roots grown at the closer spacing and lifted while young, are the best to eat.

SWEET CORN

Select a warm sheltered site for this crop in cooler districts — plenty of sun and well cultivated garden soil are the growing requirements. Remember to add plenty of rotted organic matter to poor soils.

Sow directly into the growing site from mid-May on or when frost danger has passed, placing two or three seeds every 12—15 in. (30—38 cm) down the rows, which should be 30—36 in. (76—91 cm) apart. Thin seedlings to one, once they are established.

Pollen from the male tassels which form at the top of the plant floats down in the wind to pollinate the female cobs which are formed in a sheath of leaves lower down the plant. Complete wind pollination is most likely if you grow plants in a block of several rows; never plant in a single row.

The ears of each variety of hybrid sweet corn will ripen at about the same time. If space is available sow two or more varieties of different maturity times to avoid a glut. On small plots, try some of the midget varieties thinned to 6—8 in. (15—20 cm).

TOMATOES

Tomato growing gets easier each year for home gardeners because of the vigor, productivity and disease resistance of the new hybrids.

Tomato growth habits are now described as indeterminate (vines with long stems that are best staked and pruned); determinate (bushy, compact growth that can be unsupported and is best for containers); and semi-determinate (vines that fall in between but do best with some support such as wire hoops.

Sunshine is the one real requirement for tomato growing. The brighter the light, particularly early in the year when raising young plants, the better the

Below left: Male and female sweet corn flowers are carried on the same plant.
Below right: Harvest cobs when milky sap flows from the grain when pressed.

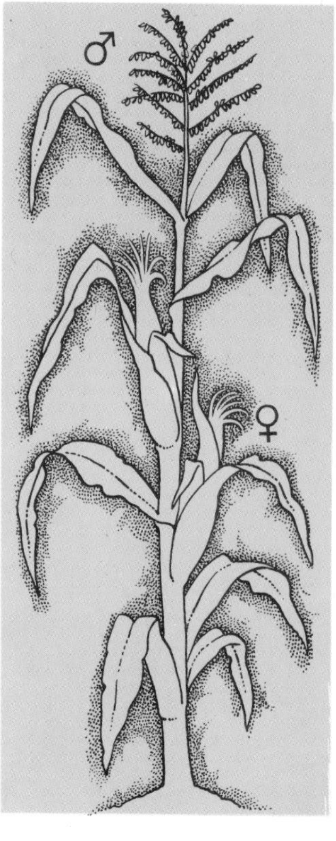

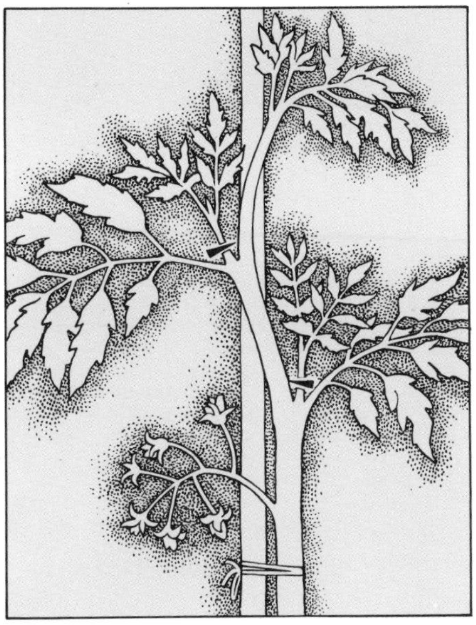

Remove side shoots from tomatoes as soon as they appear.

Raise tomato plants in pots to the stage where the first fruits form before planting in fertilized peat-filled growing bags, an English innovation under experimentation here.

growth and the better the flavor. Most garden soils are adequate but those improved by rotted manure and compost give superior results. Use any of the proprietary potting mixes to fill pots and other containers.

Very good tomato transplants can be purchased from local outlets but it is quite easy and satisfying to raise your own from seed in a sunny window or under fluorescent tubes. Start the seed about six-eight weeks before the last killing frost in your region (see map on page 142). Plant two seeds in a Jiffy 7 pellet and after germination pinch off the weaker of the two seedlings. Harden the seedlings before planting outdoors. When the weather is warm, set outside. You can plant out earlier if you use Hotkaps for protection from a late frost. Mulch the plants with compost, decaying leaves, hay or whatever you have to save moisture and control weeds.

Staked plants can be set as close as 18—24 in. (45—60 cm). The latest support method is to "cage" the plants in 5 ft. (150 cm) lengths of construction wire with a 6 in. (15 cm) mesh, bent and wired together to form a cylinder. For most varieties, the diameter of the cages should be about 18 in. (45 cm). The fruit is picked through the meshes. Be sure the cages are firmly anchored to the ground.

There are many blights and bugs that can trouble tomatoes, but the truth is that few turn up in most home plots and even when they do, fail to spoil the entire crop. Buy a general purpose tomato dust and use it according to directions. It may foil early and late blight, aphids, whiteflies and flea beetles. Follow a rotation of crops to foil soil-borne diseases and select modern hybrids that are resistant to nematodes, verticillium and fusarium wilts.

TURNIPS

Any garden site is suitable for turnips, but avoid those that are heavily shaded. All well-cultivated garden soils are suitable, but the best shaped roots grow in soil that has been manured and enriched for previous crops.

Sow succesionally outside from early to mid-spring using fast-maturing varieties like 'Tokyo Cross' (35 days) and 'Early Purple Top Milan' (45 days). Sow again in late summer for fall harvest. Turnips do not grow well in hot weather. In the deep South and along much of the Pacific coast, turnips grow well in winter. 'Just Right' is a good variety to grow for roots (60 days) and greens (27 days). Sow the seed in rows 12 in. (30 cm) apart and cover very lightly with soil.

As the seedlings produce the first rough leaves, thin them out to stand 4 in. (10 cm) apart along the row.

Very swollen and distorted roots will be produced on soils infected by club-root disease. If the soil has been proved to contain this disease it is best to avoid growing turnips or use the control given under broccoli. Flea beetles cause neat round holes in the foliage. Spray or dust with rotenone. Use diazinon in the soil, according to directions, to control root maggots.

Turnips should be pulled while still young to be eaten at their best.

Herbs

Herbs can make all the difference to a meal, and no garden should be without at least some of the more popular kinds. Usually just one or two plants will provide sufficient seasonings for most families and there's always space for the smaller-growing species.

A wide range can be grown without even encroaching on the vegetable plot—a number of herbs make very attractive plants in their own right and do not look amiss in shrub and flower borders. The evergreen bay, the powder blue flowers of rosemary, the rich mauve flowers on chives and the ground-covering purple and cream variegated, shrubby sage (where hardy) are good examples.

Many herbs can be grown in containers on the windowsill, on the back step, in small troughs and in hanging plant containers. The perennial kinds like mint, sage and thyme are good for this, and so is parsley. They all respond to regular picking and this prevents indoor plants getting too thin, long and drawn.

An ideal site is one that can offer a well-drained soil in full sun, as good sunlight helps to produce the strongest flavor. This isn't essential, however, as most most common herbs will grow satisfactorily in all soils. The only problem is likely to occur on heavy, wet soils, which make for a short life for most herbs.

It's sensible to position a herb border near the kitchen door. We only require a small quantity of herbs for flavoring, and it is convenient to nip out and pick a sprig of mint for new potatoes or a sprinkling of chives for sour cream. If there isn't a suitable bed, a few plants can be grown in pots, tubs or planters on the terrace.

Never be afraid to pinch back the shoots of most herbs regularly to achieve bushy growth.

Basil

Basil has a sweet, licorice-like flavor and aroma. The green leaves, as fresh in appearance as lettuce, are essential in Mediterranean cuisine and tomato recipes. 'Dark Opal' is a purple-leaved variety. Sow the seeds indoors in early spring, outside later. Basil is an annual.

Bay

The bay will eventually grow into a small tree, but it also responds to pot culture, either as a low bushy plant, possibly trimmed to a pyramid, or grown on a stem to form the typical standard "round-headed" plant seen in

Bays can be trained in a variety of shapes, and are suited to pot culture.

tubs outside restaurants. It isn't difficult to keep plants nicely shaped, but do the trimming with pruners, not shears as these cut the leaves in half. They will need a trim two or three times a year.

Although it is a hardy evergreen, try to avoid exposure to cold easterly winter winds which burn back the leaves. Plants grown in pots must be taken into a light garage or put in a window for protection in the depths of winter except in mild climates.

New plants can be produced by rooting young tips when stems start to harden in July and August. Well rooted cuttings should be potted and summered outdoors.

Fresh and dried leaves of this herb are used in combination with other herbs in a bouquet garni as well as on their own to flavor many different kinds of dishes the world over.

Leaves can be dried by placing several in a shallow tray in a very cool oven.

Dried leaves are likely to have a stronger flavor than fresh leaves.

Short rows of chives produce masses of leaves. One plant is often sufficient.

Chives

Once you have chives established they really look after themselves — and they make a very attractive border with lots of grass-like foliage and masses of mauve flower heads if you allow them to bloom.

Chives flourish in a shaded border and once established should be cut back to the soil regularly to encourage the new growth used for flavoring. Established clumps should be lifted and divided every few years in April or September. If you want fresh supplies all the year, grow a few seed-raised crops indoors.

The grassy foliage is chopped into small pieces which give a delicate onion flavor to salads, egg dishes, cream cheese, soups and sauces. The bright green color is lost if the leaves are dried so it is better to keep supplies of fresh leaves coming along (or you can put some into the freezer).

Dandelion

It is debatable whether the dandelion should be classed as a herb or a vegetable, as the leaves are sometimes eaten raw in salads (special large-leaved varieties are available from specialist seedsmen), cooked like spinach or used as a flavoring for soups. Equally it can be regarded as a culinary herb, for its roots may be roasted and ground to make a coffee substitute or additive. Unlike most other herbs, however, it likes a shady spot and a moist, fertile soil if it is to produce large leaves.

Early spring is a good time to sow dandelion, preferably in small groups. Thin the plants so they are eventually 6 in. (15 cm) apart.

If you want blanched leaves for salads, cover the plants with an upturned pot or box the following spring. After blanching and picking the leaves, give the plants a rest to rebuild their vigor before blanching a few more leaves.

Dandelion roots can be harvested any time after the growth has begun to slow down in the autumn.

For the biggest, most succulent roots, it is best to wait until October or November when the foliage has really stopped growing.

Dill

Dill is one of the annual herbs, which means fresh plants have to be raised each year. But it makes up for that by growing quite vigorously, and its thin feathery foliage will grow to about 3 ft (90 cm) in height. If you are growing several plants you can space them 9—12 in. (23—30 cm) apart.

Both leaves and seeds are used, and they have a flavor akin to caraway and aniseed; but use them sparingly for the flavor is quite strong. Chopped leaves can be used to flavor soups, sauces and savory stews. Seeds can be added to vinegar to produce dill vinegar for pickled gherkins. To give cucumber sandwiches a new tang, try sprinkling the slices with a little dill seed.

The feathery foliage of dill is attractive as well as being useful in the kitchen.

The popular Florence fennel is an attractive plant in the garden. Draw soil around the base of the plant to blanch the swollen leaf bases.

Fennel

There are two plants called 'fennel' — common fennel, *Foeniculum vulgare*, a perennial herb and Florence fennel or finocchio, *Foeniculum vulgare azoricum.* This has similar feather foliage but is also grown for its swollen leaf bases.

Common fennel can be sown from March to May, in rows 15 in. (38 cm) apart, but if you want seed heads to develop sow early. Thin the seedlings to 12 in. (30 cm) apart. Both kinds are grown as annuals in cold climates.

As the leaves do not store easily, it is a matter of freezing some for winter use or potting up a few plants to grow indoors.

Cut seed heads in September and October and hang them upside down in paper bags to dry. Seeds soaked in water are said to make a good soothing liquid for stomach ache.

Florence fennel is best sown in April in rows 20 in. (50 cm) apart and thinned to 9—12 in. (23—30 cm) apart. This plant needs a warm, well-drained, humus-rich soil in a sunny position in the garden.

As the leaf bases of Florence fennel start to swell, hoe soil up around them to give the blanched white color. These are eaten raw in salads or cooked to flavor stews.

Garlic

As everyone knows, garlic is a very pungent herb, but one that is justifiably popular with cooks.

It is a member of the onion family and can be grown in just the same way as shallots and onion sets. Divide a bought bulb into cloves and plant these 6in. (15 cm) apart in rows 12 in. (30 cm) apart.

The cloves can be planted in fall in mild climates for harvestable bulbs in spring and summer or elsewhere in spring for bulbs ready in October. Lift when the leaves start to yellow, then put them in trays to dry.

Horseradish

Horseradish is probably better known in a sauce than in the garden, but there is every reason to find room for a few plants.

Plant sparingly, however, because once established the deep searching thongy roots soon become very invasive and take some digging out. The leaves will grow 2 ft (60 cm) or so high. Although any small piece of root will grow, the top crown-shoot part (which

Even the smallest garden has room for a short row of garlic.

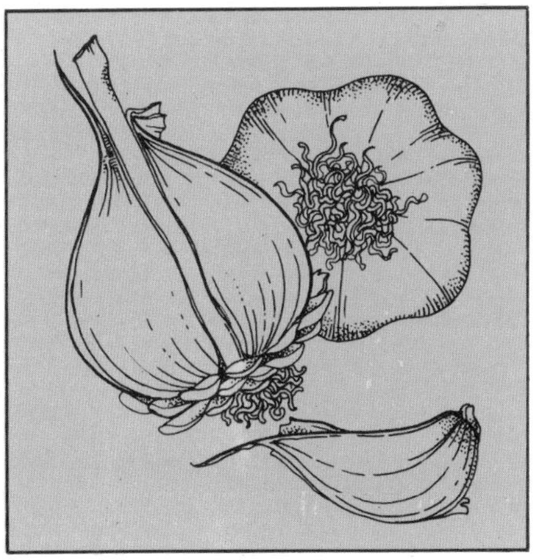

Horseradish root cuttings. Slant the base to ensure planting the right way.

is no use for culinary purposes anyway) is best. Plant in spring, 18 in. (45 cm) apart.

Lift the roots in late autumn and store in sand and peat moss for use when the soil is frozen.

Shredded slivers from the white cylindrical roots used fresh in cream sauces provide the traditional, hot mustardy flavored relish to go with roast beef. Fresh root scrapings can also be used as a sauce on raw shellfish dishes to give a pungent flavor.

Marjoram

Sweet marjoram *(Origanum marjorana)* is actually a perennial, but it is best treated as an annual as it can die outdoors in winter in all but the more sheltered spots and mild climates.

The seed should be sown indoors in March and the seedlings planted out in late May or early June, 9—12 in. (23—30 cm) apart. Alternatively they can be sown direct into the cropping position in mid-April. In either case they need a warm, sunny position.

Gather the leaves as they get large enough and before the plant develops flower heads. Chop them for use fresh and dry some for winter supplies. They are a useful ingredient in mixed herbs, or as a substitute for thyme.

For a stronger flavor and to provide fresh leaves in winter, it is best to grow oregano (*O. vulgare*) as a pot plant in a sunny window. There are several variants of this species, also known as pot marjoram. One form, 'Aureum', has golden foliage. Although oregano is a perennial, it is not reliably winter hardy in most northern regions. Grow in a warm, sunny position in the garden. Sow the seeds indoors in early spring, later outdoors. Keep the plants about 12 in. (30 cm) apart. In mild climates, use oregano as a ground cover on sunny slopes.

Mint

Mint is a plant often taken for granted, yet there are many kinds and most are worth cultivating.

The common mint or spearmint, *Mentha spicata*, is the species most frequently found in gardens and is most recommended for mint sauce. Another type worthy of note is *Mentha suaveolens*, the round-leaved or apple mint, a type not affected by rust disease. Many claim this is the best mint to use with new potatoes. There is a very attractive white variegated form of apple mint.

You are unlikely to have any difficulty growing mint — it usually needs restraining rather than encouraging. A good tip is to plant the pieces of root, from which new plants are grown, in an old plastic bucket (or similar container) with a hole in the base. Bury this in the garden up to 2 in. (5 cm) of the rim and fill it with soil. The mint roots will be contained and not spread all over the garden.

It's a good idea to lift some roots in the autumn and grow them in pots indoors to supply young sprigs through the winter.

Parsley

This is one of those herbs that grows like a weed when allowed to self seed. It is not quite so easy when we try to raise plenty in the garden.

The main difficulty usually lies in getting the seed to germinate. It is a slow germinator, and the old cottage gardener's tip of pouring boiling water along the drill sometimes speeds things along. Be sure to use fresh seed and sow indoors in pots of seed compost for certain success.

Sow in rows 9—12 in. (23—30 cm) apart in spring for summer and autumn use, and late July or early August for winter use in mild climates. Thin to 6—12 in. apart (15—30 cm).

Parsley is a biennial which will produce leaves for several seasons if the flowering stems are cut before they fully develop. It will stand some shade and produces a lot more leaf if it is given an occasional liquid feed.

One of the most useful herbs, parsley is ideal for garnishing, or in sauces and stuffings, and as a constituent of bouquet garni. Fresh leaves are by far

Several low-growing herbs, such as marjoram, make good ground-cover plants.

There are many species of mint. All need the root run restricted.

Parsley seedlings can be transplanted into pots for indoor cultivation.

the best, but you can ensure additional winter supplies by air-drying bunches of foliage in summer and rubbing it down before storing in sealed jars. To retain the color, dip fresh leaves in boiling water for a minute or so, shake dry and then dry in a cooling oven.

Rosemary

This is a plant that grows quite large and it looks well towards the front of a small shrub border where it is winter hardy in parts of California and other mild-climate regions. If kept trimmed back each spring it will not reach more than 2—3 ft (60—90 cm) high.

Rosemary responds well to being grown in a pot in a sunny window.

Plants can be raised from seed sown in spring and summer, or from cuttings taken in August, September or October. Light soils suit the plant best.

Sage

Sage is another shrubby herb. As well as the true species with its attractive grayish-green leaves, there are purple-green and cream, and pink and green variegated forms.

The best flavored foliage comes from young plants grown in well-drained soil in a warm, sunny site.

All species can be raised easily from seed sown from March to June. Alternatively they can be propagated from cuttings rooted in sandy compost in September.

Trim off the purple flowers before they open, and cut plants back to get a harvest of shoots and also to encourage more basal growth and foliage.

It takes some time to dry the rather thick leaves and woody stems, and they need a warm, airy place. Once dry, just rub the leaves in your hands to break them up, then store in an airtight jar.

Rosemary is an attractive flowering shrub as well as a popular herb.

Tarragon

Tarragon (*Artemisia dracunculus*) is a tall, bushy perennial that needs winter protection in the North. Its leaves are used to flavor vinegar, sauces and chicken. It needs sun. Some plants lack flavor — before you buy — pinch off a leaf and taste it.

Thyme

The comon garden thyme (*Thymus vulgaris*) is a really attractive low-growing decorative shrub. Planted close to a path or near the back door, you will be aware of the delicious fragrance every time you brush by. If the young shoots are not cut for drying, the 8—12 in. (20—30 cm) plants are covered with purple flowers in June.

Among the many thymes is a golden-leaved form, *Thymus vulgaris* 'Aureus'. Another particularly attractive type is the lemon thyme, *Thymus* × *citriodorus*, which has silver and golden-leaved forms.

Thyme needs a sunny site and light, sandy soil. You can propagate by cuttings taken with a heel in May or June, or raise common thyme from seed sown any time from March to July. Once established, put out young plants 9—12 in. (23—30 cm) apart.

Sage and thyme are popular shrubby herbs, and make a good planting combination.

Greenhouses

Greenhouses are not the panacea to all garden problems and you will achieve greater success if they are viewed as an extension to the outdoor growing season. Enclosing an atmosphere with glass or polyethylene keeps out wind and rain, and some of the larger pests can also be kept out, but we need to be at hand to control moisture and temperature.

Higher average temperatures under cover mean more rapid growth, not only of plants but also of diseases and multiplication of pests, so protected crops need more frequent attention.

Automatic systems for heating, ventilating and watering make things much easier for us, especially for those gardeners not at home in the day to operate ventilators, adjust heaters and do the watering. Even so, I advise the progression slowly; gain experience first by gardening outdoors and on the windowsill, then use frames and other protection before adding a greenhouse. Choose a cold or intermediate house to start with.

The margins for error are much wider where the plants are growing in the open with a large volume of soil in which to spread roots. Restrict the roots in small pots and checks to growth are more likely because of dryness, fluctuating temperatures and excessive feeding.

These warning remarks must, of course, be treated only as sensible caution, for greenhouses really can give tremendous satisfaction. They protect us from the cold weather to make gardening more comfortable and allow an even greater variety of plants to be grown. The smell on a warm day when the paths are damped down and a whole range of plants is growing strongly really can't be described. It is the breath of life to true gardeners. But like all pieces of equipment greenhouses need proper handling and the instructions carefully followed.

Careful siting of greenhouses and frames is important to capture the most light.

Where the spare-time gardener leads a busy life, various cold frames will be more easily handled. They give protection from the weather, bring crops forward a few weeks and extend the fall season. Ventilation, more crudely provided, is less critical.

Once some experience is gained then all these protective structures can be used in association with one another. Many seedlings and cuttings raised in heated greenhouses and small propagators need to be moved to a cold greenhouse or frame to harden off.

Where space is very limited a specialist interest like orchids, carnations, cacti and tropical plants may demand just one small heated house. A small cold greenhouse is ideal for alpines and here the less energetic and physically disabled gardener can get much pleasure at little cost.

The cheapest way to heat a greenhouse is to build a lean-to on the side of the house and draw warmth from the house heating system. Ideally built on to the south-facing wall, or west-facing for second choice.

Commercial growers make good use of plastic-covered houses and I see these structures being used increasingly in gardens. They do not have the disadvantage of glass which seems to tempt balls where there are children in the family! Ventilation systems are crude, rather like frames, and they prove ideal for the simple and yet so popular and practical plan of growing fall, winter and spring salad crops and anything else that will survive 45°F (7°C) temperatures.

The polyethelene house would make the perfect winter cover for a sandpit where there are small children!

Polyethylene tunnel cloches are inexpensive and can amply repay their cost in the vegetable garden by advancing and extending the growing and harvesting season.

CLOCHES AND OTHER PROTECTION

Cloche, the French word for bell, is used to describe individual plant protectors, and is a practice more familiar to British and European gardeners then American. However, there are well-known American cloches, the Hotkaps, wax-coated paper domes that are sold by mail-order seed and nursery firms as well as garden centers. Unlike most of the cloche materials described below, Hotkaps are a strictly temporary means of protection and are always discarded after use. They are most often used in spring in the North to protect tomatoes, eggplants and other vegetable plants from cool nights and late spring frosts. They do heat up inside and should be slit at the top to allow air circulation.

There are three other main choices of material for cloche construction. The cheapest in the long run and the material which best retains heat is glass. Panes of glass held on galvanized frames are the most practical but it takes careful handling and some knack to use over a number of years without breaking the glass.

Rigid, clear corrugated plastic is also brittle in cold weather but very much easier to handle and the better materials carry a 10-year guarantee against breaking. Beware of cheap, light clear plastic which will fracture in the cold and when exposed to strong sunlight. The small lightweight plastic cloches with poor anchorage also blow away in strong winds.

Thin polyethylene film is the cheapest material and can be used to cover tunnel cloches, (see drawings below). Select film which has been ultra-violet light inhibited, usually marked U.V.I. on the packs. This film will last two full winters and one summer before disintegrating. Where the sheet is stored out of sunlight in summer it may last three or more seasons.

Be sure to anchor both ends of the polyethylene sheet over tunnel cloche hoops very securely before fastening each top tensioning wire. Set the wire hoops out first, bury one end of the sheet, unroll over the hoops, pull tight and then bury the second end. Finally fix the tensioning wire. In very exposed positions it is worth pulling a little soil up over the two edges of the polyethylene to give even greater anchorage.

POLYETHYLENE

Another idea from England that might be tried is to cover the soil with polyethylene sheets, into which slits and perforations have been cut, once crops are sown and planted. Then as the crop develops it lifts the film, forming its own support. Potatoes, lettuce, radish and hardy annual flowers have all responded well to this treatment. The slits allow irrigation and rainwater through so quite a wide bed can be covered. A good system for short period cover but not very adaptable in windy regions.

A Plan for Cloche Gardening

While not all the ideas for using cloches that follow are adaptable to all regions of the USA, gardeners in mild climates where some gardening is possible all year

Tie one end of the polyethylene to a stake or bury it.

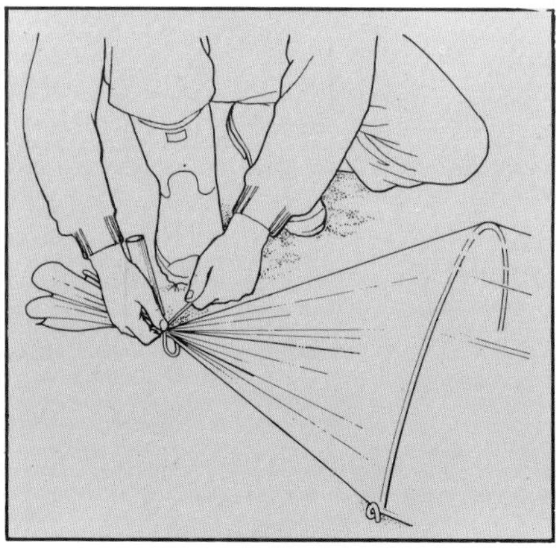

When both ends are secured, adjust the tension to hold the polyethylene.

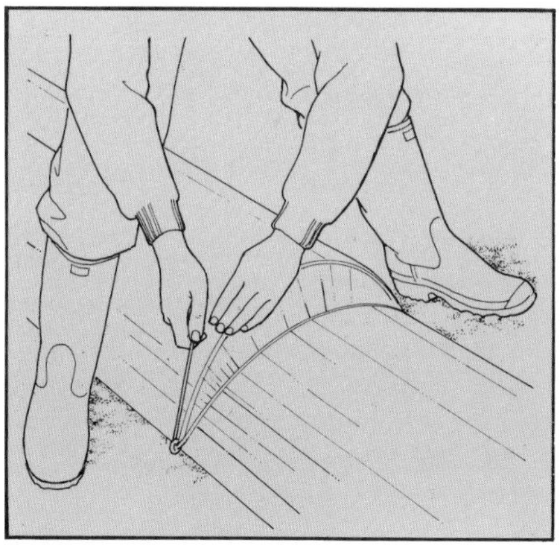

To weed or tend crops, simply slide the polyethylene back over the wires.

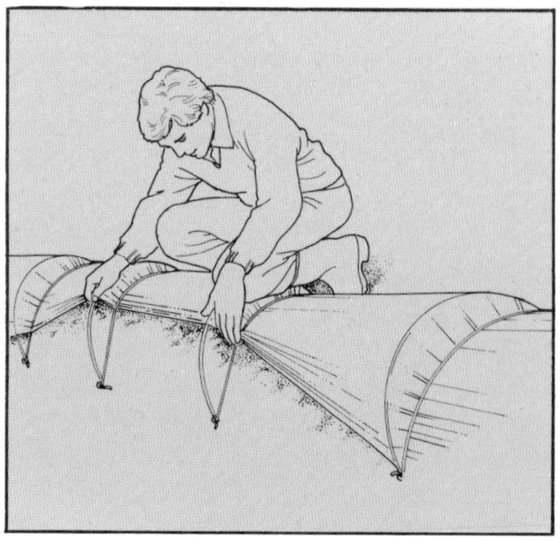

Cloche-grown fall sown lettuce, sweet peas and larspur in early spring.

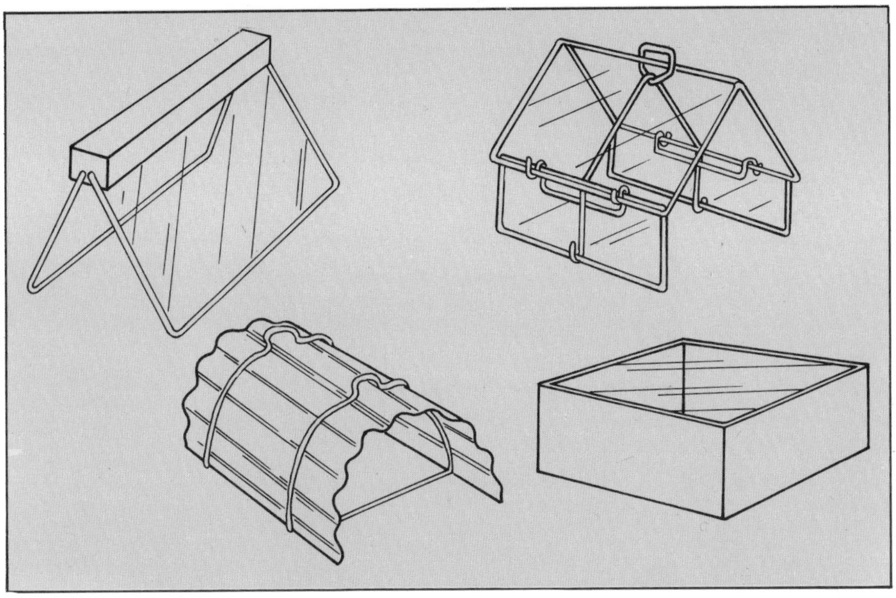

There are many kinds of cloche, but the principal types are tent (top left), barn (top right) and tunnel (bottom left). Even a box with a glass top can be used and in the USA, more often is.

can certainly benefit. And those in the North will find that adaptations of the cloche can profitably extend their growing season in both spring and autumn.

There are several absolute musts for cloches, and lettuce is first and foremost. Sown in late September or early October outside and covered with cloches, beautiful hearted lettuce can be cut in April and May.

Strawberries are the second choice, with cloches protecting the flowers from frost and the fruit from wet and birds, apart from the earlier fruiting.

In the North, a tunnel cloche can be used very successfully over lima and snap beans in the fall.

Think of the cloche growing year in four parts. First the autumn-sown over-wintered crops like salad onions, cabbage, lettuce, sweet peas and other hardy annuals.

Over-winter protection will extend harvests quite considerably and a late September sowing of broccoli will overwinter well to bear in May. Cabbage, cauliflower and broccoli seedlings can also be overwintered in this way and transplanted outside in spring to give early crops. Transplanting will delay the harvest by 2—4 weeks to help achieve succession.

The second period is early spring, where cloche-warmed soil can be used for earlier sowing and planting. Often one row of cloches can be used for two crops. Early peas, carrots, turnip and broad beans first, then over potatoes and snap beans.

The third period is late spring when they can be used to cover squash cucumber, melon plants or seeds and bush tomatoes very successfully.

Fourth comes the autumn cropping which is really an extension of the outdoor summer fruit and vegetables. August-sown lettuce given protection can be cut right into November and radish sown in succession will bear till Christmas. Cloches used to cover strawberries from February to June and tomato plants can be moved over everbearing strawberries to fruit through the fall.

Autumn protection given to parsley, spinach and endive again provides pickings to Christmas.

Care needs to be taken from spring on when the sun can be very hot and scorching may occur where leaves touch the cloche.

Some rigid cloches can be stood on end in pairs to form a tube around single tomato plants tied up a cane or stake.

The cheap way to achieve this summer protection is to push in three or four canes and pull a clear plastic bag, with the base slit open, over them.

While cultivation for crops under cloches is much the same as for the open ground there are one or two significant points. At first sight it appears that crops will be very short of water. In practice the surface soil under cover remains dry but water running over the cloche and in from both sides keeps the sub-soil nicely damp.

Excepting mid-summer, even in hot weather running the hose over the outside of the cloche gives the plants underneath all they need. If you really want to cosset plants like melons and tomatoes run a length of 2 in. (5 cm) wide black plastic pipe, with tiny holes punched every 8 in. (20 cm), alongside the plants and drip water through this.

Although the surface of the soil beneath cloches often appears dry, the roots of crops penetrate to the moister soil beneath, dampened by run-off water.

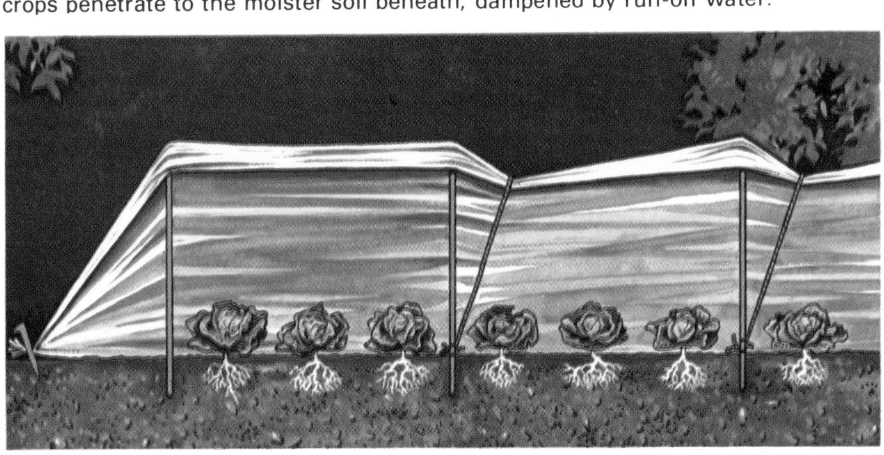

FRAMES AND PROPAGATORS

Frames

Although cloches are moved to the crops, frames are usually sited permanently, often close to the greenhouse where they are used to harden off plants — that is acclimatize them to colder conditions — before transplanting outside.

There are, however, two types of frame that are moved. One is the simplest of frames, constructed from a bottomless box with a pane of glass over the top, and this type can be moved to shelter tender rock plants and other single plants. The other movable kind is the original single or double Dutch light frame, (see illustration).

The single Dutch light system is easily moved from one crop to another. The front and back boards are held in place by driving stakes into the ground on both sides of the board.

A good plan for Dutch light frames planting in the upper South is to sow lettuce, beets, and carrots, cabbages and other hardy vegetables in the fall for winter harvests. As these are harvested, others can be sown or planted in their place. Later the frame can be moved to strawberries.

Much more common are the traditional garden frames with high backboard and lower front board, the glass sloping to the south to catch all possible light and warmth. There are many types made of wood, metal and plastic.

If you are buying one or making your own see that it is a good size, 4 ft × 6ft (1.3m × 2m), at least, so that it holds a good volume of air. Tiny frames will heat up furiously, and having little volume of soil to hold the warmth will cool down quickly.

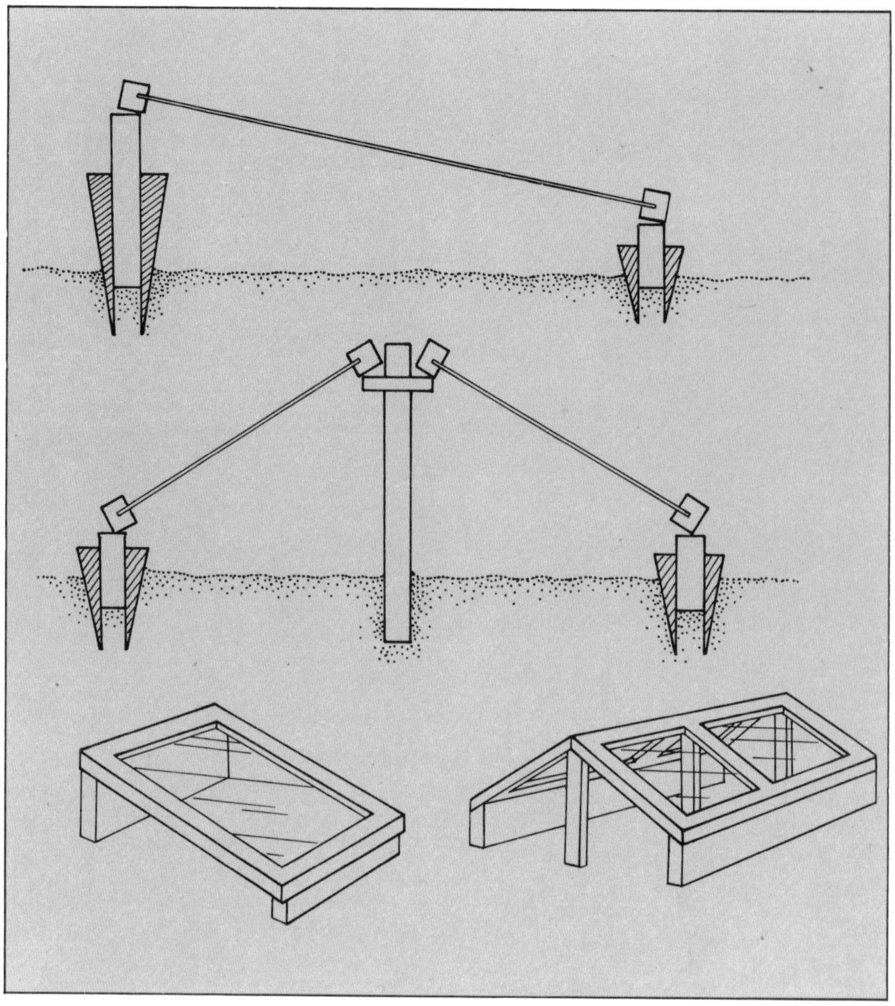

Dutch light frames, a large sheet of glass framed with wood is supported on two boards for a single span frame. Double spans are made with two low edge boards and ridge board supported on stakes. Edge boards are held between short stakes.

Before the days of electricity, old gardeners built 'hot beds' of rotting manure. The heat from the decomposition was used to raise early crops.

A pit is dug first, the fresh manure stacked in it, firming and adding leaves to extend the period over which heat is released. The manure is covered by several inches of soil and the frame stood on the soil.

An alternative to manure is a mixture of such materials as hay, straw, sawdust, kitchen refuse, leaves and fertilizers. Use about 1 lb. (.45 kg) of urea and 1 lb. of 5-10-5 for a frame area about 4 ft × 6 ft. (1.3m × 2m). Excavate the soil to 18 in. 45 cm), pack in 4-in. (10 cm) layers of organic matter sprinkled with fertilizer to 1 ft. (30 cm), water well, add 6 in. (15 cm) of soil and close the frame.

Warmth is needed to get the rotting process under way — ideally a temperature of 50°F (10°C). Once the heat has started it will be self-generating. Expect a high temperature for four weeks and then a steady fall over eight to ten weeks. If a hot bed is started in late February, for example, it will give heat to late April, or early May when the weather is getting warmer.

Raise the soil temperature just a few

Soil-warming cables make it possible to raise many seedlings and cuttings in cool greenhouses that require a high temperature. Lay the cables in parallel lines.

degrees and get early harvesting of crops such as lettuce, carrots, radish, turnips and spring onions. Even if you're not too successful with the heating, the rotted result is beautiful stuff to improve soil in frames, greenhouses and outside.

Electric soil warming cables are the modern-day equivalent to the old hot bed, but frames must be located close to a source of electricity. Soil cables with built-in thermostats are available from nursery supply firms. The cables are buried 4—5 in. (10—12 cm) deep to warm the soil and nicely raise the temperature in the frame.

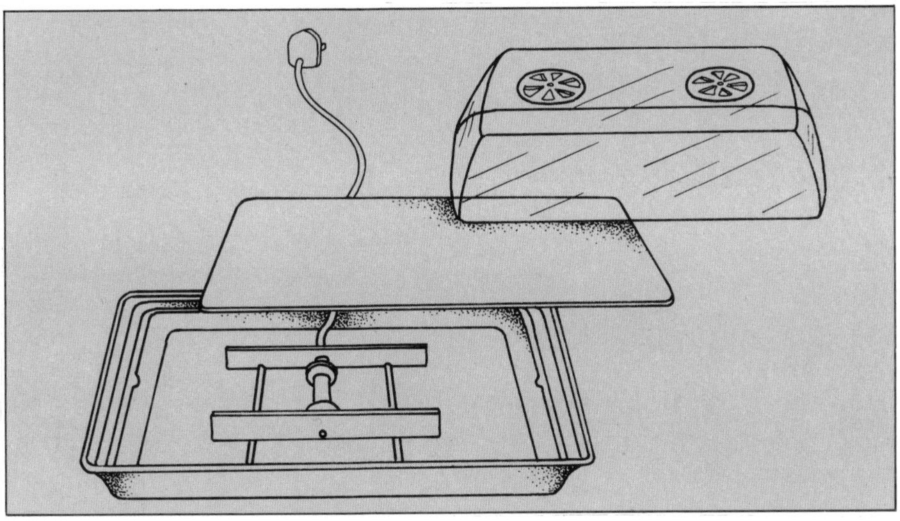

A shallow tray of water is heated by a sealed electric tropical fish tank heater for this seed and cutting raiser.

Propagators

Soil-warming cables are a common heat source for small propagators and for seed and mist propagating benches in greenhouses. When the cable is sold it has a watt loading to give heat output. Input needs to be 12—16 watts per sq ft (77 sq cm) for a cold frame in the North, 8 watts for a propagating frame, and 16—18 watts for a mist propagator where bottom heat to 75°F (24°C) is required.

Experimental work has proved that crops in warm soil can be grown satisfactorily in an air temperature 3°C lower than normally recommended. The use of soil cables therefore allows earlier planting in cold frames and greenhouses.

The most even distribution of heat across the soil occurs when the cables are spaced a distance equal to the depth to which they are buried. A good rod thermostat in the soil is needed to control the temperature; bury this just 1 in. (2.5 cm) deep at right angles to the wires. Cables are usually buried in sand for seed and mist propagators. See they are put down in parallel lines with the ends gently curved.

Several other heating methods are used to warm small propagators. One simple homemade system uses a 40 watt light bulb, and a low-priced proprietary single seedtray propagator has a sealed heat pad.

Small tropical fish tank heaters are also used to heat water under other seed propagators.

Check with your local electrician to be sure your electrical sources are adequate. I cannot emphasise enough the need for care where electricity is used to ensure there are no shorts. Professional wiring and great care to avoid piercing the covering on 240-volt soil-warming cables when cultivating crops are essential.

Where cold frames are not large enough to hold the small propagators either bring them indoors or, much better, use them in a cool greenhouse where any heat lost from the propagator will then help to warm the greenhouse.

If sunlight has to pass through a window to reach one side of the propagator and then pass through the propagator hood before reaching the seedlings, very soft, light green and drawn growth results.

Put one of the large proprietary propagators, with automatic misting nozzles and heating cables, in any greenhouse and the gardener's scope to raise many kinds of seedlings and cuttings is greatly enlarged.

Exercise a little control in the numbers of young plants raised early in the year if the size of the heated area you have to move these young plants into is limited.

Bottom heat and automatic misting really make rooting soft cuttings child's play. Watch the automatic leaf, two electrodes in a plastic block, which allows current to flow when wet. When dry the contact is broken and the misting valve is opened. A piece of cutting over the 'leaf' or hardness from water continually drying will interfere with this control.

Mist propagators can be used the whole year round, using them for slow

There are many types of proprietary propagators available, but it is also possible to make one by using a 40-watt light bulb as a heat source.

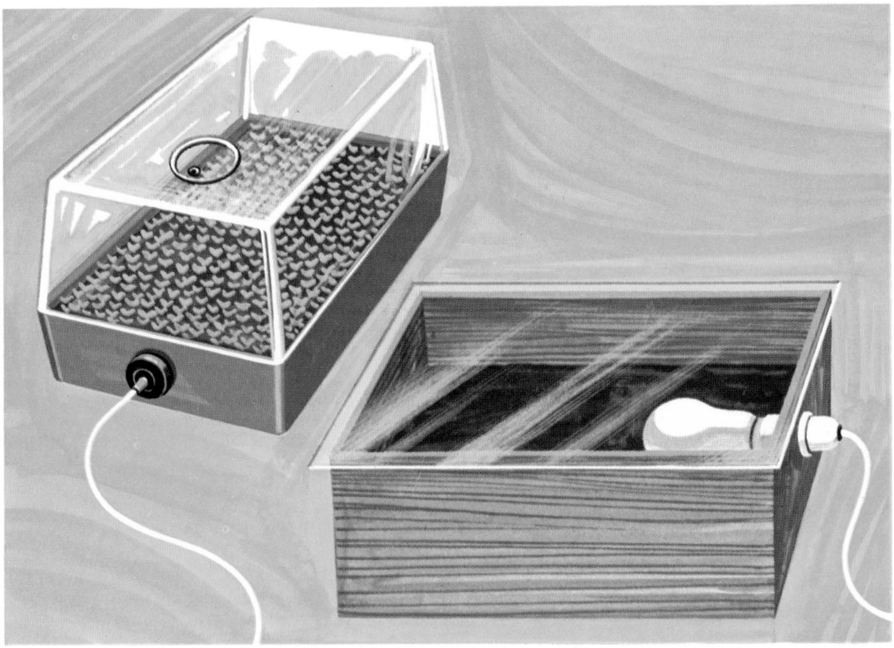

Although there are clear pros and cons for metal or wood greenhouses, many gardeners have a clear preference for the aesthetic qualities of one or the other.

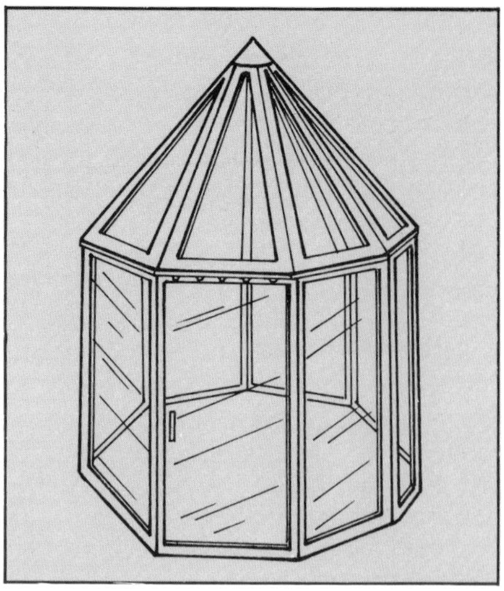

There are more decorative greenhouse shapes, such as this octagonal type.

rooting evergreens, such as *Chamaecyparis* and ×*Cupressocyparis*, in the autumn and winter.

GREENHOUSES

Choosing the structure

Glass Modern, well-designed aluminum structures are best because the lightweight glazing bars cast least shadow, the metal needs no preserving treatment and glazing seals are very good.

These houses did have the difficulty of fixing crop support wires, but now special bolts with split rings are available. Two flat sides are filed on the bolt head to fit into the extruded channel in all glazing bars.

Prefabs are so carefully made that all the metal is packed in a large cardboard box and easily transported.

Next choice is western red cedar (wood from *Thuya plicata*) which usually comes treated to improve the waterproofing and gives a natural reddish look. While regular maintenance is not required, treating the wood occasionally with preservative oil will extend its life.

There is a greater heat loss with metal frames than with wood, a consideration in very cold regions.

Where white painted timber is required for the sake of visual appearance, it is quite satisfactory but the need to paint regularly is expensive.

After deciding on type of structure look next at the shape and ventilation. Free-standing and lean-to houses can have either glass to the ground, perhaps a better choice in mild climates because of heat loss, or low brick, concrete or wooden bases where staging is to be installed for pot plants growing at waist height.

There are also semi-globular and octagonal shapes which can look attractive in the overall garden design. The outside surface area on these is big in comparison with cubic capacity, however; a factor which increases heating costs.

Where the glasshouse has a low brick wall base it is no bad idea to construct either cold frames or a rock garden with a second retaining wall against it to retain heat.

Adequate ventilation is essential and very small houses desperately need big vents. The rule of thumb figure is window openings to an area of one-sixth of the floor area. The greenhouse door may well provide ventilation, and on small lean-to houses it would be wise to try to fit automatic ventilators on the door.

Three traditional types. A lean-to (top) is easy to heat; brick- or cement-based (left) is good for pot plants; Dutch type (right) is good for crops grown in the border.

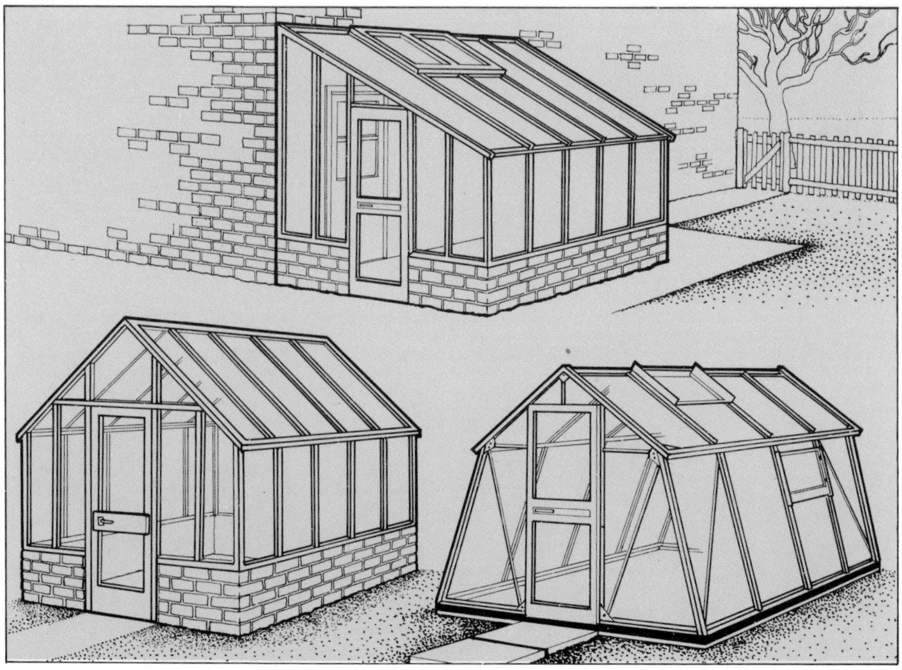

Sliding doors are generally preferable to hinged doors because they are less likely to be caught by the wind when people go in and out. It can be a distinct advantage to have a door which will slide open sufficiently to get a wheelbarrow through.

If a greenhouse has insufficient ventilation one improvement is the installation of an electric fan. Fit the fan in the top of one end of the house and then fit a louvered ventilator in the base of the opposite end. The fan will be switched on and off quite easily with a thermostat to control the temperature.

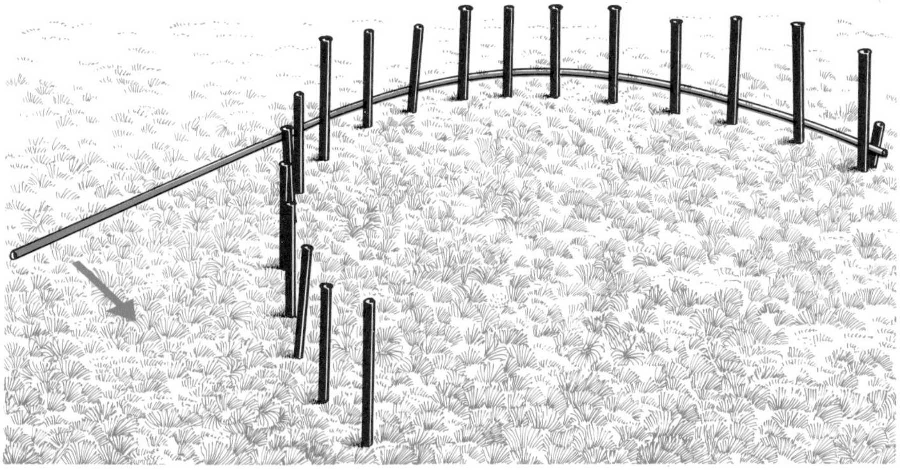

To bend the galvanized pipe for polyethylene house described below, use posts driven into the ground. An extra post at the end is needed to hold the pipe.

Polyethylene and plastic houses

Corrugated rigid clear plastic sheet on a timber framework makes a reasonable greenhouse and in a very small garden doubles nicely as a storage shed.

Polyethylene can be used to produce a very cheap house but has the disadvantage that heat is lost through this film more quickly than glass and plastic.

One complete sheet of the film does not have the draughts which pass between sheets of glass and it is excellent for cold house crops.

There are a number of polyethylene designs but for me the half circular 'tunnels' with ends buried for anchorage are preferable. Light polyethylene structures really do gather up the wind and secure anchorage is essential.

Whether you buy this kind of house or build your own the ventilation again is critical. All houses must have ventilation both ends. If the ventilation is by a door at one end only the wind will blow in and literally blow the house away. Allowing the wind to blow right through releases the destructive force.

Cheapest and simplest are roll-down doors. Roll *down* because where just a little ventilation is needed hot air can be let out of the top of the house and there is not a cold draught whistling across at floor level.

Building a polyethylene tunnel house is quite simple for a DIY enthusiast.

The instructions below are for the construction of a polyethylene house which would completely cover a 10 ft × 12 ft (3m × 4m) plot. If you reduce the height, the width and the area of soil cover will be correspondingly increased.

The materials needed are:

3 × 21 ft (6.4m) lengths ½ in. (1 cm) bore galvanized water pipe (for hoops)

2 × 5 ft (1.5m) lengths ½ in. (1 cm) bore galvanized pipe (for ridge pieces)

6 × 2 ft (60 cm) lengths 1 in. (2.5 cm) bore galvanized pipe (for foundation stakes)

1 × 20 ft (6 m) length of 10-gauge galvanized fencing wire

4 × 8 ft (2.4m) lengths of 2 in × 1 in. (5cm × 5cm) timber (lintels for doors)

2 × 4 ft (1.2m) lengths of 2 in. × 2 in. (5cm × 5cm) timber (lintels for doors)

4 × 6 ft (1.8m) lengths of 2 in × 1 in. (5cm × 2.5cm) timber*

2 × 4 ft (1.2m) lengths of 2 in. × 1 in. (5cm × 2.5cm) timber*

Quantity of laths for roller blind door

Quantity of nails

**Any thin lath wood; alternatively staples and wire can be used.*

The framework of polyethylene house described above, ready for construction of the doorway and eventual covering.

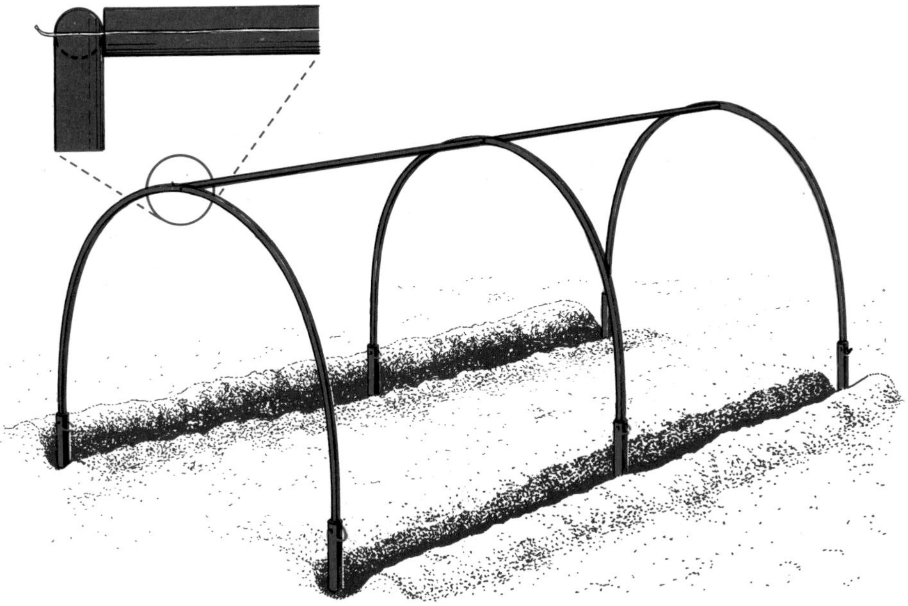

The door frame in position (see finished house on next page).

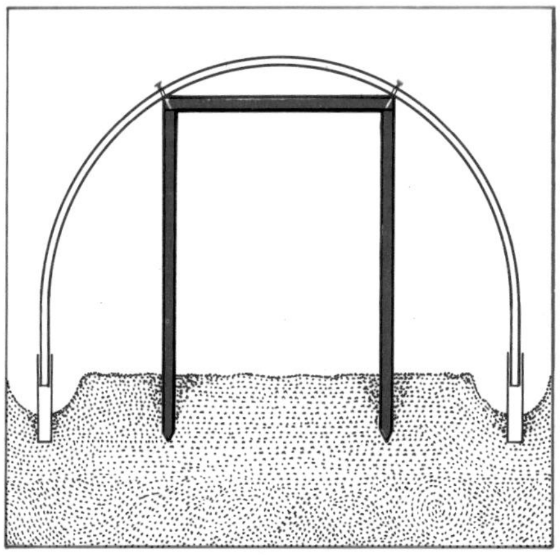

Polyethylene houses can be successful for crops like tomatoes and lettuce, and can be moved every couple of years.

Drive a series of short posts into the ground and bed the three 21 ft (6.4m) lengths of pipe round them to form a semi-circular hoop 12 ft (4 m) in diameter (see illustration). Then measure the site to mark out a 10 ft × 12 ft (3 m × 4 m) area. Take out a trench 10 in. (25 cm) wide and 12 in. (30 cm) deep around the outside, 2 in. (5 cm) out from the marked plot. Throw the excavated soil out of the area, *not* into it. Drive the 2 ft (60cm) foundation stakes firmly into the ground, positioning one at each corner and one in the center of each side. Leave 6—9 in. (15—23 cm) protruding above ground.

Drill a hole through the foundation stakes and the end of each hoop and place the hoops in the foundation stakes to erect the main structure. Secure by putting a short piece of wire or bolt through both holes you have drilled.

If the polyethylene cover becomes slack you can lift up the hoop a fraction, drill another hole and secure in the same way to take up the slack.

Drill a hole horizontally through the top of each hoop, but make sure it is in the top and center. Thread wire through the hole in an end hoop, then the length of one ridge piece, through the center hoop, then the next ridge pipe and finally through the other end hoop. Secure both ends of wire to form a rigid structure.

Bury the base of the 8 ft (2.4 cm) long 2 in. × 2 in. (5cm × 5cm) wooden uprights 4 ft (1.2m) apart into the soil to construct the door lintels. Drive nails through holes in the hoops, through the cross-pieces and into the uprights, to hold the 4 ft (1.2m) cross-timbers in place. (Alternatively use thick strips of rubber over the pipes and nail them to the cross-pieces and uprights.)

All rough or sharp edges should be covered with insulating tape or strips of plastic, then the structure can be covered with the polyethylene sheet.

Use 500-gauge (125 micron) film 24 ft × 24 ft (7.3m × 7.3m). Be sure it is ultra-violet inhibited (UVI). The sheet must fit firmly to give the whole structure strength and wind resistance. Fit the cover in warm weather because as the film cools it will shrink and tighten further.

Make sure the "skirt" around the base is the same length all the way round, then fill in the trenches with soil — firming it to tighten the film.

Cut out the film inside the lintels and fold the edge around the lintels, nailing it securely with timber laths and nails. Make the doors either as lift-up blinds or as polyethylene covered frames secured as sliding doors. (Both doors must be open to ventilate the structure adequately.)

Wood-framed doors on hinges are tidier and easier to get in and out. The film doesn't keep flapping in the wind if stretched over timber. Leave

Primula malacoides is a good plant to grow in a cool greenhouse.

the top square of a wood-framed door clear of the film and cover with plastic net for ventilation. At night and in the winter small plastic blinds can be used to cover the net to keep in more heat.

Polyethylene does attract more condensation than glass inside but top ventilation soon dries it out.

A film of moisture helps retain heat in cold weather when the house is closed.

Siting a greenhouse

All greenhouses need to be sheltered from the wind and away from trees and buildings which cast a shadow and reduce light.

Timber structures will cast much more shadow than the thin aluminum glazing bars. It is important, therefore, to see that wooden glasshouses are sited east-west, then the heavy timbering on the end doesn't block valuable light entering from the south.

Where the wooden end and door does face south some 60 per cent of light can be obstructed in the winter compared to a 30 per cent obstruction with an east-west house.

A cold greenhouse with ample ventilation is an ideal environment for alpine plants and spring-flowering bulbs.

COLD GREENHOUSE CROPS

The cold or unheated greenhouse is not very practical for most regions of the North, although special structures like the sun-heated pit have had devoted practioners in New England and similar climates for years. And with the advent of polyethylene, so much cheaper than glass, many northern gardeners have felt they could afford to experiment.

In fact, building a polyethlene house like the one described here is a very good introduction to greenhouse gardening.

Northerners, depending on the severity of their climates which can also differ from year to year, can use such houses in the spring and fall, and in some regions through the winter if they are satisfied to grow really hardy crops such as lettuce, kale and the like.

Lettuce is a very worthwhile cold greenhouse crop.

Generally though, the cold greenhouse is for mild climates that are frost-free or where only occasional freezes can be expected. The information below is mostly intended for them, but those in the North are bound to pick up a few ideas, too.

Cucumbers and melons are very tender and mid to late May is soon enough to plant. Once the summer crops are finishing in the autumn, clear the house, wash down the superstructure and house pot-grown autumn chrysanthemums.

Chrysanthemums are then cut by November and lettuce can take their place to heart in April and complete the cropping sequence.

Many variations can be added to this basic scheme. Pot-grown shrubs like forsythia and camellias can be brought inside in mid-winter for protected early flowering. All the spring-flowering bulbs can be given the same treatment.

Pot-grown peaches can be brought in once the flower buds show color, to protect them from the frost. Take them out once the fruits have set and the weather is warming.

Bring in pot-grown strawberries and roses in February to fruit and flower in May. Grape vines like 'Black Hamburg' can be grown in the house; the vine is either planted in the border soil or outside with the rod trained through a small hole in the wall or glass.

Hardy annuals can be sown in early autumn and grown both in the border soil or in 5—7 in. (12—18 cm) diameter pots to flower April or May. Good varieties for this are calendulas, pansies, stocks, antirrhinums (sown in July or August) and myosotis (sown in May or June). Sweet peas are a good cut flower to grow in the border soil and train up strings.

Dahlia tubers can be planted in April to give early summer flowers but choose the dwarf-growing varieties.

Many of the seed-raised pot plants like coleus, celosia, browallia, exacum, and impatiens will grow well and decorate the cold greenhouse in summer, but the seedlings need heat in the spring.

Stocks are very rewarding plants for a cold greenhouse, making ideal cut flowers, but buy types where you can select double seedlings.

Begonias, fuchsias and pelargoniums can be given similar treatment, raised from seed or cuttings in heat and then grown in the cold greenhouse through the summer.

You will find the cold greenhouse useful to carry chrysanthemum clumps through the winter.

Given a mild winter, with no more than a few degrees of frost in the house, fuchsia and geraniums can be over-wintered in pots if the soil is kept on the dry side and old yellowing leaves cleaned off.

Herbs grown in pots will continue to provide fresh leaves well into winter and from early spring, given cold glasshouse protection. Parsley, mint, sage and chives in pots are good examples.

Cucumbers, peppers and tomatoes are all likely to be infected by soil-borne diseases where they are grown for several years in the same soil. Even where tomatoes and cucumbers are alternated the disease verticilium wilt is likely to occur. After no more than two years' growing in the border soil it is advisable to change their location or fresh soil.

Polyethylene greenhouses really come into their own here because when the plastic cover needs changing at the end of the second year the house is easily moved to a fresh site and the old site exposed to the weather and given a rotation of crops.

HEATING A GREENHOUSE

Some control of ventilation is essential for all home greenhouses. There are a variety of automatic controls that are available; one type being a thermal unit that expands in heat to open the ventilators. Once you have the facility to cool houses in hot, sunny weather then heating can be introduced to increase the range of plants to grow in autumn, winter and spring.

Consider the energy source and heat output required when purchasing a greenhouse heater. The first thing to remember is that each 5°F (3°C) lift in temperature between inside and outside will double the heat requirement. A good thermostat sited out of direct sunlight and away from the heat source will give accurate heat control and avoid wasting fuel.

Set the thermostat so that the heating cuts off well before the automatic ventilators start to open.

Electricity is the easiest heat source to operate but remember the cost of bringing a cable to the house and wiring up the heater. Electric fan heaters give air movement which can help to reduce botrytis and other fungal diseases in crops like tomatoes and chrysanthemums.

Gas heaters need pipe installation where house supply is used, and if bottle gas is used the price of two gas containing bottles should be included in the cost comparison. An automatic changeover from one bottle as it empties to another will be needed.

Natural or bottled gas is the cheapest source of greenhouse heat. Electricity is expensive and almost prohibitive if the greenhouse is not a lean-to type attached to the main house.

Two figures are needed to find the size of heater for any greenhouse. First is the temperature lift. Where the coldest winter temperature you are likely to get is 20°F (—7°C) and you just wish to hold an inside temperature of 40°F (5°C) then a 20°F (12°C) temperature lift is needed.

Next to be calculated is heat loss; some materials hold warmth better than others. Heat loss is usually described in 'U' values, the higher the number, the greater the loss. Some examples are glass 1, asbestos 0.8, brick $4^1/_2$ in. (11 cm) thick 0.6, 500 gauge polyethylene sheet 1.4, rigid clear plastic 1, glass lined with polyethylene 0.5.

If you calculate the surface area and multiply by 1.4 this covers all surfaces and gives some spare. Multiply the total heat loss figure by the degree lift to get the Btu rating and the heater required. Convert the Btu figure to kilowatts for electrical heaters by dividing by 3,412.

COOL GREENHOUSE CROPS

Running a cool greenhouse will keep heat costs down yet offer a wide choice of plants. There are very many seed-raised winter-flowering pot plants which survive in a 45°F (7°C) minimum temperature.

Calceolarias, cinerarias and freesias from seed sown in March and corms planted in September, cyclamen, primulas *(P. malcoides, P. obconica, P. sinensis)* and schizanthus are always popular. Wash the glass regularly in the

Columnea is a spectacular hanging basket subject for a warm greenhouse.

Make use of all space in a greenhouse.

Increase the heat and you increase the harvest period and yield of tomatoes like this tasty cherry tomato and sweet and hot peppers.

winter so that these plants get all possible available light, then very sturdy plants will develop in the cool conditions.

Where the temperature is down to 45°F (7°C) at night and 10—15 degrees higher in daytime, be careful with the watering. It is better to keep a little on the dry side rather than risk botrytis and other wet rots.

Aphids also welcome the winter protection so spray or fumigate regularly, especially if calceolarias or cinerarias are grown.

Among vegetables, lettuce can be cut from autumn to late spring, and all summer fruiting plants can be planted a few weeks earlier to give a longer harvest period and a heavier crop.

Cacti need to be rested through the winter. Kept frost-free and dry they will shrivel back naturally before swelling up and bursting into growth with more warmth and moisture in late winter and spring.

Other plants for a cool house are azaleas, hardy spring bulbs and camellia. Stocks grow well in these conditions. Buy types where you can select doubles and raise the seedlings indoors or in a heated propagator. Once up, move to the cool greenhouse and all the double flowering forms will turn yellow. Save these and throw away the dark green healthy looking singles! 'Column' and 'Beauty of Nice' stocks can be grown in the border soil to cut or in 5—7 in. (12—18 cm) pots. The bigger the pot and wider the spacing in the border, the larger the flower spikes will be.

Calla lilies are another good pot plant for a cool house. Pot up the rhizomes (swollen root bases) in 6—10 in. (15—25 cm) pots of a good loam-based potting compost and bring under glass in early autumn. They will grow strongly through the winter and early spring, demanding plenty of water. Dry off after flowering.

Where a little heat is used to bring pot roses into early flowering the bushes need potting up in good time and the new roots established before forcing into growth. By potting one bush into an 8—10 in. (20—25 cm) pot of a good loam-based potting compost in early October, it can be gently forced from the following February. Rested in autumn and early winter, the bush can be forced for several years with just a little fresh compost added to the top of the pot. Have a second batch of potted roses to flower up to Christmas. These bushes are rested from mid-winter to early spring out of doors, and dried off a little before putting them out. Grow them outdoors all summer and house them with pot chrysanthemums in September.

Select glasshouse cut flower varieties of rose for this treatment; 'Sweet Promise' (also known as 'Sonia') is recommended for this.

A number of perennial foliage plants can also be used to decorate the cool greenhouse the year round. Several raised from seed such as *Asparagus Sprengeri*, *A. setaceus* and *Grevillea robusta* can be recommended. Climbing *Passiflora caerulea* is also raised

Automatic ventilators prevent the greenhouse from overheating while it is unattended.

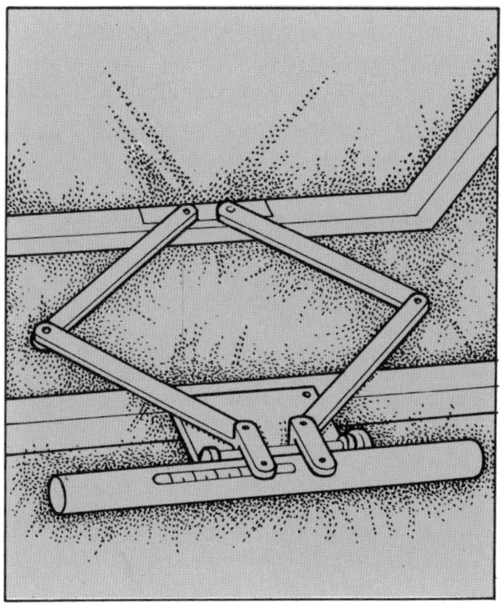

Different varieties of cinerarias will give a range of height and flower size. Sow in several batches from July to August for a succession of flowers.

from seed and flowers well under cool glass. Cut it back in spring and grow it in a pot to restrain the growth.

HEATED GREENHOUSES

If you can hold a minimum temperature of 50°F (10°C) in a greenhouse in winter it will be possible to grow semi-tropical plants. Take the temperature up to 60°F (15°C) and the tropical plants, including quite demanding cultivars of croton, ferns and orchids, often described as stove-house plants, can be accommodated.

There is less use for propagators in these temperatures. Seed pans and trays of cuttings placed over the heat source will be kept quite warm enough to give good germination and rooting.

Many plants, attractive in summer outside, can be kept in good form given the extra heat. Coleus is a good example. Tender evergreen climbers such as *Hoya carnosa*, *Jasminum polyanthum* and *Stephanotis floribunda* can be trained over roof wires to fill the house with flower, fragrance and foliage. Most tender climbers, but not hoya, are best cut back in early spring when they have outgrown the space available to them.

High temperatures will really push up the fuel bills in cold weather and erecting a polyethylene tent within a greenhouse is one way of reducing the cost and housing a smaller quantity of plants within the tent at the higher minimum temperature.

Strong winds blowing over a glass or plastic house can increase heat loss by 15—20 per cent, so a sheltered site is essential. Lining the inside of the house with plastic sheet to give a double glazed effect does save heat. It also causes a loss of light in winter when the light levels are already very low.

Lining the whole house reduces light by 35 per cent and I would prefer to line just the north-facing side to save heat and reduce light by no more than 18 per cent.

Where warmth comes from soil cables within the house a polyethylene tent over the crops in and on the heated area will reduce heating costs by 16—20 per cent. Using cloth rather than plastic to cover only during darkness can achieve a 22—24 per cent heat saving.

Soil

Border soil needs preparing well if plants are grown directly in it. Start with the best available garden soil. Mix seven parts of soil with three parts of peat moss and two parts coarse sand to make a general purpose mix. The soilless mixes, available at garden centers, can also be used.

Most plants will grow well for many years in such well prepared soil. It is possible to remove all the soil to two spades' depth, wash down with a soil sterilizer and refill with a new soil mix to grow repeatedly with tomatoes and carnations. A tiny piece of infected soil can quickly reinfect the whole area, however, and I prefer either rotation or the switch to fertilized peat-filled growing bags and similar container growing methods with soilless mixes.

At least two thorough cleanings right

Heavy crops of eggplant are possible in a warm greenhouse.

TEMPERATURE CHART

Inside Temperature	Glass to Ground	Brick to Bench Height	Polyethylene House	Lean-to Glass to Ground
4°C (38°F) just frost free	1.5 kw	1.25 kw	1.75	1.25 kw
7°C (45°F) cool greenhouse	2 kw	2 kw		1.75 kw
10°C (50°F) temperate house	2.5 kw	2.5 kw		2 kw
15°C (60°F) store house	3.5 kw	3 kw		2.75 kw

Guide to heat input for 20°F heat lift in 6 ft × 8 ft (1.8 m × 2.4 m) greenhouse.

Vine weevil grubs eating a primula root. Other crops are also affected.

through the greenhouse will be necessary, especially where the house is heated and kept filled the year round. Early spring and autumn are the ideal times. Clear a section at a time, wash down the glass inside and out, scrub the superstructure, then freshen up the benches and all pot-grown plants.

Constant moving of plants is also necessary, rearranging to give more space as each plant develops. Rake over gravel or expanded clay granules on the bench, wash capillary watering mats and keep everything fresh and clean.

Watering

A watering can with a long spout is sufficient for small greenhouse purposes, although a switch to hose saves time in hot weather and where the house is quite large. Damping down the path and base of the house in hot weather will give a good growing atmosphere.

Keeping the can filled with water on the path allows warm watering of very succulent plants like saintpaulias. Apart from this exception tap water temperature is quite acceptable for most plants.

There are a variety of capillary watering systems which are invaluable to greenhouse owners away in the daytime. Simplest is a polyethylene lined bench covered with 1 in. (2.5 cm) of fine sand. The sand is kept wet and the plants draw up what moisture they need from the sand. After settling pots on the sand, water once from above to set up capillary water movement.

More sophisticated are the sand beds and various kind of capillary mats which are kept wet automatically. There are several systems where water is released either when the reservoir level falls or when the mats dry.

Commercial growers also use systems with a separate drip or trickle nozzle to each plant. One or two of these are now available in smaller sizes to suit garden greenhouses. Even the fertilized peat-filled growing bags can be stood over a water-holding tray and the peat kept damp via capillary wicks.

Plant growth is much improved where checks from water shortage are avoided. In cool and cold greenhouses, however, be sure to reduce watering in winter. Where plants are just kept alive over the winter in cool temperatures, wet compost can bring death.

Fumigation

Although pests and diseases can multiply and spread rapidly in the warm confines of a greenhouse, they can be controlled with fumigants and smokes. Choose a still evening after the sun has lost its strength for greatest effect. Strong winds will speed the removal of the fumigant from the house and some chemicals can scorch the plants in hot sun.

Once the smokes are lit beat a hasty retreat and shut the door. Any big smoke leaks from the house should be noted because heat is likely to be lost continuously from these spaces.

Ventilate well before working again in the house. Check the instructions on all containers and follow to the letter. Ferns, for example, are damaged by several chemicals and will need removing from the house before fumigating.

Fruit trees in pots

Apricots, peaches, nectarines, grapes and figs are all possibles for pot cultivation. All these fruits can be grown in the border and trained against the wall of a lean-to greenhouse. They take up rather a lot of room, however, and pot culture allows more plants to be given protection, even if the yield from the pots is considerably lower.

Keep the stone fruits outside all winter and bring under cold glass just as the buds begin to burst. This protects the flowers from frost and gives a good set if the blooms are dusted over with a brush at midday. Once fruit has set, is swelling nicely and the chance of frost has passed, the potted trees can be moved outside for the fruit to develop fully and ripen.

Plunging the pots in soil reduces the need to water, which will be twice a day in hot weather. Pots from 12—18 in. (30—45 cm) diameter are required. Pot the trees up in proprietary potting compost and replace the top few inches of compost each year.

Watering is sometimes a problem with peat-filled bags in a greenhouse, but special trays are now available which maintain moisture by capillary wicks, seen here in the inverted bag. These bags are now being tried in the USA.

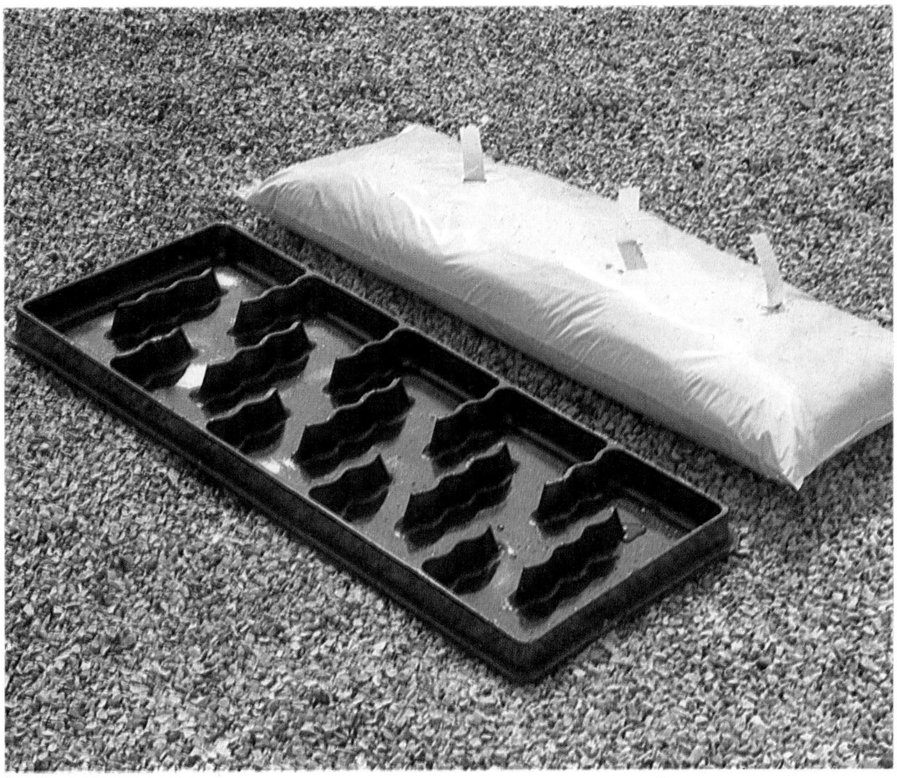

Calendar of Work
WINTER November-January

There is no substitute for the weathering of freshly cultivated land to produce easily worked crumbly soil in spring. Cultivate a little at a time to ensure all bare soil is cleared and cultivated by the end of this period. Mechanical rotary cultivators are best *not* used at this time, especially if the soil is heavy.

Dig the vegetable plot over one spade's depth, mixing in well-rotted compost as you go. In rose beds, shrub borders, in the fruit garden, under hedges and in perennial flower borders just skim the surface. Use the spade almost horizontally to cut off and invert the surface inch or two of soil. This disturbs the roots as little as possible and yet leaves a clean weed-free surface. Hoeing this crumbly surface soil in spring and summer will then be easy.

Woody plants ordered by mail often arrive at this time. If the soil is too wet to plant, dig out a trench and cover the roots with soil or damp peat until conditions improve. In much of the North, November is about the last time for planting lilies and spring bulbs.

Lawns

Rake off all leaves and debris to keep the lawn tidy; where the weather is mild and grass continues to grow it can be cut. In the South and parts of the West, existing Bermuda lawns go dormant at the onset of cool weather. For a green lawn in winter, overseed with annual ryegrass, Kentucky blue or other cool-season grasses.

Ornamental garden

A good period to construct new features; paved areas (in mild climates), rock garden, walls and flower beds. Roses and other bare-root woody ornamentals can be planted when the soil is frost-free.

In cold regions of the North, where snow cover is uncertain, place evergreen boughs (use discarded Christmas trees) over flower beds once the ground freezes. This helps keep the ground frozen and prevents plants from being heaved up during thaws and refreezing.

This is a good time to move large deciduous trees and shrubs which have out-grown their space. It is best to knock heavy accumulations of snow from evergreens.

Vegetables

After the first of the year, seed catalogs start arriving in droves. The good catalogs give more than mere lists of seeds to order so study them carefully for lengths of time from sowing seeds to their harvesting. Paying attention to these dates is one way to avoid having too much of one kind of vegetable ready at the same time.

In much of the South, this is harvesting time for endive, kale, cabbage, leeks, spinach and parsnips. In cold frames, sow lettuce and other hardy vegetable seeds.

Fruit

Check ties are secure to stakes. Throughout much of the South and South-west, dormant sprays can be given to fruit trees.

Prune deciduous trees when the wood isn't frozen. Autumn-planted cane fruits can also be cut back now. If you want to try your hand at grafting new fruit varieties on to your trees, now is the time to cut scion wood and store it by just pushing the end into the soil.

Greenhouse

Bring in bulbs, rhubarb crowns and chicory roots a few at a time to force. Wash down the glass and clean the structure thoroughly.

EARLY SPRING February - March

Spring seems closer in the still-frozen North, if you cut witch hazel, forsythia and pussy willow branches to force into flower indoors. When such indoor bulbs as amaryllis and veltheimia finish blooming, continue watering — until late spring for veltheimia, and through fall for amaryllis — before resting them.

Lawns

Where raking the surface to remove debris, moss and old grass was not completed last autumn there is a chance to do this now. Once completed, early spring is a good time to apply ground limestone, if needed. Wood ashes from the fireplace can be spread over the lawn in place of lime. In the South, sprigging of grass can be done.

Ornamental Garden

Just as soon as the surface soil starts to dry, hardy border plants can be transplanted. This is a good time to split Michaelmas daisies, *Chrysanthemum maximum* and similar perennials. Pansies and other bedding plants over-wintered in frames can be hardened off to prepare them for outside planting.

Prune back hard all bush, standard and perpetual climbing roses at the end of this period. Late summer and early autumn flowering shrubs like buddleia, caryopteris, and large-flowered clematis can also be cut back hard.

If you did not transplant lilies in the autumn get to it now to develop a strong root system.

Established rock plants will benefit from some new compost worked in around them. Prune back heathers and mulch them with damp peat.

Vegetables

Outdoors hardy vegetables like peas, broad beans, cabbages, radish, broccoli raab and spinach can be sown. Indoors sow seeds of tomatoes, eggplant and peppers.

General fertilizer can be spread over dry land and cultivated into the surface in preparation for spring planting. Shallots, onion sets and Jerusalem artichokes can be planted.

Lift parsnips and any other root vegetables before they make new leaf growth and the roots shrivel. Once lifted store in damp peat in a cool place.

Fruit

Apply a general fertilizer around all fruit—early in the season if the plants are in grass, later if in open cultivated soil. Once the fertilizer has been worked into the surface, mulch under trees and bushes with well-rotted compost to retain moisture and smother weeds. Where spring frosts are a problem, damaging blossoms, delay mulching until after the fruit has set because the bare soil radiates warmth and reduces frost damage.

Complete all pruning of fruit trees and grape vines. Continue dormant sprays in the North. Prune all autumn-fruiting raspberries back hard. The tips of summer fruiting kinds can also be cut back to remove dead tips and tidy the canes.

Greenhouse

The busiest season in the greenhouse starts now. Cuttings need to be taken from geraniums, fuchsias, chrysanthemums and other summer-flowering plants. The cuttings will need warmth to root.

Sow seeds of vegetables and annuals. Even if you are running a warm greenhouse—and a necessity if you have a cool house, some bottom heat will be needed to germinate the seeds. Even an electric light bulb in or under the propagating box will raise the temperature five to fifteen degrees more than outside the box.

SPRING March - April

This is the big seed-sowing, propagating and planting period. Plants established now will have the whole summer growing period before them. Once the surface soil starts to dry get the hoe working in all parts of the garden with bare soil. A large area can be covered in a little time where the soil is crumbly and there are no weeds, I like to hoe right through the garden at least once a fortnight if not once a week. No weed, however deep-rooted, can withstand being sliced through every week.

Lawns

Sow grass seed on well-prepared soil for new lawns and re-seed bare patches once the surface has been scratched over and a little fresh soil worked into the area.

A general lawn fertilizer should be evenly spread at this time.

Ornamental Garden

Evergreens can be transplanted in showery weather. Move as big a root and soil-ball as possible to reduce the check to growth, and syringe over regularly with water to reduce moisture loss in mild climates.

Prune back frost damage on shrubs like hebes, fuchsias and tender evergreens in mild climates where these shrubs grow outdoors all year. In the North, plant bareroot perennials such as bleeding heart, phlox and astilbe.

Hardy annual flowers need to be sown outdoors now for masses of summer color. At the end of the period some half-hardy annuals like asters can also be sown where they are to flower.

Prune shrubs like forsythia and flowering currants after flowering. Just cut out some of the flowered branches to retain shape and size.

Vegetables

This is the time to sow very many of the vegetables. It is worth spacing out the sowings to get a succession of crops. A few lettuces sown every 2—3 weeks for example. See there is at least three weeks of *warm* weather between sowings of peas for succession; if the weather is cold delay the next sowing. This is important even when early and midseason varieties are used.

Plant potatoes, onion sets, asparagus and in the far North, first sowings of peas, broad beans and spinach.

Thin out seedlings down the row once they are well established, remembering to leave enough carrots, turnips and similar root vegetables to pull young ones to eat while leaving alternate plants to develop fully.

Work a high-nitrogen fertilizer around cabbages to speed growth. Toward the end of this period, in the North transfer indoor-grown tomatoes and peppers to the cold frame.

Fruit

Watch all fruits for signs of pests and diseases. When in doubt about the right time to spray fruit trees, contact your county extension agent (listed in the telephone book under the county government) for help and regional guidance.

Strawberry plants can be set out. Feed established beds and replenish the straw mulch which will suppress weeds and keep fruits clean. Remove flowers from newly-set June plants and everbearers. With latter, leave flowers after July for fall crop.

Greenhouse

Still time to sow annual flowers such as marigolds and zinnias and such vegetables as squash, cucumbers and melons, but sow the last three in peat pots so there will be no root disturbance when they are set out later in the garden.

Pot up rooted cuttings of chrysanthemums and fuchsias and once established, harden off in cold frame.

LATE SPRING May - June

Warm sunny weather brings tremendous speed of growth. Late frosts are still a possibility until well into this period, so be prepared with large sheets of newspaper. Put these over tender plants and hold the paper in position with stones to give protection to bedding plants, strawberry flowers and tomato seedlings when the skies are clear at night and frost is forecast.

Sunny weather and rapid growth means heavy demand for water. Watch evergreens in tubs — they will need daily watering in hot weather. Established plants are better watered twice to ensure the compost is wetted throughout.

Lawns

When weeds are growing rapidly is a good time to apply selective weedkillers. If a fertilizer is used at the same time, use a soluble one or water the lawn a day or so after applying dry powders in the absence of rain.

Rapid growth demands regular mowing for the best lawns. Grass underplanted with bulbs and left uncut can be mown at the end of this period.

Ornamental garden

The tender summer-flowering subjects need planting now, and very tender subjects like zinnias can be sown where required to flower. This is the time to sow many biennials and perennials.

Spring-flowering primulas can also be sown, and *P.* 'Wanda' and *P. rosea* can be lifted after flowering, split up and transplanted.

Spray roses where mildew, blackspot and aphids are seen.

Put in support for tall-growing herbaceous plants and start spraying of delphinium to control cyclamen mites.

Vegetables

Keep up the successional seed sowing of salads and root crops. Corn, snap, lima and soy beans can be sown now, along with all the winter green vegetables such as kale, savoy and winter cabbage, sprouting broccoli and cauliflower.

Towards the end of the period sow seeds of squash, cucumbers and melons. Still time to buy tomato plants. Or apply a mulch and save yourself from hoeing!

Fruit

Maintain the pest and disease sprays; several are timed after petal fall because it is necessary to avoid spraying when bees are pollinating the flowers. If you have been troubled with small maggots in raspberries then two sprays with rotenone at 10-day intervals will prevent this.

Developing strawberry fruits need lifting from the soil on to straw or polyethylene to prevent mud splashes.

Red blistered leaves on peaches are caused by peach curl and can be picked off but spraying to control is done at bud burst and leaf fall.

Melons can be planted now but keep them warm for the best results.

Greenhouse

Glasshouses can be filled to capacity at this time. Shade the glass in hot weather and dampen the paths at midday if possible. Orchids, especially will need extra shade from now on. It may be easier to put them outside in the filtered shade of trees.

Chrysanthemums and all pot plants growing strongly can be moved up into larger pots. Pinch out tips of chrysanthemums twice during this period. They can be moved outdoors for the summer.

All softwood cuttings will root quickly in the warmth. These include geraniums, coleus and begonias.

SUMMER June–August

This is the time to enjoy the results of earlier activities. Warm dry weather slows the speed of grass growth and dry surface soil reduces weeds so there is time to enjoy the flowers, fruits and vegetables.

Water the outdoor garden well and mulch areas with well rotted compost to control weeds and retain moisture if you are going away for a week or two. Set up capillary watering systems for container plants on the terrace. Moving the plants, where possible, into shade will help.

Try to visit garden centers, nurseries, flower shows and well-maintained parks to pick up other good ideas for your garden.

Lawns

Water very well in dry weather. Selective weedkillers can still be applied to kill weeds. August is the best time in most regions for sowing grass seed.

Ornamental garden

Summer months are ideal for putting down paving if winter frosts prevented construction work of this kind. Hedges will need trimming if new growth is to cover the cuts by winter. Keep the garden tidy by cutting off all dead flower heads. Where plants like delphiniums are cut back hard another flush of flower will be produced in the autumn.

Transplant seedling biennials to produce bushy specimens. Take cuttings from pinks and rock plants like helianthemum. Chrysanthemum and dahlia flower stems will need disbudding to produce large flowers on a single stem. Propagate iris by division and shrubs like hydrangeas from softwood cuttings.

Prune shrubs like lilac, philadephus, spiraea and weigela after flowering.

Vegetables

Try sowing swede seed in early summer if you have had difficulty growing good roots. There is still time to sow salads, beets, snap beans and carrots. In mild climates cabbages need sowing at the end of this period.

Plant out the winter greens, such as kale, and see that they are well watered to get them growing well. Watch for gray and white aphis curling the leaves; early sprays with rotenone will knock them out.

Pinch the growing tips from broad beans at the first sign of black aphids. Pinch out the growing tip of outdoor tomatoes once four trusses of fruit have set.

Plenty of water and liquid fertilizer applied to leaf crops, tomatoes, celery and onions will increase the yields considerably.

Fruit

Water applied in dry weather to fruit trees and bushes will increase this year's yield and help build up reserves for next year's crop. Prune out all the fruited canes from summer raspberries once picking is complete.

Tie in the fast-growing new shoots on loganberries and blackberries to ensure a good crop next summer.

Thin out the fruit on apples, pears and plums where the fruit set is heavy. One apple every 6 in. (15 cm) of branch is usually ample.

Greenhouse

Any large-flowered chrysanthemums should have their stems reduced to two or three. Carnations may require disbudding. Continue to take soft-wood cuttings.

Be merciless! Throw out plants that have had their day, especially those that are being replaced by cuttings.

AUTUMN September - October

Harvest time, the big clean up and a start on the new gardening year. Spread the well-rotted compost from your heap over the soil to mix later. This gives plenty of space to fill with leaves and all the old plant remains as flower and vegetable beds are cleared.

Shorter days will mean slower growth and more time for the reconstruction of garden features, whether from living plants or inanimate landscape materials.

Lawns

Sow seed in early autumn or lay turf for the best results. Mow the lawns less regularly as the speed of growth slows.

Ornamental garden

All the summer bedding plants must be cleared as they finish flowering. It is better to sacrifice a few flowers and get the new planting established before winter. Plant all the biennial flowers and inter-plant with bulbs. See that the small bulbs are planted in early autumn to reduce the chance of shrivelling while out of the soil.

Lift early-flowering chrysanthemum clumps and over-winter in frames. Hardy annual flowers can be sown outdoors late in this period. Try fall-sowing larkspur. Sow stocks in greenhouses for early flowering next year.

A fine net placed on canes over ornamental ponds will catch falling leaves and stop them fouling the water.

Vegetables

Once the tops have fallen naturally, onions can be lifted and dried for winter storage. Lift potatoes and store in strong, multi-walled brown paper sacks or cardboard boxes. Be sure they are kept out of the light to prevent them going green.

Plant cabbages (in mild climates), and spray all brassicas to prevent caterpillar damage. Start to blanch endive for fresh salads. Lift chicory roots, screw off the tops and store in peat moss to force in the winter.

Sow endive varieties to over-winter in coldframes for spring harvest.

Fruit

When picking apples and pears keep the early ripening varieties away from the late keepers. The release of ethylene gas from ripe fruit speeds the ripening and decay of fruit nearby.

Choose a cool, slightly damp atmosphere for apple and pear storage. If the atmosphere is dry the fruits tend to shrivel.

Spray trees subject to peach leaf curl with liquid copper as leaves fall. Take hardwood cuttings of soft fruit bushes. Gooseberries root better if the cuttings still carry a few leaves.

Prune plums and damsons immediately after the fruit is picked. This usually means no more than the removal of unwanted branches.

Greenhouse

Plant up bulbs to force into early flowering and bury pots in trenches to root. Bring in potted chrysanthemums and freesias. Also bring in specimen fuchsias in pots and tubs to overwinter.

Clean down the superstructure and wash the glass to gain all possible light.

Ventilate freely on sunny days to reduce the chance of mildew on grapes, chrysanthemums and other crops.

Pot up seedlings of winter-flowering primulas, schizanthus and similar plants.

Pests and Diseases

Well-tended plants growing strongly are less likely to be infected by pests and diseases, and good cultivation is the first step to keeping these problems at bay. Garden hygiene is the next most important defence. Pests like mice, slugs, pillbags and vine weevil love to hide in old leaves and accumulated garden rubbish. Many diseases too are carried over from one year to another on old leaves, stems and infected fruits and roots.

After hygiene comes an alert eye; control measures taken at the first sign of attack are more effective and less damage is done to the host plant.

Chemicals to control pests fall into three main groups: those which kill by direct contact with the pests; stomach poisons which fall on the leaf, are eaten by the pest and kill from the inside; and systemic insecticides which are absorbed by the plant sap and kill both by contact and by insects sucking the sap.

Many fungicides, especially those we have used for a number of years, are protective. A coating of fungicide protects the leaves from infection by mildew, botrytis soft rots, rusts, black-spot, scab and similar fungal diseases. Modern systemic fungicides, however, are absorbed into the plant sap, transmitted through the plant and kill the disease as well as affording protection for the next two or three weeks.

Chemicals which can be diluted in water and sprayed on to the plants are the most commonly used, and are often the cheapest to apply. Aerosol canisters are easy and handy for spot application, especially to houseplants. Smokes and fumigants are very effective in the greenhouse. Dust can be applied to plants but it is difficult to achieve an even distribution. If applied when the plants are covered in dew the dusts will stick more effectively to the leaves. However, dusts and granular preparations are generally best used as soil treatments.

It is important that sprays are evenly distributed over stems and leaves. The sprays easily cover the upper surface but it is difficult to cover the undersides of leaves, which is where many pests live and multiply. Systemic materials really come into their own for this underside control.

While good cultivation and physical means of control (such as covering a row of carrot or cabbage seedlings with muslin to prevent rootfly attack) is to be preferred, I have no hesitation in using chemicals to keep plants healthy. It is essential, however, to follow the makers' instructions to the letter. Higher rates do not improve the kill, and the stated time must be left between spraying and harvest of fruit and vegetables.

Bees will also be killed by *some* insecticides, so choose carefully when spraying plants in flower, and even when spraying plants surrounded by flowering weeds.

Where pests and diseases occur repeatedly year after year it may well be necessary to apply a regular protective spray program.

If you do use repeated chemical applications try to apply a few different chemicals. This prevents the build-up of strains resistant to one specific control.

There are several biological methods of pest control. There are bacteria which just kill caterpillars, and there are insect parasites of aphis, whitefly and red spider.

Such insect parasites need to be used with understanding, however, for they seldom work if introduced when the pests have already reached epidemic proportions.

Red spider mites can be especially troublesome in a hot dry atmosphere. The webbing develops with very heavy infestations and the tiny spiders are clearly visible.

PROBLEMS AND SOLUTIONS

Aphids or aphis are also called greenfly, but cover blackfly, gray mealy cabbage aphis, rose aphis, and several more. Some have wings and some are wingless — all multiply at an alarming rate.

The old-fashioned remedy was to spray with soapy water, which washes the pests off or to rub them off with your fingers, messy but efficient for small clusters. I prefer very swift chemicals

Aphids usually cluster on above-ground growth but some attack roots.

like resmethrin, rotenone and malathion.

Birds, deer and rabbits can be a nuisance in rural areas. Throw a small-mesh net over blueberries and other fruits to elude the birds. Cats help deter rabbits and they and deer can be repelled by thiram but fences are the best solution.

Black spot of roses is easily recognized on foliage. Spray weekly during growing season with Benlate.

Cabbage worms are green larvae of small white butterflies and attack all brassicas. Hand pick and/or spray with *Bacillus thuringiensis* or spray or dust with rotenone.

Leaf miners are little maggots tunnelling between the upper and lower

The tunnels made by leaf miners are unmistakeable and disfiguring.

surfaces of leaves. The grubs can be pinched with the thumbnail, but if this does not appeal, systemic chemicals like Di-Syston also give control. Chrysanthemums, cinerarias, hollies, birches and columbine are all susceptible to this pest.

Mice and voles can be serious in some areas but the populations fluctuate. In bad years, roses, fruits, hollies, and tulips and many perennials are ruined. Cats help. Consult county extension agents for regional controls. Moles are carnivorous but do provide mice with runways.

Red spider mites are tiny spider-like creatures. There are two kinds; the fruit tree red spider mite is seen on strawberries, peaches, apples, pears and other broad-leaved trees and

Leaf mottling may be one of the first signs of red spider mite attack.

shrubs in hot dry weather; indoor red spider mite attacks many houseplants. Symptoms of both kinds are the same, a bronzing of the leaves, and cobwebbed leaves with heavy infestations. Spray with rotenone, dimethoate or malathion; several sprays may be needed to achieve control. Syringe regularly with water as this also helps to reduce attack.

Cyclamen mites are invisible but they cause distorted growth on such plants as delphinium, strawberries, cyclamen and African violets. Spray with Kelthane.

Scale insects are tiny shell-like creatures that cling to the stems of plants. They can be removed from woody deciduous plants by spraying with miscible oil in late winter. Scales can be a problem in the house or greenhouse on orchids, citrus, ferns and other foliage plants. Spray with malathion or dip the plants in a

Slugs and snails are well known, but can be controlled quite easily with baits.

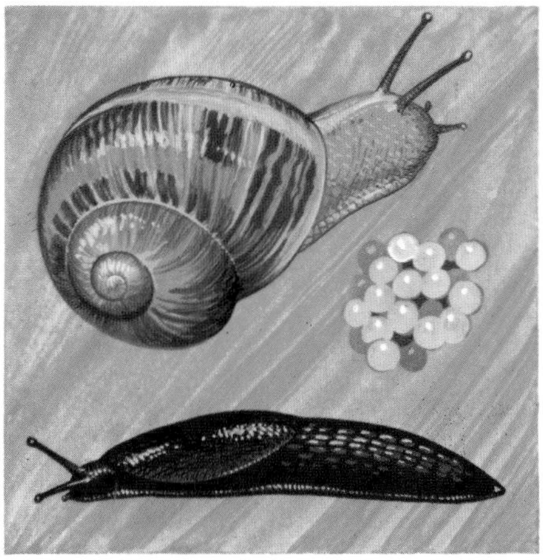

malathion bath. A few scales can be controlled with a swab dipped in alcohol.

Whitefly can be a very persistent pest indoors and outdoors on fuchsia, impatiens and ageratum. It is necessary to spray once every three days for at least 14 days with either malathion or resmethrin to gain control. Encarsia is a parasite which can be introduced into a greenhouse, but a miniumum temperature of 50°F (10°C) and long daylight hours are needed.

Botrytis, which is also known as gray mold, can be particularly troublesome

Whiteflies are tiny insects, often found on the undersides of leaves.

on peonies and greenhouse plants. Winter lettuce also tend to fall victim. This fungus disease shows itself as a fluffy gray mold that develops on new growth. Control with dusts and sprays containing benlate, Bordeaux or thiram.

Bulb and corm rots are sometimes troublesome. Dipping many bulbs and corms in a benomyl solution before planting will help reduce such diseases as freesia fusarium, botrytis of gladioli, freesia, narcissus and tulip fire, and scab and core rot of gladioli.

Damping off is caused by several fungus diseases which attack developing seedlings. Typical symptoms are apparently healthy seedlings falling over in a patch. The stem at ground level goes to a black thread. The new soilless mixes, such as Promix, Redi-earth, Jiffy Mix, etc., are sterile and their use virtually eliminates the disease.

GARDEN CHEMICALS

Garden chemicals often have complicated-sounding names, but there are also proprietary names for the same substance. These are usually easier to pronounce, but there can be several proprietary names for the same active ingredient. The chemical names are always listed on the label. The chart below is a guide but some states ban or restrict the use of certain chemicals and regulations are constantly changing.

Chemical	Description and Uses
Bacillus thuringiensis	A biological control used as spray for inch (or canker) and cabbage worm and caterpillars.
benomyl	Systemic fungicide, available as Benlate. For rose black spot, gray mold, mildew, rust and fruit scabs. Toxic to fish.
Bordeaux mixture	Copper sulfate and hydrated lime (in equal parts in water) used as spray or dust to control fungous and bacterial diseases such as gray mold, leafspots, molds.
calomel	Mercurous chloride, a fungicide, to dust in soil to control clubroot of cabbages and other brassicas.
captan	Fungicide used as dust or spray to control black spot on roses, gray mold and many fruit diseases. Toxic to fish.
carbaryl	Dust or spray insecticide available as Sevin. For caterpillars, Japanese beetles. Toxic to bees and fish.
diazinon	Dust, granule or spray insecticide (available under various trade names including Spectracide) to control radish and cabbage maggots, flea beetles, corn borer and earworm and others. Toxic to bees, fish and birds.
dichlofluanid	Fungicide used as spray or dust to control botrytis or gray mold, black spot on roses, tulip fire and some tomato and fruit diseases.
dicofol	Miticide, available as Kelthane, to spray on African violets, cyclamen, delphinium. Can be used as dip for houseplants.
dimethoate	Systemic insecticide available as Cygon, etc., to control scale insects, aphids, mealybugs and two-spotted mites. Toxic to birds and bees.
dinocap	Fungicide, available as spray or dust, to control mildew (Mildex) and some mites (Karathane). Toxic to fish.
ferbam	Fungicide used as spray for black spot on roses and other leaf diseases and for fruit rusts and scab. Sold as Fermate.
lime sulfur	Fungicide for use against certain fruit diseases, including peach leaf curl, when temperature is below 29°C (85°F).
malathion	Insecticide as dust, spray or granules for scales, leafminers, mealybugs, aphids, whiteflies and lacebugs. Toxic to fish and bees. Do not use on ferns or maples.
metaldehyde	Slug bait usually available as pellets under various trade names, such as Snarol, Bug-Geta, etc.
methoxychlor	Insecticide used as spray or dust to control many chewing pests, especially on fruit trees, and to control squash vine borer. Toxic to fish.
milky spore disease	Biological control dust containing spores of *Bacillus popilliae* for use on lawns to control Japanese beetle grubs.
miscible oil and oil emulsion	Insecticides used as dormant sprays on some shrubs, trees and fruit trees to control scales and eggs of caterpillars and mites.
nicotine sulfate	Best known as Black Leaf 40 spray but also available as fumigant for greenhouses. For thrips and aphids.
oxydemeton-methyl	Systemic insecticide (Metasystox-R) used as spray to control aphids, mites, leafhoppers.
PCNB (quintozene)	Fungicide, available as Terraclor, in spray or dust form to control clubroot of brassicas, including wallflower, and some bulb and lawn diseases.
pyrethrum	Insecticide used as spray against aphids and whiteflies. Do not spray cyclamen, maidenhair fern or poinsettia. Toxic to fish.
resmethrin	Insecticide used as spray or in aerosols to control aphids and whiteflies. Toxic to fish.
rotenone	Insecticide, also known as derris, used as dust or spray to control aphids, thrips, and flea beetles. Toxic to fish.
thirem	Fungicide spray used to control many diseases, including gray mold, rusts, downy mildew, it is also a seed protectant and animal repellant.
zineb	Fungicide used as spray or dust on fruits and vegetables. Available as Dithane.

ALWAYS FOLLOW THE MANUFACTURER'S INSTRUCTIONS TO THE LETTER.
Used as instructed all these chemicals will be quite safe, but some can be dangerous if not mixed and used properly. Before buying or using any garden chemicals check on the label that it is safe for the plant you wish to use it on (certain chemicals may damage some species or varieties and this will be indicated). If you are using chemicals on food plants, be careful to note the time lapse between applying them and the crop being safe to eat. Remember also that some chemicals can be harmful to fish, birds and pets. Most will also harm beneficial insects such as bees.

Index

abies 70, 78, 80
acer 42, *42,* 49, 54
Achillea filipendulina 97
achimenes 107, 112
acidanthera 86
aconites 86
adiantum 108, 112
aechmea 106
aeration, lawns 29
aerial layering 109
aesculus 41, 43
African violets 103, 105, 107, 108, 110, 112, 113
ageratum 91
agrostis 24
Ailanthus altissima 43
ajuga *96*
alder 43
allium 87
alnus 43
alpines 92 *et seq*
Althea rosea 95
alyssum 90, 91 *92,* 93
amaryllis 86, 109, 113
amelanchier 43, 49, 54, 63
ananas 112
anemone 88, *88,* 97
annuals, hardy 83, 85, 175, 185
Anthemis nobilis 26
antirrhinum 175
anthurium 107, 112
ants in lawns 33
aphelandra 105, 107, 112
aphis, apple 127, 132
  blackberry 133
  cherry 132
  conifer 77
  currant 135
  peach 129
  pear 130, 132
  plum 132
  strawberry 139
apples 124 *et seq, 126, 127,* 184, 185
arabis 93
aralia 62, 106
araucaria 80, 107, 112
Arbutus unedo 43
artichoke 146, *146*
ash (tree) 41, 44
ash (wood) 10
asparagus (vegetable) 142, 143, 144, 145, 146, *146*
asparagus (fern) 108, 112, 177
Asperula odorata 26
aspidistra 106, 110, 112
Asplenium nidus 107, *107,* 108, 112
aster 90
astilbe 106
Atlas cedar 80
aubretia *92,* 93
aucuba 54, *54,* 62, 106
Austrian Pine 70, 80
avocado pear 110
Axonopus affinis 24
azalea 17, 54, 63, 104, 106, 107, 110, 112
azalea gall 54

Bacillus thuringiensis 149
bahia grass 24
balsam (conifer) 78
barberry 54, *54*
basil 162
bay 162, *162*
beans, broad 147, *147*
  lima 142, 143, 144, 145, 147
  other 147
  runner 148, *148*
  snap 142, 143, 144, 145, 147, *147*
bedding plants 90 *et seq, 90*
beech 35, 37, *37,* 38, 39, 41, 44
beet 142, 143, 144, 145, 148
begonia 90, 91, 98, *98,* 105, 107, 110, 112
Bellis perennis 94, 95, *95*
beloperone 107, 111
berberis 35, 36, 39, 54, 63, *95*
bent (grass) 24
bergenia 97
Bermuda grass 24
betula 43, 49
biennials 94
billbug *32,*
birch 43, 49, *52*
birch bark cherry 46
birds, damage to apples 127
  damage to currants 135
  damage to plums 132
  on lawns 33
bird's nest fern 107, 108, 112
blackberry 132, 133, *133*
  training *134*
black currant *134*
black-spot 121, *121*
blueberries 134
bonfire tree 45, 49
bonsai 110
Boston ivy 66
botrytis 111, 139
bottle gardens 106
box 36, 39, 54
box elder 42
brachycome 86, 90
broccoli 142, 143, 144, 145
broom *53,* 56
browallia 175
brown rot 132
Brussels sprout 142, 143, 144, 145, 149, *149*
buddleia 53, 55, 63
bulbs and corms 83, 86, 87, 109
buttercup *33*
butterfly bush 55
buxus 36, 39, 62

cabbage 142, 143, 144, 145, 149, 150, *150,* 169
  root fly 149, *151*
  white butterfly 149
cacti and succulents 109, *109,* 177
caladium 88, 110
calceolaria 112, 176
calendula 84, 175
California lilac 55
Californian Poppy 84, 85
Californian Redwood 73
callicarpa 62
calliopsis 84
calluna 55, 63
camellia 55, *55,* 62, 63, 106, 112, 175
campanula 93, 95, *106,* 112
Canadian hemlock 77, 80
Canary Island ivy 106
candytuft *84*
canker 127
cankerworm 132
cane spot 135, 139
Canterbury bells 94, 95, *95*
capsicum 107, 111
carnations 98, *98*
carpet grass 24
Carpinus betulus 24, *35,* 37, 39, 43, 49
carpenteria 63
carrots 142, 143, 144, 145, 150, *150,* 169
caryopteris 53, 63
castanea 41, 43
cast iron plant 112
Catalpa bignonioides 43
caterpillar, apple 127
  cabbage 149
  rose *120,* 121
cauliflower 142, 143, 144, 145, 150, 151 169
ceanothus 55, 63
cedar of Lebanon 80
cedrus 71, *71,* 78, 80
celeriac 142, 143, 144, 145, 151, 152, *152*
celery 142, 143, 144, 145, 151, *152*
celocia 175
centipede grass 24
Cercis siliquastrum 43, 49
chaenomeles 51, 55, *55,* 62, 63
chafer, rose *120*
Chamaecyparis lawsoniana and cultivars 37, 39, 69, *69,* 71, *72,* 74, *75,* 78, 80
C. nootkatensis 80
C. obtusa cultivars 78
C. pisifera cultivars *12,* 73, 74, 75, 78
chamaedorea 112
chamomile 26
Cheiranthus cheiri 95
cherry, flowering 46
chervil 142, 143, 144, 145
chestnut, chinese 43
  horse 41, 43
  sweet 41, 43
Chewing's fescue 24
chicory 142, 143, 144, 145, 152, *152*
chimonanthus 51, 55, 63
chinch bug 33
Chinese cabbage 142, 143, 144, 145, 152, *153*
chlorophytum 106, 112
choisya 55, 63
Christmas cactus 104, 109, 113
  cherry 109
  rose 96
chrysanthemum 98, *99,* 107, 112, 175, 177
  annual 84
C. maximum 97, *97*
cineraria 113, 176, *178*
cissus 103, 106, 110, 112
citrus 106
clary 84
clay soil 7
clematis 44, 64, *64, 65*
clerodendrum 62, 63
climbing shrubs 64 *et seq*
cloches 141, *141,* 167 *et seq, 168, 169*
clover *33*
club-root 149
codiaeum 105, 112
codling moth 127
Colchicum autumnale 88
Cold greenhouse crops 175
coleus 112
Colorado spruce 77, 80
columnea 105, *176*
colutea 62
compost, garden 9
  heap *10*
  potting/seed 15, 16, 105
conifers 69 *et seq,* 97
cool greenhouse crops 176
coral spot 135
cordon fruit *131, 136*
corkscrew hazel 56
cornflower 84
corn salad 142, 143, 144, 145
cornus 43, 49, 56, 62
corticium fungus 33

corylus 56, 62
cotinus 56, *56,* 62
cotoneaster 17, 35, 36, 39, 56, 62
crab, ornamental 45, 49
crabclaw cactus 109
crabgrass 32
crataegus 37, 39, 43, 49
creeping juniper 78
creeping myrtle 26
cress 142, 143, 144, 145
crocus 86, *87,* 88, 109, *109*
croton 105, 112
crown imperial 88
Cryptanthus bivittatus 107
Cryptomeria japonica 'Elegans' 77, 80
cucumber 142, 143, 144, 145, 152, *153,* 175, 176
X*Cupressocyparis leylandii 11,* 38, 39, 71, 75, 80
Cupressus macrocarpa 71, 80
cuttings 17, *17,* 18, 110
cyclamen, hardy 86, 88
  indoor 107, 110, 112
  mite 111
Cynodon dactylon 24
cyperus 106, 112
cryptanthus 112
Crytomium falcatum 108
cytisus 56, *56,* 62, 63

daffodil 86, 87
dahlia 91, 99, *99,* 175
daisy *33*
daisy, double 94
damping off *16*
damson 131
dandelion *33,* 162
daphne 56, 63
date 110
day-lilies 83, *97,* 101
dead-heading bulbs 87
  bedding plants 91
delphinium 96, 97
deodar 80
design 11 *et seq*
deutzia 17, 56, 63
dianthus 93, 95, 98
dicentra 97
Dichondra micrantha 26
dieffenbachia 105, 112
digging 8, *8,* 9, *9,*
digitalis 95
dill 163, *163*
dogwood 43, 51, 56
dollar spot 33
Douglas fir 80
dracaena 112
dragon plant 112
drainage, for lawns 23
drumstick primula *93*
dumb cane 112

earth star 112
Easter cactus 109, 113
Echinops ritro 97
Edelweiss 93
egg plant 142, 143, 144, 145, 178
elaeagnus 37, 57, 62
elm 38, 41, 47
Endymion hispanicus 89
endive 142, 143, 144, 145, 153, *153*
English daisy 95
English ivy 26, 65
English yew 37
epimedium 97
episcia 112

Eranthis hyemalis 88, *88*
Eremochloa ophiuroides 24
erica 57, 62, 63, 93
eryngium *97*
Erypimum asperum 95
erythronium 86
escallonia 36, 57, 63
eschscholzia 85
Eucalyptus gunnii 44
euonymus 36, 39, 57, *57,* 62, 76
euphorbia 108, 113
evergreen azalea 112
evergreens, pruning 54
exacum 175

fairy rings 33
fagus 37, 39, 41, 44
false cypress 70
fan-trained fruit 131
fatshedera 106, 113
fatsia 62, 106
fennel 142, 143, 144, 145, 163, *163*
ferns 105, 108
fertilizers 9, 10
  for lawns 24, 30, 31
  for pot plants 105
Festuca rubra commutata 24
ficus 103, 105, 107, 109
Filipendula ulmaria 96
fireblight 130
firethorn 39, 60
fittonia *106*
flagpole cherry 46, *46,* 49
flame nettle 112
flame-violet 112
flaming sword 113
flamingo flower 112
florence fennel 163, *163*
flowering currant 37, 39, 53, 60
foliar fertilizers 10
forget-me-not 94, 95
forsythia 17, 37, *52,* 53, 57, 63
foxglove 94, 95
frame 167, 170, *170, 171*
fraxinus 41, 44
fritillaria 88
fruit 123 *et seq*
fuchsia 39, 53, 57, 63, 100, *100,* 106, 108
fusarium patch 33

gage 131
galtonia 86
garlic 142, 143, 144, 145, 163, *163*
Garrya elliptica 51, 58, 62
genista 58, 62, 63
gentiana 93
geranium 97, 103, 108
Ginko biloba 69, 80
gladiolus 86, 87, 100, *100,* 101
Gleditsia triacanthos 'Sunburst' *43,* 44, 49
globe artichoke 146, *146*
gloriosa daisy *91*
Gloriosa rothschildiana 110
gloxinia 98, 107, 110, 113
godetia *85*
golden chain 49
golden rain tree 44
gooseberry 17, 135, 136, *136*
  sawfly 136
grape 128, *128*
grape ivy *103,* 106
greenfly (see also aphis) 111
  on soft fruit 139
greenhouse 167, *167,* 172 *et seq, 172*
  polyethylene, making 173, *173,* 174, *174*
green manuring 9

Grevillea robusta 113, 177
guelder rose *62*
gum tree 49
gypsophila 84

Hamamelis mollis 35, 51, 58, *58,* 63
hawthorn 37, 43, 49
heaths 51, 55, *73*
heathers 55
hebe 39, 58, 62
hedera 26, 62, 65, 106, 113
hedges 35 *et seq*
  cutting 38, *38,* 39
helenium *97*
helianthemum 93
helichrysum 85
hemerocallis 97, 101, *197*
hemlock 39
herbaceous plants 96, *96,* 97, *97*
herbs 162 *et seq*
hibiscus 58, 63, 108, 110
hippeastrum 113
Hippophae rhamnoides 39, 62
holly 39, 58
hollyhock 95
honesty 94, 95
honey fungus 77
honey locust 44, 49
honeysuckle 65, *66*
hornbeam 35, *35,* 37, 39, 49
horseradish 18, 142, 143, 144, 145, 163 *164*
houseplants 103 *et seq*
Howea forsteriana 108
Hoya carnosa 178
hyacinth 86, *86,* 87, *87,* 88, 109
hydrangea 58, 62, 63, 65, *65,* 106, 108, 110
hydroculture *104,* 105
Hypericum calycinum 26, 58, *58,* 62, 63

Iceland poppy 94, 95
ilex 39, 58, 62
impatiens 90, 175
Indian bean tree 43
indigofera 63
inkberry 58
iris 86, 87, 89, 96, 97, 109
Irish juniper 78
Irish yew 80
ismene 86
ivy 26, 65, 104, 106, 113
ixia 86, 88

Japanese andromeda 59
Japanese beetle 33
Japanese Holly Fern 108
Japanese Quince 51, 55, *55*
Japanese Umbrella Pine 80
jasmine 17, 62, 65
jasminum 59, 63, 65, 178
Jerusalem artichoke 146, 146
Judas tree 43, 49
Juglans regia 44
June beetle 33
Juniperus chinensis cultivars 75, 78, 80
J. communis cultivars 74, 75, 76, *76,* 78
J. horizontalis cultivars 76, 78
J. Xmedia 'Mint Julep' *76*
J. procumbens 'Nana' 74, 75
J. sabina 'Tamariscifolia' 77, 78
J. scopulorum cultivars *69,* 73, *73,* 74, 80
J. squamata cultivars *75,* 76, 78
J. virginiana cultivars 76, 78

kalanchoe 113
kale 142, 143, 144, 145, 148
kalmia 59, 63
kangaroo vine 112
kentia 108
Kentucky blue grass 24
Kerria japonica 59, 62, 63
Kilmarnock Willow 49
kniphofia 98
Koelreuteria paniculata 44
kohl-rabi 142, 143, 144, 145, 153, *154*
kolkwitzia 63

laburnum 44, *44,* 49
larkspur 84, 85
larch 69, 75, 80
larix 70, 80
laurus 62
laurel 37, 39
lavatera 84
lavender 36, *36,* 39, 54, 63
lavandula 36, 39
lawns 23 *et seq*
  calendar of work 30
  cutting, 27, *27*
  diseases 33
  feeding 10, 30, 31
  grassless 26, *26*
  laying turf 26, *26*
  mowers 28, *28*
  pests *32,* 33
  preparing site, 23, *23,* 24
  sowing 24, 25
  watering 29, 30, *30*
  weeding 31, 32, *32, 33*
Lawson's Cypress 37, 39, 69, 71, 73, 76
  80
leaf cutter bee *120,* 121
leaf hopper *120*
leaf roller 132
leaf spot 139
leeks 142, 143, 144, 145, 154, *154*
legumes (for green manuring) 9
leontopodium 93
leptosiphon 86
lettuce 142, 143, 144, 145, 154, *154,*
  155, 169, 170, 175, *175*
leucothoe 62
Leyland 38, 39, 69, 80
ligustrum 36, 39
lilac 53, 61
lilies 83, 86, 89, *89*
Limnanthes douglasii 84
linaria 84
linden 47
Liquidambar styraciflua 45, 49
Liriodendron tulipifera 45
lithospermum 93, *93*
lobelia 90, 91
loganberry 133, *133,* 134
  training *134*
Lolium perenne 24
London plane 41, 45
lonicera 35, 36, 39, 62, 65, 66, *66*
love-in-a-mist 85, *85*
love-lies-bleeding 84
lunaria 95
lythrum 97

magnolia 45, 49, 59, *59,* 63
mahonia 36, 39, 51, 59, 62, 63
maidenhair fern 108, 112
maidenhair tree 69, 80
Malabar spinach 159
mallow 84
malus 45, 49
maple, Japanese 42, *42,* 49, 54
  Norway 42, 49
  snakebark 42, 49
maranta 105, 113
marigolds 90, 91, *91*
marjoram 164, *164*
marrow 154, *155*
mealybug 77, 111, 129
melon 142, 143, 144, 145, 169, 175
Mexican orange blossom 55
Michaelmas daisy *97,* 99
mignonette 84
mildew on apples 127, 132
  blackcurrants 139
  gooseberries 139
  peaches 129, 132
  roses 120, *121*
mile-a-minute vine 66, *66*
mimulus 93
mint 164, *164*
mock orange 37, 59
mole, control 32
monkey puzzle 80
monstera 105, 109, 113
montbretia 86
Monterey cypress 71, 80
mother-in-law's tongue 106, 113
mother of thousands 113
mother-of-thyme 26
mountain ash 47, 49
mountain laurel 59
mowers, types 28, *28*
muscari 87, 89, 94
mustard 142, 143, 144, 145
myosotis 95, 175

nasturtium *84,* 85
narcissus 86, 87, 88, 89
Neanthe bella 108
Nemophila insignis 84
Neoregelia carolinae 106
nepeta 97
nerine 86
New Jersey tea 55
New Zealand spinach 143, 145, 159, *159*
nicotiana 83, 91
nigella 84, 85
Nikko fir 80
Nootka cypress 80
Norfolk Island pine 107, 112

oak 41, 47
okra 142, 143, 145
olearia 63
onion 143, 145, 155, *155*
orange peel clematis 64
Oregon-grape 59
origanum 164
osmanthus 59, 62

Pachysandra terminalis 26
paeonia 59
palms 108
pansy 94, 95
Papaver nudicaule 95
parlor palm 108, 112
parsley 143, 145, 164, *165,* 175
parsnip 143, 145, 155, 156, *156*
parthenocissus 62, 66
Paspalum notanum 24
Passiflora caerulea 66, 177
passion flower 66
pea 15, 156, *156*
peach 128 *et seq, 129,* 175
  leaf curl 46, 129, *129,* 132
  borer 132
peanut 110
pear 129 *et seq, 130*
  leaf blister 130
  midge 131
  psylla 132
  rootstocks 124
  scab 131
pelargonium 108
peony 59, 96, 101
peperomia 113
pepper (edible) 143, 145, 156, 176
pepper (ornamental) 112
periwinkle 26
pernettya 62
petunia 90, 91
pH 9, 23
philadelphus 37, 59, 63
philodendron 106, 113
Phoenix canariensis 108
phlox 18, *92,* 93, 96
phytophthera 77
picea 70, *73,* 74, 75, 76, *77,* 78, 80
pieris 59, 62
pineapple 110, 112
pinus 70, 71, 78, 80
pips, plants from 110
planning 7, 11 *et seq*
plantain *33*
planting 20, 21, *21*
  conifers *71*
  hedges 38
  roses 118, *118*
  shrubs 52, 53
  trees 47, 48, *48*
planting-out time 83
platanus *44,* 45
platycerium 113
plum 131, *131,* 132
  cuculio 132
  rootstocks 124
Poa pratensis 24
poinsettia 104, 108, 113
polyanthus 94, *94*
polygonum baldschuanicum 66, *66*
poppy, annual 84, 85
poppy, Iceland 95
poplar 17, 46, 49
populus *45,* 46, 49
potato 143, 145, 157, *157*
potentilla 53, 59, *59,* 60, 62, 63, 94
prayer plant 113
pricking out *15, 16,* 17
primula *93,* 113, *174,* 176
privet 17, 36, 37, 38, *38,* 39
propagation 14 *et seq*
  houseplants 109, 110
  roses 120
propagators 171, *171*
protected cropping 141, 167 *et seq*
pruning fruit 127 *et seq*
  roses 118, 119, *119*
  shrubs 53, *53*
  trees 48, *48*
prunus 35, 36, 37, *37,* 39, 45, 46,
  46, 47, 49, 63
Pseudotsuga menziesii 80
pteris 108
purple leaf sand cherry 36
purple leaved plum 37, 49
pyracantha *12,* 17, 35, 39, 51, *52,* 60, *60,*
  62
pyrethrum 96, 97
pyrus salicifolia 'Pendula' 46, *46,* 49

quercus 41, 47
quickthorn 39

radish 143, 145, 157, 158, *158,* 168, 181
Raoulia australis 94
raspberry 123, *123,* 136, 137, *137*
  beetle 133, 137, 139
red currant 135, *135*
red spider mite 77, 111, *120*
Rhipsalidopsis gaertneri 109, 113
rhododendron 17, 60, *60,* 62, 63
rhoicissus 110
rhubarb 143, 145, 158, *158*
rhus 56, *56*
ribes 39, 60, 63
Robinia pseudoacacia 41, 47, 49
rock garden 92 *et seq*
rock rose 93
root cuttings 18
rootstocks 123, 124
root weevils 139
rosa 63, 117, 120
rose 115 *et seq*
  climbers and ramblers 116, *116*
  floribunda 116, *117*
  grandiflora 115
  hybrid tea 115, *116*
  miniature 116, *116*
  pests and diseases 120, *120*, 121, *121*
  pruning 118, 119, *119*
  shrub 117, *117*
rosemary 165, *165*
rubber plant 103, 109, *110,* 113
Russian olive 37
Russian vine 66, *66,*
rust, on roses 121, *121*
rutabaga 143, 145, 160, *160*
ryegrass 24

sage 165, *165*
St. Augustine grass 24
saintpaulia 105, 107, 108, 113
salix 47, 49, 60, *60,* 62
salsify 142, 143, 158, *159*
salvia 90, 91
sandy soil 7
sansevieria 106, 110, 113
Santolina chamaecyparissus 36, 39, 54
sawfly, apple 127
  gooseberry 136, 139
saxifraga 93, 113
scab 127, 132
scabious 97
scale insect 111
schlumbergera 109, 113
Sciadopitys verticillata 80
scilla 86, 87, 89
scindapsus 107
sclerotinia 33
scorzonera 158, *159*
Scots pine 69, 70, 80
sea buckthorn 39
sedum 26, *26, 92,* 96, 97
seeds, sowing 14 *et seq*
  storing 15
sempervivum *92,* 93
senecio 36, 39, *61,* 62, 113
Sequoia sempervirens 73
Serbian spruce 70, 73, 80
service berry 54
shadbush 49
shallots 143, 145, 155
shrimp plant 107, 112
shrubs 51 *et seq*
  planting 52, 53
  pruning 53
Siberian wallflower 95
silk oak 113
sinks for alpines, making *92,* 93
sinningia 98, 107, 113
skimmia 51, 61, 62, 63
slipper flower 112
slugs and snails 154
snapdragon 90
snowberry 61
snowdrop 86, 87, *88,* 109
sod webworm *32,* 33
soil 7 *et seq*
soilless composts 16
solanum 108, 113
Soleirolia soleirolii 106
sorbus 47, 49
sorrel 143, 145
sowing, indoors 15, 16, *16*
  outdoors 14, *14,* 15, *15*
Spanish broom 61
sparixis 86
spartium 61, 63
spider plant 106, *108,* 112
spinach 143, 145, 159, *159*
spiraea 37, 61, *61,* 63
spur blight 134, 137, 139
squash 143, 145, 154
Stachys byzantinus 97
stardust 86
star of Bethlehem 112
Stenotaphrum secundatum 24
stephanandra 61, 62
Stephanotis floribunda 109, 178
stocks 83, 91, 94, *94,* 95, 175, *176,* 177
stag's-horn fern 113
strawberry 138, *138,* 139, *139,* 169, 175
strawberry tree 43
streptocarpus 110
sumach 60
swamp cypress 70
swan river daisy 86, 91
swede 160, *160*
sweetcorn 142, 143, 144, 145, 160, *160*
sweet gum 45, 49
sweet pea 84, 101, *101*, 169, 175
sweet potato 143
sweet William 94, 95, 98
sweet woodruff 26
Swiss chard 142, 143, 144, 145, 148
Swiss cheese plant 109, 113
sycamore 42
symphoricarpos 61, 62
syringa 61, 63
Sythrum virgatum 97

tamarix 62, 63
tampala 159
taxodium 70
taxus 37, 39, 70, 80
terrarium 107
Thanksgiving cactus 109, 113
thuja 39, 76
T. occidentalis cultivars 37, 77, *77,* 78
T. orientalis 'Aurea Nana' 75, *75*
T. plicata 75, 77, 80
T. p. 'Atrovirens' 37, 39
thyme 93, 165, *165*
thymus 26, 165
tigridia 86, 87
tilia 47
toadflax 84
tomatoes 143, 145, 160, 161, *161,* 169
  176, *177*
tools 18, *18*
topiary, cutting 39
tortrix moth damage *120*
tradescantia 106, 113
trees, 41 *et seq*
  planting 47, 48, *48*
  pruning 48, *48*
tree of heaven 43
tsuga 39, 75, 78, 80
tulip 86, 87, 89, *95,* 109
tulip tree 45
Tulipa spp. *86,* 89
turnip 143, 145, 161, *161*
turnip flea beetle 161
turnip-rooted celery *152*

ulmus 41, 47
umbrella grass 106, 112
urn plant 106

Vancouver (conifer) 80
vegetables 141 *et seq*
  sowing dates 142
verbascum *97*
veronica, shrubby 39
viburnum 35, 62, *62,* 63
Vinca minor 26
viola 95
Virginia creeper 66
Virginian stock 84
viscaria 84
vriesia 113

wallflower 83, 86, 87, 94, 95, *95*
walnut 44
watering equipment 19, *19, 30, 104*
water melon 143, 145
weed control in lawns 31, 32
weedkillers, hormone 32
weeping pear 46, 49
weeping willow 47, 49
weevil, root 139
weigela 17, 62, 63
western red cedar 39, 69
whitebeam 49
white currant 135, *135*
whitefly 111
white grub *32*
white pine 80
willow 17, *47,* 60
winter aconite 88, *88*
winter cherry 113
winter jasmine 59
winter sweet 55
wireworm *32*
wisteria 67, *67*
witch hazell 58, *58*
woolly aphis 127
worms, in lawns 33

xeranthemum 85

yarrow, *33*
yew 39, 70, 80

zebra plant 112
zebrina 113
zinnia 90, 91, 92
zoysia (grass) 24, 26

Acknowledgements
We are indebted to the following for permission to reproduce photographs:
Michael Warren
Bernard Alfieri
Peter McHoy
Pat Brindley
Kenneth Scowen
Floraprint Ltd (copyright I.G.A.)